Dedication

This book is dedicated to Donald Deneck, who was the editor for John Wiley geology textbooks for many, many years. Students often do not appreciate the underpinning to their education provided by editors of the great textbook companies. Don acquired geology texts for thousands and thousands of practicing geologists, who owe the quality of their educations to his dedication to his profession. His responsibility took him through numerous editions of the physical geology text by Longwell, Flint and Skinner, the important mineralogy manual by Dana, Hurlbut, and Klein, and structural geology books by G. Davis, Ragan, and Hobbs. Don and his family have now moved from New York to his beloved Virginia, where he will not only enjoy the genteel life but will be out there convincing professors to use this and other Wiley textbooks. This one certainly would not have happened if Don had not aggressively sought me out. Don, I sincerely thank You.

R. N. A.

Contents

Where Did All That Ocean Come From?

Any of us fortunate enough to have sailed so far from shore that we could no longer see land must have wondered where all that water came from. There is enough water to cover 70 percent of the planet's surface, not just surficially, but with a coat averaging two miles thick from sea level to sea floor. Yet no other planet in our solar system has even a lake-sized deposit of water on its surface. What makes us so different? Why don't Mars, Venus, Saturn, or our Moon have water at the surface? In order to begin to understand how our Earth works, we must discover where all the water comes from. And we will find that the secret locked within the origin of the oceans also holds the key to the way the planet began.

Although we still have not solved the entire puzzle of how the Earth and its neighbors were formed, several rigid constraints of the Earth's formation exist. For example, we have never found a single rock that is older than 3.7 billion years old on the Earth. Yet we know the solar system is 4.5 billion years old. How can we be so sure of the age of the solar system if we can't find rocks on Earth of that age? The truth is that there are indeed rocks on Earth that have **radioactive-decay** (called **radiometric**) ages of 4.5 billion years, but these are all **meteorites** that have fallen to the Earth from space. Also, the greatest geological expeditions of all time, the Apollo missions to the moon, recovered rocks that were at least 4 billion years old. And missions to Mars and Venus leave us with little doubt that all the planets formed at about the same time.

The paradox is that the Earth has no old rocks but the moon has no young rocks. So where did all the old rocks from the surface of the Earth go? And could the missing rocks have anything to do with the oceans we now have? A hint to the answer to that question is found in the composition of the oldest Earth rock. There is indeed something very special about that 3.7-billion-year-old rock; it was deposited as soft mud under the ocean. If there was already an ocean, there had to be a bottom to that ocean made up of rock.

But where is the record of all that rock? Since we cannot have ocean without rock underneath, the oldest covering on the planet must have been destroyed and replaced with younger rock. What kind of catastrophe could have wiped out the entire surface record of the planet for its first 1.8 billion years of existence? Such a cataclysm would make present theories that the dinosaurs were wiped out by a large **meteor** impact seem of trivial dimension. In fact, when we look at the early history of the Moon, Mercury, or Venus, we see that meteor impacts were the dominant geological event in the early solar system. But the massive meteor-impact craters that surely hit the early Earth are gone along with every other trace of that time period.

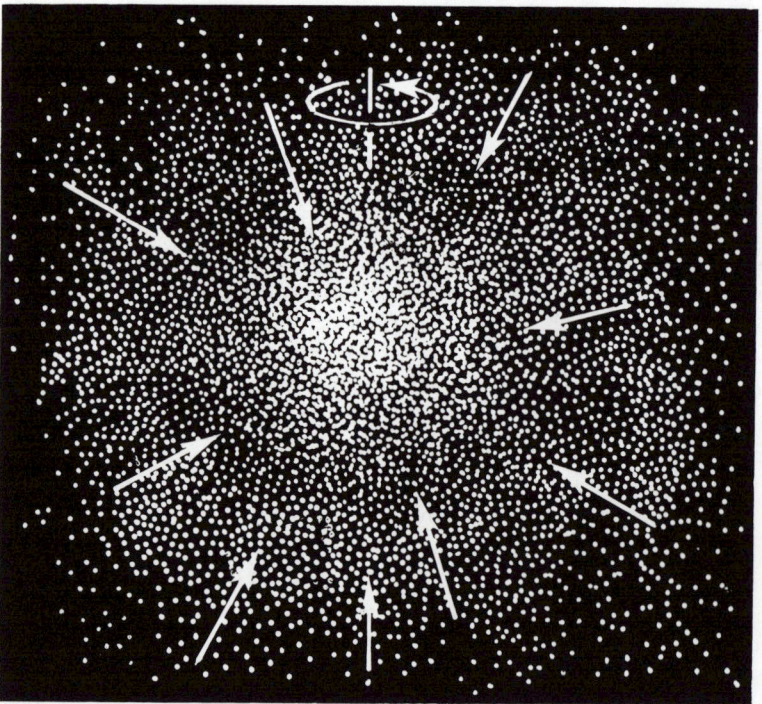

Figure 1-1. The solar system formed from the gravitational coalescing of a stellar dust cloud. As the cloud condenses, it begins to rotate faster and faster (from Turekian, 1972).

The Early Solar System

The key piece of scientific information that we have for what did occur in the early days of our planet's existence comes from physical and chemical constraints on what the Earth must have been like in order for it to have evolved into a planet covered by so much water (the oceans themselves). Obviously, we must have been different from Mars or the other planets, but what made us so different? Although we don't know the exact mechanism, the planets **accreted** from what are called **planetesimals.** All the planets revolve not only in one direction (counterclockwise) but also in one plane about the sun (except for Pluto). Also, there is a consistent spacing of the planets; they are not randomly distanced from one another. They seem to have acted as "vacuum cleaners," sweeping the debris from each of their orbits into first small protoplanets, then into planetesimals, and finally into one major celestial body for each orbit. Just as we do not yet know the physics of how this vacuuming occurred, we also do not know why it failed in one particular orbit next to Mars where an **asteroid** belt exists instead of another planet.

There is another peculiarity of the solar system which tells us something of how the Earth began. The sun has 99 percent of the **mass** of the solar system, whereas most of the **angular momentum** of the system is in the planets (c.f., Press and Siever, 1982). Angular momentum is mass times velocity, so either the sun is rotating too slowly or the planets are rotating too fast for their mass. For this anomalous momentum to have resulted, the solar system must have begun **cold.** But how do we jump to such a conclu-

Figure 1-2. The rotation flattens the dust cloud into a disk. The center becomes hotter and more dense until nuclear ignition fires the sun. The resulting explosion distributes 99 percent of the angular momentum of the solar system into the orbits of the newly forming planets. The dust somehow accretes first into proto planets, then into planets and moons (from Turekian, 1972).

sion about temperatures from mass and velocity? How could the mass and velocity have gotten out of balance? The only way the physics makes any sense is for the system to have begun as a ring of cold gas and dust swirling around a central nucleus. As gravity pulled more and more dust (mass) to the center, the nucleus heated up, much as a bicycle tire pump will get hot as air is compressed in its chamber (Figures 1-1 and 1-2). Bang! The center became so hot that a nuclear explosion ignited the sun, but the blast blew enough heavy dust back out to the planets to disrupt the mass-velocity balance of the solar system. The system had to begin cold, then heat enough to ignite a nuclear explosion in order to explain the peculiar occurrence that the planets spin too fast. The awesome powers of the laws of physics and chemistry give us the ability to see into the very origins of our existence.

The dust driven away from the sun first accreted into planetesimals, then into planets, and the solar system was formed. What kept any of these new planets from getting too hot and exploding into suns themselves? That is how binary-sun systems happen. The outcome depends only upon how much dust there was in our particular galactic neighborhood when our solar system began to form. Jupiter very nearly became a companion star to our Sun, but there was not quite enough dust to compress Jupiter to ignition temperature. This was just one of a string of fortuitous events that resulted not only in our planet being the only one with oceans, but also the only planet with elaborate forms of life (in our solar system, that is).

How Hot Was the Early Earth?

The early Earth must have been much like Mars or Venus are now. The surface was surely pockmarked with craters. But the planet must have accreted cold. Again we jump from seemingly unrelated observations to temperatures. How do we know that the planet did not accrete as a volcanically molten body? The answer comes from the truly unique constraints placed upon the formation of the Earth by the presence of the vast oceans. Again we return to the existence of oceans as a critical difference between Earth and its planetary neighbors. Where did all the water come from? It must have been trapped in the earth. But how? The only way was as minerals. Water forms an important constituent of a whole set of minerals known as **hydrates.** The one common characteristic of all hydrated minerals, however, is that if they get too hot, they **dehydrate,** or release their water. Did you every wonder how a pottery kiln works? A soft and wet clay blob is molded into a pot, then put into a kiln to make it hard. What happens physically is that in the kiln, heat dehydrates the clays, driving out their chemically bound water which then becomes steam and evaporates. The resulting pot is hard and dry.

The Earth must have saved its kiln days until relatively late in its history.

Why? Because an atmosphere is required in order to capture water that is **outgassing** and turn it into an ocean. The reason for this is that the water must be insulated enough to form a liquid. An atmosphere of gases is a natural insulator from radical temperature fluctuations and therefore would have been required to form oceans. Why is there no water on Mars then? The famous canals may indeed have resulted from early water on Mars, but all the water is gone now. Coincidentally, Mars has very little atmosphere. Also, Mars is considerably smaller than the Earth, and as we shall soon see, size controls how hot the planet's kiln becomes. Perhaps Mars still has most of its water inside because its kiln was never fully fired.

The Great Cataclysm

One additional piece of the early history puzzle comes from the composition of the Earth's present atmosphere compared to that of the Sun. But how do we know the composition of the Sun? The **spectrum** of the light given off by the Sun is a function of the gases burning to produce that light. And the Sun has one million times more neon, krypton, argon, and all the other **inert gases** than the Earth (c.f., Press and Siever, 1982). These gases are called inert because they do not bind chemically with any other element. So if the Earth has much less of these gases than the Sun, it must have lost great quantities. It lost one entire atmosphere! Our atmosphere, like the rock surface, is the second that existed on the planet; consequently, it is short of inert gases. The plot continues to lead to a catastrophe of unimaginable dimensions. Not only have we lost all record of any rock existing at the surface of the planet for its first 1.8 billion years of existence, but one entire atmosphere has been lost as well. And we are about to learn how the surface of the planet was then covered by trillions and trillions of gallons of water.

In order for so much water to have been available for the second atmosphere, it could not have been outgassed during the first 1.8 billion years of the Earth's history. A planet with a cold interior was required. Otherwise, the kiln would have cooked out all the water early on in its history. Yet the very fact that an ocean ultimately formed indicates that the kiln was eventually fired. This story is slowly leading us to the other most prominent physical part of our Earth besides the oceans—the **core.**

What do we know of the present temperature inside the Earth? You can be assured that it was hotter then than it is now. When one goes deep into the Earth, it gets very hot very quickly. Just ask a South African gold miner. The average amount of heat coming out of the Earth's surface per second is one microcalorie per square centimeter (1 μcal/cm^2/sec). This flow of heat can be converted into temperatures inside the Earth by multiplying by the distance down to the point of interest. To the center of the Earth, the distance is 6400 km. Then divide by the thermal conductivity of the rock in between (a measure of the ease with which the heat is transported through a solid). To illustrate, a silver teaspoon gets very hot in a cup of coffee, but a trivet insulates a table from a hot tray. The **thermal conductivity** of silver is much higher than that of asbestos. So the temperature at the center of a silver earth would be much lower than that at the center of an asbestos earth for the same surface heat flow, since we divide a constant by a larger number in the silver example. What is happening physically is that the silver earth conducts the fixed quantity of heat faster and more readily to the surface and thus cools it off faster, resulting in cooler temperatures at any given time. But if we convert surface heat flow to temperatures at the center of the Earth using thermal conductivity values appropriate for rock, we get a temperature at the center of 100,000 degrees centigrade (°C)—hotter than the sun. How can that be?

This puzzle has been a famous paradox in geology for centuries. Lord Kelvin actually fell prey to another form of the same paradox 150 years ago. He was interested in the age of the Earth, so he calculated it assuming that the entire body began at 1200°C, the temperature of **magma,** or molten rock. (He wanted a maximum possible age so he assumed the most extreme case.) He knew the present-day surface heat flow and the thermal conductivity of rock so he calculated the time it would take to cool from molten conditions to a present-day surface heat flow of only one microcalorie per square centimeter per second. His answer of 45 million years directly contradicted the views of paleontologists who knew of dinosaurs and ancient seas.

Lord Kelvin had made the same mistake as that of the French Count of Buffon in the 1700s (see Boorstin 1983). Having an avid curiosity, this gentleman made a series of progressively larger-diameter molten spheres and measured the length of time each took to cool. He reasoned that the Earth began as a molten ball, so he plotted the time to cool versus the diameter of each molten sphere, and then extrapolated that rate from his largest ball, which was two feet across, to the diameter of the earth. His estimate of the Earth's age was tens of thousand years—not much more incorrect than Lord Kelvin's scientifically derived age. Their mistake was one of ignorance. At that time heat was known to travel only conductively (from grain to grain by transferring vibrations) or convectively (by moving and carrying the heat with it). At about this time Marie Curie discovered **radioactivity.** The Earth is much older than Lord Kelvin calculated because additional heat is constantly being generated within the earth by radioactivity to replace that lost through the surface. Also, the center of the Earth does not have to be 100,000°C because heat is constantly being generated throughout the earth's diameter, allowing the center to be much cooler.

Radiation also provides the mechanism both to have begun the Earth cold and to have eventually fired the kiln. But the amount of heat generated in the first 1.8 billion years far surpassed that of a kiln, instead reaching that of an iron smelter. (See Figure 1-3.) Not only did the Earth heat up to the dehydration state, but it also became hot enough to melt iron in its interior. And liquid iron is both mobile and heavier than rock. It first melted in the mantle, sank to the center of the Earth, displacing light rock upward. This frothing of the entire planet was the cataclysm to end all cataclysms.

This catastrophe is called **differentiation,** in which the heavy elements of the Earth sank to the center and the light elements frothed toward the surface (Figure 1-4). Why it happened has to do with a bit of chemistry called the **Clapyron curve** of iron. The pressure–temperature relation above which melting occurs and below which a solid form of the element is stable is called the Clapyron curve for the element. As the Earth gradually heated from within through radioactive decay, the pressure and temperature appropriate for the melting of iron was gradually approached. Upon crossing the Clapyron curve (Figure 1-3), iron melted throughout the Earth's interior, but primarily midway down in the region called the **mantle.** Molten iron is heavier than rock, so it sank. Light elements such as granite rose to the surface to form the beginning of our continents. This overturn destroyed all evidence of the original surface of the planet. The frothing also drove off the first atmosphere.

The heat source was KUTh, or potassium (chemical symbol is K), uranium (U), and thorium (Th). These three radioactive elements provide 99 percent of the internal heat generation within the Earth, and each has a **half-life** (the time required for half its total mass to have decayed radioactively) of about a billion years. So about one twentieth of the original KUTh present

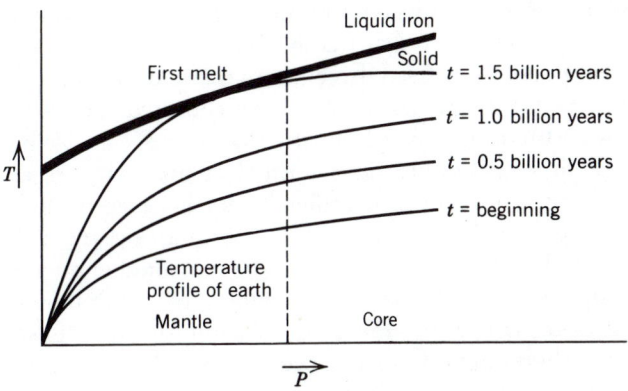

Figure 1-3. The melting relation of iron in pressure and temperature space. Superimposed upon this plot is the temperature history of the Earth. At about 1.5 billion years after accretion, the mantle reaches the melting temperature of iron. The liquid iron then sinks to begin formation of the core, and planetwide differentiation begins (from Jordan and Anderson, 1974).

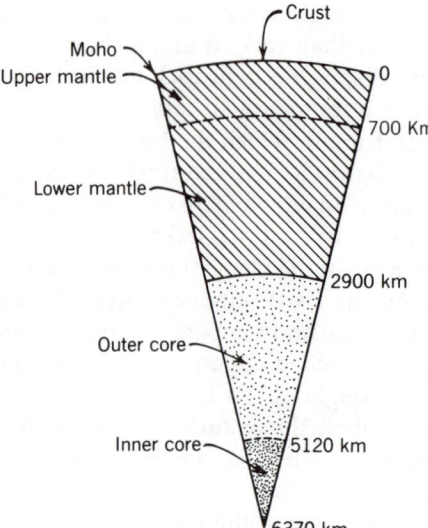

Figure 1-4. Cross section of the Earth showing the core–mantle–crust divisions.

at the formation of the Earth is still generating heat inside the Earth today. The rate of heat generation is so many calories per gram of KUTh present, so the total heating within the first billion years of the Earth's history is purely a function of the *amount* of KUTh originally present. There is a limited amount of KUTh in any cloud of cosmic dust, so the amount of heating is completely a function of size or diameter only. Here is the first fortunate coincidence affecting our present Earth's environment. If the earth had been too large, there would have been so much KUTh that the kiln would have fired too early and water would have been driven from the hydrous minerals too early in the Earth's history for water to have been captured. The water would have escaped with the inert gases from the first atmosphere. When the iron finally melted, the core would have formed at the center of the Earth, but the surface would have been completely dry because no more water would have been left inside to be expelled to form an ocean. If the earth had been too small, the planet still would not have heated enough to fire the kiln. Did this happen on Mars? If the iron smelter fired, then the kiln fired, but Mars has no core. It is likely that water existing in Mars is still present largely because differentiation has not occurred yet. Why not? Not enough KUTh, simply because the planet is too small. Mars is about half the size of the Earth.

How do we know that Mars does not have a core? We certainly can't go inside the planet to prove it. If you were to attach a tennis ball to a string and sling it rapidly about your head, the ball would flatten at the poles from its original spherical shape into an ellipsoid. If instead you attached a string to a baseball and slung it around, it would deform or flatten much less. Why? Because it has its heaviest mass at its center, whereas a tennis ball is hollow with all its mass near its surface. By simply observing Mars with a telescope we can see that it is much more elliptical than the Earth. Mars therefore has little or no core.

This simple illustration of how basic physics is applied to deductions of the origin and thermal history of Mars is exactly how geology is practiced on Earth. We cannot go more than a few miles into the Earth even with a drill bit, yet we can make observations and deductions based upon the constraints imposed by the laws of physics and chemistry. You will soon be surprised by how much a geologist can learn from some seemingly scanty information. Let's take an astronomical tour through the planets to demonstrate the technique before we turn our further attentions solely to our planet Earth.

Mars

Beginning with Mars (because we have been concentrating on its contrasts with Earth), its most visible features are the remarkable canals and the polar ice caps. Mars is still heavily cratered as well. Mars also has a single volcano, which is 500 km in diameter and has a summit 23 km high. Surrounding this and other smaller volcanoes on the surface are smooth, flat deserts believed to be seas of **Lava** that flowed from the volcanoes as recently as 200 million years ago. Weather definitely occurs on Mars; dust storms of enormous proportion can be seen even from Earth (Figure 1-5). Thus, the young age of the lava flows is indicated because weathering would have eroded the lava seas if they were old relics of a long-dead planet. Yet there was just not enough heat to completely wipe out the original surface of Mars; therefore, craters from the original formation of the planet still can be seen on the surface. The canals definitely were formed by running liquid of some sort. They form tributary networks, and the degree of crosscutting implies millions of years worth of liquid flow. Yet the surface did not have large accumulations of liquid in lakes or oceans. It is as if rains came, water flowed, and then space claimed all the water back.

Water is indeed the likely liquid that flowed on the Martian surface, but carbon dioxide is another possibility. The polar ice caps, and the entire present atmosphere, are made mostly of carbon dioxide. The size of the volcanoes compared to those on the Earth also tells us that the surface of Mars has been stagnant for billions of years. As we shall see, Earth has an active surface where entire continents drift relative to the molten source region for lavas, so no volcano stays above that source for a long enough time to form such large volcanoes as are found on Mars. A likely history, then, is that the planet heated enough early-on to expel sufficient water as steam in volcanic

Figure 1-5. The rubbly surface of Mars as seen from the Viking 1 lander. The rocks are likely basalt chunks thrown out from impacts of meteorites. The red color of the surface is from rusting of the iron-rich soil. Most of the oxygen on the surface is tied up in this rusting process (NASA photo).

eruptions to produce rain and river runoff, but not enough heating occurred to differentiate the planet into an iron core. The water eventually escaped through Mars's thin atmosphere, leaving behind the heavier carbon dioxide to eventually dominate the surface of the planet. It is likely that in approximately 4 billion years the Earth will look as Mars does now. By then our heat engine will have died down to that of the present Mars.

The Moon

The other planetary body that tells us the most about how our planet works is our own moon. The Moon is of course dominated by craters from great meteor impacts, most of which occurred more than 4 billion years ago. The fact that this original impact surface is preserved tells us that the body is dead thermally. But it does have vast mountain ranges, made mostly of granitic rock, and large lunar seas, each called a **Mare** (pronounced mah-ray), made of basaltic lava. The **granites** are light-colored rock, whereas the **basalts** are black. Which are heavier? The blackness comes from heavy elements such as iron, magnesium, and potassium. The light-colored minerals (especially quartz) making up granites are lightweight elements such as silicon, aluminum, sodium, and calcium. The mountains were formed by a minor differentiation event whereby the basalt separated from the granite. It is also known that a small core was formed in the early history of the moon because a weak **magnetic field** exists in rocks brought back by astronauts. As you will later see, a molten iron core is required to form even a weak magnetic field around a planet.

The answer to the major question that has intrigued scientists for millennia—Where did the Moon come from?—is still not certain. In the early 1960s, one of the major reasons scientists suggested manned lunar exploration to the Kennedy Administration was to discover the origin of the Moon. Kennedy then seized upon the concept as a way to demonstrate American technical superiority to the Russians, and this geological goal was all but lost. The irony is that by the time Neil Armstrong set foot on the Moon, virtually every geologist considered this puzzle solved. The Moon appears to have been captured from a close orbit during the early formation of the Earth. Certainly the existence of moons in the solar system is the rule rather than the exception. However, the idea that the Moon was ripped away from the Earth somehow has also been espoused for hundred of years. This explanation has been given, for example, for the origin of the Pacific Ocean, claiming it is the hole left behind by the moon.

The mission to the Moon interestingly reversed some of the certainty that the moon was a captured extraterrestrial body. The chemical composition of trace elements (those high up the periodic table with abundances in the range of one part per billion of a rock) from lunar rocks have unmistakable links to abundances found in Earth rocks. But these trace elements are not found in extraterrestrial meteorites. So we must step back from our certainty of the Moon's origin and say that, if indeed it was captured, it must have formed within the same orbital swath as the Earth and have been more of a small sister than a foreign asteroid that simply came too close. We do not know what kind of upheaval the capture event caused on the surface of the Earth, since the record is long gone.

Mercury

Being so close to the sun, Mercury is difficult to observe. We did not even know that its period of rotation was different from its year until 1965. The temperature at the pole rises to 430°C during the day, hot enough to melt lead. The nighttime temperature reaches −170°C. Mercury is heavily cratered, but it is crisscrossed by deep **scarps,** which appear so much like wrinkles on the skin of a dried-up apple that the **bulk contraction** of the planet after overheating is the favored explanation for the scarps. Mercury also has a weak magnetic field, first detected by the Mariner 10 spacecraft. Although active early on in the history of the solar system, no evidence for geological activity is found from 4 billion years ago to the present.

Venus

Venus is a planet of considerable interest because its diameter is almost exactly that of the Earth, yet its evolution must have been quite different. For example, the direction of Venus's rotation is opposite that of the other planets in the solar system. Until 1962 it was thought that the period of that rotation was four days. Scientists could not explain how one planet, rotating at about the same speed as the other planets, could rotate in the opposite direction. Radar finally penetrated the cloud cover of Venus in 1962 to find a planet spinning once every 243 days (Figure 1-6, color insert). That means the atmosphere consists of one continuous jet stream blowing at 100/m/s above the surface. The form of the surface revealed by radar is much more weatherbeaten than that of the Earth. What few craters there are have been almost flattened by the hurricane-force winds. Again, that is what we thought until direct observations were finally made.

As we progress through this book to look at geology under miles of water, our conclusions should be tempered by what the Soviets found upon landing unmanned probes on Venus. In 1970, the Venera 7 spacecraft set down on Venus *without* photographic equipment. The expected low light level through the opaque venusian atmosphere would prevent the taking of photographs. In the 15 minutes that the spacecraft worked, there was plenty of light and only a gentle breeze blowing. So the next Soviet spacecraft was able to take a few quick photos of Venus's surface, showing a boulder-strewn desert.

We are left to explain the massive erosion of its surface without the hurricane-force winds that blow in its upper atmosphere. Venus has a thick atmosphere made almost completely of carbon dioxide. There is so much carbon dioxide in the atmosphere that no **limestone** rock could exist on the planet. Limestone chemically bonds carbon dioxide with calcium to make one of the predominant forms of rock deposited beneath the Earth's oceans. But where did the water for oceans go on Venus? It is likely that the planet expelled all the chemically bound water because, being the same diameter as Earth, it has the same amount of KUTh. Although Venus has no magnetic field indicative of a molten core, it still underwent differentiation, and likely has a solid core because it is not as elliptical as Mars, but rather, spherical like the Earth. What happened to the water on Venus is both sobering and relevant to the present Earth environment. How delicate a balance it is.

All the water was *boiled off* by the temperature in the atmosphere. How did it get so hot? We hear on the news about the dangers of carbon monoxide pollution in our atmosphere. It forms carbon dioxide, which enhances the **greenhouse effect** of the atmosphere, causing the atmosphere to trap more heat from the sun than it gives off. This could cause the Earth's temperature to increase by a degree or so in our lifetime. Not much, you may think, but melting of the polar ice caps would flood every major coastal city in the world. Twenty percent of the solar radiation that penetrates the atmosphere is converted to **infrared** or longer wavelength radiation at the surface and is reflected back into space. Carbon dioxide clouds are opaque to this infrared radiation, so the heat stays in the atmosphere. The Earth might itself one day have a carbon dioxide atmosphere at 400°C. On Venus it became so hot that a limestone kiln was fired up, not only boiling all water off the surface of the planet but freeing all carbon dioxide from the rocks as well.

Moons of the Outer Planets

Jupiter and the planets beyond are gaseous and have no rock surfaces. They are so distant from the sun that not much rock-forming dust was blown out that far, and what little there was went into their moons. These moons have provided some of the truly great solar-system discoveries of our time. Jupiter, for instance, has 14 moons. One, Io, was photographed in the midst of volcanic eruption by the Voyager spacecraft in 1979 (Figure 1-7, color insert). No active volcanism other than eruptions on Earth had previously been seen in the solar system. Io is halfway between Jupiter's powerful **gravitational pull** and that of the next moon out, Europa. Heat from the **tidal pull** of these two bigger bodies causes the volcanism. But Io is remarkable for another reason: It has so much volcanic activity that its water is long gone. The **volatiles** now being blown into the atmosphere of Io are mostly sulfur. Io may have a small ocean of liquid sulfur, and when it rains, it rains sulfuric acid.

Europa, on the other hand, is completely covered with ice (Figure 1-8). Here we may have found a counterpart to the Earth's oceans, except that, being so far from the sun, it is an ocean of ice over 100 km thick. The whole moon is crisscrossed with ice **crevasses**. These cracks are likely caused by **tidal friction**, but water wells up into the cracks from below, renewing the surface into a perfectly smooth sphere. This contrasts with the next moon out, Ganymede, which is larger than Mercury and is one gigantic snowball with no solid center at all (Figure 1-9). Yet the surface is pockmarked with craters, so this moon must have been dead forever.

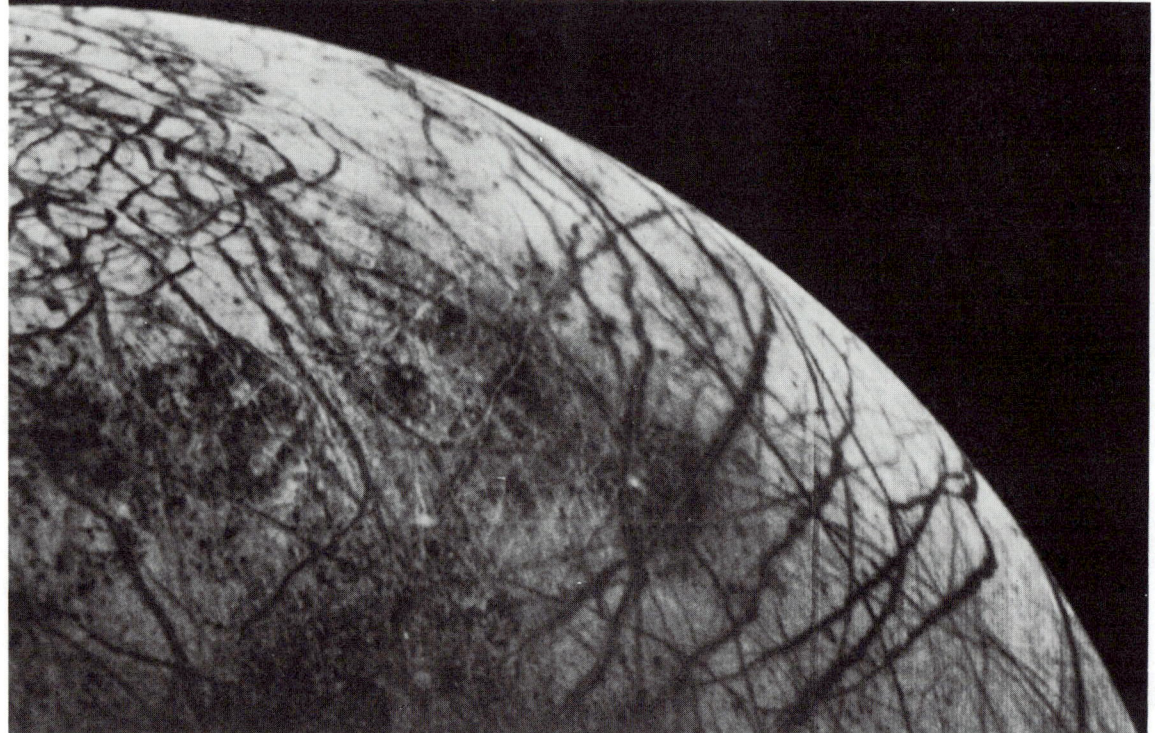

Figure 1-8. Europa, the moon of Jupiter between Io and Ganymede, has a surface covered by a thick sheet of ice. Black fractures are crevasses that indicate some kind of activity within the moon. For speculation of how similar to our solar system the moons of Jupiter are, read Arthur C. Clarke's book *2010: Odyssey Two*, in which Jupiter becomes a companion sun to our own and life evolves in a sea under the Europa ice sheet (NASA photo).

Summary

When we see the variety of planetary forms in the solar system, we can only be in awe of this magnificent planet Earth. Here life evolved so precariously as to tolerate a temperature range of only -100 to $+150°C$ in a solar system where *no other member* has temperature extremes even vaguely falling within that range of values. Arthur C. Clarke, in his book: *2010: Odyssey Two*, speculates about life evolving on the Jovian moons we have been discussing, and in many ways Io, Europa, and Ganymede are not that much different from Venus, Earth, and Mars. If Jupiter had been just a little bigger, it might have been a sun and we might have living companions in this solar system.

Clarke, A. C., 1982, 2010: Odyssey Two: New York, Ballantine.

Francis, P., 1982, The geology of the solar system, *in* D. G. Smith, ed., The Cambridge Encyclopedia of Earth Sciences: New York, Crown/Cambridge Press.

Milton, S., 1982, The Earth in space, *in* D. G. Smith, ed., The Cambridge Encyclopedia of Earth Sciences: New York, Crown/Cambridge Press.

Press, F. and Siever, R., 1982, The Earth, 3rd ed.: New York, Freeman.

2

History of Geology under the Sea

To understand the Earth, one must understand how it works under the sea. Not only is 70 percent of the Earth's surface covered by the ocean, but the undersea world is simpler to understand than the terrestrial world. Why is marine geology easier to understand than continental geology? Because the continents are an amalgam of countless collisions and **rifts** from the past and are the major players in **continental drift.** Just as the Sahara Desert was once at the South pole, so Antarctica was once a tropical coal forest. The Rockies were once the western shore of North America. Some of the centers (called **cratons**) of the continents are 3.5 billion years old.

In contrast, the ocean floor is young, geologically speaking. The time scale for geological movements and rock deformation is quite different from that of our lives. North America will slide perhaps six feet across the Pacific plate along the San Andreas Fault of California in one average lifetime. Yet in the last 10 million years, that seemingly insignificant movement along the San Andreas Fault has been enough to open the entire Gulf of California. Baja California used to be attached to Sonora, Mexico. As a further illustration of the complexities of the Earth, consider that the oceans themselves are 20 times older than the oldest sea floor (Figure 2-1). Understanding this apparent paradox will take us a long way toward learning how this planet works.

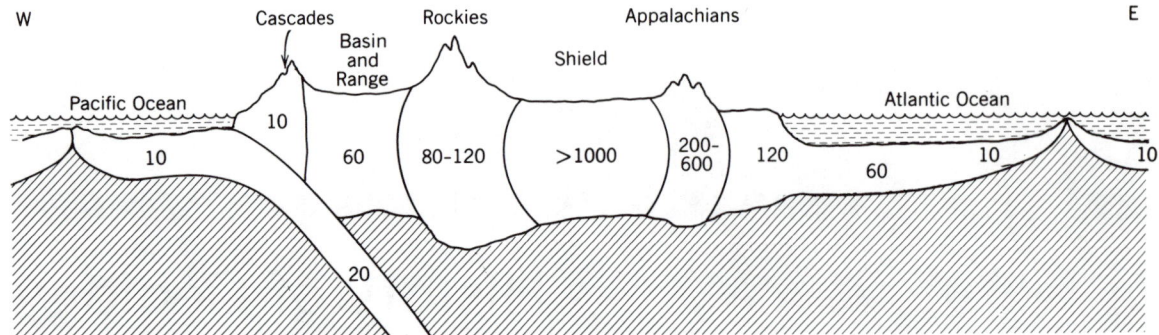

Figure 2-1. A cross section of the North American continent from the Pacific to the Atlantic Oceans. The rough ages of each of the primary geological provinces are shown. Hatching indicates the mantle below the oceanic and continental lithospheres.

How Do We See Beneath the Sea?

First we must realize that it is not easy to see what's beneath the sea. Now we do it by satellite as well as ship, but in the past we only knew what was directly beneath a ship as it sailed a particular path across the ocean. Over the entire seafaring history of man, ships have not crossed the first one percent of the surface area of the oceans. These ships provided only a fleeting glimpse of the form of the sea floor. But satellites have begun to change all that. In 1978 an oceanographic satellite called **Seasat** was launched (Figure 2-2). Its primary mission was to map sea-surface temperatures, wind directions, and wave heights. An **altimeter** was included to measure continuously the distance from the satellite to the sea surface. This was done by precisely measuring the travel time of microwave radar pulses. The radar scan produced an accurate image of the topography of the ocean's surface (with wave height averaged out).

The satellite failed because of an electrical problem after only 100 days of operation. Coincidentally, NASA was undergoing drastic cost cutbacks and no funds were available to analyze the Seasat data. More than three years went by before the altimetry data were looked at, but Seasat's radar observations will as surely revolutionize our concepts of how the Earth works as Marie Curie's discovery of radioactivity did. The sea surface is called a **geoid,** implying a free-floating surface that automatically seeks a level of equal gravity everywhere. Gravity is a direct function of mass, so if more mass lies near Hawaii than off New York, as is the case, the sea level

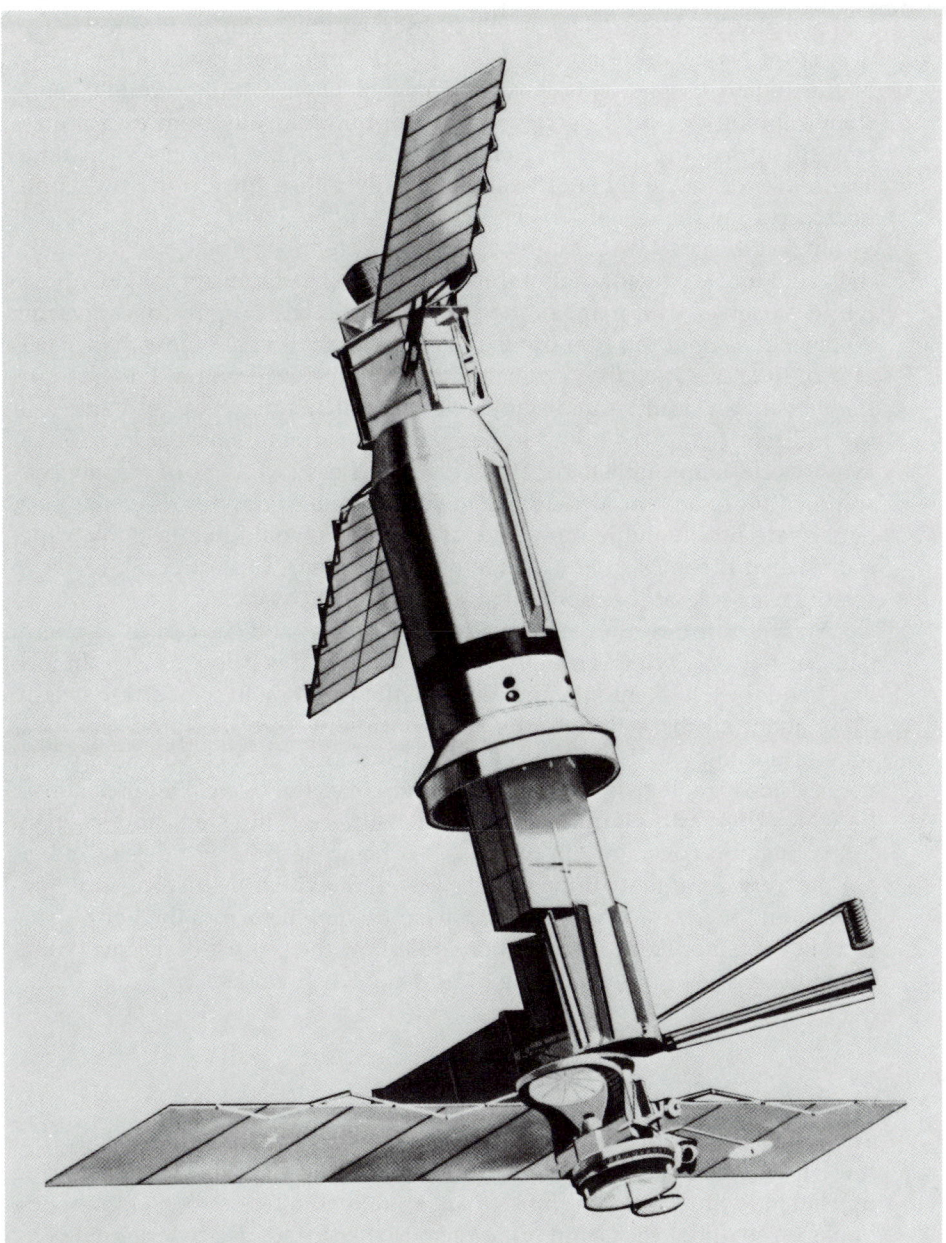

Figure 2.2. The Seasat oceanographic observation satellite returned a vast amount of information about the gravity field of the ocean floor. The satellite covered 90 percent of the ocean surface in 100 days, whereas all ships in human history have covered far less than 1 percent of the oceans (from William F. Haxby).

will actually be deeper. The satellite observed the ocean surface to be 1 m deeper off New York than off Hawaii. A 100-m trough exists in the center of the Indian Ocean. This basin, somewhat like an imperceptibly gentle slope running downhill over thousands of miles, results from excess mass beneath Africa and Australia versus that beneath the Indian Ocean floor. The seawater in the Indian Ocean is actually pulled toward the two continents, creating the trough.

In fact, Seasat saw enough of the oceans in only 100 days to determine the geoid for 90 percent of its surface (Figure 2-3, color insert). Suddenly we found ourselves with maps of the sea-floor mass based upon coverage from 90 percent as opposed to those made from ship coverage of less than 1 percent of its area. Of course, errors in our old maps were found. For example, Kerguellen, an island equidistant from Australia, Antarctica, and Africa in the Indian Ocean, was found to be many miles from its proper location on every world map published before 1978. It is easy to think of ourselves as so much more advanced than the great Portuguese navigators of the past, but we are not infallible nor so advanced as we would like to think, especially when it comes to knowledge of the sea floor. It is, after all, easier to see the near side of the moon than the floor of the ocean.

Mass is not directly converted to topography, and the Seasat altimetry data see not only what is on the sea floor, but what is below as well. In fact, we get our best look into the mantle from the variation in sea-surface height. More about all these things later, but for now we see the rather primitive state of our knowledge of the sea floor. Without even a cursory glimpse of the sea floor, geologists were unable to discover the overriding mechanism by which the Earth's surface moves. That surface is not static and stagnant but young and constantly in turmoil. It is being destroyed and renewed, as are the very continents upon which we reside, which themselves ride piggyback on the great plates that are constantly moving across the Earth's surface. Let's step back into our history and follow the process of discovery that led to our present understanding of how the Earth works.

The Early Days

The British were, not surprisingly, the first to do serious marine geology. But it wasn't the famed *H.M.S. Challenger* that started it all. Cable ships repairing transatlantic lines were the first to snag (accidentally, of course) grappling hooks on sea-floor rocks and bring them to the surface. Discoveries made by these cable ships, such as the existence of a plateau of shoal topography between North America and England, led directly to the British admiralty's charge that the *H.M.S. Challenger* spend 1872 to 1876 searching the world's oceans for "basic knowledge and the betterment of man" (Figure 2-4).

Figure 2-4. A facsimile of the original oceanographic exploration ship, the *H.M.S. Challenger*, which sailed the oceans in the 1870s.

But our view of the earth beneath the sea progressed only very slightly from the *Challenger* era to World War II. It is interesting that technological development was (and still is) the controlling factor in the expansion of our knowledge of the ocean floor. While the rest of the world was at war once again, the neutral Swedish government sponsored expeditions to attempt to return to the surface the soft material covering the sea floor. This **sediment** or mud was difficult to retrieve because it is often "soupy".

The invention of the piston corer laid open a whole new world of the Earth's past (c.f., Sullivan, 1978). The first experiment consisted of driving the barrel of a pipe into the mud with explosive charges. The technique consistently failed, however, because in addition to the hazards of handling explosives at sea, the tube pushed the sediment down and around the outside of the pipe rather than passively filling the barrel. The Swedes invented an alternative (Figure 2-5), which is still used worldwide to this day—the piston corer. As the barrel passively falls through the mud, a piston fires upward from the bottom of the barrel, sucking mud into the pipe.

What came to the surface in these first "cores" was a layered history of the sea floor going back millions of years. The mud turned out to be com-

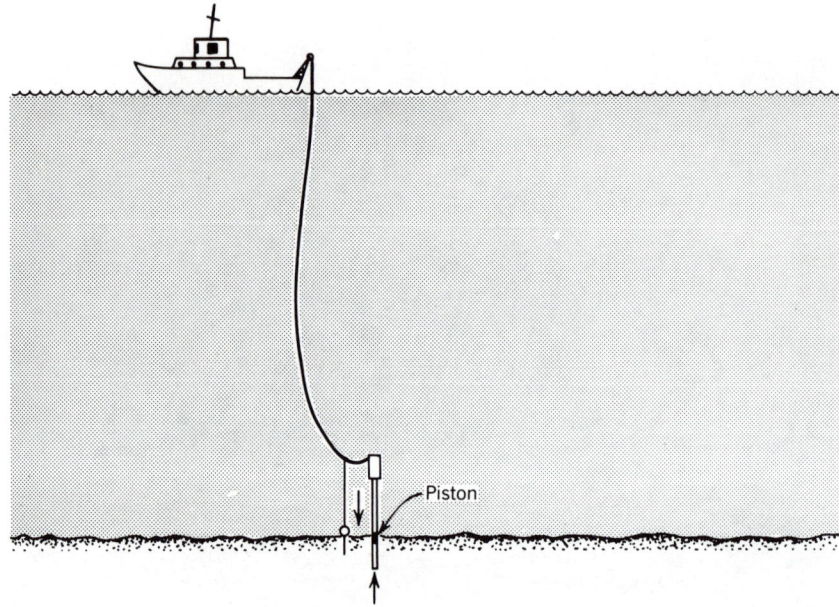

Figure 2-5. A piston corer that is designed to take samples of sediment on the sea floor by drawing mud into a steel barrel at the same time that the apparatus is thrust into the sediments. A wire cable lowers and returns the piston corer to the surface ship.

posed of shells of dead microscopic marine organisms that once lived near the surface (Figure 2-6). They would die and gently rain downward to build up over the millennia a blanket of sediments covering the rock. The discovery that the evolution of these organisms was preserved in the shape and form of these shells launched the profession of marine geology. Because the rate of growth of the sedimentary blanket is so slow (as slow as 1 m per million years), the history of that sea floor for the last 10 million years could be laid bare on the deck of a ship in a 10-m piston core.

Acoustic Imaging of the Sea Floor

Other advances in sea-floor physics were proceeding within the U.S. Navy during World War II. The advent of **sonar** allowed for mapping the topography of the sea floor during the normal progress of any ship across the sea. In fact, deep-sea volcanoes called **guyots** and **seamounts** were discovered

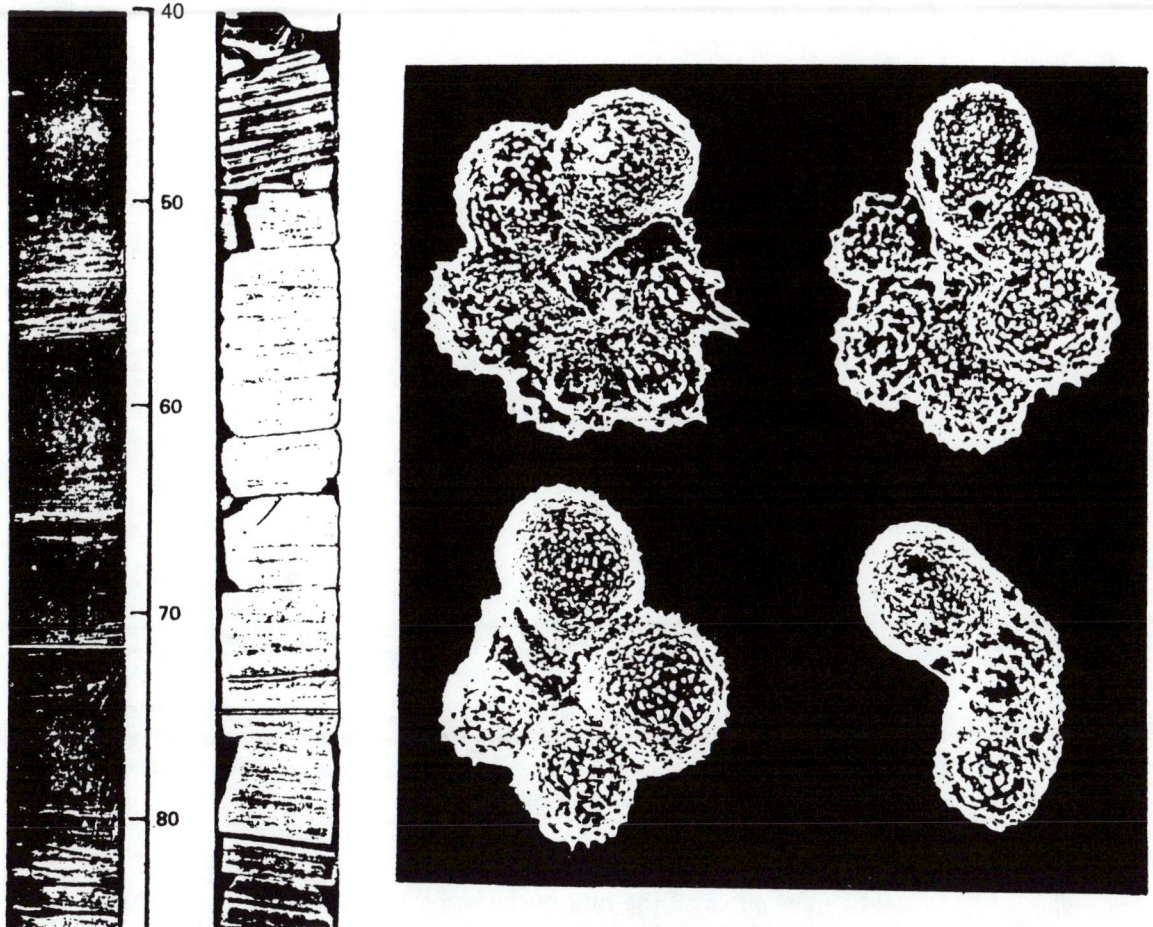

Figure 2-6. A representative mud core from the drilling vessel *Glomar Challenger*. Depth is given in cm below the seafloor. A smear of the mud placed under a microscope reveals foraminifera shells, which are the primary component of calcium carbonate sediments under the sea (from Kennett, 1981).

by a naval troop carrier making routine runs from Hawaii to tiny western Pacific islands (Figure 2-7).

Those early sea-floor scanning techniques pale in comparison to today's sophisticated acoustic tomography, multiswath profiling, and three-dimensional sidescan imaging. The early image was from a broad outgoing beam some 60 degrees wide. This beam of sound would be emitted from an acous-

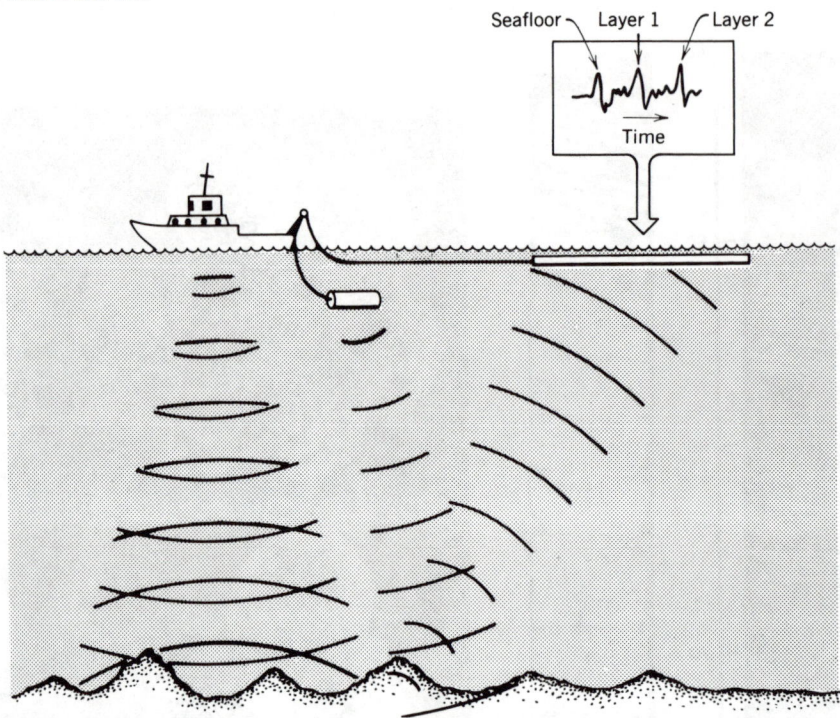

Figure 2-7. Seismic reflection profiling (right) detects the major boundaries under the sea floor that reflect sound energy. Echo sounding (left) uses a higher frequency sound source that does not penetrate the sea floor, but instead reveals the topography of the surface.

tic transmitter on the hull of the ship. It would travel outward and downward to hit the first sea floor it encountered and to reflect back to the ship's hull. The problem was that a large mountain off to the left or right of the ship would reflect the sound just as quickly back to the ship as the sea floor directly under the ship. The resulting topographic profile of the sea floor was a crudely averaged depth to sea floor under the entire 60° of the echo sounder's beam width. The new techniques utilize either multiple transmitters with narrow beam widths or deeply towed sidescan transducers, which can easily distinguish topography off to the side of a ship's course from that directly beneath the hull.

As an excellent example of the current state of the art in sea-floor imagery, consider the stereoscopic sidescan view of a submarine canyon off the east coast of the United States prepared by John Farre of Lamont-Doherty Geological Observatory (Figure 2-8). This 5-km wide stereo sonar image follows the path of Carteret Canyon off New Jersey from shallow water at the bottom of Figure 2-8 to the deep-water terminus of the canyon along the

J.A. FARRE   L-DGO

J.A. FARRE   L-DGO

Left eye

Right eye

Figure 2-8. Undersea sonic images in stereo show submarine canyon of the Hudson River off the east coast of New Jersey. White line interrupting each eye's image is data gap where towed receiver hit sea floor. A sharp drop in topography crossing the canyon just above the lower data gap produces a submarine waterfall as the slurry of river debree slides down the canyon toward the deep sea.

continental slope-rise boundary at the top of the figure. A submarine canyon is the subsurface extension of the current of a major river pouring its heavy erosional debris into the ocean. Think of it as a river that extends far out into the ocean. The depth of the water is 1500 m at the bottom of the figure and 2300 m at the top. The white stripe passing lengthwise through the center of the photo is the path of the towed vehicle emitting the sidescan acoustic pulses. The images to the left and right of the vehicle are reflections off the sea floor. Whites are strong reflectors; blacks are acoustic shadows. The horizontal white gaps are missed intervals caused by the need to change magnetic tape for the recording of the digital images.

The three-dimensional image is displayed at a ten-to-one vertical exaggeration to blow up topography changes on the sea floor. The separation of each data point in the left versus right-hand images is offset to produce the appropriate perception of depth for unaided stereo viewing. Unfocus the eyes as if viewing a far object and the two images merge and become stereoscopic. Better results are achieved using a mirror-style stereo viewer, especially one with magnification.

The image shows that Carteret Canyon is not a simple v- or u-shaped valley, but that along its lower reaches a very narrow canyon crosses a steep cliff forming an "underwaterfall." It then is almost stranded on the flat plain beneath the falls where it feeds into one of several flat-floored, steep-walled erosional chutes. These grooved chutes terminate abruptly at the slope–rise boundary. This is the site of an oblong depression that drains toward the left. In the upper left-hand corner of the image is a strongly reflective, angular object—perhaps a sunken ship.

Submarine Detection Methods

Attempts at submarine detection led not only to the development of sonar but to the measurement of the Earth's magnetic field at sea as well. Submarines could be found by scanning the magnetic field of the Earth and identifying the large positive perturbations that are caused by the magnetic body of the submarine. Depth charges provided the first energy sources to bounce sound waves through the outer skin of the ocean floor and record the reflected and refracted waveforms (seismology) beneath the sea floor itself.

Meanwhile, the transatlantic cable industry reappeared on the horizon to rekindle scientific curiosity about the geology of the sea floor. After the war, the Lamont-Doherty Geological Observatory was founded as part of Columbia University on the Palisades Cliffs across the Hudson River from New York City. The continual loss of offshore cable service due to breakage led Maurice Ewing and Bruce Heezen of the observatory to relate some of the breaks to sea-floor **earthquakes** and subsequent landslides. Scanning through past records they found that one particular earthquake that occurred east of Cape Cod in 1929 resulted in the instant severing of six cables within 95 miles of the epicenter. To the south, however, Heezen and Ewing found that cables snapped in sequential order depending upon their distance from the earthquake. They found that an undersea landslide had traveled 800 km to the south at an initial speed of 83 km/h under water depths ranging from tens to thousands of meters (Figure 2-9). Such astounding undersea events

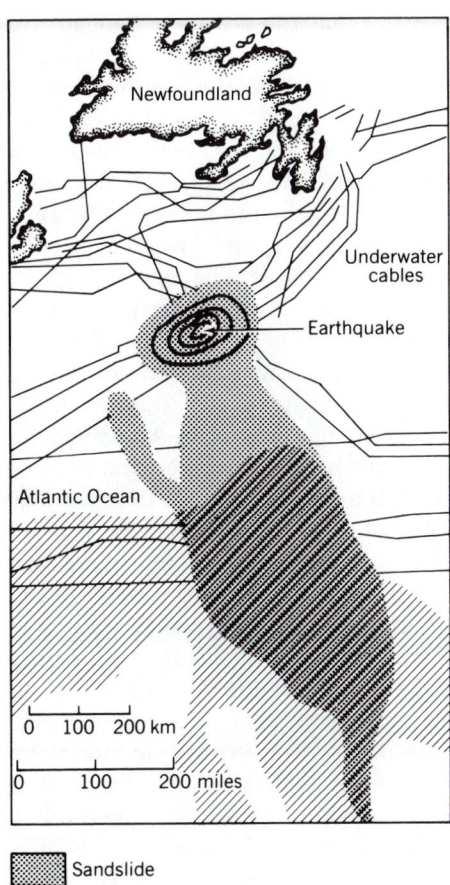

Newfoundland

Underwater
cables

Earthquake

Atlantic Ocean

0   100   200 km

0   100   200 miles

▨ Sandslide

▨ Abyssal plain

Figure 2-9. Undersea mud slides (dots) from an earthquake off Newfoundland were discovered by Bruce Heezen and Maurice Ewing to be the cause of severed trans-Atlantic telephone cables (black lines). Prior to this time, the deep sea (hatching) was thought to be a geologically inactive place (from Sullivan, 1978).

are now known to be commonplace throughout geological time and are called **turbidity currents,** for the murky, turbid appearance of the heavy slurry that comprises the slide.

A View of the Sea Floor

Full-time oceanographic exploration of the sea floor was then launched by Lamont and other great United States oceanographic institutions, such as the Scripps Institution of Oceanography in San Diego, California, and Woods Hole Oceanographic Institution on Cape Cod in Massachusetts. The resulting discoveries show clearly and concisely that the sea floor beneath the oceans is in a state of constant motion. Its history is one of birth by volcanic fire, death by **subduction,** and rebirth by earthquake and volcano again and again throughout the earth's history.

To give an example of the spectacular scenery beneath the ocean, the **topography** of the sea floor is dominated by the world's largest mountain range. Higher than the Himalayas, this world-encircling midocean **ridge** is, in fact, a crack into the molten interior of the planet. New lava is constantly spewing forth along this 40,000-mile mountain range. The crest is high for the same reasons that Hawaii and other volcanoes pour lava from their tops: Hot rock expands to greater volume than cold rock. The midocean ridge is one continuous series of volcanoes of almost unimaginable dimensions. Its smoothly sloping flanks extend from the exact center of the Atlantic Ocean, for example, all the way to both the American and European–African shores of the western and eastern Atlantic, respectively. Bruce Heezen first realized the geologic significance of the **mid-Atlantic ridge,** but thought that because of its magnitude, it must be the site of an expanding Earth.

Scratched into these mountain flanks like long fingernail marks are fracture-zone rifts delineating the paths of the flanks away from the volcanic ridge crests. At the other end of many of these flanks are extremely deep trenches. These trenches are up to 10 miles deep, and are the deepest features on the planet. Here cold rock is subducted back into the molten mantle, there to be remelted and eventually have a rebirth back at the other end of the massive conveyor belt: the midocean ridge. Thus, expanding mountains are compensated for by subduction zones, which keep the Earth from expanding. Pockmarked seemingly at random across these great ocean bottoms are individual volcanoes, called seamounts, that exist because the heat below each seamount was too great to deny lava its eruptive day at the surface.

Summary

Thus the ocean and continents are 3.5 billion years old, but the oldest sea floor is only 160 million years old. Ocean water is not subducted but instead floats above this great conveyor belt. The continents too are carried on the back of the conveyor belts, but they do not drift aimlessly about on the soft ocean floor. Rather, they ride on the back of giant plates, which form a mosaic-like pattern across the Earth's surface. These plates move relative to each other following precise geometric laws of motion on a sphere; these laws were laid before us by Euclid but a flicker of geologic time ago. In order even to begin to understand the Earth, including that beneath the sea, we must establish the physical and chemical laws by which these great plates are born, destroyed, and move across the Earth's surface. The theory that unites these diverse processes under one grand hypothesis has created a revolution in the Earth sciences as great as Darwinian evolution in biology or Einsteinian relativity in physics. Called **plate tectonics,** it is the greatest discovery ever in our attempts to understand how the Earth works.

Further Reading

Heezen, B., 1954, The mid-Atlantic ridge: *National Geographic,* August.

Sullivan, W., 1978, Continents in Motion: New York, Freeman.

Plate
Tectonics

The modern concept of plate tectonics began with the theory of continental drift proposed by Alfred Wegener in the early part of this century. He was a meteorologist who spent his winters on the ice in Greenland. It was during these periods of isolation that he contemplated the Earth and wrote about continents that drift about like icebergs in the sea. He deduced this theory from the remarkable geometric fit of the east coast of South America and the west coast of Africa. His book *The Origin of Continents and Oceans,* first published in 1915, sparked a great deal of controversy. The centerpoint (Figures 3-1 and 3-2) of his contentions was that South America fits perfectly into Africa because they had once been a single continent that was somehow torn apart. In the great geological past, a tremendous rifting of the large continent occurred and South America floated off to the west of Africa, carrying with her identical biota and similar geological features along her common coast. Evolution took care of the rest, developing diverse fauna that adapted to different living conditions on the now separate continents (Figure 3-2).

The idea was not well received, however. Geologists did not take kindly to a meteorologist dabbling in their profession. They seized upon the lack of a mechanism for such an outlandish occurrence. The physics of how a continent could be so mobile was missing. Did the continents plow their way through the ocean floor? Impossible! The existence of diverse but related flora and fauna on different continents was a well-established fact, but the prevailing explanation was that land bridges once connected the continents allowing for migration of animals across them. These bridges had somehow

31

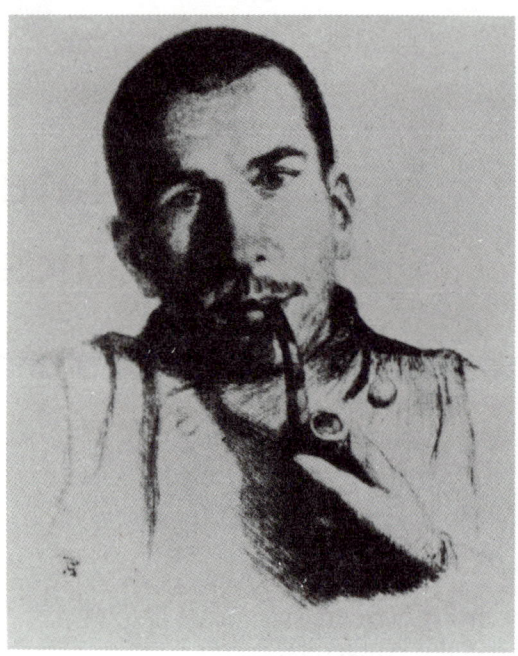

Figure 3-1. Alfred Wegener with his best fit of Africa into South America.

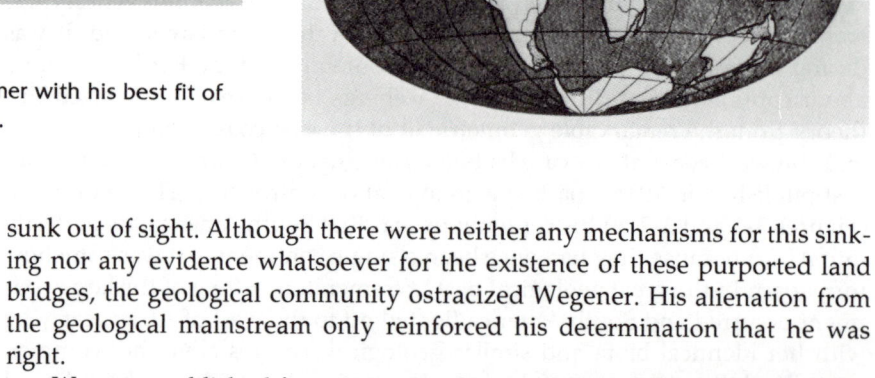

sunk out of sight. Although there were neither any mechanisms for this sinking nor any evidence whatsoever for the existence of these purported land bridges, the geological community ostracized Wegener. His alienation from the geological mainstream only reinforced his determination that he was right.

Wegener published four revisions of his book, the last claiming in a publication note that continental drift had just been proved (1927) by the latest longitude measurements between North America and Europe, which showed that the two continents had moved apart by 32 cm/yr from 1914 to 1927. These rates are 10 times the actual rate of movement, and probably say more about the inaccuracy of determining longitude in the early 1900s than about continental drift. Wegener's last revision reads like the desperate pleading of a scientist who has become a defender of his life's philosophy rather than a proponent of a scientific theory. We know that he was working on another version of the book when he met his untimely death in the win-

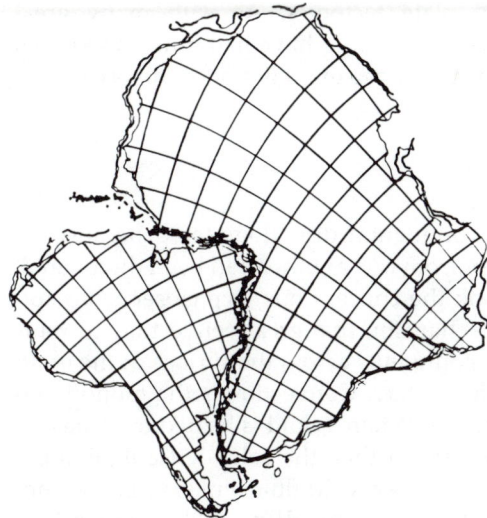

Figure 3-2. The present-day best fit of South America and Africa requires that the continental margins, not the coastline, define the edges that were initially rifted apart. Earthquakes from the mid-Atlantic ridge (black dots) are held fixed and the two continents are rotated about a pole of rotation back together. Note that a good fit requires that the Falkland continental margin be included as part of South America (from Smith et al., 1977).

ter of 1930 on the Greenland ice cap. No traces of either his body or his manuscript have ever been found.

To judge Wegener an amateur or a buffoon would be foolish indeed. He was not only one of the great explorers of Greenland, finding almost single-handedly the most favorable route across the island from east to west, but he was also a great meteorologist and the first to measure the true thickness of the inland ice sheet: 1800 m. The foreword to his last revision to *The Origin of Continents and Oceans* carries some profound predictions:

Scientists still do not appear to understand sufficiently that all earth sciences must contribute evidence towards unveiling the state of our planet in earlier times, and that the truth of the matter can only be reached by combining all this evidence. . . . I believe that the final resolution of the (continental drift) problem can only come from geophysics, since only that branch of science provides sufficiently precise methods.

If he were to include **geochemistry,** he would be exactly right about how continental drift was finally resolved as only one component of the bigger theory that unifies all the movements at the surface of the Earth into an all-encompassing paradigm called plate tectonics. As with many great pioneers, one wonders what fun Wegener would have had if he had known what we know about the geological bonanzas that lay under the oceans.

Convection in the Mantle

As we said earlier, the theory of continental drift floundered because no mechanism to carry continents away from one another had been discovered. Arthur Holmes in 1928 to 1936 took the concept one step closer to acceptability by proposing just such a mechanism: that great convection currents in the mantle (Figure 3-3) carry the continents across the surface of the earth as a large conveyor belt carries bales of hay. Convection is the motion you see in soy soup in a Japanese restaurant. When a fluid is heated from below, the hot liquid expands and becomes lighter than the cold, dense fluid at the top. The light, hot liquid rises and the dense, cold fluid sinks. This does not happen erratically; concentrated patterns of **upwelling** and **downwelling convection cells** appear in the fluid.

But does convection really exist in the Earth's mantle, and if so, does it carry the continents across great expanses of ocean? Not enough observational evidence existed to answer these questions until the 1960s. It was the exploration of the ocean floors that provided the necessary evidence. In 1964, Harry Hess of Princeton University looked at the accumulating evidence from deep-sea soundings of depth to the sea floor and found that they demonstrated clearly the form of a giant range of mountains submerged between the African–European Atlantic Coast and North America. Hess proposed that this mid-Atlantic ridge was the site of a process he termed sea-floor spreading.

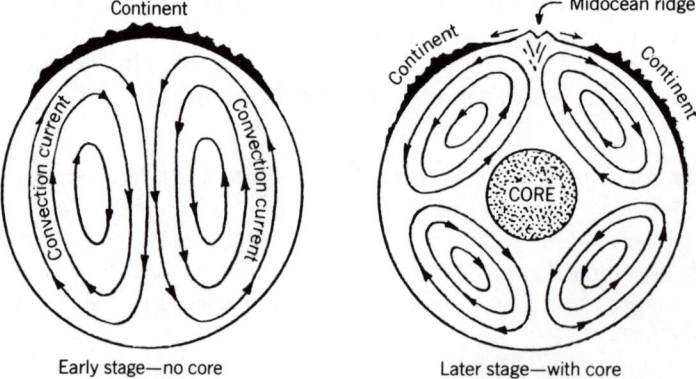

Figure 3-3. The convection hypothesis of Arthur Holmes and Vening Meinez to explain why Wegener's contintental drift happened (from Holmes, 1978).

Sea-Floor Spreading, Subduction Zones, and Transform-Fault Plate Boundaries

The mid-Atlantic ridge consists of a string of volcanoes that produce new sea floor when they erupt. Lava cools and spreads away from these volcanoes to become the conveyor belt upon which the continents ride, hence the name sea-floor spreading. This process forms new rock, then moves new lava away from the mountain range as even newer lava replaces it at the midocean ridge crest. A lithospheric plate is so formed.

In the late 1960s, the remaining pieces of the puzzle were synthesized into the theory of plate tectonics. For example, how is new sea floor formed in the Atlantic, and South America separated from Africa without the earth's expanding? Plate tectonics proposes that the Earth's surface is broken into large mosaic-like plates that move relative to each other in a precisely determined way. Geometry explains the motion; convection controls the interactions. The Earth does not expand because plates can interact in two ways besides sea-floor spreading. The opposite end of the conveyor belt exists at deep-sea trenches, such as that off the west coast of South America (Figure 3-4), where old rock from the surface plunges downward, back into the man-

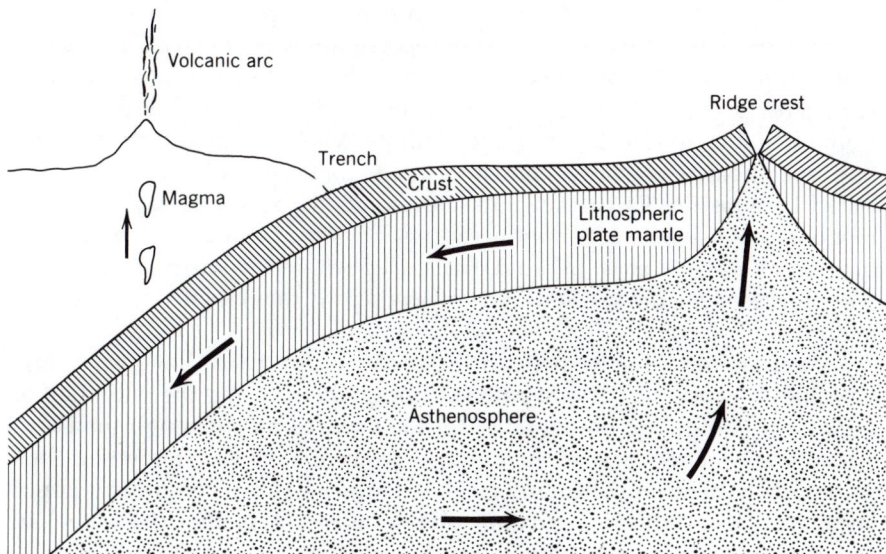

Figure 3-4. Schematic drawing of cross section from a midocean ridge (right) to a subduction zone (left). Sea-floor spreading generates new oceanic plate, and subduction consumes the plate back into the mantle as if the system were one big conveyor belt.

tle. Subduction zones mark the collision of two plates. One plate must ride over the other, forcing the weaker plate back into the mantle (Figure 3-4). There are mountain ranges at both of these boundaries. A third type of plate interaction occurs when two plates slide past each other. A long linear fracture in the earth called a **transform fault,** such as the San Andreas, results. Here the Pacific plate is sliding to the northwest across the North American plate.

Each of these three plate boundaries is characterized by a different kind of force: **tension,** or extension at sea-floor spreading boundaries; **compression,** or collision at subduction zones; and **shearing,** or tearing at transform faults.

Plate Tectonics

Let's look in detail at the accumulated evidence that the Earth is indeed covered with a mosaic of rigid plates. These plates move about as solid entities and interact with each other only at their common boundaries. The overriding discovery at the foundation of plate tectonics is that the surface of the Earth is capped by rigid outer plates overlying a soft, partially liquid mantle.

How do we know what is inside the Earth? When an earthquake happens, for example, the Earth shakes with a precise group of vibrations. The primary wave of energy is called a **compressional wave** (also called the primary wave or the P-wave) because the particles in the Earth push and pull each other as the vibration is passed (think of it as shaking exactly away from, then toward, the center of the earthquake). The second form of vibration is a **shear wave** (also known as the secondary wave or S-wave), so called because the Earth transmits the vibrations by a sideways shearing motion. This wave is important because solid must be in contact with solid for a shear wave to pass. If liquid exists deep within the Earth, shear waves will be absent for the portion of the wave's path that crosses through that region.

Waves going directly through the center of the Earth have very slow velocities because part of that path is through the core and the outer half of the core is liquid. The time it takes for the wave to pass through the Earth appears to be slow because the liquid core absorbs shear energy and thus slows down the wave. The surficial layer of the Earth is a fast transmitter of shear waves, and thus is rigid and solid. However, less than 100 km below the surface, a low velocity zone exists (Figure 3-5).

The low velocities are caused by molten rock, not much—perhaps 1 percent—but enough to slow down shear waves and to provide lava to the surface whenever a crack appears in the surface lid. We call this lid the **lithosphere;** it is the material of which the plates are made. The partially molten mantle below is called the **asthenosphere.** The lithosphere, being made up

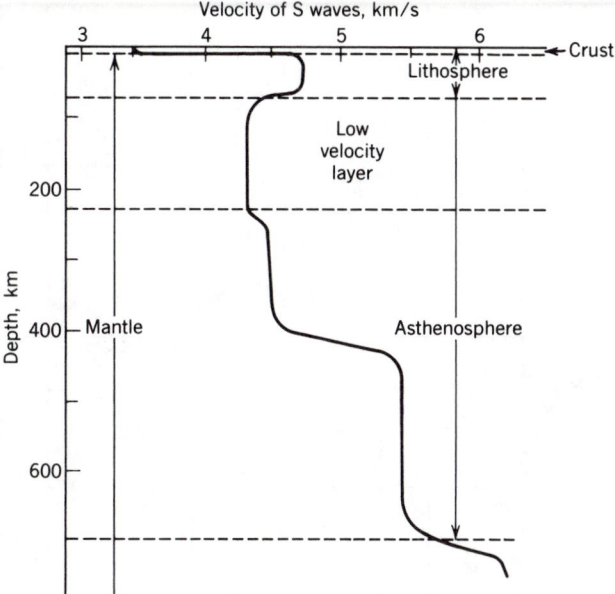

Figure 3-5. Velocity structure as a function of depth for the transmission of shear waves. Partial melt zones slow the shear wave propagation dramatically. The lithosphere of solid, cold rock stands out abruptly as a major seismic boundary (from Dewey, 1972).

of cold, solidified lava is gravitationally unstable in that it is heavier than the asthenosphere below. In fact, plate tectonics is a large convection pattern. But the surface motions of that convection pattern are governed by very precise laws because the lithosphere is a rigid solid. Plates were discovered because they are so rigid that they obey strict rules of motion. These patterns were quickly noticed after observations of the sea floor brought in enough information to map the plates and their boundaries.

Two solids on a sphere can do only one of three things and remain rigid: pull apart from each other, collide, or slide across each other. Tear a sheet of paper in two, then hold one piece in each hand. Any motion of the left-hand piece relative to the right can be described by one of these three motions *if and only if they remain on the same plane of motion.* Sound familiar? Substitute the surface of a sphere, and these are the three forms of plate boundaries described in the last section. The plates interact only at their edges, not within their solid interiors.

The data to prove this theory was provided to the geological community beginning in the 1950s, when the United States was preoccupied with the detection of Soviet nuclear bomb tests. The Eisenhower administration built a worldwide network of 125 seismic stations to record ground shaking from nuclear tests, and this network also recorded every large earthquake that

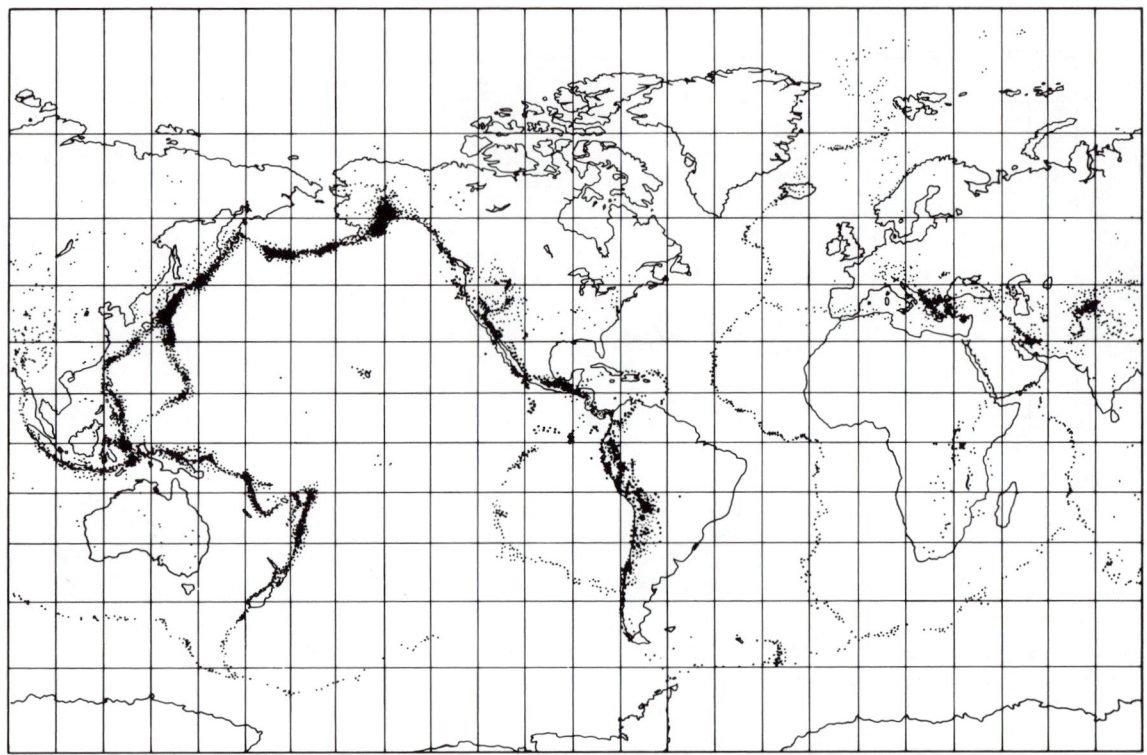

Figure 3-6. World seismicity, 1961 to 1969. Black dots are individual earthquakes.

happened anywhere in the world. By the late 1960s the network had accumulated enough earthquake locations to plot them on a world map. It became clear that earthquakes do not occur randomly on the surface, but in linear belts that wrap around the Earth (Figure 3-6). This remarkable fact had escaped detection until the seismic network was constructed.

But what controls earthquakes so precisely as to align them into belts? Moreover, when the locations of all known volcanoes are added to the same world map, they fall along the same belts as the earthquakes (Figures 3-6 and 3-7). It took a simple but elegant intellectual leap for geologists to recognize that these belts of seismic (earthquake) and volcanic activity are the boundaries of interaction among a few large and rigid plates that cover the surface of the Earth.

Plate tectonics, as originally defined by Tuzo Wilson (University of Toronto), Dan McKenzie (Cambridge University), Xavier Le Pichon (University of Paris, but then at Lamont), and Jason Morgan (Princeton University),

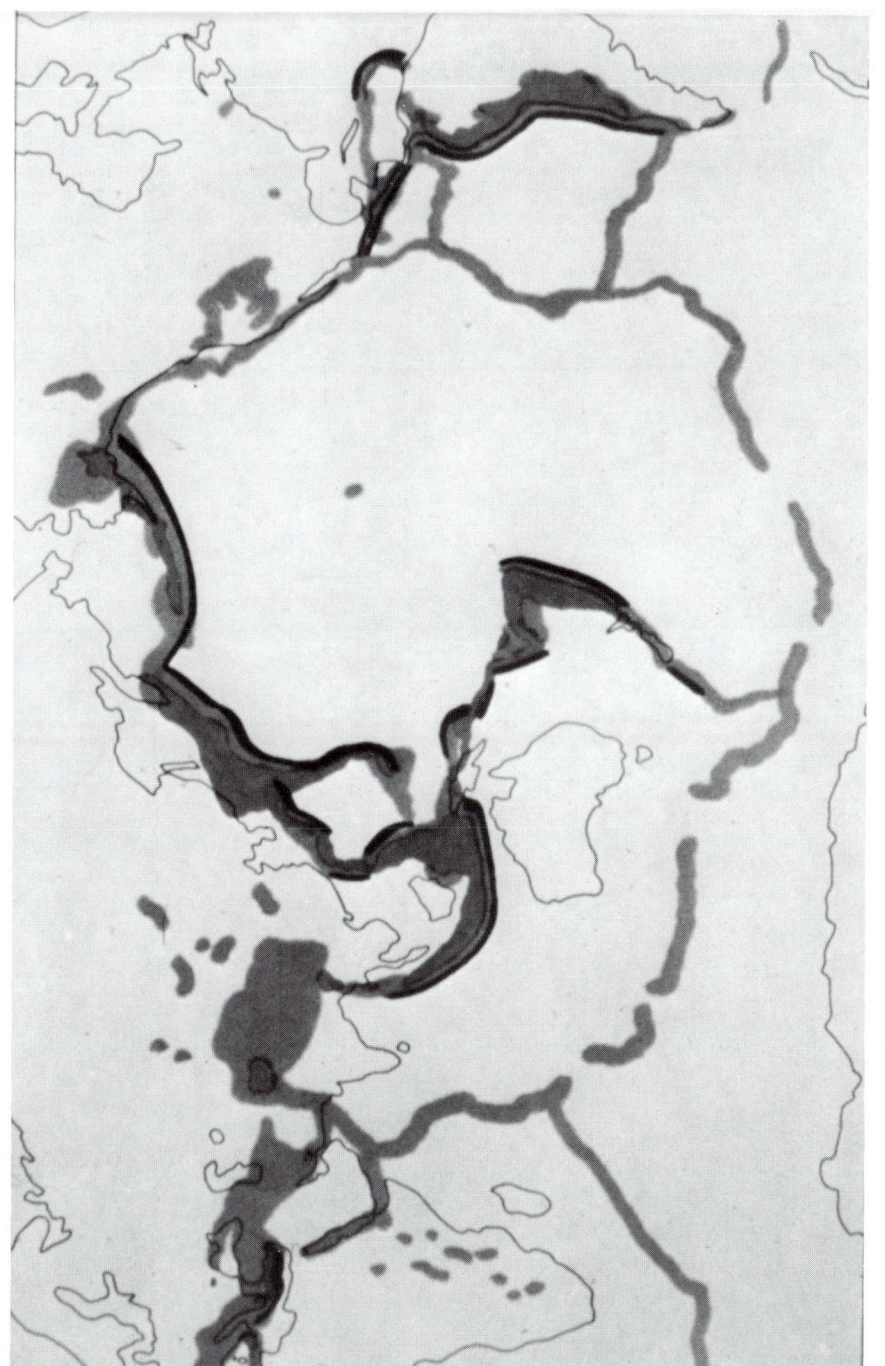

Figure 3-7. Active volcanism on the planet. Solid black lines are subduction zones. Shading are areas with presently active volcanoes (From John Dewey).

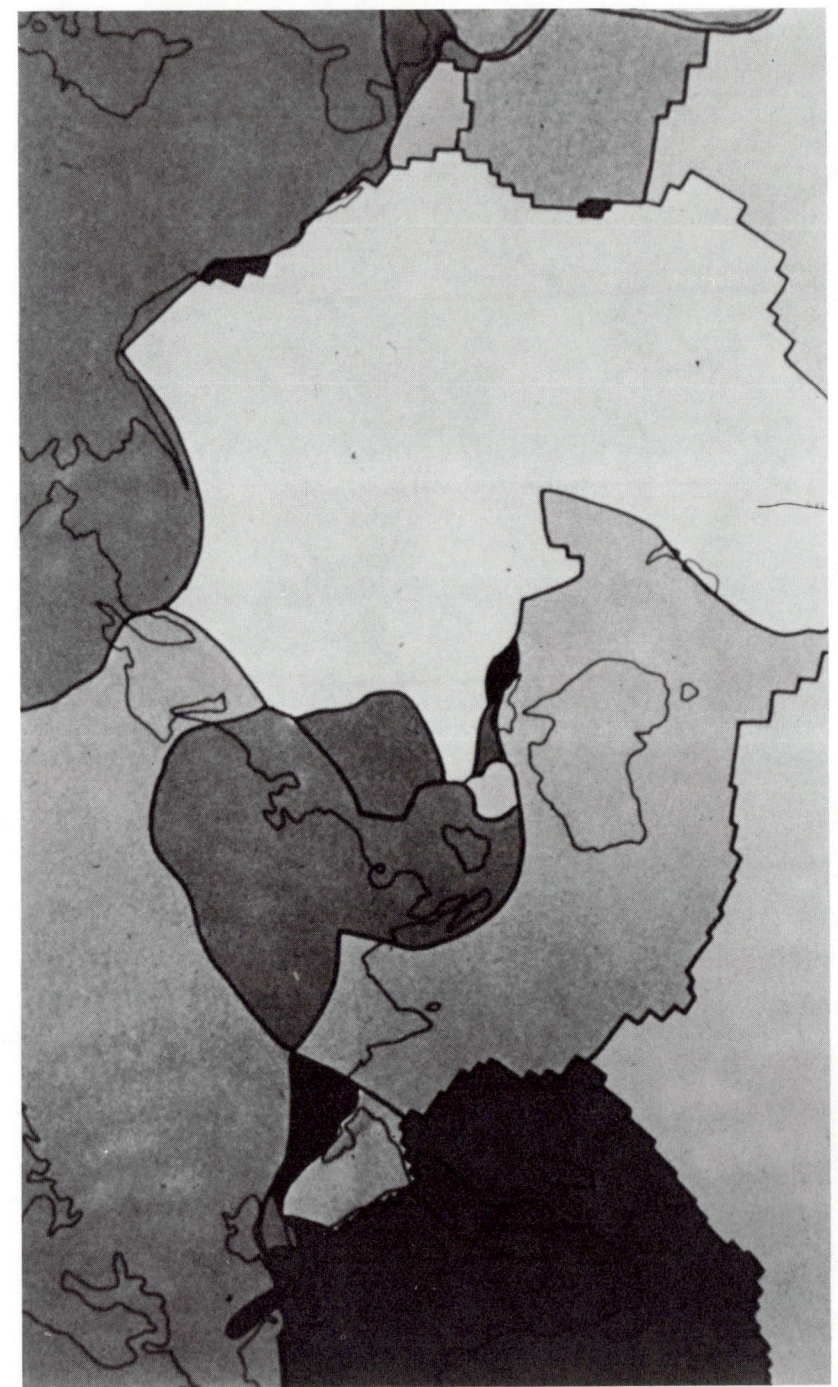

Figure 3-8. Individual plates of the Earth's surface (from John Dewey).

Figure 3-9. A classic example of a transform fault is the San Andreas Fault in California, which separates Pacific plate (left) from North American plate (from Robert E. Wallace, United States Geological Survey).

describes the relative motion of such plates but does not deal directly with the forces within the mantle that cause these motions. It is simple and predictive, but only for surface motions. The Earth's surface is covered with approximately 12 large, stable lithospheric plates. They move relative to

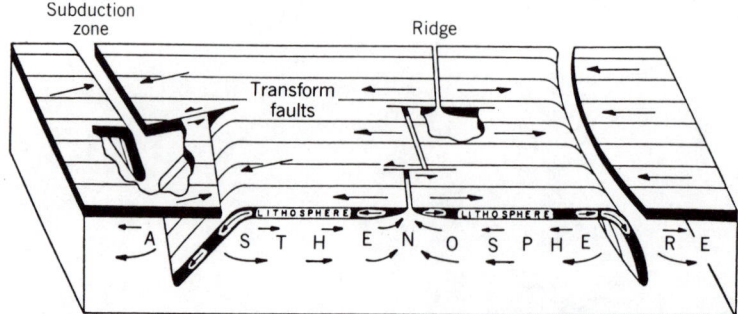

Figure 3-10. Schematic drawing of all three plate boundaries possible between two plates in plate tectonics (from Isacks et al., 1968).

each other causing tectonic activity only at their boundaries where interactions with other plates occur. Almost all the earthquakes and volcanoes on the surface of the earth happen at these precisely defined boundaries (compare Figures 3-6, 3-7, 3-8).

The elegance of plate tectonics goes far beyond just describing where earthquakes and volcanoes occur. There are processes occurring at these boundaries that allow us to determine the direction of motion of plates on the surface. For example, we can predict that if the Pacific plate continues to move to the northwest relative to the North American plate as defined by the San Andreas Fault (Figure 3-9), San Francisco will collide with Alaska in 40 million years. You might say that this information is not of much use, but plate tectonics also allows us to infer that San Francisco used to be attached to Sonora, Mexico, and that gold mines found there might "have brothers" ripped off Sonora and carried a thousand miles to the north.

Plates that move apart have transform faults scratched into their surfaces (Figure 3-10). These always point in the direction of the relative motion of the two plates involved (Figure 3-11). If we can map the direction of these transform faults (Figure 3-12), we can determine a pole of rotation of the two plates. Eighteenth-century Swiss mathematician Leonhard Euler showed that two rigid bodies moving on a sphere can only rotate about a single pole. Thus, we can exactly describe the motion of any two plates relative to each other by some angular rotation velocity about a pole located somewhere on the Earth. This pole is not tied to the Earth's pole of rotation. That is, the rotation of two plates is relative only to each other; it is not related to a fixed reference frame within the Earth such as the Earth's rotation axis. We can prove that Eulerian geometry holds for the motion of, for example, North America versus Africa. First we locate the direction of transform faults marking the sea-floor spreading motion of Africa away from North America (Figure 3-12). These will define small circles or lines of latitude about the pole of rotation. Then we draw great circles, or lines of longitude, perpendicular to these lines of latitude in the North America–Africa

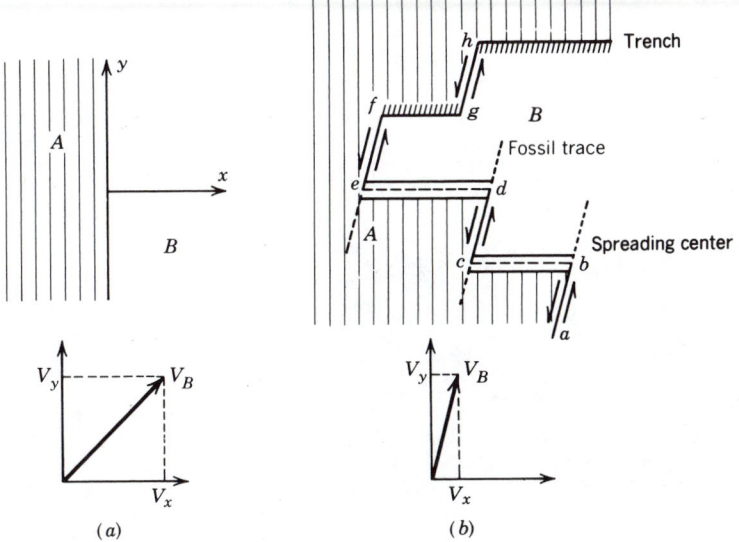

Figure 3-11. *Left,* simple extensional plate boundary where, in Cartesian coordinates, the velocity of *B* with respect to a fixed *A* is the result of *B*'s *x* and *y* components of motion. *Right,* a more complex plate interaction between two plates, where *B* is both extending away from *A* at a spreading center and being subducted by *A* at a trench (Hatched). The relative velocity of *B* relative to a fixed *A* is calculated from the spreading rate at the midocean ridge (double bars), and the direction of the resultant motion vector of *B* relative to *A* is determined from the direction of the transform faults (single lines with arrows) (from LePichon et al., 1973).

reference frame. Euler predicts that these great circles intersect at two and only two points on the globe, the poles of rotation. Sure enough, the real data converge upon a point just south of Greenland (Figure 3-13). There is another pole on the exact opposite side of the Earth. Euler further predicts that the velocity of separation will vary with angular distance from the pole, and as seen in Figure 3-14, this also is true.

The same test can be applied to every plate with a sea-floor spreading or transform-fault boundary with another plate. But Eulerian geometry also predicts that three plates must be in contact many places in the world. Similar geometric laws allow us to vector sum around such **triple junctions** to determine the relative motion of three plates in contact. Consider the easiest of such junctions: where three spreading centers intersect. If we know the direction and velocity of opening of any two of them, we can uniquely determine the velocity and direction of motion of the third relative to the other two (Figure 3-15). But what if a spreading center does not separate two or

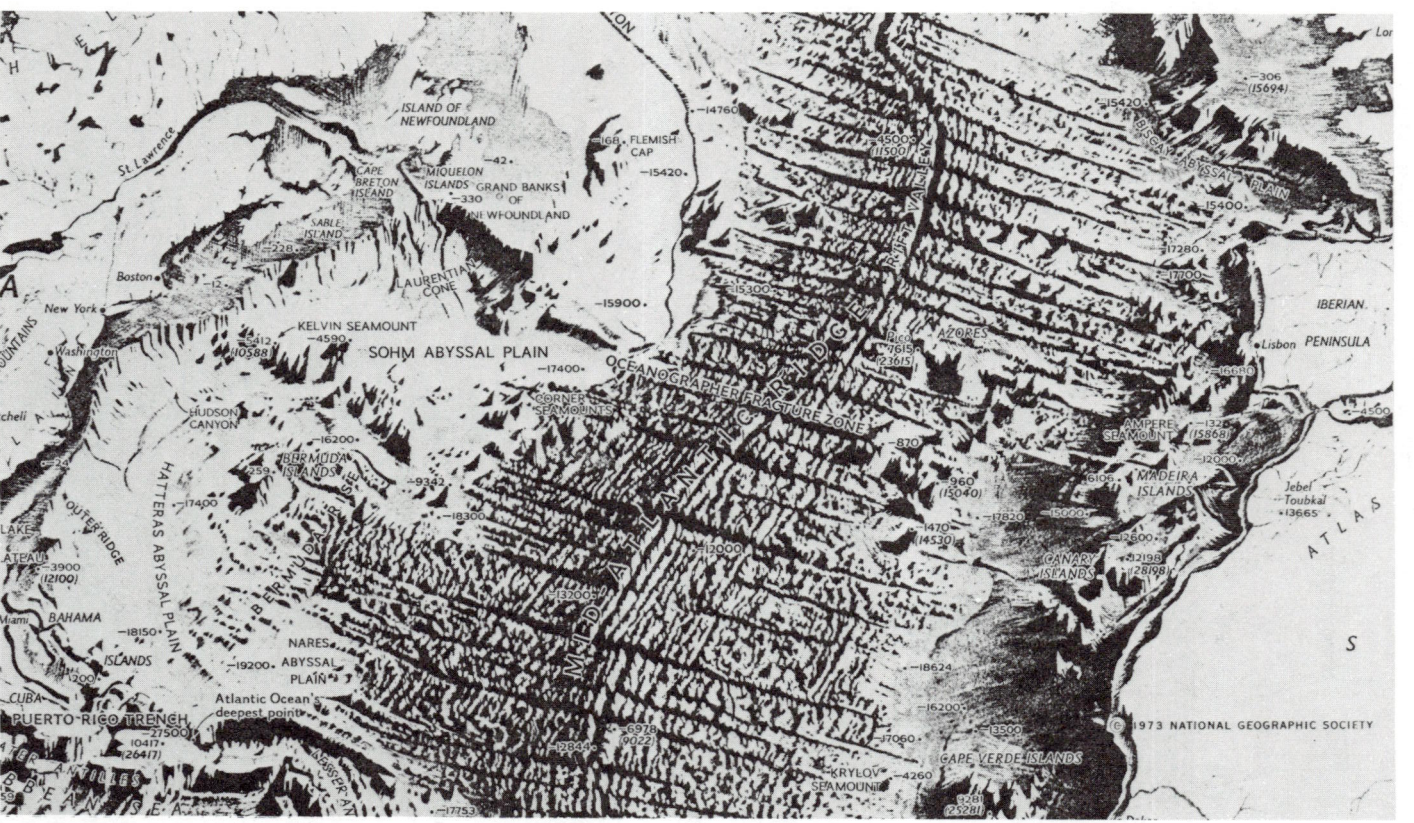

Figure 3-12 Physiographic map of the Atalntic Ocean north of the equator. Note the topographic expression of the mid-Atlantic ridge, with its many fracture zones (northwest–southeast lines), central rift valley (northeast–southwest trending), and gentle slope toward continents on both sides of the ocean (from Heezen and Tharp, 1977) ©Marie Tharp.

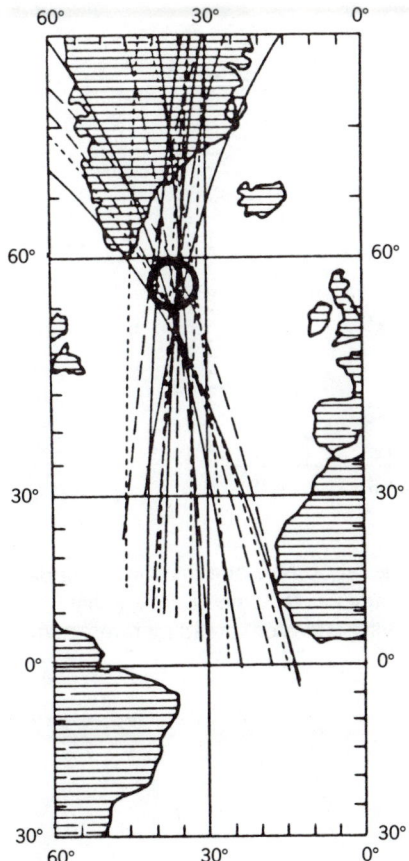

Figure 3-13. Convergence of poles of rotation determined from various fracture zones in the North Atlantic Ocean for relative motion of North America away from Africa. The circle marks the 90 percent confidence limits for the location of this pole. Each line is a great circle perpendicular to the fracture zone in question. (from Morgan, 1968).

three plates? How do we determine relative motion, or even more. interestingly, how do we know what kind of motion is occurring along that boundary?

It is possible to define the boundaries of plates by the type of tectonic activity associated with each. But it is important to realize that the continent–ocean transition is an insignificant barrier compared to the thickness of a lithospheric plate. Therefore, a continent–ocean boundary can occur well within a single plate, and in general such edges of continents have little to do with plate boundaries. The continents are, however, large enough to weigh down plates that contain significant surface area of continent, but the continental crust is insignificant compared to the dimensions of a plate (greater than 100 km thick and often several thousand kilometers across). That is, plates with continents appear to move more slowly than those without, such as the Pacific plate; but they still move by the same geometric laws (Figure 3-16).

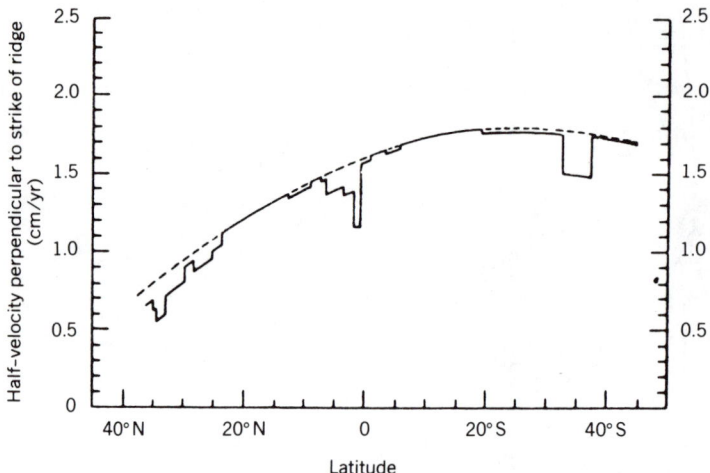

Figure 3-14. Spreading rate away from the pole (at 60°N) along the plate boundary between Africa and North America. The rate varies as the sine of the angular distance from the pole, thus the smoothly varying curve of spreading rate versus distance from the pole (from Morgan, 1968).

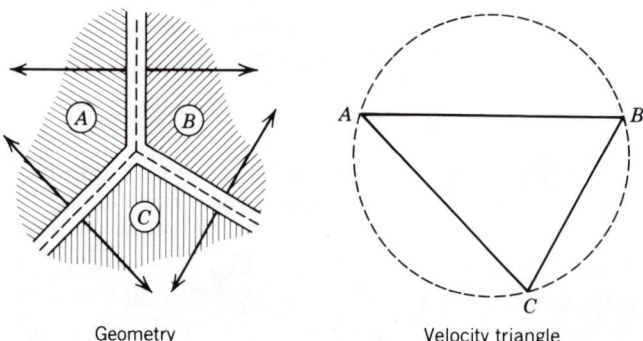

Geometry   Velocity triangle

Figure 3-15. A triple junction where three spreading centers meet at a single point on the Earth's surface. If we fix the location of plate *A*, then the motion of plates *B* and *C* can be determined from vector addition. The motion direction is determined from fracture-zone orientation and the velocity is derived from the determination of spreading rate. The velocity triangle then connects the vectors where the directon of the lines is the relative plate-motion direction and the length of the lines is the velocity. The rate of opening of *C* relative to *A* can be determined from *A* and *B* by the length of line needed to complete this triangle, even if no other information exists for spreading rate between *A* and *C*.

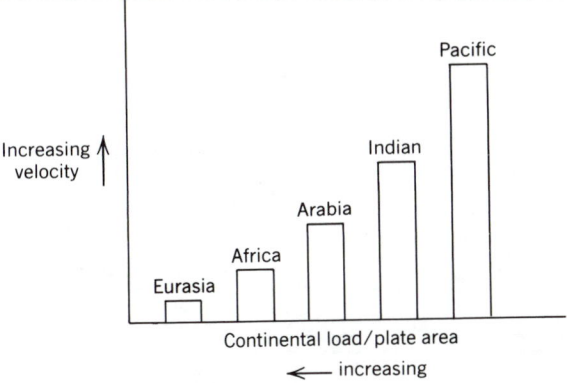

Figure 3-16. Relative velocities of various plates measured against a fixed mantle. The plates with significant continental area move decidedly more slowly than plates without continents (from Forsyth and Uyeda, 1975).

Earthquakes and Focal Mechanisms

Plate tectonics is a powerful geological tool because it is predictive. One can determine the type of plate boundary interactions by studying the **focal mechanisms** of earthquakes, for example. North American–Pacific plate interaction can be determined by studying the orientation of the fault planes along this boundary (Figure 3–17). These earthquake mechanisms have distinct orientations that tell in what direction two plates are converging or diverging. They are of different form, depending upon whether the fault motion causing the earthquake was tensional (a **gravity,** or **normal, fault** in which the motion is in the same direction as gravity's pull), compressional (a **thrust fault** caused by collision where motion appears to be against gravity), or **strike-slip** (as the name implies, one plate slides across the other) (Figure 3-18). Earthquake focal mechanisms can be used equally well to determine the pole of rotation of Pacific–North America motion, as transform faults determined North America–African plate motion in the previous example.

The visual displays of earthquake focal mechanisms, called **balloons,** are really the simplest information one can get from an earthquake. An earthquake literally shakes the entire Earth. But there is a pattern to this shaking. As the compressional wave passes any given location on the Earth, the ground either heaves up or sinks down. The planet cannot move only in two halves like an orange sliced by an earthquake fault (the knife blade). Consider the San Andreas Fault: If half the globe west of California heaved

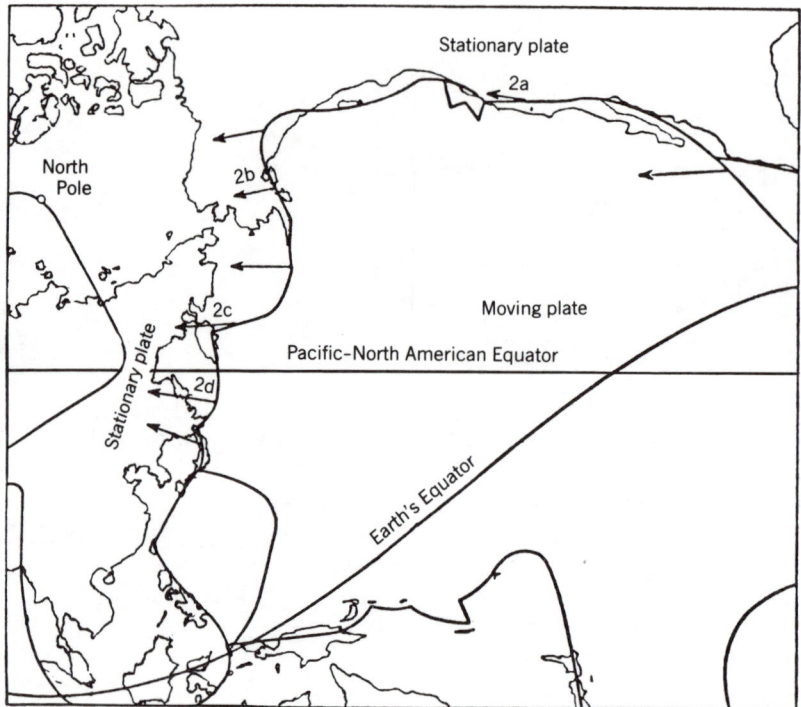

Figure 3-17. Move the reference frame of the Pacific plate from the Earth's axis centered at the North Pole to an axis centered at the pole of rotation of the Pacific plate about a fixed North American plate. The equator of this pole of rotation is now the center horizontal line across the figure. All motion vectors of Pacific North American motion should now be along latitudinal (or horizontal) lines, and the data (arrows) clearly are (from McKenzie and Parker, 1967).

and slid to the north after the San Francisco earthquake and the other half east of California sank and moved to the south, the rotation of the Earth would be disrupted. It would be as if one were to slice a tennis ball in half, then glue it back together with the two halves offset. Throwing the tennis ball would cause it to carom wildly off to one side. The Earth cannot do the same. It must spin smoothly in orbit. The secret of how the Earth accommodates the splitting motion of an earthquake is found in that familiar axiom: For every force in one direction, there must be an equal and opposite force (one of Newton's laws of motion). If the Pacific moves to the north, then the Indian Ocean in the opposite quadrant of the Earth must move counter to it to balance the net force on the Earth. Otherwise, our rotation would be disrupted. This means that the Earth moves in *quadrants* during an earthquake, rather than in halves.

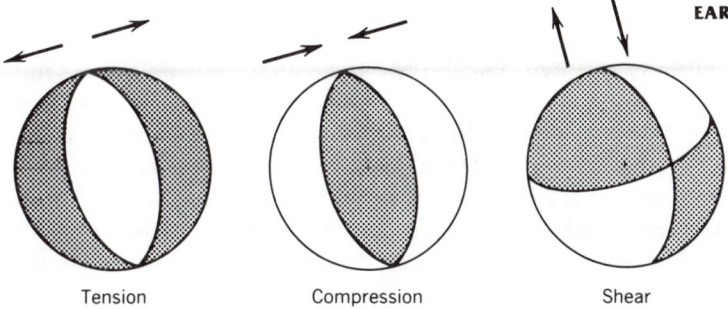

Tension   Compression   Shear

Figure 3-18. The three types of earthquake focal mechanism balloons. Black is the upward motion of the Earth projected from the spherical surface of the planet onto a plane located so that the earthquake is at its center. White areas show downward first motion of the ground after the earthquake. The Earth moves in quadrants in response to any earthquake. The type of motion along the fault that caused the earthquake can be determined from the pattern of up versus down motion recorded on seismometers from throughout the world.

Consider a gravity, or normal, fault where the Earth breaks along a 45-degree slope and the rock slides downhill in the direction of the gravitational pull. Tensional forces cause such faulting. Somewhere on the opposite side of the globe, the Earth must move in the opposite direction to counteract this force. There are now more than 125 seismographic stations around the world that have instruments that record the motion of earthquakes. By recording whether the **first motion** of the ground was either up or down after an earthquake, the mechanism or type of earthquake can be determined. A normal fault will cause all stations near the downthrown side of the fault to record downward first motions. Stations on the other side of the fault will record upward first motions. By examining enough seismograms from the four quadrants of the planet centered on the **epicenter** of the earthquake, the two regions that moved up can be determined. Ninety degrees from these quadrants will be two regions that moved down. By projecting the spherical earth onto a plane, a balloon, or focal mechanism, can be constructed. The pattern of the balloon allows one to determine the type of earthquake that occurred, even if the event was located hundreds of miles at sea.

Consider now a mysterious earthquake that occurred in the center of the Indian Ocean in May of 1971. Visual inspection of the fault is impossible, yet we can determine not only what type of event it was, but also the orientation of the quadrant boundaries will show the orientation of the fault. In Figure 3-19 we display the seismograms from 14 stations around the world, recorded minutes after the Indian Ocean earthquake happened. We then plot up or down motion on the station map for the projection centered at the earthquake's location (Figure 3-20). As can be seen, the southeast quadrant literally had a first motion where the ground moved up, the northeast quadrant all moved down, the southwest quadrant moved down, and the northwest quadrant moved up. Here is observational proof that the Earth really does move in quadrants during an earthquake, as described earlier. Such motion is called **double-coupled,** since each of two opposite quadrants is coupled to the other. This earthquake was neither a tensional normal fault nor a compressional thrust fault, but instead, a strike-slip transform fault because of this checkerboard pattern recognized from its focal mechanism

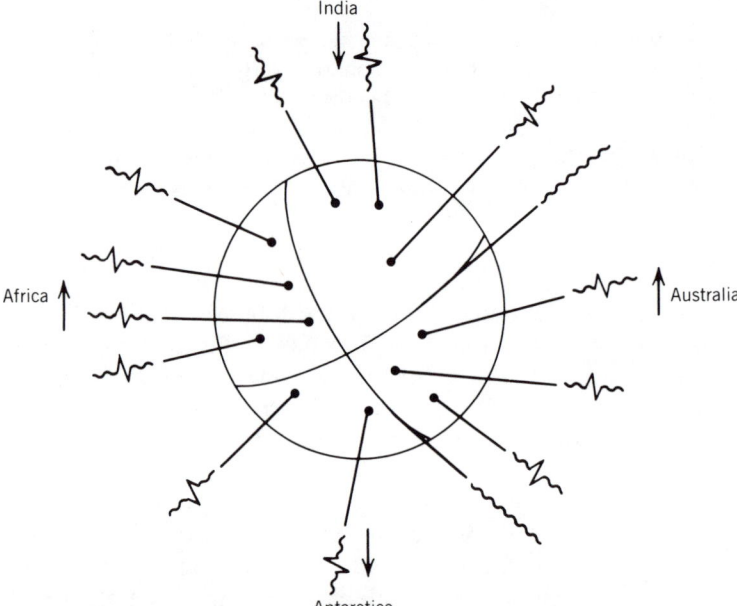

Figure 3-19. An earthquake has occurred along a transform fault in the middle of the Indian Ocean. Seismographs in India and Antarctica record downward first motion, whereas those in Africa and Australia move upward at the first passing of the P-wave. Plotted onto a focal mechanism balloon, we can see that the fault is strike-slip and oriented either northwest–southeast or northeast–southwest. We cannot tell which.

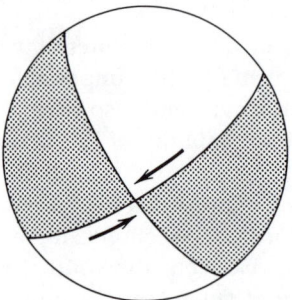

Figure 3-20. Because it fits the direction of opening of the Indian plate relative to the African plate, we choose the northeast–southwest plane as the most likely direction of motion.

balloon. A normal fault would have all of India and Antarctica moving down with Africa and Australia moving up, and a thrust fault, vice versa.

By determining the balloons from the earthquakes occurring under Japan, we can describe the physical processes occurring during subduction. Not only do we see the Pacific plate hanging beneath Japan as outlined in the locations of the earthquakes, but the focal mechanisms on the upper plane of the plate are all compressional or thrust earthquake balloons. Those on the bottom plane are all normal fault balloons (Figure 3-21). The plate is either sagging into the mantle from its own weight, producing compression on the top of the plane and tension at the bottom, or it is unbending after being bent at the trench axis. Such forces can be replicated by sliding a sheet of paper over the edge of a table. Because the paper is elastic, first it bends then unbends as it passes over the edge of the table. The balloons have allowed us to see forces present for hundreds of miles beneath Japan.

Earthquakes have been precisely recorded only since the late 1950s, and plates, though they move slowly (about six feet in the average person's life-time), move to the geological time scale. So plate tectonic theory would not be very powerful unless it could be extended back in time long before the 1950s. Earthquakes take us back through our lifetime and sometimes through recorded history. They go back even further than that when we see the seismic definition of a plate plunging 700 km into the mantle beneath a subduction zone, because we know that at a rate of 10 cm/yr, 7 million years of that plate's motion is outlined to us along that 700-km path (Figure 3-22). But we need an even longer-lived geological recording of the past motions of plates, and the magnetization of the Earth provides just such a record.

The Sea-Floor Magnetic Map

The dilemma of how to extend the geological record back millions of years is eased by the ocean floor, which provides us not only with the history long into the geological past of plate motions, but also with a critical Eulerian requirement that we mentioned earlier: the velocity with which one plate moves away from another can be determined. This velocity must also be known if descriptions of motion are to be made mathematically. Fortunately, sea-floor spreading has been recorded on the sea floor with the precision of a map—and a magnetic map at that. The Earth's magnetic field originates in the liquid outer core. Convection currents are again responsible, this time for moving electrons. This motion results in an electrical field, and through Maxwell's equations, a magnetic field.

Because of the instability of these convection currents in the core, a unique phenomenon has occurred randomly throughout the history of the Earth—**polarity reversals.** The north pole flips to become the south pole and vice versa (Figure 3-23). That is, the repellent magnetic pole suddenly

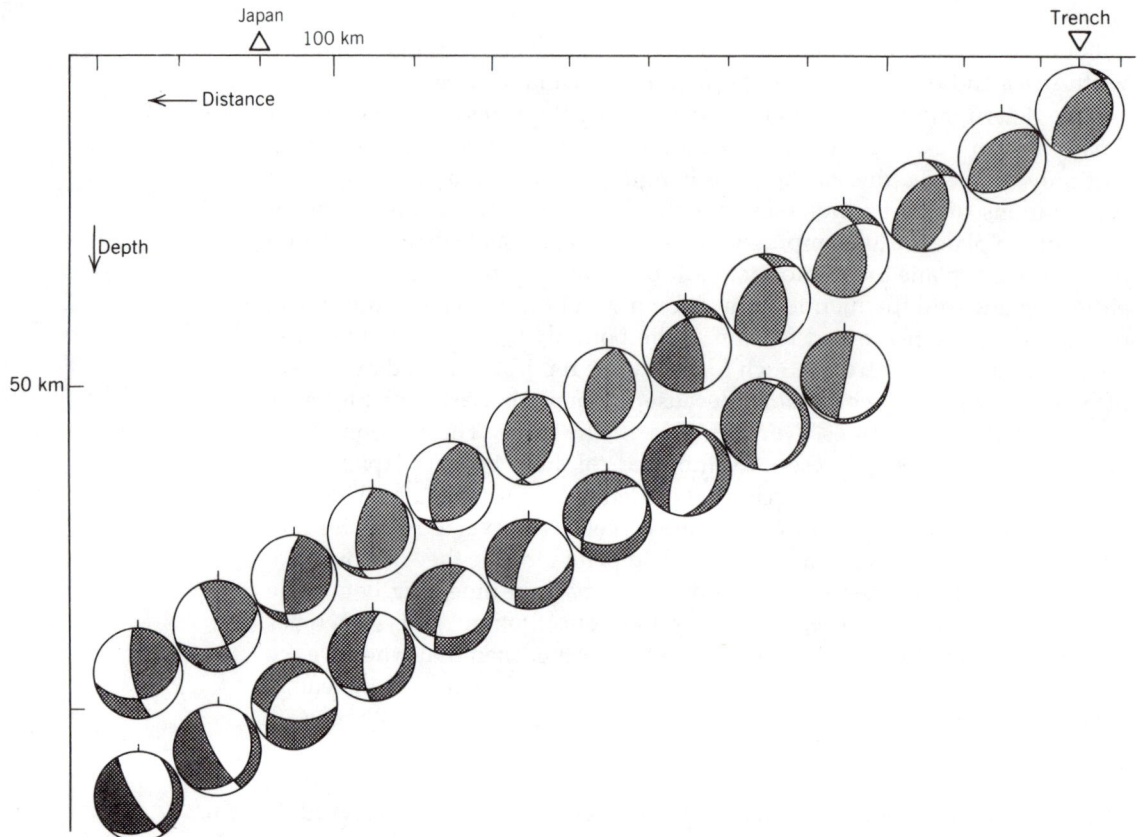

Figure 3-21. The seismologists of Tohoku University in Japan have compiled focal mechanism balloons for literally hundreds of earthquakes occurring on the downgoing subduction zone beneath Japan. They find not only that the earthquakes are ordered into two planes, one along the upper surface of the plate and the other outlining the lower edge, but also that the top plane is made up of compressional or thrust earthquakes and that the bottom earthquakes are extensional or tensional. The forces acting to cause these two planes of earthquakes are therefore different (from Hasegawa et al., 1978).

flips to become the attractant pole. To observe rocks with reversed magnetic poles is easy (one need only use a fancy compass), but the explanation of why the Earth's magnetic field reverses randomly is mostly unknown. Still, one can begin to appreciate the imaginations of the founders of plate tectonics to recognize so simple yet so bizarre a phenomenon as magnetic pole reversals. They must have wondered whether anyone would believe such an outlandish concept.

The Earth's magnetic field exists as if a large bar magnet or dipole were at the center of the Earth. The present configuration of north and south is

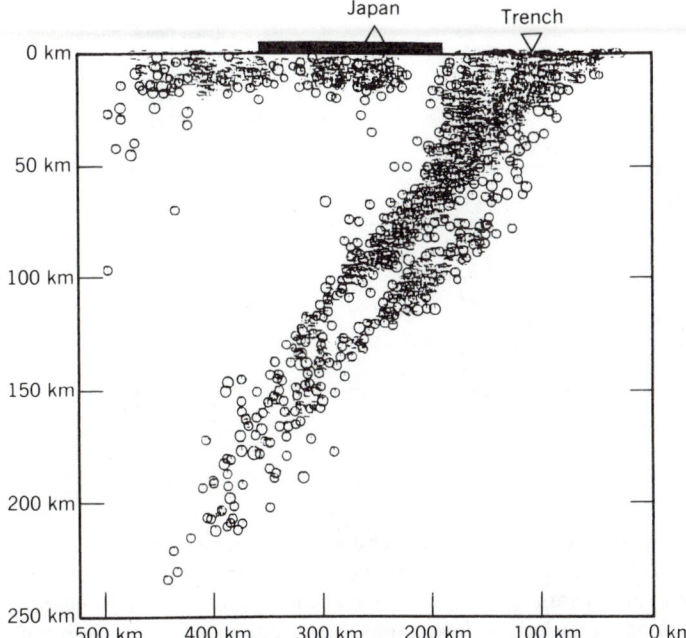

Figure 3-22. Seismic activity beneath Japan clearly delineates a cross section of the Pacific plate moving at 45 degrees downward into the mantle. The open circles are earthquake locations from events recorded by the Tohoku University seismographic network from April 19, 1975 until December 31, 1977. The upper and lower seismic planes are thought to be the top and bottom of the rigid, brittle portion of the Pacific plate (from Hasegawa et al., 1978).

called *normal*. It was *reversed* 700,000 years ago. If you go to Iceland at the center of the mid-Atlantic ridge and pick up a rock, its magnetic memory—that field that existed on earth when it cooled down from lava to rock—will tell you that the north pole is up toward the present pole. If, however, you drive a few miles from the center of the island toward the eastern or western shores of Iceland and pick up a slightly older rock, a compass held close to it will show the incredible fact that the south pole of the rock faces up toward the present north pole. The rock's magnetic field was reversed when these rocks cooled from lava. A compass of the earth's past magnetic field was recorded within the rock (Figure 3-23).

If you take a ship and steam east to west several times across the Reykjanes ridge south of Iceland with a magnetometer, stripes will appear on your shipboard magnetic field recording device (Figure 3-24). These stripes are parallel to the mid-Atlantic ridge and to the coasts of Europe and North America. They represent successively older rock as one goes away from the mid-Atlantic ridge toward the continents. The pattern of normal (black-

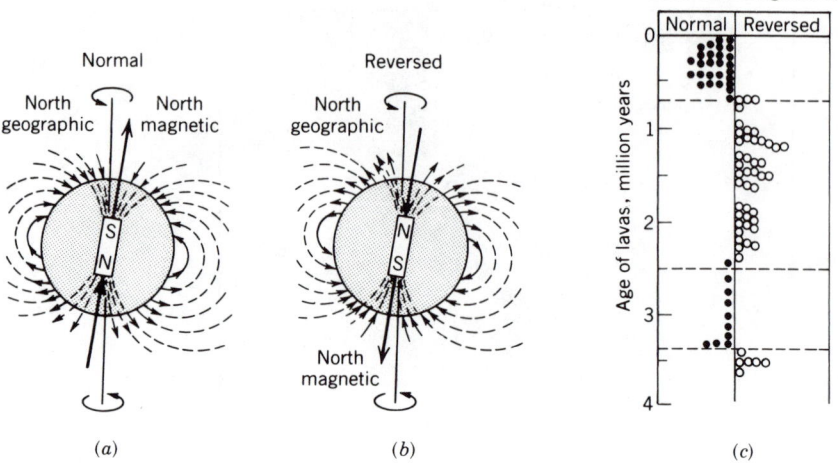

Figure 3-23. Dramatization of magnetic pole changes, which happened frequently in the past. The north-seeking magnetic pole of the present (a) was at the South Pole one million years ago (b), but back at the North Pole three million years ago (a). These facts are derived from measuring the magnetic orientation of rocks of varying ages into the past. Why the reversals occur is poorly understood, but has to do with changes in the convection pattern in the core of the Earth (from Opdyke et al., 1968).

striped) and reversed (white-striped) magnetic anomalies is as distinctive as a fingerprint, telling the age of the sea floor (Figure 3-25). The earth's magnetic field reversed scores of times during the formation and cooling of successive segments of Reykjanes ridge sea floor. As the North American plate spread away from the European continent, these stripes of younger and younger lava cooled onto the edges of the receding plates, only to record permanently the compass direction of their age.

The validity of this "fingerprint" was proved by the deep sea drilling vessel *Glomar Challenger*. Named for the original oceanographic vessel (see Chapter 2), the *Challenger* has proved to be one of the most powerful tools ever devised for obtaining scientific information about the sea floor (Figure 3-26). Over 600 holes have been drilled into the oceanic lithosphere. Dates from the rock and sediment at these sites have proved beyond a shadow of a doubt that the sea floor spreads, that the continents drift, and that magnetic-reversal stripes record the history of that movement (Figure 3-26). Yet we would surely still be arguing about such an outlandish theory if the drill bit had not actually returned specimens to the laboratory to prove the theory. Since the late 1960s, hundreds of oceanographic ships have scoured the oceans recording the magnetic anomalies of the ocean floor, and consequently, the age of the sea floor has been largely determined (Figure 3-27).

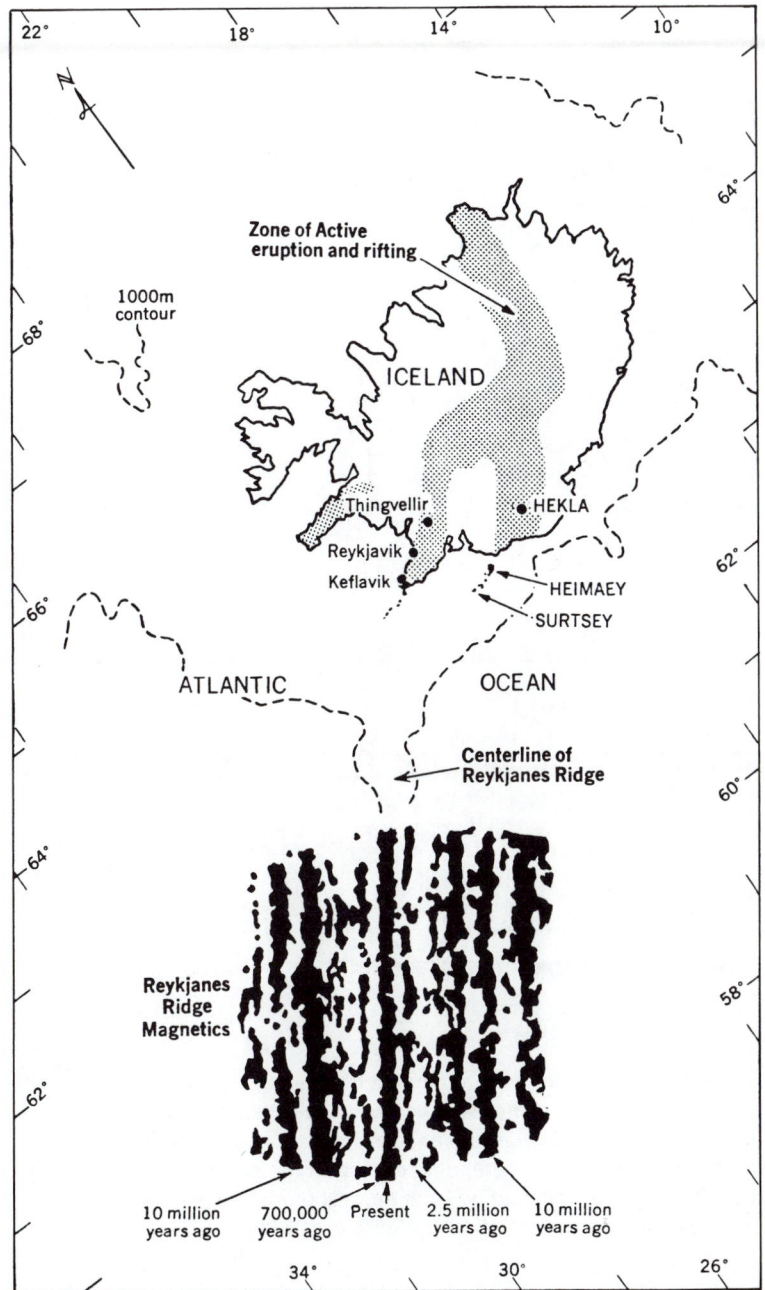

Figure 3-24 The black and white striped pattern represents bands of sea floor with the rock magnetized as it is today, with the north pole pointing north (black stripes), and rock magnetized so that the north pole of the rock points in the reverse direction, to the south (white stripes). This pattern can be used to age-date the sea floor, as shown in the figure (from Heirtzler et al., 1968).

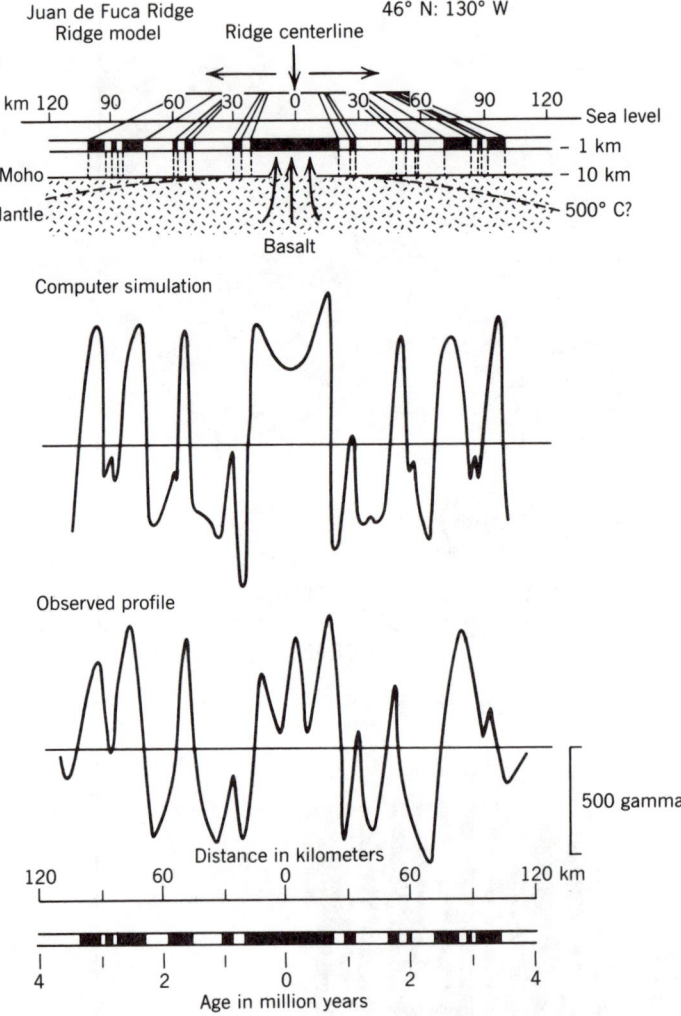

Figure 3-25. Our understanding of magnetic field reversals and plate tectonics allows us to model the intrusion of basalts with normal and reversed magnetization in chronological order at sea-floor spreading centers *(top)*. The observed magnetic field over the spreading center on the Juan de Fuca Ridge off Oregon can be faithfully reproduced by such models (compare *middle* versus *bottom*) (from Vine and Wilson, 1965, after Sullivan, 1974).

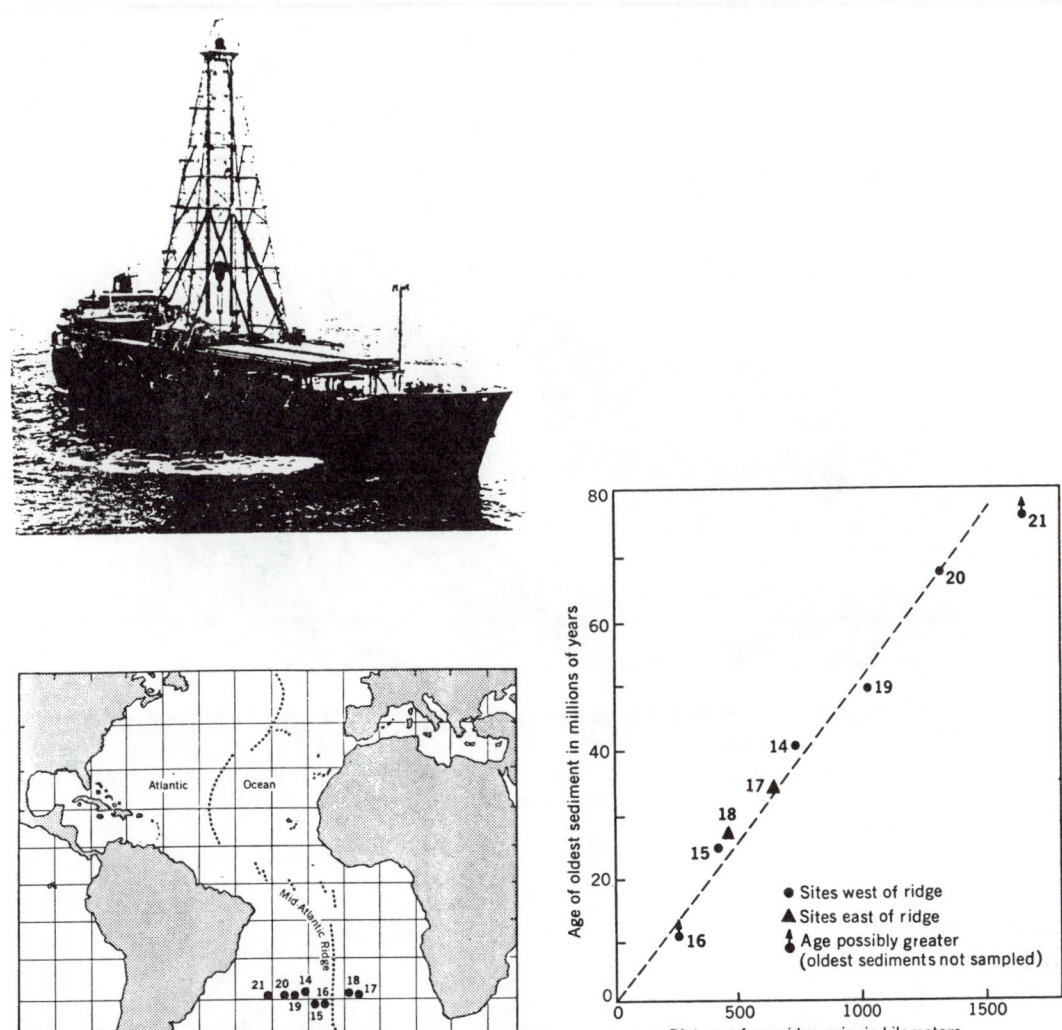

Figure 3-26. The drilling ship *Glomar Challenger* has revolutionized our understanding of the sea floor by delivering samples of sediment and rock from over 600 locations throughout the world's oceans. But the most famous results are still those from leg number 3 out of a total of 96, when the ship drilled a profile across the midocean ridge in the south Atlantic. Chief scientists Dick Von Herzen of Woods Hole Oceanographic Institution and Art Maxwell of the University of Texas and their crew returned mud resting just above the basalt that had aged away from the ridge crest, just as plate tectonics and magnetic reversals had predicted. This provided the first direct proof of the theory (from Maxwell, Von Herzen, et al., 1970, after Sullivan, 1974).

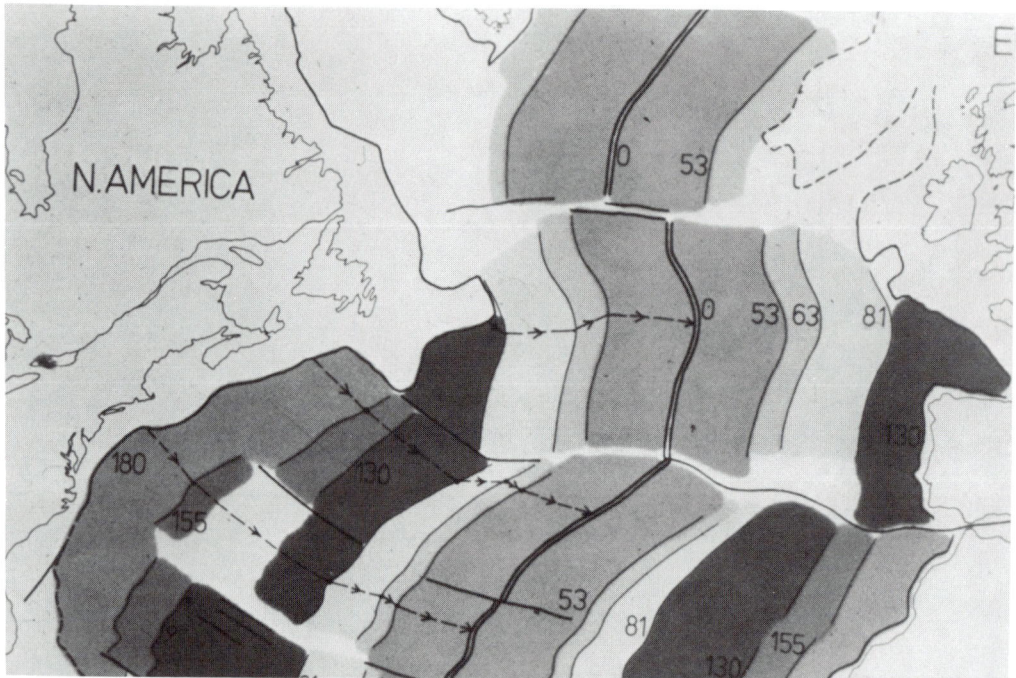

Figure 3-27. Similar age progression was found in the North Atlantic, where the ages (numbers in millions of years) get younger along flow lines (dashed arrows) as the *Challenger* sampled from the edges of the ocean toward the center at the mid-Atlantic ridge (from Dewey, 1980 after Talwani et al, 1971).

The Ocean Floor and Continents

The plates are indeed geologically young, because subduction carries the oceanic lithosphere back into the mantle whenever collision with another plate occurs. The oldest ocean floor is only 160 million years old, whereas the oldest continent is 3.7 billion years old, and the ocean itself has been deep and blue for the same 3.7 billion years. The continents actually grow by this same collision process because (1) they are made up of rock that is lighter than oceanic rock and thus more difficult to subduct and (2) at subduction zones, the oceanic plate is melted back into the mantle. Some of this melt, the lightest rock, invariably escapes back to the surface forming volcanoes and large mountain ranges such as the Andes, the Sierra Nevadas, and the Pacific Ring-of-Fire (Figure 3-28). These mountain ranges are the predominant mechanism by which the continents accrete new rock. This

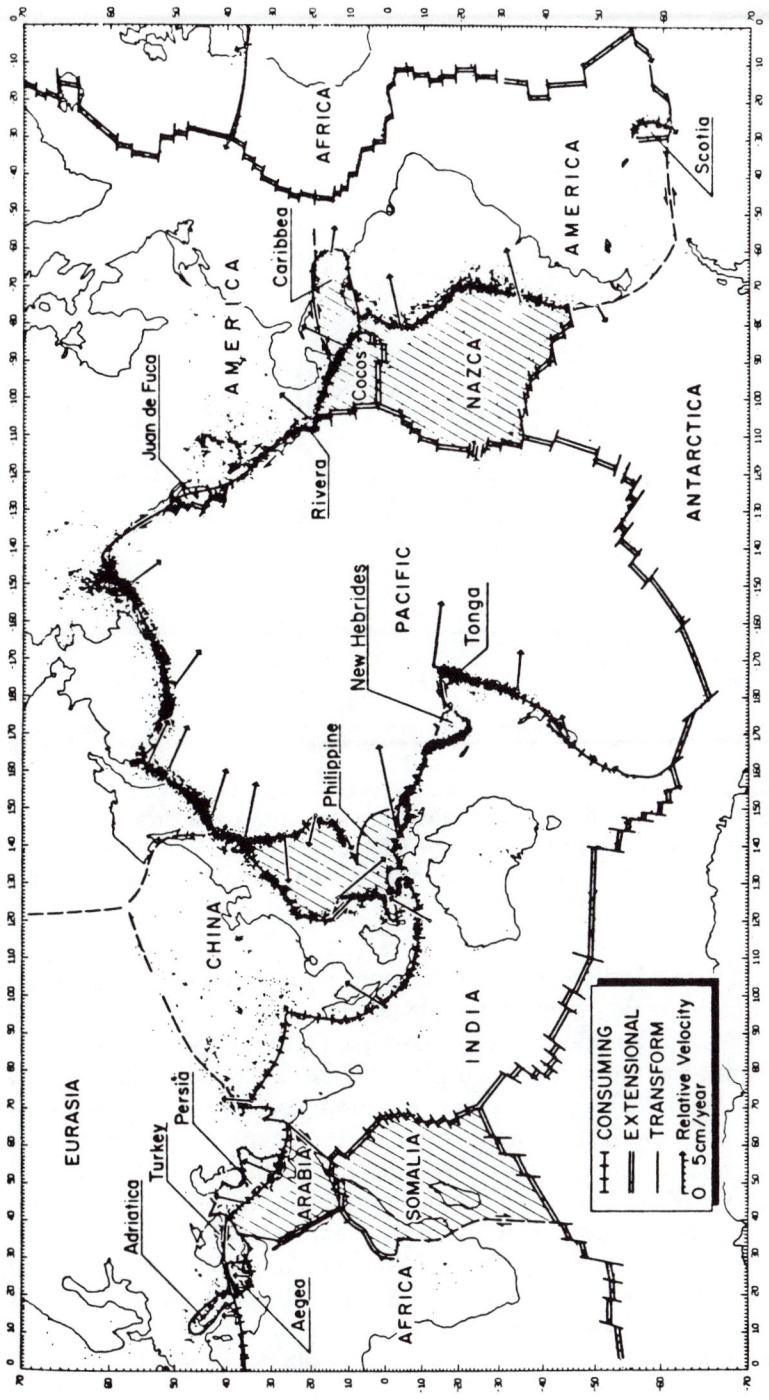

Figure 3-28. Midocean ridge system along with transform faults and trenches outline the major plates of the Earth's surface. In plate tectonics all the action occurs at the edges of plates. Arrows indicate some motion vectors with velocity a function of the length of the arrows. Dots are earthquake locations (from LePichon et al, 1973).

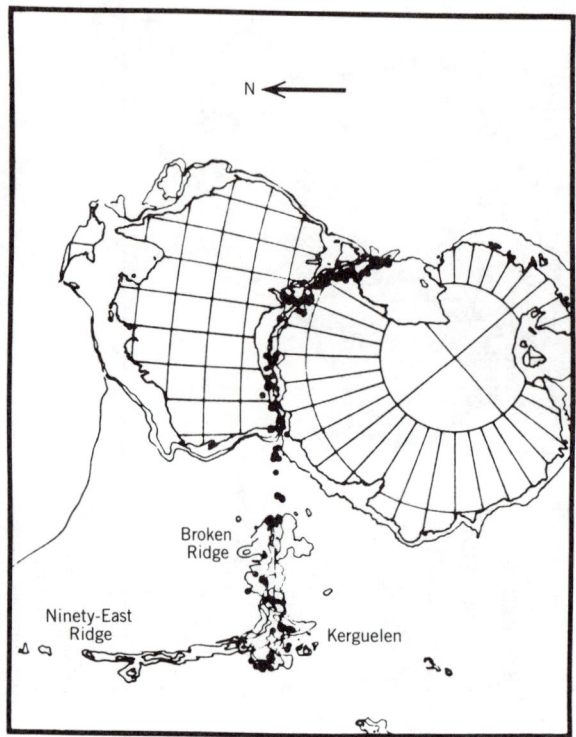

Figure 3-29. Australia and Antarctica rotated back and refit along the midocean ridge between them (located by the earthquakes shown by black circles). From the south, the Island of Kerguelen from the far southern Indian Ocean refits snuggly into the Broken Ridge—Ninety East Ridge complex from the north (from McKenzie and Sclater, 1971).

subduction process is also one of the reasons why earthquakes and volcanoes occur at the same places on the planet.

The Earth's surface motions and tectonic activity can be described using only 12 plates. The motion of each plate can be described relative to any other one if we fix its location in time. For example, Figure 3-28 shows the Indian plate as being fixed or assumed to be stationary, and the motion of other plates relative to it. Because the plate tectonic theory is geometric, no knowledge of the driving force pushing and pulling the plates in this complex pattern of interaction is required. This is particularly fortunate because one of the great remaining mysteries of how the Earth works is the driving force for plate tectonics. That is, we can describe the directions and speeds of all the plates on the surface of the Earth without knowing what forces are directly responsible for pushing and pulling the plates in these trajectories.

The Complex Continents

The sea floor is relatively simple geologically because it is never at the surface for very long. All sea floor older than 160 million years has been subducted back into the mantle. Complexity is bred by multiple overprinting events through a long geological history. The longer a feature remains on the surface, the more complex and more difficult to decipher it becomes. Thus, plate tectonics was not discovered until the simplicity of the ocean floor was realized. The continents are light, and they float like blocks of wood in the bathtub of the heavy ocean-floor rock. They float because they are made of some of the lightest rock on the planet. Continents are hard to force down a subduction zone because they are so light. Therefore, continents have grown throughout geological time and so are much more complex than the oceans.

Summary

In the remaining chapters we look in detail at the evolution of sea floor as it is born at the ridge axis, ages in the center of plates, is subducted, and sometimes reappears to be accreted onto the continent. We point out how the predictive nature of plate tectonics allows us to find metal ores, hydrocarbons, and other industrial necessities while avoiding cataclysms such as volcanic eruptions and earthquakes. And we show how this remarkable theory of plate tectonics unites the diverse scientific disciplines needed to study how the Earth works. We will see how tightly Australia used to be fitted into Antarctica, for example, and we will learn how they came to be rifted apart (Figure 3-29). Finally, we learn that, as powerful as this theory is, it still does not explain everything that happens on the surface of the Earth. Many puzzles remain for new generations of geologists, particularly questions about how the continents and the mantle work deep below the surface.

Further Reading

Le Pichon, X., Francheteau, J. and Bonnin, I., 1973, Plate Tectonics: London, New York, Elsevier.

Wegener, A., 1966, The Origin of the Continents and Oceans: London, Dover.

4

The Oceanic Lithosphere

The most fundamental unit in plate tectonics is the lithosphere, or plate. We have already seen that the continents ride along the backs of the lithosphere, so let's look in detail at what constitutes this predominant component.

The primary structure of the outer skin of the earth, the lithosphere, includes both the crust and the upper mantle. The term lithosphere means "rocky layer." **Atmosphere, hydrosphere, lithosphere,** and **asthenosphere** are the outer layers of the earth. The boundary between lithosphere and asthenosphere is a seismic low velocity zone thought to be caused by the presence of a small amount of molten rock. Thus the asthenosphere is the soft, partially molten mantle beneath the solid, rock-like outer plate. The depth to this low velocity zone beneath the lithosphere becomes deeper as you go away from the spreading center into older and older oceanic lithosphere (Figure 4-1). Thus, the lithosphere has the physical appearance of a slowly thickening lid over the partially molten asthenosphere (Figure 4-2). The simplest explanation for this thickening is that the lid is slowly cooling. The lower boundary, which marks the depth to the first molten rock, becomes progressively deeper with age as more and more magma cools and solidifies onto the bottom of the lithosphere. As we will see, this simple cooling phenomenon can account for a remarkable number of physical observations about the lithosphere.

For instance, the lithosphere itself is not completely rigid. Hawaii, like other islands in the middle of the ocean, consists of a pile of volcanic rocks

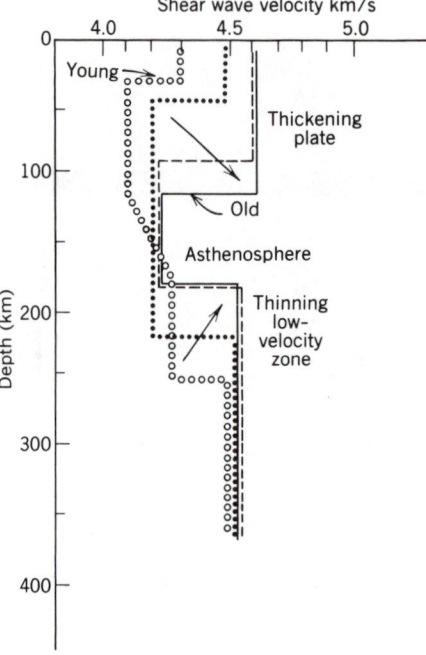

Figure 4-1. Shear waves move more slowly in partially molten mantle, which can be seen in Asthenosphere under faster velocity plate. The mapping of this structure beneath progressively older plate shows how plate thickens as it cools away from the midocean ridges. These observations depend upon the worldwide network of seismometer receivers monitoring earthquakes from all over the surface. Interestingly, the molten zone also thins away from the ridges. (from Don Forsyth, 1974).

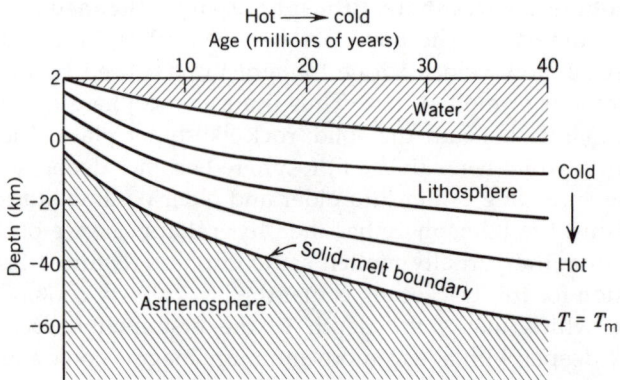

Figure 4-2. Lithospheric plate model explains form and change in elevation of the plate with age as purely a function of temperatures and cooling away from the ridge crest. Note the increased water depth away from the ridge (at left). T is temperature and T_m is melting temperature for rock.

"loading down" the lithosphere. A moat surrounds Hawaii where this load has sunk into the plate (Figure 4-3). Tony Watts of Lamont, presented this concept as loading on a lithosphere consisting of two layers—a *brittle* upper surface and a *plastic* lower region. The brittle top is needed to prevent the whole island from sinking into the lithosphere, and the plastic bottom must be present to allow for the flow of softer material away from Hawaii needed to form a moat. In order to match the exact shape and dimensions of the moat, Watts found the brittle layer must be about 30 km thick, with the plastic layer extending about 50 km below that to the partially molten asthenosphere.

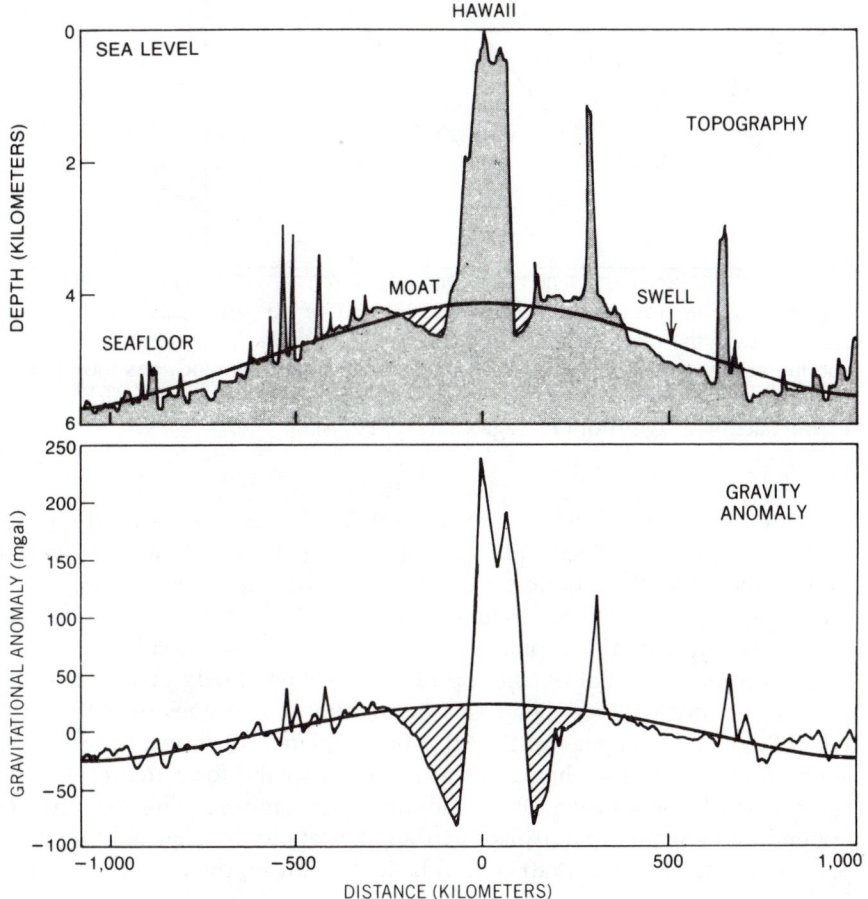

Figure 4-3. The plate is rigid, so a load will cause it to respond by sinking. Here, Hawaii has a moat around it (Hatched) caused by the load of lava from the volcanic activity. The broad swell on which Hawaii and its moat sit (solid line) is the bulge from the mantle hot spot that created Hawaii in the first place (from Watts et al., 1985).

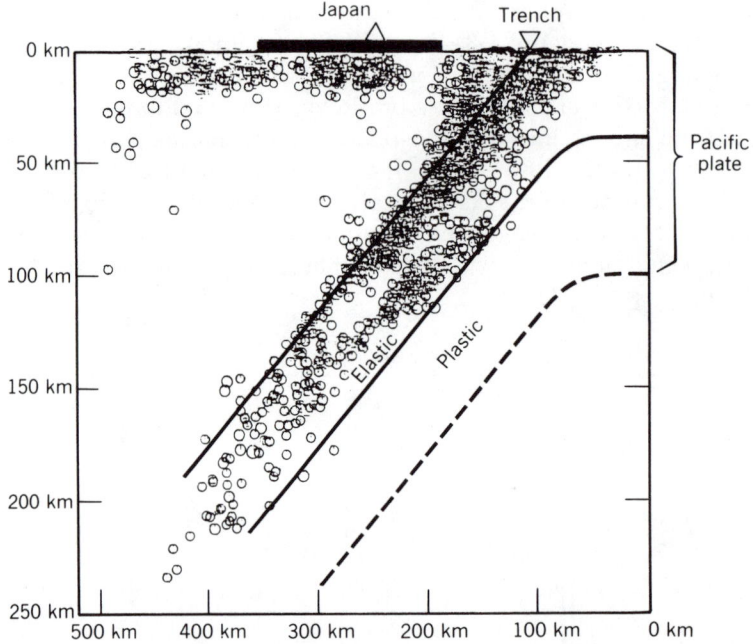

Figure 4-4. The cross section of earthquake locations beneath Japan (circles) shows clearly the brittle top and bottom of the elastic Pacific plate being subducted beneath Japan. The thermal thickness of the plate includes this elastic thickness plus the hotter bottom, which flows plastically rather than deforming by earthquake breakage (from Hasegawa et al., 1978).

One can see the thickness of the elastic layer by observing the earthquake pattern on the Pacific plate being subducted beneath Japan (Figure 4-4). To subduct a lithospheric plate, it must be physically bent to force it into the asthenosphere. The earthquakes show that the subducted plate then straightens out again as it plunges into the mantle. As noted before, if you set a piece of paper flat on the top of a table then slowly push it over the edge, the paper will first bend and then unbend as it goes over the edge. Why? Because the paper and the lithospheric plate both have enough elastic strength to rebound to their original shapes after the force that caused the bending (collision with another plate) has been removed. This bending and unbending beneath Japan causes earthquakes along the edges of the elastic part of the plate. Just as Watts found beneath Hawaii, the Pacific plate has a 30-km thick elastic zone, as can be seen from the distance between the top and bottom earthquake zones beneath Japan (Figure 4-4).

By measuring the moat dimensions around literally hundreds of volcanoes that dot the surface of the Pacific plate, Watts was able to show that, like the base of the lithosphere, this elastic layer thickens as the plate ages. This he also relates to the cooling process.

The elastic–plastic boundary stays at the 350° to 650° C temperature zone within the lithosphere, with cooler rock being brittle and warmer rock being plastic. As the plate cools away from the midocean ridge spreading center, the depth to those temperatures sinks deeper into the plate, and so the brittle–plastic boundary also becomes deeper with age (Figure 4-5).

The base of the lithosphere is an *isotherm* (a constant temperature surface) above which mantle material is plastic but solid and below which it is partially molten (Figure 4-1). The **pressure** and melting **temperature** of the rock controls the isotherm at which this transition occurs. **Thermodynamics** is the branch of physics that provides the laws defining the effects of pressure and temperature on the physical state of elements and compounds, and we will soon see its predominant importance in defining how the Earth works. Thermodynamics controls where the boundary between lithosphere and asthenosphere is located.

Structurally, the lithosphere consists of an outer crust of light basaltic rock and a deeper residual, called **ultramafic rock,** which composes the mantle of the lithosphere. The term mantle is confusing because there are two mantles: the lower 90 percent of the lithosphere and the entire asthenosphere. Also, the lithospheric mantle is part brittle and part plastic. How can this be? The term mantle is a remnant from pre-plate tectonics days and is a generic term for the ultramafic layer of the Earth. Ultramafic rock can be plastic, elastic, or partially molten, depending on the pressure and, more important, the temperature at the depth where it resides.

If you took the mantle below the lithosphere and melted it, the light rock

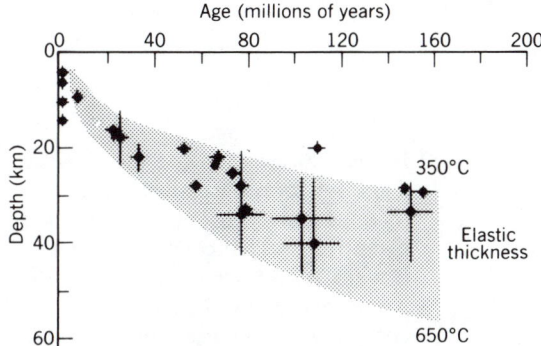

Figure 4-5. The dimensions of a moat that forms around any seamount or island are a function of the thickness of the elastic part of the plate. If thick, then only a small moat will form, and vice versa. Mapping of the increase in elastic thickness determined from the size of moats made by seamounts (solid dots, with error bars) shows that the elastic-plastic boundary closely follows the sinking of the 350 to 650°C isotherms. As the plate cools, the isotherms sink deeper into the plate and more and more of the plate becomes brittle (from Watts, 1982).

floating to the surface would be basalt; the residual heavy rock would be ultramafic **peridotite.** This is exactly what happens at a midocean ridge. Asthenospheric mantle rises buoyantly into a zone of extension between two plates. As it rises, the lighter components separate from the heavier rock. Sound familiar? This is differentiation similar to the formation of the core early in the Earth's history. The light basalt forms the topmost layers of the lithosphere, called the crust, and the heavy peridotite forms the ultramafic mantle of the lithosphere. If you were to grind up the whole lithosphere then heat it just to its melting point, the resulting rock would exactly match the composition and form of the asthenosphere.

The Oceanic Crust

The boundary between the crust and mantle in the lithosphere is a **seismic discontinuity** between slow velocity (light basalt) and fast velocity (heavy peridotite) rock called the **Mohorovičić discontinuity,** or **Moho.** It is the matching of seismic velocities recorded under the ocean with laboratory measurements of sound velocity in rocks of known composition that allows us to identify the kinds of rocks making up the oceanic crust and mantle near the Moho (Figure 4-6). Deep-sea drilling, dredging of the surface of the litho-

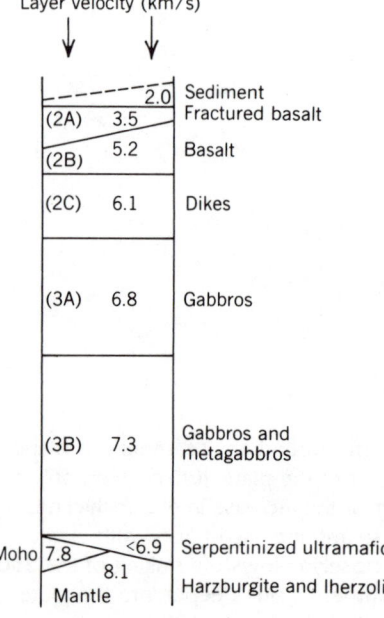

Figure 4-6. Seismic energy travels as if in layers of progressively faster material in the crust at the top of the plate. The rock within each layer is characterized by these velocities. The basalts and gabbros thought to compose the oceanic crust have the same velocities when measured in the laboratory as those measured in the ocean floor. Below the Moho, mantle rocks called ultramafics are required to produce the very high velocities observed (from Harrison and Bonatti, 1981).

sphere with steel baskets, and sampling by deep-diving submarines give us real rocks with which to cross-check that remote-sensing identification.

The current hypothesis for the compositional variation of the lithospheric crust is shown in Figure 4-6. We have succeeded in drilling only through the sediment and the first layer of the oceanic crust; verification by the drill bit still is awaited. The deep-sea-drilling ship *Glomar Challenger* did succeed in penetrating these outer layers, however, encountering highly **fractured** and rubblelike **pillow basalts** in **layer 2A. (Layer 1** is sediment and is discussed later.) Pillow basalts form when lava pours out of a fissure beneath water. The water **quenches** the shell of the lava, but the interior can cool only by conduction, which is very slow compared to the convection of heat away from the surface of the lava by water. Thus the interior remains molten for a long time, and the lava continues to flow downhill. Round tubes form and periodically break off as chunks of lava that resemble a pile of pillows. The result is a pillow basalt. This eruptive phenomenon has been observed directly on Hawaii, where a lava flow was followed down the side of Kilauea volcano into the sea. Divers then took movies for the first time of pillow basalts forming underwater. **Cores** returned to the surface by the *Challenger* have the same curved edges as Hawaiian pillow basalts. An **ultrasonic imaging** device has even been lowered into the *Challenger's* drill hole to produce a picture of the inside of the Earth, the borehole wall. Elliptical images, which can only be from pillow basalts, are clearly seen in the images of the borehole wall from layer 2A (Figure 4-7).

Beneath layer 2A the *Challenger* encountered more pillow basalts, but the **void spaces** between them were thoroughly filled with **clays** and other **alteration minerals.** Also, the pillows were of much smaller diameter. This zone makes up seismic **layer 2B** of the oceanic crust. Beneath that, the form changes from the kind of lava that pours out at the surface **(extrusive)** to internal feeder **dikes (layer 2C)** that supply the lava **intrusively** to the surface. This layer 2C was also drilled into by the *Challenger.* Below that, the frozen remains of the **magma chamber** that supplied the lava in the first place are thought to make up **layer 3** (Figure 4-8). This zone has never been penetrated, so we must rely upon other evidence for its composition. We will direct Chapter 5 toward what are believed to be slivers of ancient oceanic crust that were sliced upward onto the continents as accidental remnants of past subduction events. The structure and chemical composition of these **ophiolites** strongly influence what we think is below **layer 2** of the oceanic lithosphere.

Below the **gabbro,** or frozen magma chamber basalts, is the Moho. What lies below this sharpest of all seismic boundaries has intrigued geologists for decades. The Deep Sea Drilling Project actually began as a fantastic adventure to drill one hole into the Moho. We are lucky that **Project Mohole** had to be diverted to over 600 shallow holes because the technology did not exist 20 years ago to drill 7 km into rock beneath 5 km of ocean. Instead of one

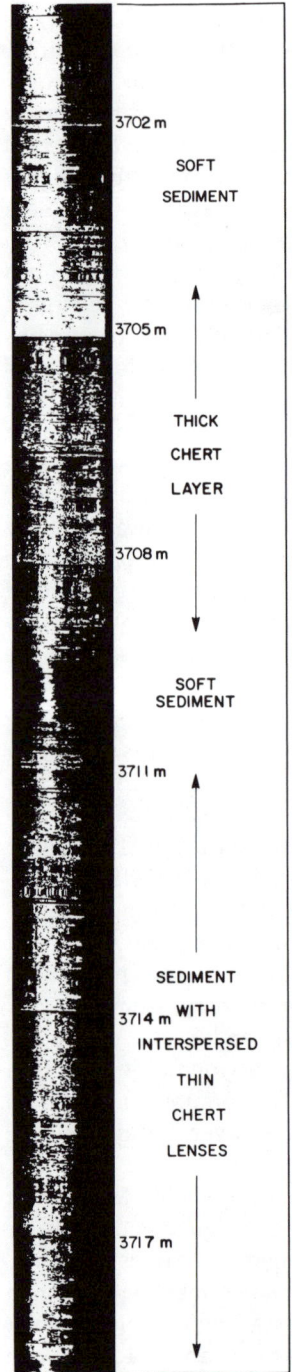

3702 m

SOFT

SEDIMENT

3705 m

THICK

CHERT

LAYER

3708 m

SOFT
SEDIMENT

3711 m

SEDIMENT
3714 m WITH
INTERSPERSED
THIN
CHERT
LENSES

3717 m

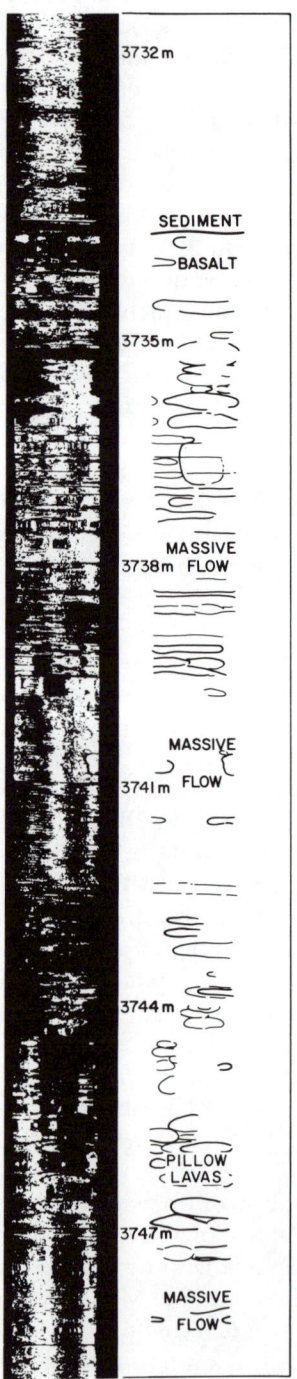

3732 m

SEDIMENT
BASALT

3735 m

MASSIVE
3738 m FLOW

MASSIVE
3741 m FLOW

3744 m

PILLOW
LAVAS

3747 m

MASSIVE
FLOW

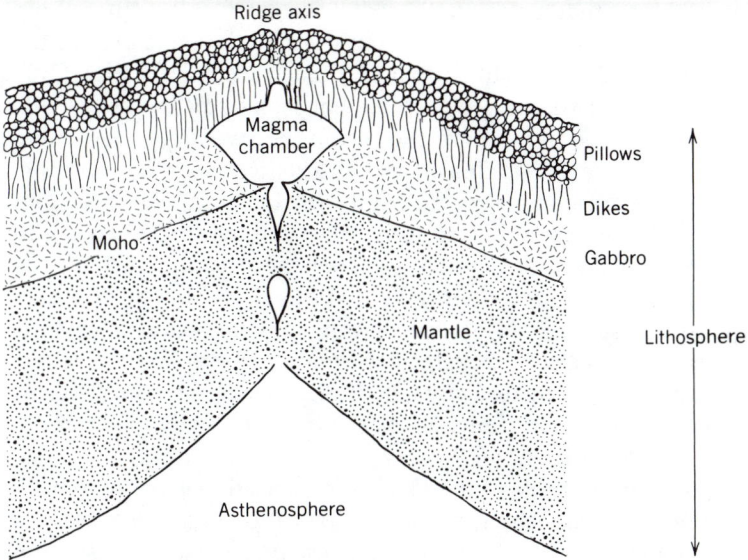

Figure 4-8. Structure of a mid-ocean ridge crest with the magma chamber at the axis freezing into the gabbros off-axis to form the solid lithosphere.

deep hole, we now have a thorough reconnaissance of the sea floor upon which to finally base a Moho drilling attempt. A new 15-year phase of deep-ocean drilling is now launched. Called the Ocean Drilling Project, it has the technical capability to reach layer 3 and perhaps the Moho itself.

The Oceanic Mantle

What do we know of the material below the Moho? The Moho itself is a large velocity boundary where seismic waves traveling mostly within the crust above the Moho are so much slower than similar waves traveling

Figure 4-7. Borehole televiewer images from inside a *Glomar Challenger* drill hole into the pillow basalts (depth in meters below sea level). On the left are the sediments that accumulate above the pillows. On the right, elliptical structures are parts of pillows penetrated by the drill bit, about 30 m below the sediment basalt boundary. These images are made from ultrasonics. Just as medical technology allows us to see inside a pregnant woman's womb, so can we "see" inside the Earth (from Zoback and Anderson, 1982).

mostly below the Moho that they actually arrive at a receiver later than those from below the Moho, even though they both left the same source at the same time and the mantle waves had to travel a much greater distance. Only two kinds of ultramafic rock have velocities that fast, and they are of reasonable composition to be made from the residue of basalt: peridotite and eclogite. As we hinted earlier, we think peridotite is the correct composition, mainly from a process of elimination. **Eclogite** is exactly the same composition as basalt, but a higher pressure form. The volume of molten basalt would thus increase from that needed to make the oceanic crust to that required to make the entire lithosphere. We do not believe that much basalt exists in the asthenosphere. Also, the oceanic mantle exhibits **seismic anisotropy,** or directionality, whereby faster and slower velocities are thought to be caused by elongated crystals of **olivine.** These crystals grow at the ridge crest in a preferred direction. Peridotite is partially made of olivine crystals, but eclogite has none.

This is an excellent example of the kind of logic used in geology to decipher the structure and composition of the portion of the planet inaccessible to human examination. Peridotite is not the rock that forms the asthenosphere, though. That rock is code-named **pyrolite,** for an imaginary mix of three parts peridotite to one part basalt. Three fourths of the lithosphere is peridotite and one fourth is basalt. Remember the mixed-up and melted lithosphere scenerio. As you can see, if pyrolite were to melt and separate out, a lithosphere would result. We have never recovered a single grain of pyrolite rock from anywhere in the entire solar system; but we still think our asthenosphere is made of this composition of rock.

The Plate Model

The oceanic lithosphere can be modeled very successfully as a cooling plate of rock of finite thickness that is in **isostatic equilibrium** (that is, like a block of wood in a bathtub, it is floating at its natural level in the liquid mantle). The top of the plate is an isotherm, the cold bottom of the ocean. One edge of the plate is the sea-floor spreading center where new hot rock is continually added, and the bottom of the plate (Figure 4-2) is the 1200°C isotherm, the temperature that is required to partially melt mantle rock. All cooling is essentially vertical, even though the plate consists of material that is spreading away from a midocean ridge at a rate of several centimeters per year. The reason that most heat is lost vertically is that all rock is about the same temperature as that touching it in all horizontal directions, and the only cold surface through which heat can be effectively lost is upward into the ocean.

The lithospheric plate model predicts that the amount of heat coming out of the top surface decreases **exponentially** with age. That is, for each doubling of age, the amount of heat loss is squared. But the model further predicts that the depth of ocean water above the sea floor is entirely dependent upon this cooling as well. As the oceanic lithosphere cools, it contracts or shrinks, so the sea-floor depth should be only a function of its age and should decrease exponentially away from spreading centers (Figure 4-9). Put another way, the ocean should become deeper with distance from a hot mid-ocean ridge. Dan McKenzie of Cambridge University, John Sclater of The University of Texas, and Jean Francheteau of the University of Paris actually predicted this relationship before we were able to verify it empirically throughout the oceans. This observation alone gives one

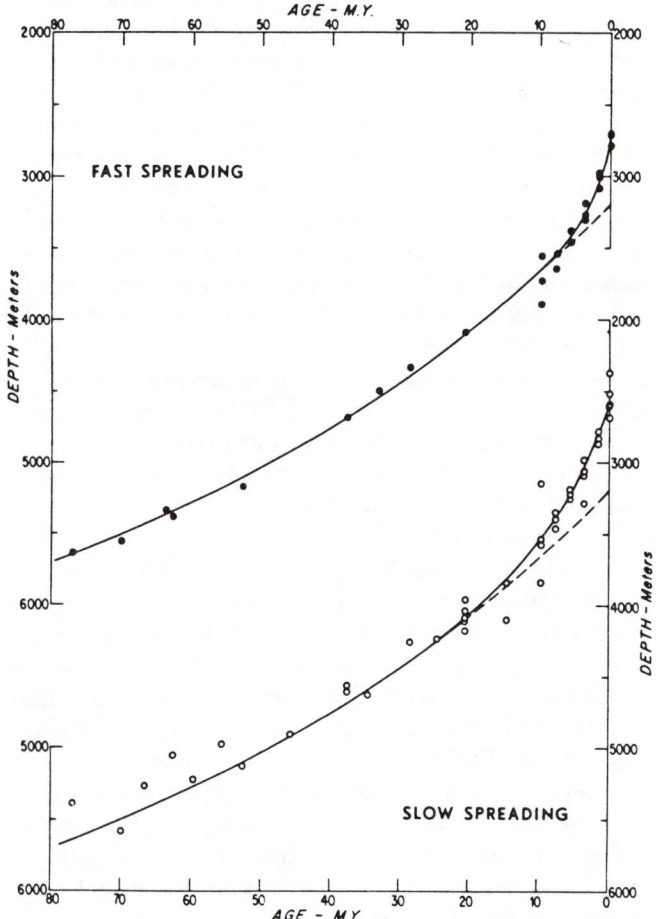

Figure 4-9. Both fast- and slow-spreading rate ridges subside exponentially away from the volcanic centers as the rock slowly cools. Eighty million years after formation, the lithosphere is still cooling and sinking because of thermal contraction. (from Le Pichon et al, 1973).

some idea of the power of the plate tectonics concept. With one simple cooling model, if we know the depth of the sea floor, we can predict the age of virtually the entire ocean.

The plate model's prediction that oceanic heat flow also decays exponentially away from spreading centers turns out to be a more complex issue, however. The amount of heat flowing out of the top of the plate is a rather easy measurement to make. Stick a few thermometers into the mud at successive depths and measure the conductivity of the mud to heat. **Heat flow** is the product of the increase in temperature with depth times the thermal conductivity. The first measurements ever, by Sir Edward Bullard of Cambridge University in 1954, indeed showed high heat flow near spreading centers. But as more and more measurements were made (now there are more than 10,000 in the oceans), a large scatter in values close to the midocean ridge axes became apparent (Figure 4-10). Also, the mean value of measurements near the spreading center was found to be much colder than it should be. After all, the volcanic spreading center should be the hottest place on the oceanic lithosphere, since it certainly is the youngest.

As David Kitts of the University of Oklahoma pointed out in a history-of-science article on plate tectonics, it was a tribute to the acceptability of the plate tectonics hypothesis that by 1973 this low heat flow was considered to be anomalous rather than considering the plate model to be disproven. In fact, the elevation of the sea floor shows that the plate model successfully predicts the integrated heat content of the entire plate at any given age. That is, the **ridge crest** is indeed the hottest locale on the lithosphere because it is the shallowest and least contracted. The **thermal contraction** of the whole plate contributes to that elevation. The observation of heat flow measures only a skin effect of the near surface temperatures.

Now that a systematic pattern for surface cooling has been recognized throughout the oceans, it is believed that hot springs resulting from the circulation of oceanic bottom water into and out of the oceanic crust are causing both the low heat flow and the scatter in measurement values near midocean ridges. These hot springs have recently been photographed in action in the eastern Pacific Ocean (Figure 4-11). Their discovery is so important that Chapter 7 is devoted to the midocean spreading center hot-spring activity. For our purposes here, consider Old Faithful Geyser in Yellowstone Park. The ground around the geyser is cold because the hot spring removes heat extremely efficiently to the atmosphere. Only the existence of a magma chamber deep below Old Faithful keeps it active hour after hour. Still, its geological days are numbered because it will soon (within the next 10,000 years) cool even the magma chamber into solid rock.

This form of fluid circulation takes the heat out of the oceanic crust to the oceanic bottom water directly in the form of hot springs, so that heat-flow measurements in the mud on top of the lithosphere do not "feel" the

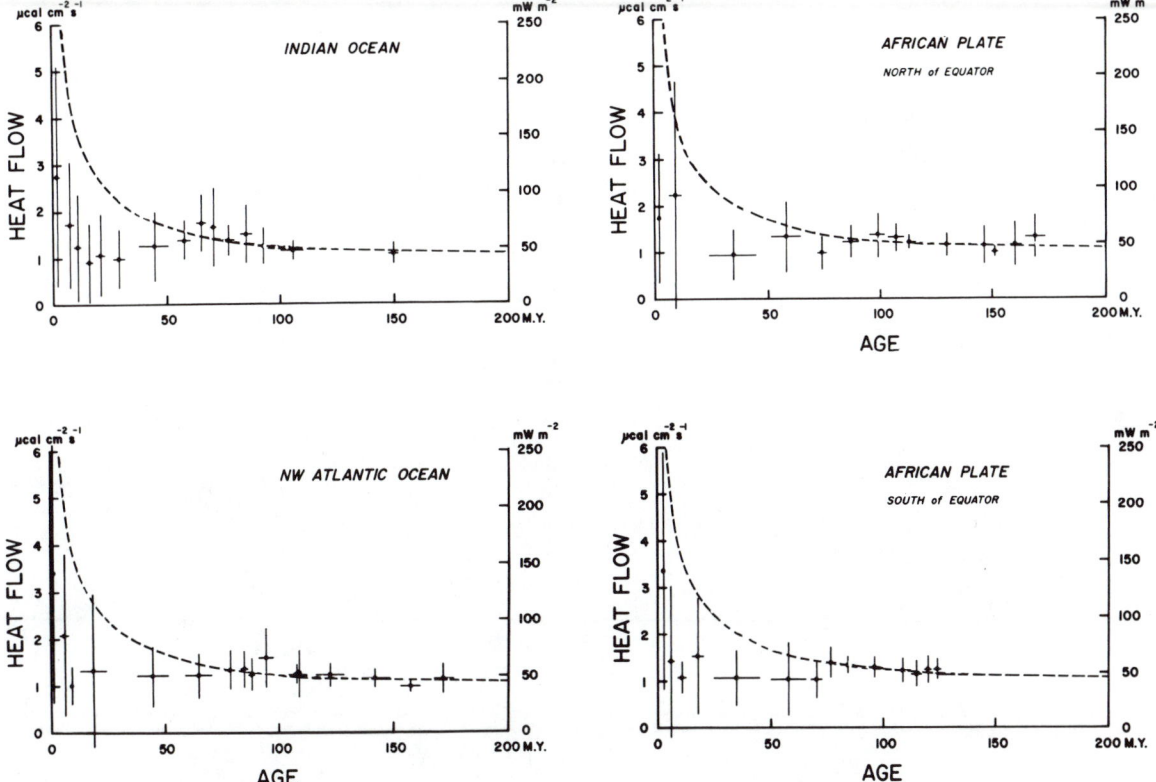

Figure 4-10. All is not explained by plate tectonics because the expected heat loss out of the top of the plate, which is predicted by the subsidence (the dashed curves above), is not observed in any ocean. Instead, all young plates have too low heat flow (solid dots with error bars). That is, these young plates are too cold. The reason is that hot-spring activity efficiently removes heat near the ridge axis. This "skin effect" has no effect on the deeper cooling of the plate that causes the subsidence (figure by Mike Hobart).

extra heat flow. When this convective heat removal is taken into account, the heat-flow observations then also agree with the oceanic plate model.

This water circulation into the crust is important for two reasons. First, major metal concentrations occur at the zones of upwelling hot water (i.e. **metallogenesis** occurs in these hot springs). Second, the oceanic crust **buffers** the compostion of the oceans. That is, the chemistry of ocean water is held within tight limits by the circulation of ocean water through the oceanic crust once every few million years. Thus the composition of the oceans has remained virtually constant throughout most of geologic time.

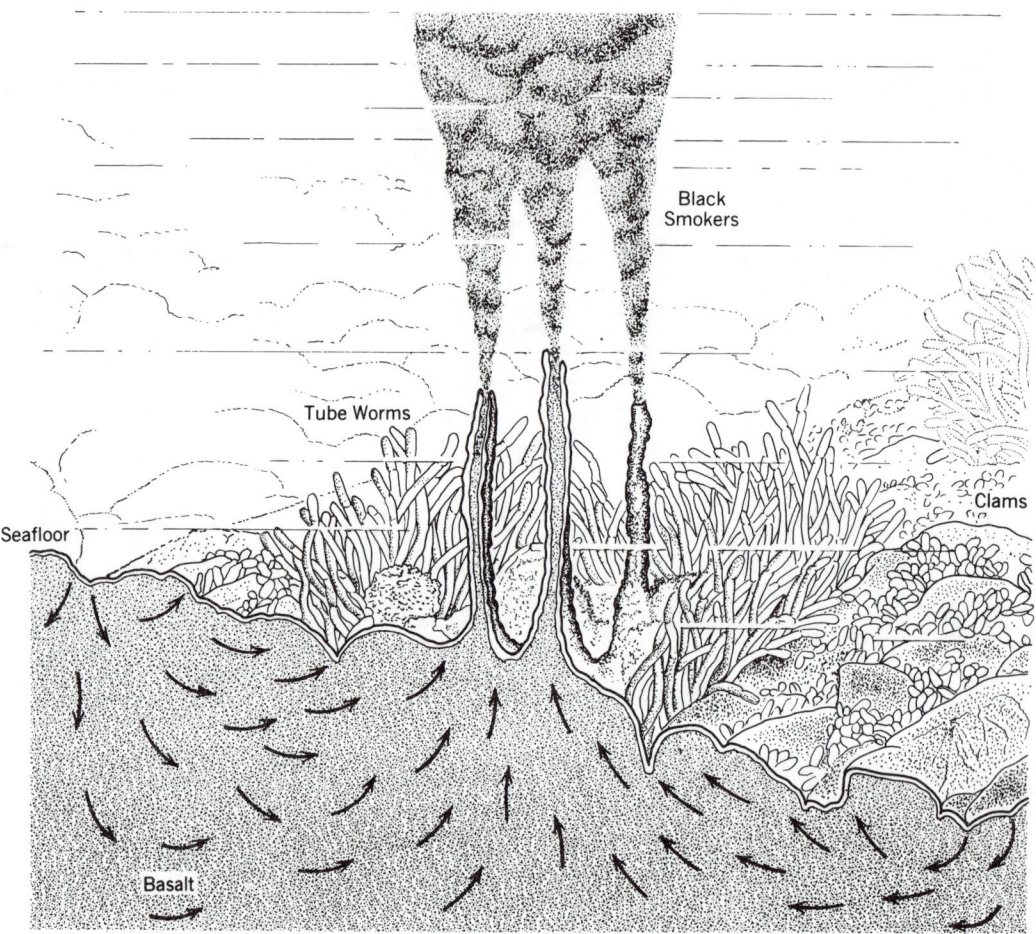

Figure 4-11. This hot-spring activity (black arrows) produces a spectacular show of spouting metalliferous effluents that contain sulfides that support perhaps the most remarkable biological community in the world (worms and clams above) (Bonatti, 1981).

Summary

We can now define a plate model and observe the shape and form of the oceanic lithosphere as it ages away from spreading centers. It is a remarkably simple slab of rock. Yet these plates have continually interacted in predictable ways to affect every aspect of Earth history, and many aspects of human history as well. But the big puzzle ever since Wegener has been, what pushes the plates around? What is the driving mechanism, the ultimate force that decides where and what kind of plate boundary interaction will occur when? The beauty of plate tectonics and its corollary, the plate model, is that we do not need to know the answer to these ultimate questions in order to understand the processes occurring at the surface of our planet.

Further Reading

Fox, P. J., and Stroup, J. B., 1981, The plutonic foundation of the oceanic crust, *in* C. Emiliani, ed., The Sea, v. 7: New York, Wiley.

Harrison, C. G. A., and Bonatti, E., 1981, The oceanic lithosphere, *in* C. Emiliani, ed., The Sea, v. 7: New York, Wiley.

Ophiolites: A Slice of Oceanic Lithosphere

Discovering the nature of the crust and mantle, which constitute the oceanic lithosphere, is inherently a difficult task. This leads to some of the charm and much of the adventure of the profession of marine geology, but getting at rocks that are two miles below a ship is an arduous task indeed. And steaming around the world looking for similarities and differences from ocean to ocean requires international team efforts involving years of research. For example, part of this chapter was written from the science office of the deep-sea drilling vessel *Glomar Challenger*. We (14 scientists) were on a two-month expedition away from family and friends over Thanksgiving, Christmas, and New Year's to try to drill the deepest hole ever into oceanic lithosphere. This was to complete the fourth expedition and eighth month of drilling at this site. A total of 60 scientists from all over the world spent two months each drilling this hole. And yet we reached only a little over 1 km into the sheeted dikes just beneath the surface layer of pillow basalts.

Other ways of recovering oceanic lithosphere are just as arduous, and one, the deep-diving submarine, is a little dangerous. We are blessed with a quirk of the subduction process, however, which allows us to walk over slivers of old oceanic crust and mantle and knock off chunks of rock with a sledge hammer. Pieces of oceanic crust and mantle sometimes are "shaved off" the descending plate at trenches and are "plastered" to the colliding landmass. These pieces of old oceanic lithosphere are then available for land-based study. Obviously, walking over a mountain with a hammer is much easier than diving for a few limited specimens with a submarine, or drilling through rock beneath miles of water. It turns out that all three kinds of studies are necessary because these land slivers are often incomplete. They must be ground-truthed into the proper oceanic framework before generalizations can be drawn from their detailed geology.

Ophiolites provide a glimpse of the lithologies and structures as well as an aerial view of the heterogeneity of the oceanic lithosphere. There are not many of them, and they are always found in obscure places around the planet, such as along the cliffs of Tierra del Fuego at the very southern tip of South America, in uppermost Newfoundland, in the Afar Desert of northwestern Africa, and in guerilla-infested jungles of Luzon in the Philippines. One of the best ophiolites in the United States is at Point Sol along the Big Sur coast of central California. Unfortunately, it is in the middle of Vandenburg Air Force Base, a prime test site for Cruise, MX, and Trident missile development. Not surprisingly, geologists have a hard time getting permission to visit Point Sol.

Ophiolite Structure

Quoting Casey, et al. (1981), ophiolites "consist of a distinctive assemblage of various mafic and ultramafic rock types with an ordered stratiform (layered) arrangement. They . . . are often associated with deep-water marine sediments and metalliferous precipitates. The range of lithologies and gross structure . . . have their correlatives in samples recovered from contemporary deep ocean basins."

These ophiolite complexes thus provide a window into the oceanic lithosphere, and the first lesson they teach is that the lithosphere must be highly variable in the thicknesses of its basic units from place to place (Figure 5-1). As we have seen before, these basic units consist of an outer layer of pillow basalts grading downward first into sheeted dikes and then into gabbros, coarse-grained equivalents of basalt that are thought to represent the cooled magma chamber. The Moho separates the gabbros from layered peridotites found beneath the frozen magma chamber. The latter make up the oceanic mantle. From one ophiolite to another, the thicknesses of these layers vary quite a bit. How much the extrusion process, which slaps these slivers onto land, contributes to this heterogeneity is still an open question. But within any one ophiolite, layers will thicken and thin over several kilometers of horizontal extent.

Beginning at the top and looking in detail at each of the tectonic layers of an ophiolite, the pillow basalts and sheeted dikes represent the volcanic carapace with its feeder network. Seismically, this upper layer shows a steep gradient in velocities from that of the nubbly lava flows of the pillow unit (3.0 to 4.0 km/s seismic velocity) to the more uniform and constant velocities of the dikes (6.0 km/s). The topmost layers are often called layers 2A

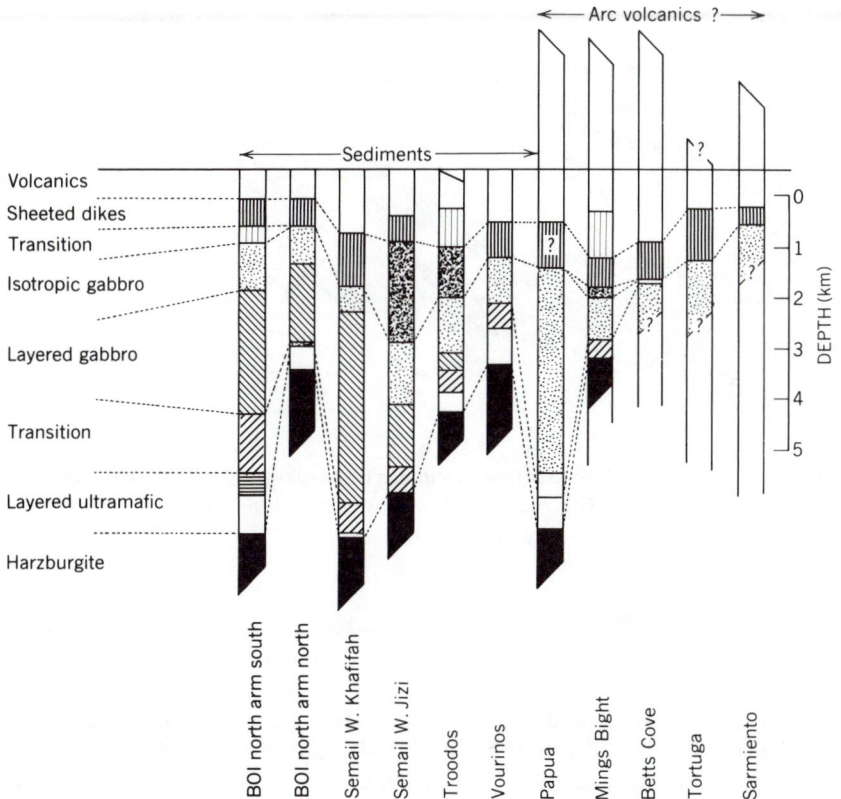

Figure 5-1. The various ophiolites of the world have different thicknesses of each oceanic crustal layer preserved. For example, the north arm of the Bay of Islands (BOI)ophiolite has a thin layer 3 gabbroic sequence preserved whereas the Semail ophiolite in Oman has a much thicker gabbroic layer. All ophiolites preserve some of each layer, however (from Casey et al., 1981).

and 2B, with layer 1 (the sediments) and layer 2C (the dikes) bracketing them. But the term layer is a misnomer, since the transition from one to the other is irregular and gradual.

Drilling into the Crust

The deep-sea drill hole into these layers found a geophysical boundary that was much more distinct than the structural transition from pillow basalts to dikes, for example. Whereas the zone with intermixed pillow basalts and dikes was 200 m thick, the geophysical parameters of the crust changed gradient over only 50 m. That is, **electrical resistivity, porosity, density,** and

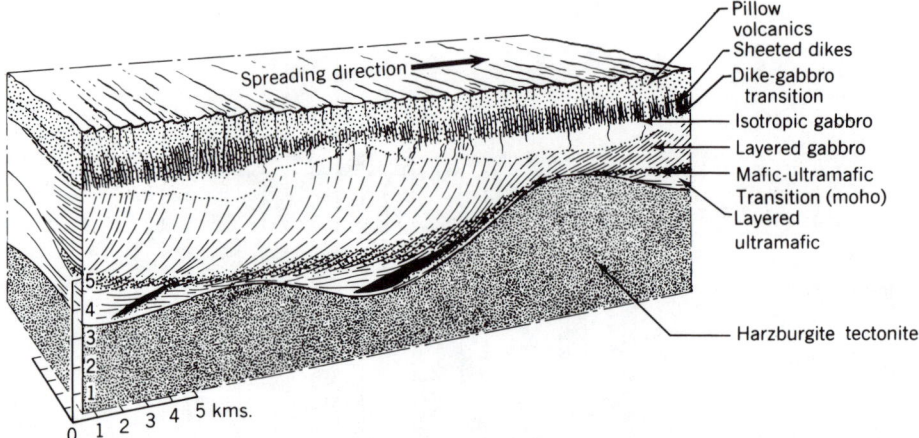

Figure 5-2. Cross section through an ophiolite displaying the various structural and compositional layers. This is thought to closely resemble the structure of the oceanic crust as well (from Casey et al., 1981).

seismic velocity all underwent more abrupt changes across the layer 2B–2C boundary than did chemical changes such as degree of alteration or structural changes such as dikes versus pillows. The structural change from pillow basalts to dikes combined with an abrupt decrease in the degree of fracturing are the likely causes of the sharp geophysical boundaries. Ophiolites show similar layering.

Although the Deep Sea Drilling Project has not succeeded in penetrating deep into the crust, the pillow basaltic layer has been extensively sampled. It is of similar composition to that found in all ophiolites. In both cases, the crust consists of a chaotic rubble pile of pillow lavas, massive flow basalts, **breccia** zones (cemented cobblestones), and clay and alteration minerals filling some or all of the extensive fracture network. In ophiolites, the dike layer is more ordered, with 10-cm- to 1-m-thick dikes neatly arranged upright one after the other (Figure 5-2), like row houses in Brooklyn. The intrusion process at the ridge axis appears to split dikes right down the middle with new dikes intruding so that thin 1-cm quenched contacts always bound each dike. Fracturing is much less severe and vein fillings die out progressively toward the base of the dikes.

The Frozen Magma Chamber

The gabbroic layer is of basaltic composition, but the rock is made wholly of large, slowly cooled crystals. The gabbro forms in thin laminar layers that are thought to be the slowly cooling walls of a magma chamber intermit-

Western Pacific

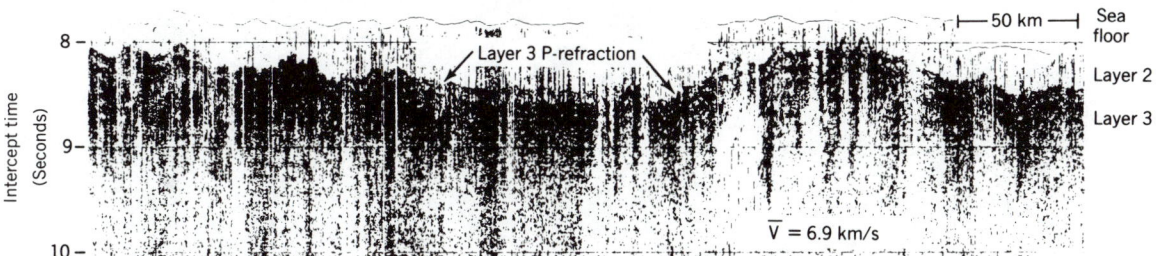

Figure 5-3. Seismic reflection and refraction profiling from a ship records sound energy that has reflected off the dike–gabbro boundary between layers 2 and 3 (from Talwani et al., 1981). The vertical axis is the time taken by the sound waves to travel from the ship downward to the boundary, then back to the surface (8 to 8.5 s) (Talwani et al, 1983).

tently replenished with magma. The boundary upward to dikes is gradational, whereas the lower boundary is abrupt at the Moho. By bouncing sound waves off the various layers of the crust, we can see the form of these boundaries. **Seismic refraction** is a technique by which sound waves are sent downward into the crust, pass along boundaries between fast and slow rock, and re-emerge at the surface at different times. Using this technique, we can form a picture of the boundary between dikes and gabbros (Figure 5-3). Interestingly, this boundary is sometimes found to be rougher than the sea floor itself. Often it is too rough or diffuse to show up at all. It has never been detected by methods that reflect sound waves off a surface.

This latter technique, which is called **seismic reflection** profiling, was perfected by oil companies to see oil-bearing structures beneath the surface. Shooting these waves of sound into the oceanic crust, we can see that the Moho is not only an excellent reflector, but is also continuous across the midocean ridge magma chamber at least in the eastern Pacific Ocean (Figure 5-4). In many ophiolites this Moho boundary is so abrupt that you can knock off a single rock with gabbro and periodotite meeting across a few inches. Below the Moho in ophiolites, blobs of **diapir-like** lower mantle ultramafics are imbedded in a background of upper mantle peridotite (Figure 5-5).

A characteristic of all drilled ophiolites and ocean crust is the alteration of the basalt into claylike minerals, particularly in the extensive fractures and cracks that shatter the crust. When hot water passes through the **permeable** pore spaces and fractures, chemical reactions similar to rusting occur. Since oceanic lithosphere is often formed under miles of seawater, it is virtually impossible to prevent seawater from entering the crust. When it does, it sets up convection currents and efficiently removes much of the excess heat in the newly erupted lava. But it also alters the basalt and takes elements such

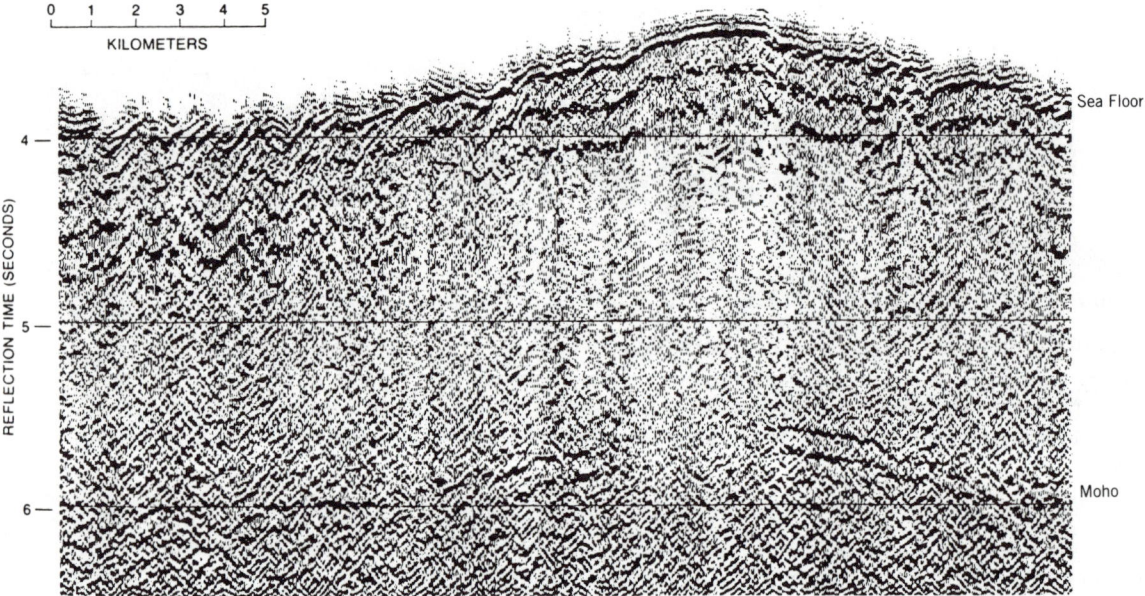

Figure 5-4. The Moho boundary between the oceanic crust and mantle can also be seen by seismic reflection profiling. In this case the sea floor is closer to the surface than in Figure 5-3, accounting for the faster travel times, but the Moho is clearly deeper into the crust (2 seconds deeper). The Moho reflector is 2 s below the sea floor as opposed to less than 1 s for the layer 2–3 boundary. To convert from time to distance, the travel time must be multiplied by the velocity of the sound waves. At an average velocity of say 5 km/s, the layer 2–3 boundary is 2 to 3 km below the surface, whereas the Moho is more than 5 km down (don't forget that the sound wave travel time records the travel *down* then *back* through the crust, so it must be divided by two before multiplying by velocity to get thickness) (from Talwani et al., 1983).

as magnesium and potassium away from the basalt, giving up calcium in return. The plumbing system through which this water flows becomes progressively plugged by clay minerals, the product of this interchange. So, as the plate ages, the water begins to flow much more haltingly because its driving force, heat, and its pathways, cracks, are both being dissipated; the heat by cooling and the cracks by precipitation.

As we go deeper into ophiolites, the minerals that fill the cracks become more and more high-temperature forms of clay. The uppermost gabbros are the most pervasively altered and at the highest temperatures in the crustal section. With further depth, the degree of alteration decreases steadily until

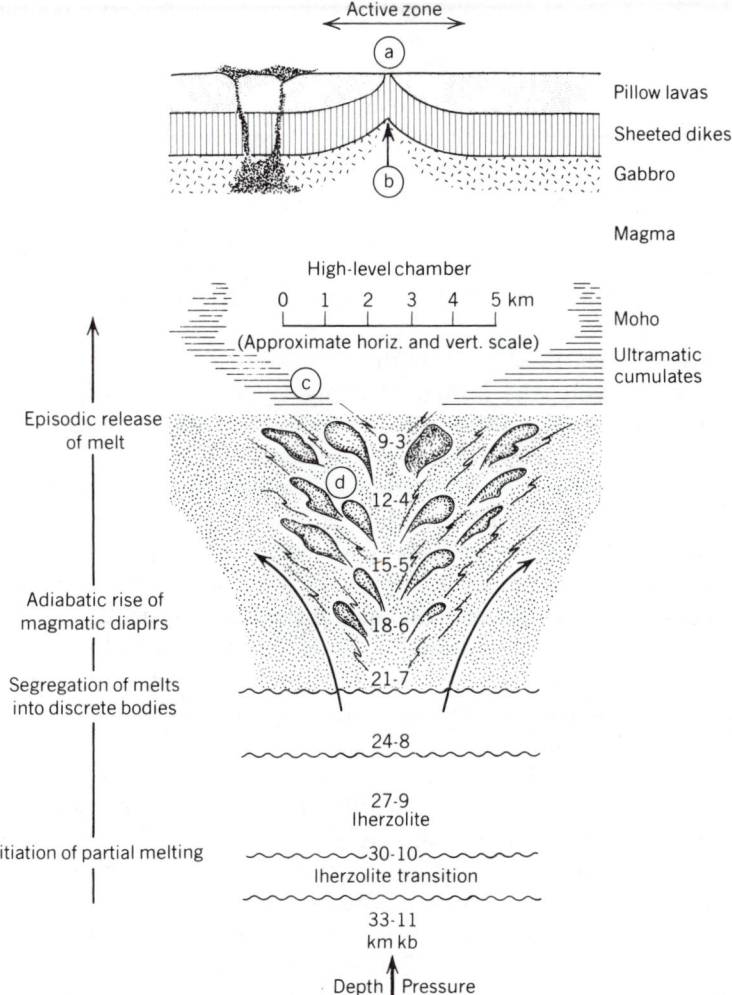

Figure 5-5. Magma chamber below the ridge axis showing the feeder blobs (d) coming from the deep mantle to replenish the magma supply in the chamber (c), as well as the mechanism by which the crust freezes into layers (b and a) (from Gass and Smewing, 1984).

the basal gabbros just above the Moho are often the freshest of the entire ophiolite section. The supply of water downward through cracks and fractures is obviously impeded at these basal depth ranges, yet the alteration above may extend 5 km into the crust. The water content of the oceanic crust is, therefore, very high, with certainly more than 2 percent by weight, and probably closer to 5 percent residing as water bound into the crystal structure of the clays.

The permeability of the oceanic crust has been measured directly at the deepest *Challenger* hole. This is an interesting but difficult experiment to perform under the extreme conditions encountered beneath the deep sea floor. A rubber tire, called a packer, is inflated against the borehole wall to prevent fluid pumped out the bottom of the drill pipe from escaping around the outside of the pipe to the ocean. Then the powerful water pumps of the drillship are revved up full speed to force the water out the pipe and into the rock. This procedure is a form of reservoir evaluation used commonly in oil fields and is called a flow test.

Permeability is measured by how the rock formation takes the forced water: If it takes it easily, the formation is highly permeable; if it takes it hard, the formation is tight with low permeability. Porosity, or the amount of space between grains of rock, is not to be confused with permeability, which depends upon porosity plus **tortuosity,** or how tortuous the path is between pores. Thus, a styrofoam cup has abundant porosity, but with no connections at all between pores it has no permeability. The permeability of the upper oceanic crust was found to be very high in the pillow basalts, about that of the best Saudi Arabian oil field, but it drops exponentially with depth into the dikes. The temperature was so high in the dikes, 160°C, that the rubber melted off the tire three different times in attempts to measure the permeability at the deepest depths in the borehole. Asbestos tires may have to be used in the future.

This form of permeability decrease agrees with alteration patterns in ophiolites in that the deepest, least-altered gabbros are also **metasomatically** altered; that is, there are no missing chemical elements. The sum of the gabbro and alteration products is exactly that of unaltered gabbro. Nothing has been removed from the system. The permeability must be very low to prevent the water from escaping with at least some chemical elements to be removed from the system. At shallower depths, the sum of basalt and alteration products is by no means equal to that of fresh, unaltered basalt, with the missing elements removed to the ocean water. From top to bottom of the crust, we move from an open geochemical system to one that is closed to chemical exchange with other layers.

The ophiolite model does not tell us much of what form of alteration if any is beneath the Moho. This deep section, when present, is often dramatically altered to **serpentine** (soapstone), but by meteoric or fresh water after emplacement on land rather than by sea water during its residence time as oceanic mantle. We must turn to geophysics and laboratory experiments on the stability of minerals to constrain the degree of alteration of the lithospheric mantle. The upper 25 km of mantle is believed to be made of **plagioclase** peridotite grading downward into heavier and heavier peridotites.

These minerals must be almost completely fresh with no water present, because altered peridotites have a velocity too slow to be a major component of the lower lithosphere.

How the Crust Was Formed

We turn now from the composition of ophiolites to what they tell us about how the lithosphere was formed. The entire oceanic crust represents the remains of repeatedly frozen magma chambers with their feeder complexes of dikes (feeding both from below in the mantle to the chamber and toward the surface from the chamber) and the extrusive lava flows of their volcanic activity. The crust consists of countless volcanoes, each split in two to be replaced by a new volcano. This process continues over millions of years until all the rock making up the floors of the great oceans of the Earth was generated. It is as if a volcano were sliced in two, then pulled apart and another volcano inserted into the gap, time after countless time. Judging from the total thickness of magma chambers now at the heart of the volcanic crust, they never contained more than 25 to 30 percent melt (magma) at any one time, so the magma chambers are more like a slush of crystals in a hot slurry. The mantle below is nothing more than the refractory residue left behind by this overwhelming melting event.

A characteristic of this magma chamber appears to be that it is periodic. That is, it heats, cools, then solidifies only to be reheated by another volcanic magma event. This shows up as cyclical minerology of the cooled gabbro and dike layers of ophiolites. Some minerals cool from a magma before others; so a banding of first, last, first, last, and so on is observed in the rocks. This must represent rejuvenation of the magma chamber with repeated new heating events. Looking at volcanic activity on land, one is hardly surprised.

Ophiolites leave us with a taste for what the oceanic lithosphere is like. Plate tectonics provides us with the mechanism with which such sustained volcanic activity can have existed on the Earth for millions and millions of years. Remarkably, the process appears to be passive. New magma fills an almost frozen magma chamber because the two great plates onto which new rock is being frozen drift slowly apart, producing cracks that extend from the surface into the magma chamber. Magma surges up to fill the cracks, and the next volcanic event is born.

Far from being complete, our understanding of ophiolites is still in its infancy. For example, the Troodos ophiolite is one of the oldest known to geologists. In fact, mines from the Troodos on the island of Cyprus provided some of the first bronze for the earliest Greek sculptures. Troodos was thought to be the typical oceanic crustal ophiolite, until a drilling team headed by Paul Robinson of Dalhousie University in Canada put the Troodos to the ultimate geological test: the drill bit.

To their great surprise they found the structure of the sea floor but the chemistry of an **island arc** volcano, which is much more alkaline (more calcium and sodium) than midocean ridge basalt (more iron and magnesium). Troodos apparently represents sea floor between two great island arc volcanoes. The structure of the plumbing system of an island arc is essentially the same as that of a midocean ridge. This is not so surprising in retrospect, however, since both are the insides of volcanoes.

Summary

At the present time, this Troodos drilling project is only 150 m from drilling through the Moho. The Moho has never before been sampled any place deep inside the Earth, and although we think we know what will be found, we can't be certain until we have samples in hand. The rock beneath the Moho is the frozen remains from *below* the magma chamber. Although it is most certainly ultramafic (heavier than any rock able to make it up to the magma chamber), we can only guess at its chemistry.

We turn now to the active formation of oceanic crust at a midocean ridge. New crust is currently being formed along the 50,000-km length of the world's spreading centers, some of which may someday slice away during subduction to form ophiolites of a future time. The processes of an active magma chamber have become some of the great new discoveries of marine geology, and within such, we will find some of the most awesome spectacles of the profession.

Further Reading

Casey, J. F., Dewey, J. F., Fox, P. J., Karson, J. A., and Ronsenkrantz, E., 1984, Heterogeneous nature of the oceanic crust and upper mantle: A perspective from the Bay of Islands ophiolite complex, *in* C. Emiliani, ed., The Sea, Vol. 7: New York, Wiley.

Gass, I. G., and Smewing, J. D., 1984, Ophiolites: obducted oceanic lithosphere, *in* C. Emiliani, ed., The Sea, Vol. 7: New York, Wiley.

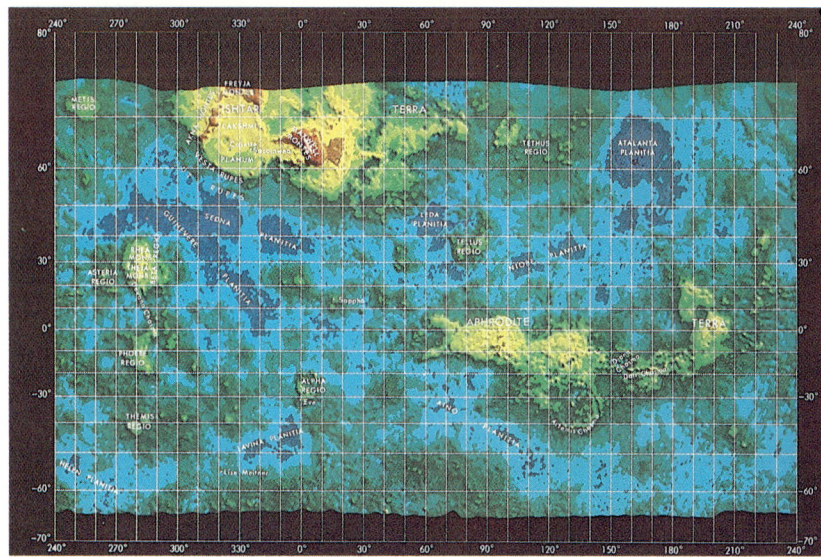

Figure 1–6. Topography of Venus as seen by radar on the Pioneer spacecraft. Yellow are elevated regions of lightweight rock, and blue are heavy, black basalts. If Venus had water, these areas would be ocean floor and the yellow would be continents. So the topographic relief of Earth is not unusual, but the existence of our oceans is (Eliason, 1982). Color scale shows topography from highs (oranges and yellows), through greens, to lows (blues and purples).

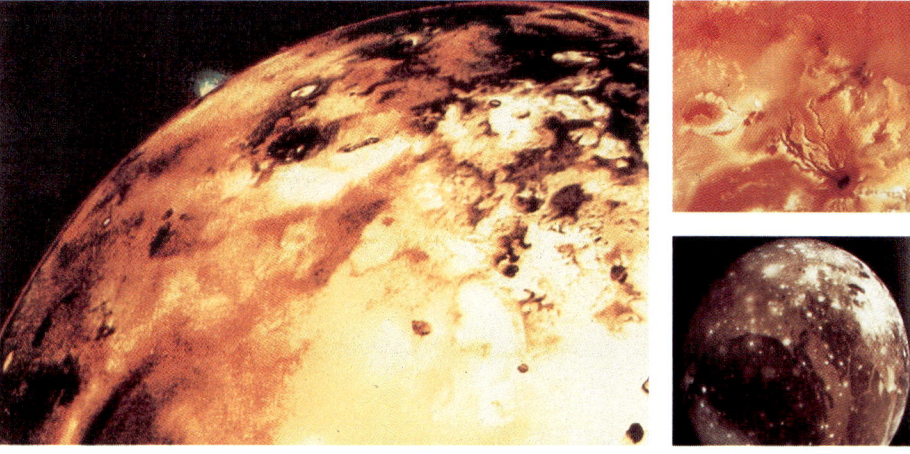

Figure 1–7. Voyager 1 photo of Io, one of Jupiter's moons showing the only recorded evidence of an erupting volcano anywhere other than Earth (on the horizon). A closeup of one Io volcano is in upper right. Lower right is photo of Ganymede, Jupiter's largest moon. White spots are impact craters. Brown regions cutting dark black are possibly newly rifted material (from NASA).

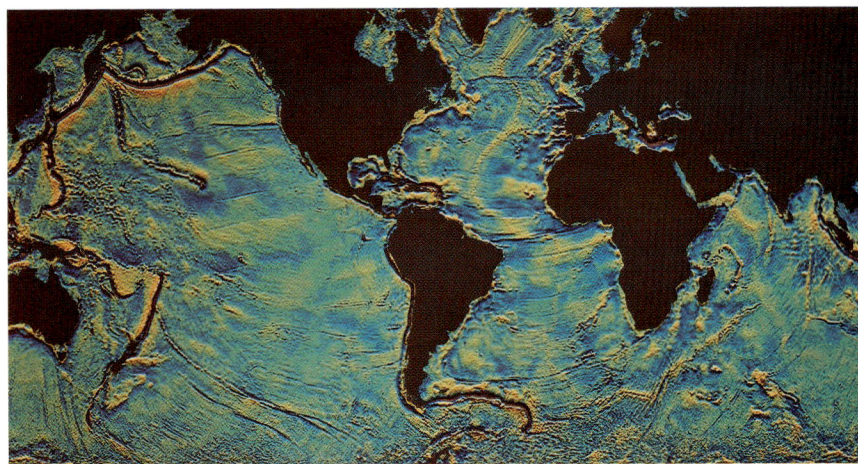

Figure 2–3. The SEASAT gravity field of the oceans. The roughness in the image is gravity, rather than topography, but the linear features must be caused by density anomalies in the lithosphere or mantle. This observational technique has revolutionized our view of the oceans because, for the first time, we have a complete image of the sea floor (from William H. Haxby).

Figure 7–2. A closeup of the tube worms called *Vestimentiferan pogonophorans*. The organism is the bright red worm inside the chitinous tube. The red worm extends more than 12 inches from the tube, which in some cases is 10 meters high. The worm's body extends for more than a meter inside the tube. They have no stomachs because the food supply is so plentiful that direct transfer of food to cells is possible. The small crabs feeding on the tubes have eye sockets but no eyes. They have adapted them into scrapers to scratch food from the microgrowth on the outside of the worm tubes (by Emory Kristof, © National Geographic Society, 1979).

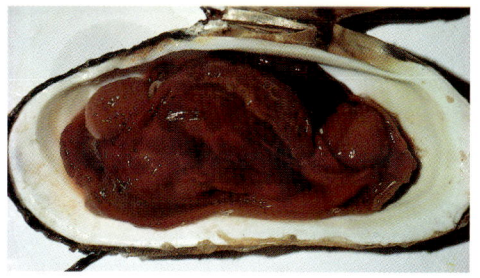  

Figure 7–3 (above). The need for hemoglobin extends to the clams as well as the worms. The meat of the black-smoker clam is beefy red. High concentrations of heavy metals also present in the black smoke make it inadvisable to eat this clam. Also, note the huge size of the clam, again an indication of the plentiful supply of sulfur-rich food (by Emory Kristof, © National Geographic Society).

Figure 7–4 (right). The black smokers exit the sea floor at "firehose velocities" as a clear liquid at up to 400°C. They immediately cool and begin precipitating their heavy metal contents. They are supersaturated in iron, copper, zinc, manganese, and most of the precious metals (by Dudley B. Foster, Woods Hole Oceanographic Institution, © National Geographic Society, 1979).

Figure 7–5. As evidence of the high temperatures present in the black smokers, consider this *Alvin* heat probe, which was inserted into the smoke to measure its temperature. The hottest waters ever encountered prior to the black smokers were 22°C, so not only did the temperature reading from this probe go off the scale, but the PVC plastic tubing melted. Melting temperature for PVC is 250°C. High-temperature platinum thermocouples were later used to measure temperatures up to 400°C in the black smokers (by Emory Kristof, © National Geographic Society).

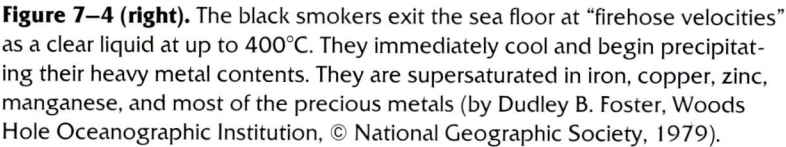

Figure 7–9. If the rising, hot limb of the crustal convection cell mixes with downgoing cold water beneath the surface, the metals are precipitated beneath the sea floor and the smoke is colder and white as it exits into the water column. Such cases preserve massive amounts of metals, which are minable millions of years later if the deposits happen to be obducted onto land as ophiolites. Troodos on Cyprus was such a whitesmoker case. The metals shown here came from a hole drilled deep into the 6-million-year-old crust south of the Galapagos Spreading Center white smokers. The "golden" mineral is pyrite or "fool's gold," but there are minable concentrations of copper and zinc present in this sample (greens) (from Deep Sea Drilling Project). (Scale is in cm.)

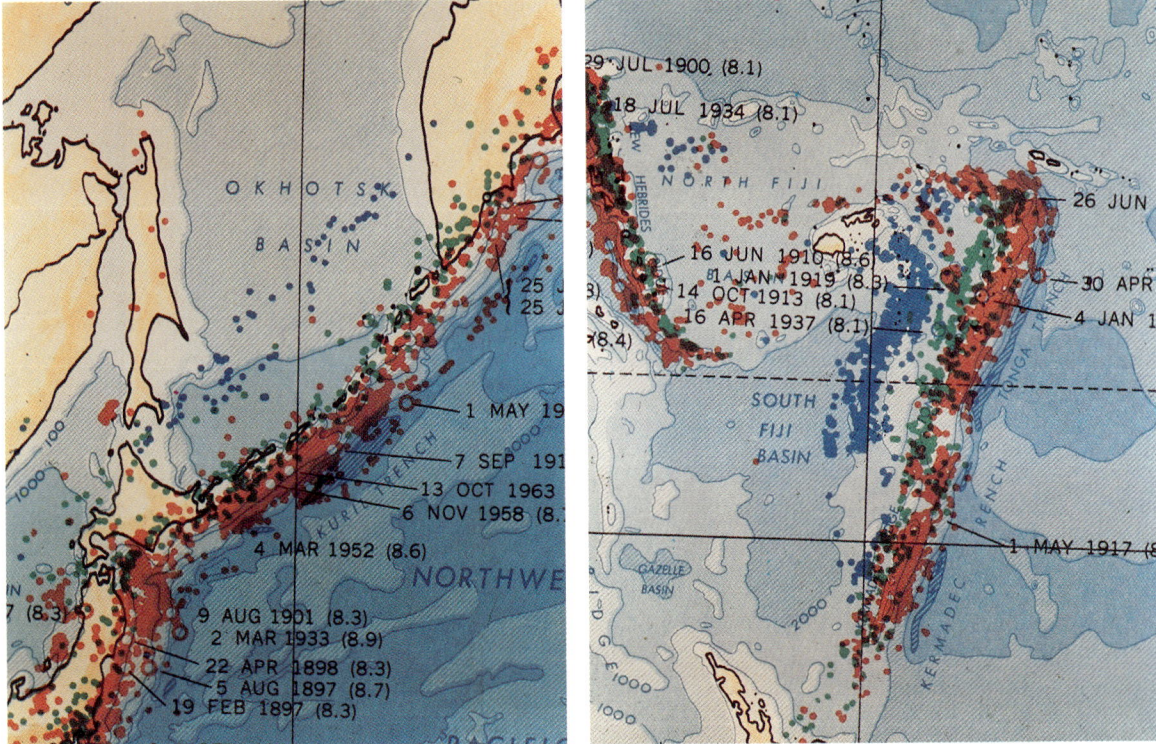

Figure 11–1 (left). Map of northern Japan and the Kamchatka peninsula with earthquakes shown as colored dots. Red dots are earthquakes that are shallower than 100 km, green events occurred from 100 to 400 km, and blue earthquakes were from 400 to 700 km deep. Large open circles are great earthquakes with dates and magnitudes given as well. Notice that the color bands move from red in the southeast to green then blue in the northwest. The projection of these earthquakes to their proper depths mark the surface of the subducting Pacific Plate beneath Japan and Kamchatka (figure from Nelson and Janse, 1979).

Figure 11–2 (right). Map of the Tonga trench in the south Pacific Ocean, with North Island, New Zealand, visible in the lower left. Earthquake locations, depths, and great event magnitudes as in Figure 11–1. The earthquakes increase in depth from east to west, again indicating that the Pacific Plate is being subducted in this direction. The color bands reverse in direction in the far upper left, where subduction of the Indo-Australian Plate is occurring from west to east beneath the New Hebrides (figure from Nelson and Janse, 1979).

Figure 11–23. Icelanders can calmly sit close to eruptions because little water comes up with lavas formed on mid-ocean ridges.

Figure 11–24. Explosive eruption occurs when water under pressure turns to steam and explodes much as a pressure cooker would if the lid were left unsecured, as in this deep sea volcano south of Japan.

Figure 11–30 (a). In 1964, an undersea volcano south of Iceland erupted enough new rock to grow above sea level and become an island. First only steam was seen.

Figure 11–30 (b). Soon Sertsey showed her central caldera.

Figure 11 – 30 (c). Sertsey eventually became quite a good-sized island.

Figure 11 – 30 (d). Sertsey grew then by lava erupting and flowing downward to the sea.

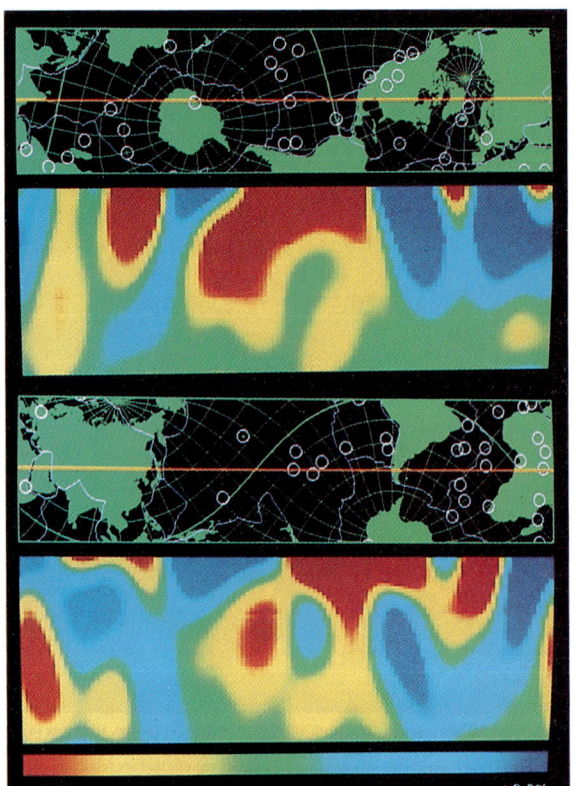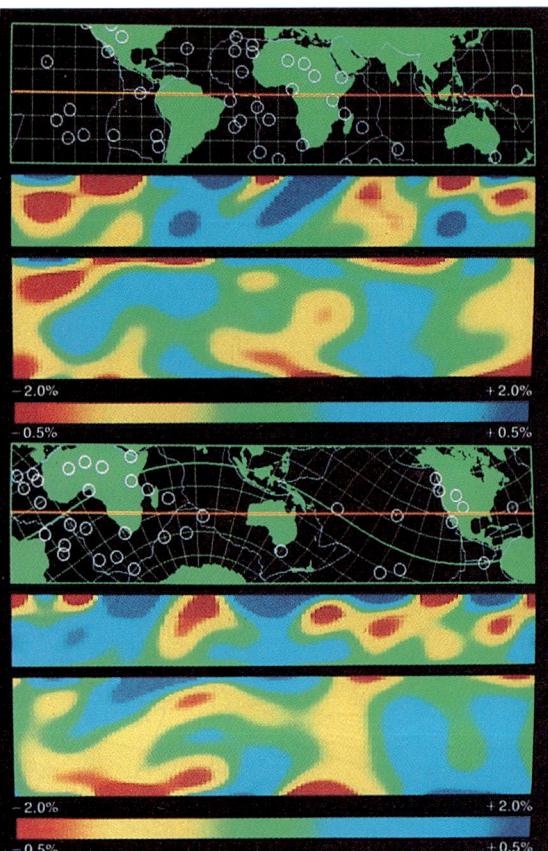

Figure 14–12 (left, top). Convection in the mantle is shown along a great circle slice from near the north pole through the south pole and from the top to bottom of the mantle (location given by red horizontal line in top panel). At the top of the color panel are Lithospheric Plates, and at the bottom is the outer core. Open circles are hot spots at the Earth's surface. This seismic tomography image is made from observing velocity differences in arrival times of earthquakes recorded across the world from where they occur. Red is slower, and consequently, hotter rock than the yellows, which in turn are hotter than the blue areas. Hot mantle is found under East Pacific Rise and Central Indian Mid-Ocean Ridge (solid, light line). Continents are above cold mantle.

Figure 14–12 (left, bottom). Seismic tomography image from Asia through the southern tip of South America and across equatorial Africa. Notice that the Tibetan Plateau above India is above hot mantle and Africa is above cold mantle. Color scale from −2% (red) to +2% (blue) velocity anomaly is shown at bottom.

Figure 14–12 (right, top). Here, seismic tomography has been used to separate the upper mantle above 700 km from the lower mantle along a slice through the equator. Notice the significant horizontal movements indicated by the velocity anomalies.

Figure 14–12 (right, bottom). Seismic tomography image of upper and lower mantle velocity anomalies from southern Africa through Australia and the southern United States. Whereas the upper mantle beneath the continents is cold, significant hot areas exist beneath continents at the core/mantle boundary (figure from Dzewanski and Anderson, 1984).

The Ridge Axis and Magma Chambers

The discovery of magma chambers at the axes of midocean ridges is a relatively new finding in the oceans. As is the usual case with this profession, it required the development of new technology. Oceanographers, in general, are technology bound. Although our imaginations wander far beyond the known, what we can see or measure always constrains our science. In a way, we are explorers. And an explorer will conduct an experiment not knowing for certain exactly what he or she is looking for or what the results will be. A scientist in a well-developed profession, such as chemistry, will conduct an experiment to extract a very specific answer. When one goes to sea with a piece of new technology, one often discovers something completely different from what one was originally looking for. This was the case with the recent discovery of the sunken oceanliner Titanic. Similar serendipity was the case with the discovery of the existence of axial magma chambers on midocean ridges, beginning in 1976. We've always known they must exist at the ridge crest in order for sea-floor spreading to occur, but the scientists involved were surprised to find them so close to the surface. After all, midocean ridges are active volcanoes, and all active volcanoes have magma chambers inside them where the lava accumulates before its eruption to the surface. But on land, the magma chamber is active only once every hundred years or so. Since a midocean ridge is pulled apart continuously, could a steady-state magma chamber exist below such a spreading center?

The breakthrough this time was made by changing the way existing seismic data are analyzed. This computer processing breakthrough, combined with a new field technique for acquiring seismic data, proved that magma chambers exist. The field of study is called marine seismology. Small earthquakes are deliberately made behind a ship with an airgun (which uses rapid release of compressed air) and are recorded miles away by an ocean bottom seismometer. Previous modeling of the results always produced planar layer solutions for the propagation path of this earthquake energy through the ridge axis. New computer processing techniques developed by John Orcutt of Scripps Institution of Oceanography allowed for vertical heterogeneity of arbitrary dimensions to be allowed for. Based on an assumed model, a *synthetic seismogram* was generated wholly by computer. The synthetic seismogram was then compared with the observed seismogram. A low-velocity zone within the crust was quickly identified as an active magma chamber (Figure 6-1).

This seismic work at the axis of the East Pacific Rise at 9°N and 21°N showed diffracted and tunneled energy 1 to 2 km beneath the ridge axis. This low-velocity tunnel disappeared from data taken from just 15 km on either side of the axis. Such low velocities occur in magma because sound energy travels faster through solid rock than through partially molten rock.

Seismic Images of the Magma Chamber

Quickly following this discovery, a shallow-water oil company exploration technique called *multi-channel seismic reflection profiling* was taken into the deep sea to look for reflections in hard rock for the first time. At 9°N, reflections from the top of the East Pacific Rise axial magma chamber were found (Figure 6-2). This technique is conclusive because it produces a profile, or picture into the crust, as if the Earth were dissected with a knife. Sound waves bounce off prominent layer boundaries, and as the profile is built with repeated sound explosions, these coherent reflections draw an acoustic picture of the subsurface structure.

Even more conclusive proof of the existence of an axial magma chamber comes from the same technique that "saw" the partially molten core and partial melt of the top of the asthenosphere. Shear waves recorded along parallel paths down the trough of the midocean ridge axis versus those just outside it have completely different appearances: The magma chamber attenuates or truncates the amplitude of shear waves traveling along the axis, but those from outside the axial zone are strong and of large amplitude (Figure 6-3). Only the existence of liquid magma below the surface could produce this observed effect.

So far, magma chambers have been found from seismic experiments at each of the seven locales examined in the eastern Pacific, but only in the

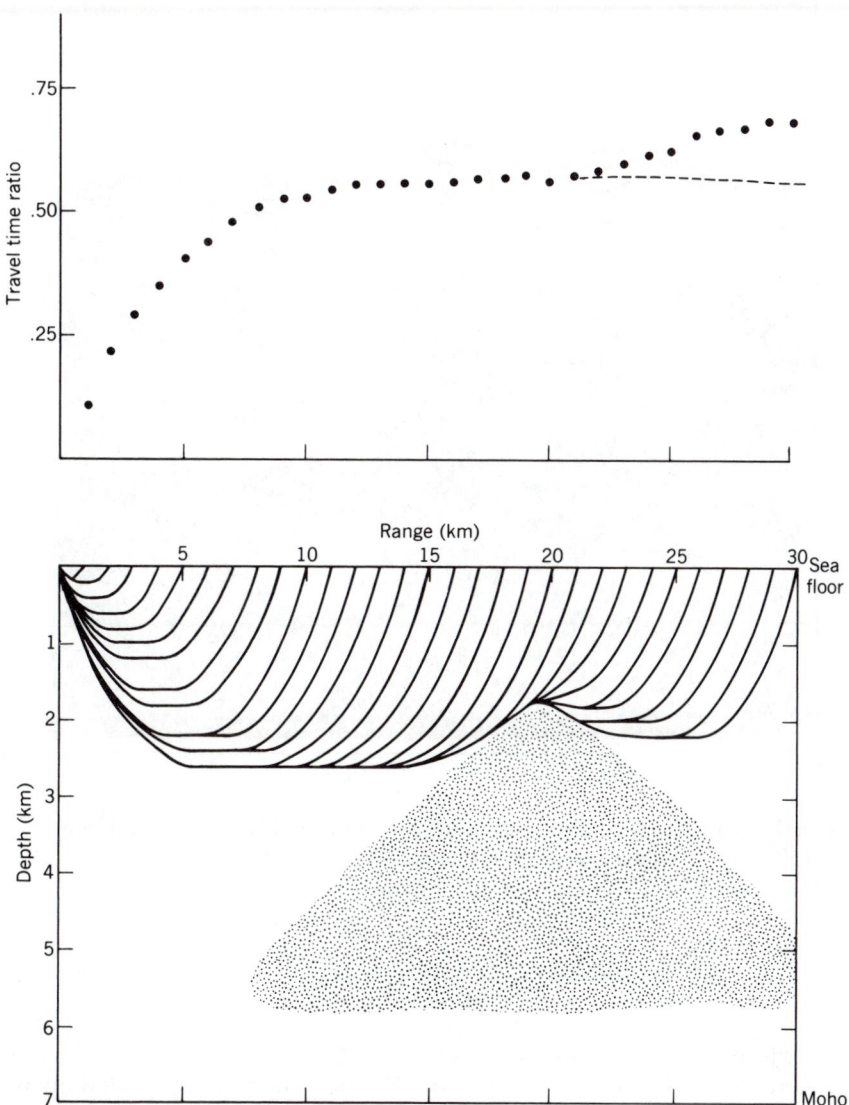

Figure 6-1. A synthetic seismogram for an explosive source at the left *(bottom)* for travel paths across an axial magma chamber (stipled) predicts travel times *(top)* that increase, flatten out, and then increase again for records obtained at each of the ranges indicated by dots. If the magma chamber were not present, the dashed travel times would be observed (from Orcutt, 1982).

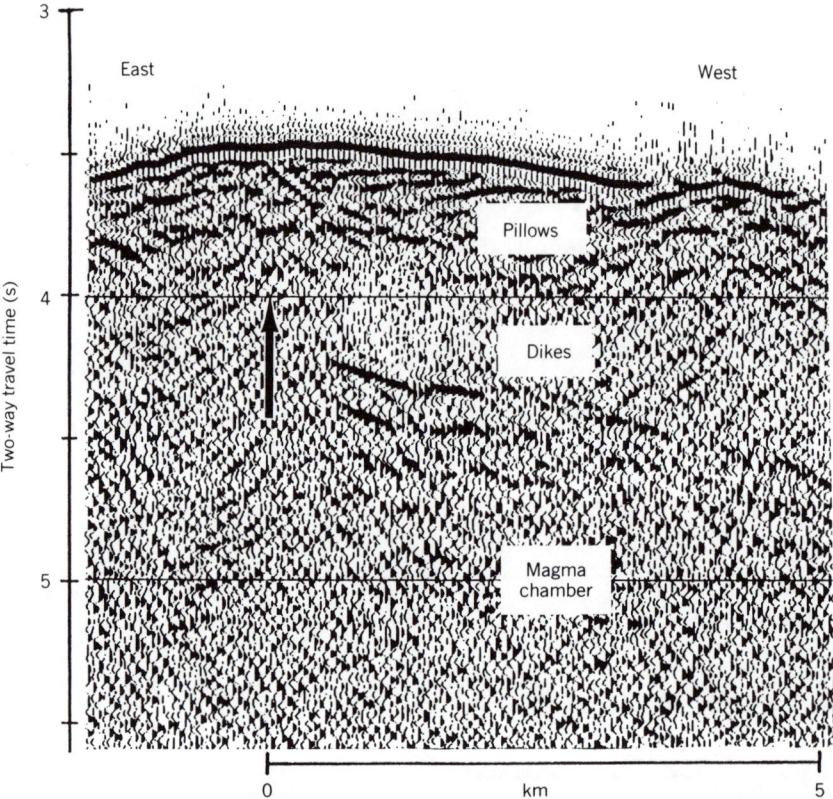

Figure 6-2. Reflections from the top of the magma chamber at the axis of the East Pacific Rise at 9 degress north. The exact center of the intrusion zone is indicated by the arrow (from Herron et al., 1982).

Pacific. Here, the mid-ocean ridge is producing new sea floor twice as fast as anywhere else in the world because the Pacific plate is being pulled away from the Cocos and Nazca plates at such a rapid rate. At slower spreading ridges, such as those in the Atlantic, perhaps magma chambers exist only once per hundred years, as on land. There the magma chambers seem to be either frozen solid or too small to see with current seismic techniques. The fact that magma chambers do not exist all the time everywhere is not as important as the fact that they exist today somewhere in the oceans. Therefore, we can study how the magma chamber makes new oceanic lithosphere in real time. That is much better than guesses based upon long-dead and fro-

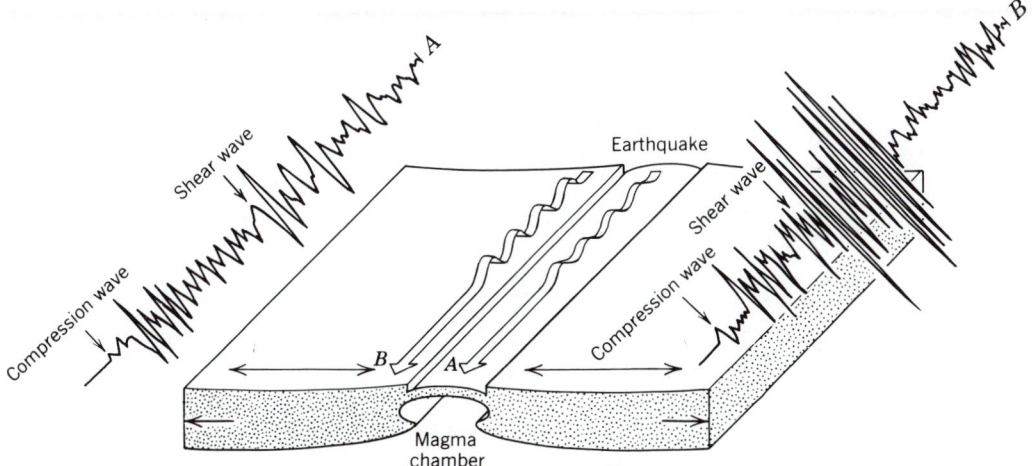

Figure 6-3. The two seismic waveforms were recorded at *A* and *B*, respectively, and represent energy that traveled through and along the side of the axial magma chamber, respectively. The highly attenuated shear wave at *A* indicates that a partially molten material has attenuated the shear energy at the axis (the magma chamber), whereas the strong shear wave at *B* indicates travel through solid lithosphere. The chamber must be narrow because *A* and *B* are only 10 km apart on the East Pacific Rise (from Macdonald and Luyendyk, 1983).

zen remains from an ophiolite. We can make educated guesses from ophiolites, then go to sea and test those theories on real, active magma chambers.

The picture seen of the ridge-axis magma chamber from this seismic evidence, as well as from the cooled remains found in ophiolites on land, is that of progressive crystal *differentiation* of a magma body with light crystals floating toward the surface and heavy crystals settling to the bottom. Repeated replenishment with new magma and mixing with this crystal slurry produces the layer cake formation of the oceanic lithosphere (Figure 6-4).

The form and regularity of the oceanic lithosphere also result from another quirk of sea-floor spreading as the newly solidified lithosphere pulls away from the magma chamber. The hot lava trying to extrude to the surface always chooses the path of least resistance to its buoyant forces of hot liquid rock. Thus the *extrusion zone* at a ridge axis is remarkably narrow. Each succeeding dike appears to very nearly split the preceding dike exactly in two. Since a dike is only about 1 m across, the entire zone from which lava flows out onto the sea floor can be mapped with a camera or acoustic mosaic system (Figures 6-5 and 6-6).

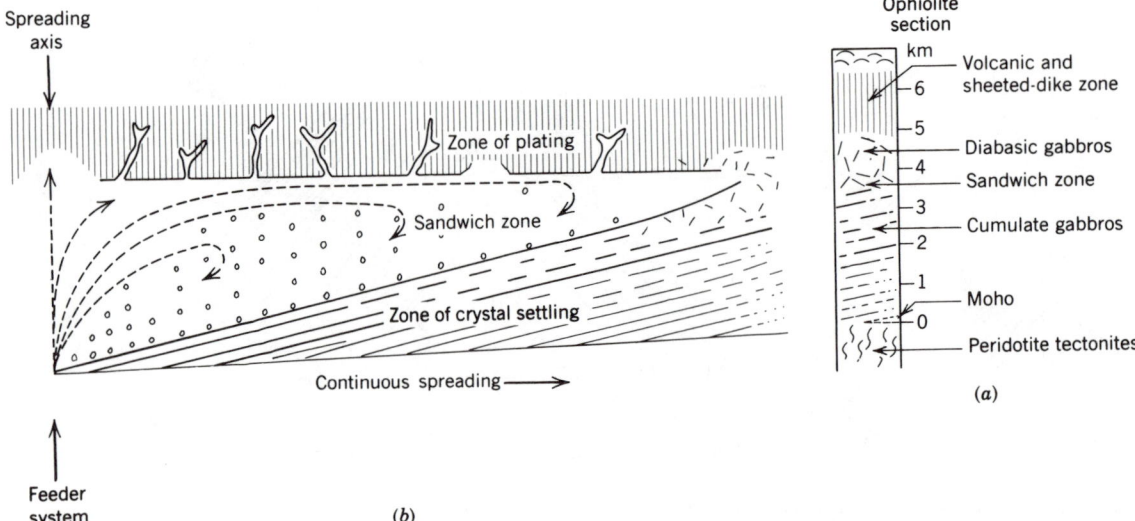

Figure 6-4. A sketch representing how the axial magma chamber crystallizes into the various layers of the oceanic lithosphere as cooling occurs away from the axis during spreading (from Casey et al., 1981).

Earthquakes and Volcanism

The ocean-bottom seismometers set at the axis of the East Pacific Rise magma chamber did more than just record sound explosions from ships. They also recorded the natural earthquakes occurring on the ridge axis. Because they sat on the sea floor so close to the source of the earthquakes, they were able to record much smaller events than we had ever before been

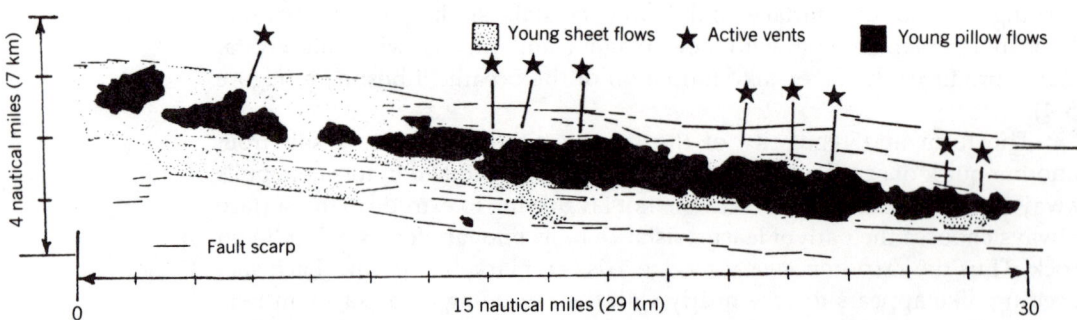

Figure 6-5. The exact center of the extrusion zone on the East Pacific Rise axis at 12 degrees north. Stars are black-smoker hydrothermal vent fields. Stiples are recent lava flows, and black areas are the most recent pillow basalt eruptions (from Ballard, 1984).

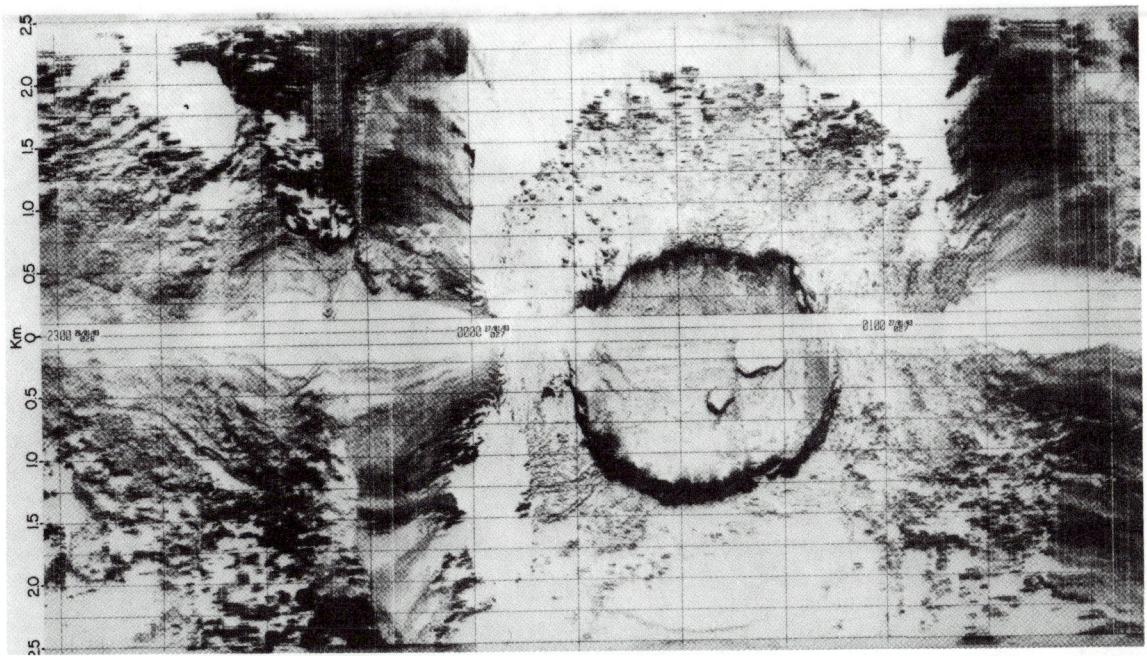

Figure 6-6. An acoustic image of an axial volcano from 12 degrees north on the East Pacific Rise lest there be any doubt about the volcanic nature of the ridge axis (from Fornari et al., 1984).

able to see. These earthquakes turned out to be completely different from normal events generated by faulting at the surface of the Earth. As Ken Macdonald of the University of California, Santa Barbara, found, the ocean bottom seismometers recorded virtually continuous harmonic tremors rather than discrete fault-generated earthquakes. Elsewhere on the Earth we have recorded harmonic tremors only at active volcanoes such as Mt. St. Helens. These oscillatory shakings are caused by lava moving back and forth within the plumbing system of a magma chamber (Figure 6-7).

Midocean Ridge Cyclicity

We can build up a picture of how a magma chamber and its related volcanic activity construct new oceanic lithosphere. One model proposed by Bob Ballard, of Woods Hole Oceanographic Institution, suggests four stages of activity, repeated time and again throughout the geological history of each midocean ridge plate boundary (Figure 6-8).

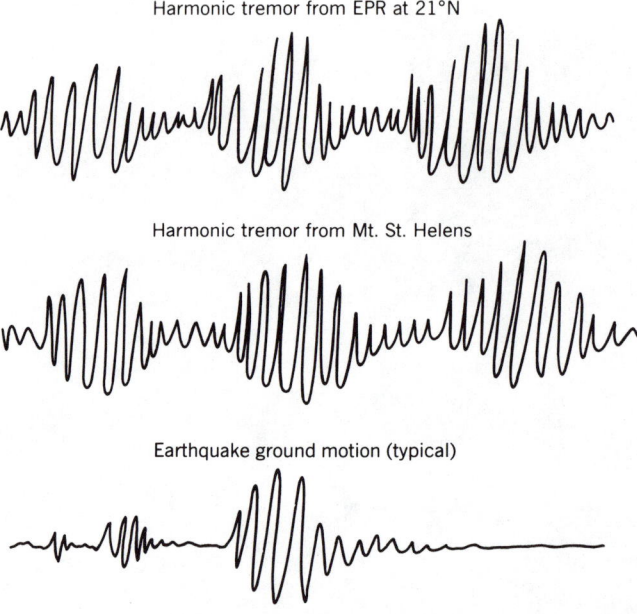

Figure 6-7. Seismological evidence of volcanic eruptions comes from ocean-bottom seismometers placed on the axis of the East Pacific Rise. Harmonic tremors similar to those recorded on Mt. St. Helens are recorded on the ridge axis rather than the typical earthquake seismograms caused by rupture of a solid. The movement of magma beneath the ridge axis produces the harmonic tremors as it surges slowly toward the surface.

1. The beginning of a new cycle is the end of the last volcanic event. The ridge axis has been pulled apart enough by the two plates involved to produce the appearance of a split volcano. The flat plain between is the locale of rapid subsidence as virtually continuous lava sheet flows fill the plain. That is, they fill the void caused by rapid extension with new dike and flow sequences. The height they reach is controlled by the hydraulic head of the rising lava. Because it is part liquid, part solid, it has a height in its tube (dike) at which it is in equilibrium with gravity. The subsidence that distinguishes this beginning and end of the cycle is caused by the rapid cooling of the entire sheet flow and dike sequence. This is the ebb period between eruptions.

2. Eventually, both subsidence and extension slow as most of the new heat from the last eruption has been dissipated. Then, faulting occurs as the two plateaus continue to creep apart, but the sheets and flows have solidified from mush. They must be broken apart by faults. In this stage, ocean-bottom

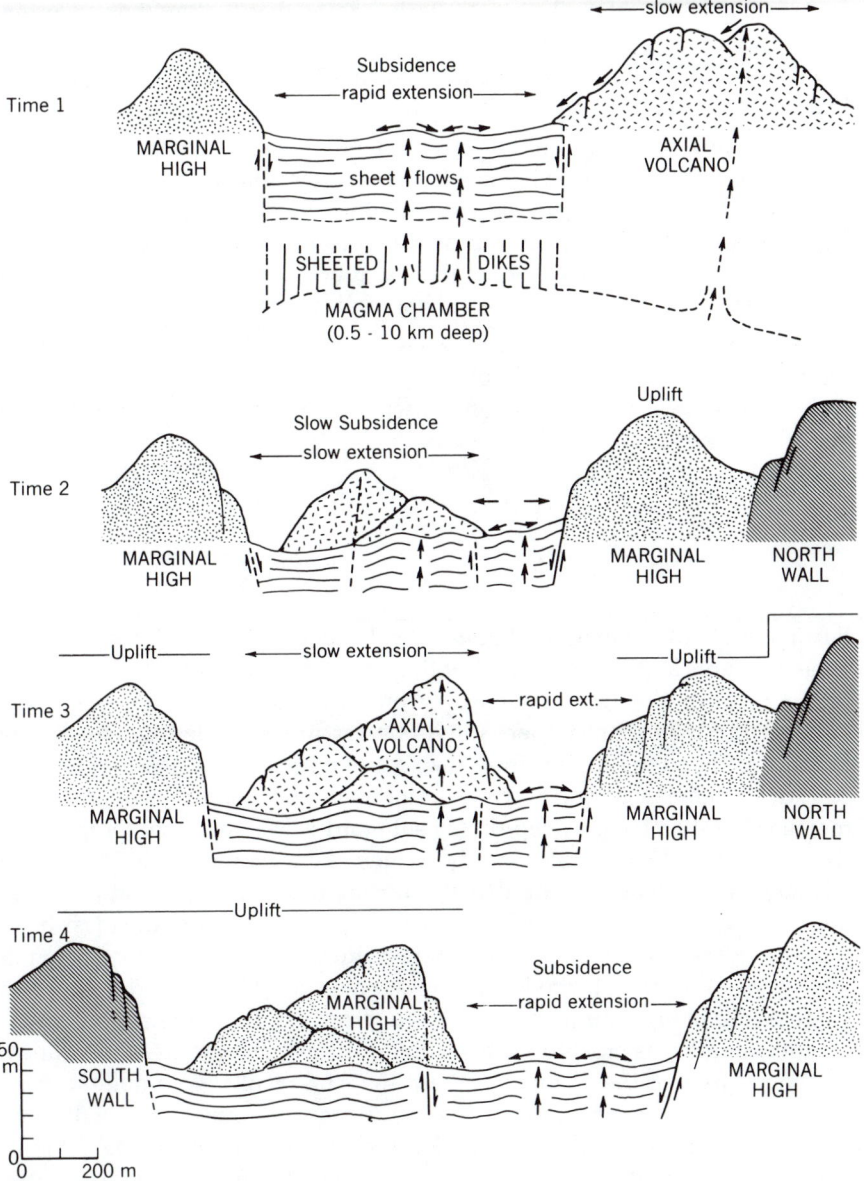

Figure 6-8. A model for the periodic sequence of eruption, subsidence, and extension that occurs on a midoceanic ridge spreading center. The sequence 1 to 4 is continually repeated for millions of years, but each step probably takes less than 1000 years (from Ballard, 1984).

seismometers record a change to real earthquakes rather than harmonic tremors. Slowly a pile of pillow lavas form at the surface. But while all is relatively calm at the surface, the magma chamber is being refilled from deep below in the mantle with new hot magma.

3. A new axial volcano forms with all the suddenness of a Mt. St. Helens, but not with the violence because, after all, there are two miles of water overhead to keep the lid on any violent eruptions. Extensive pillow lava flows from vents at the top of the volcano and fills the entire valley formed at the earlier stages. Sometimes so much lava erupts that it overflows the last valley and laps over the old split volcanoes of the last eruption.

4. Then, just as suddenly, the lava supply dries up, and the newly formed axial volcano is itself split in two. This ends this cycle of eruptive activity. The sequence repeats time after time to eventually build the great oceanic plates.

Gravity Across Magma Chambers

Further detail of the magma chamber can be gleaned from other geophysical measurements at the ridge crest, but they must be made right at the sea floor, rather than in the traditional way from ships at the sea surface. Why? Because the magma chamber is a subtle feature that blends into the surroundings if you are too far from the source with your measuring devices.

An extreme example is measurement of the gravity field above the magma chamber using a deep-diving submarine. Magma is lighter than solid rock, and thus less dense. Gravity, which is measured in the submarine, changes as a function of the density of rock below the submarine. A pendulum is swung repeatedly with the same force. The greater the mass below the submarine at a given time, the sooner the pendulum will slow down. So measuring the pull of gravity as the submarine moves slowly across the magma chamber should show a large drop in gravitational pull as the magma chamber is crossed. This technique could then be used to delineate the boundaries of the chamber, except that the results were quite different from what were expected. The low gravity zone was quite a bit smaller than the dimensions of the magma chamber seen by marine seismology, and the magnitude of the drop in gravity was so large that the light material must be just below the sea floor rather than down 2 km, as is the magma chamber. A cupola of magma was discovered at the very top of the magma chamber (Figure 6-9). A cupola is a holding chamber for a lava concentration that is just about to erupt onto the surface. So, much like the volcanologist on land who charges to the top of an erupting volcano and is killed in the eruption

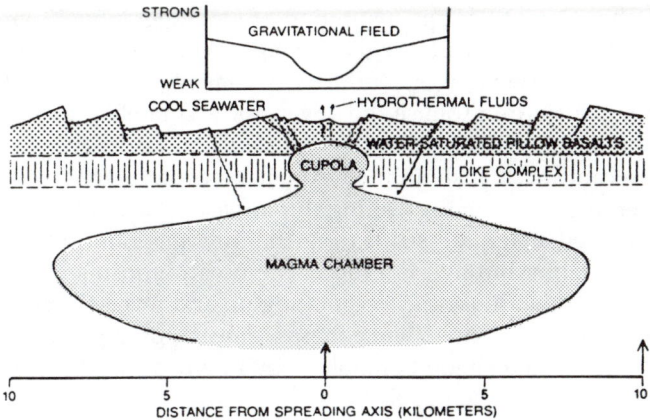

STRONG
GRAVITATIONAL FIELD
WEAK
COOL SEAWATER   HYDROTHERMAL FLUIDS
WATER-SATURATED PILLOW BASALTS
CUPOLA   DIKE COMPLEX
MAGMA CHAMBER

10   5   0   5   10
DISTANCE FROM SPREADING AXIS (KILOMETERS)

Figure 6-9. Model of the East Pacific Rise structure from a synthesis of all geophysical evidence. An intense low in the gravity field over some parts of the axis indicates that a cupola of molten lava is very close to the surface, awaiting an imminent eruption. These cupolas are episodic occurrences signaling eruptive activity. Over millions of years, all of the axis sees many magma chambers arise, erupt, then freeze again (from Macdonald and Luyendyk, 1983).

because the normal senses of prudence and logical restraint are overwhelmed and suppressed by curiosity about how the Earth works (four volcanologists were killed at Mt. St. Helens), our brave divers went right over the top of a volcano just about to erupt! Our knowledge of ridge axis volcanicity is so primitive at this time that we sometimes stumble into quite dangerous circumstances because we do not know what is there.

Electrical Conductivity and Magnetization

Electrical conductivity measurements can also be used to outline the shape of the magma chamber. In this difficult experiment, a large transmitting antenna almost 1 km long is towed just above the sea floor, and three receivers record how conductive to electricity the lithosphere is below the sea floor. With this measurement, higher conductivity is expected from magma than from rock because lava is a liquid. The only successful experiment to date was done by Chip Cox of Scripps Institution of Oceanography 12 km from the axis of the East Pacific Rise. Little if any magma chamber exists that far away from the axis because no high conductivity zone was encountered. The technique has much future promise, however, for accurately mapping the boundaries of the magma chamber.

The four-step volcanic cycle just outlined explains one of the most puzzling discoveries ever to come from the drilling ship *Glomar Challenger*. Even though clearly delineated magnetic stripes are the key age-identifier for plate tectonics, when drilling through the top of the ocean lithosphere, we often encounter both rocks with north pole pointing up and reversely magnetized rocks in the same vertical hole. Since these were supposedly erupted at different times, how could a single borehole penetrate rocks of different ages and therefore different magnetic polarities?

At the sea surface, the few "wrong-polarity" rocks at any point are lost within the signal from the "right-polarity" rocks. However, by towing a magnetometer across the axial magma chamber with a submarine, one can record the true complexity of the magnetic polarities of the ridge crest. The pattern of magnetic anomalies or stripes was found to be controlled by the degree of overflow of one volcanic cycle on top of previous eruptions. That depends mostly upon spreading rate. On the mid-Atlantic ridge, where the plates are pulled apart slowly, there is much more overlap than from the cleaner eruptive events on the fast-spreading East Pacific Rise (Figure 6-10).

Transform Faults, Propagating Rifts, and Overlapping Spreading Centers

As we saw in our plate-tectonics discussions, transform faults are not only an important plate boundary, but they also always form along small circles to the pole of rotation of the two plates in contact. Aside from a few great faults, such as the San Andreas, that separate two plates along a lateral distance of thousands of kilometers, most transform faults and their frozen remnants called fracture zones, which are used to determine the relative motion between two plates, are generated at midocean ridges as a side effect of sea-floor spreading.

If two wooden rulers are laid down in parallel onto a tray of hot wax and slowly pulled apart, the wax freezing behind almost exactly simulates the formation of new ocean lithosphere at midocean ridges. New wax coming to the surface, like lava, does so along a spreading center parallel to the rulers (Figure 6-11), but transform faults in the solid, cooled wax form perpendicular to the rulers.

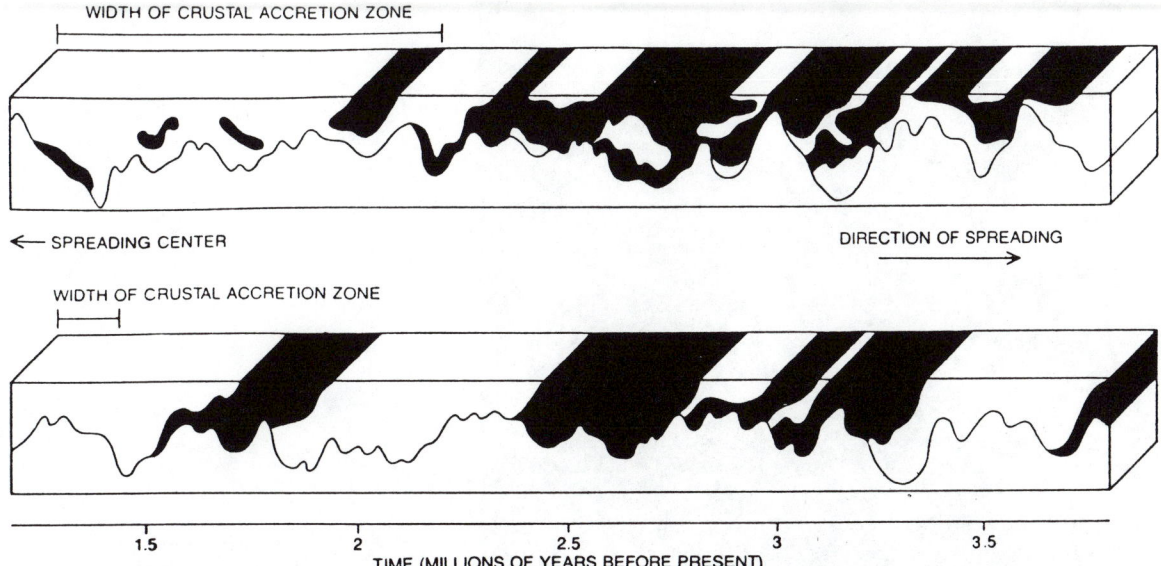

Figure 6-10. Magnetic stripes are made at the ridge axis as lava freezes and takes on the current polarity of the Earth's magnetic field. If slow spreading is occurring, a wide crustal accretion zone produces a mixed bag of positively and negatively magnetized rock as some of the volcanic activity "slops over" into older crust (*above*). Therefore, the mid-Atlantic ridge does not produce as clear a set of magnetic stripes as the fast spreading East Pacific Rise (*below*) where a narrow intrusion zone permits little mixing of magnetic polarities (from Macdonald and Luyendyk, 1983, and Schouten and Denham, 1984).

Transform faults form at regular intervals that are controlled by the spacing between the magma chambers that feed individual segments of the spreading center. The fourfold volcanic cycle described earlier is in differing stages of eruption or extension all up and down the ridge axis. Therefore, the magma chambers have finite extents in all directions (Figure 6-12). Where two chambers pinch out, frozen rock is in contact with frozen rock and a transform fault forms. The fault exists because resistance to being pulled apart is greater than the strength of the crust. It therefore breaks and a fault appears. If the magma chambers do not pinch out along the strike of the spreading center, rock does not solidify, and it instead stretches like taffy. Such a case can be generated in wax by pulling the rulers apart very fast. In the real world, fast spreading rates, such as those that occur on the East Pacific Rise, also produce this taffy effect. What is observed is a double

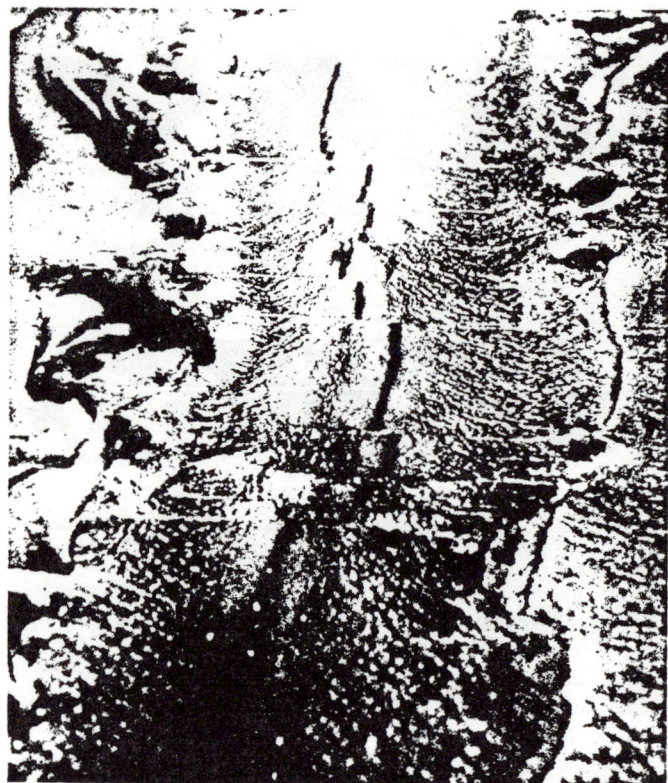

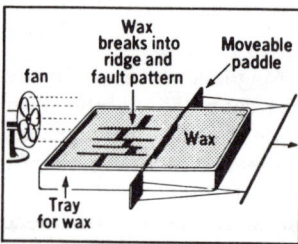

Figure 6-11. Transform faults, fracture zones, and a ridge axis are caused by the physics of spreading apart a molten material with a cool lid on top, as can be seen from a wax model as well as from the midocean ridges. Here, wax is kept melted, except that a fan cools the surface. A ruler is then pulled away from the center of the pan, and a ridge axis with all the Earth's features is formed (from Parker and Oldenberg, 1972 and Sullivan, 1973).

spreading center with overlapping zones of upwelling lava in place of the transform fault that would be present on a slower spreading ridge such as the mid-Atlantic ridge (Figure 6-13). These peculiar "69-like" structures have been observed all up and down the East Pacific Rise. Transform faults do exist on fast spreading ridges, however, but they are fewer, farther apart, and not nearly as dramatic as the deep gashes cut into the lithosphere of slow spreading ridges.

Transform faults appear to form thinner crustal basaltic layers beneath them because they are so far from feeder lavas coming from magma chambers. But they form perhaps 20 percent of all the oceanic lithosphere on slow

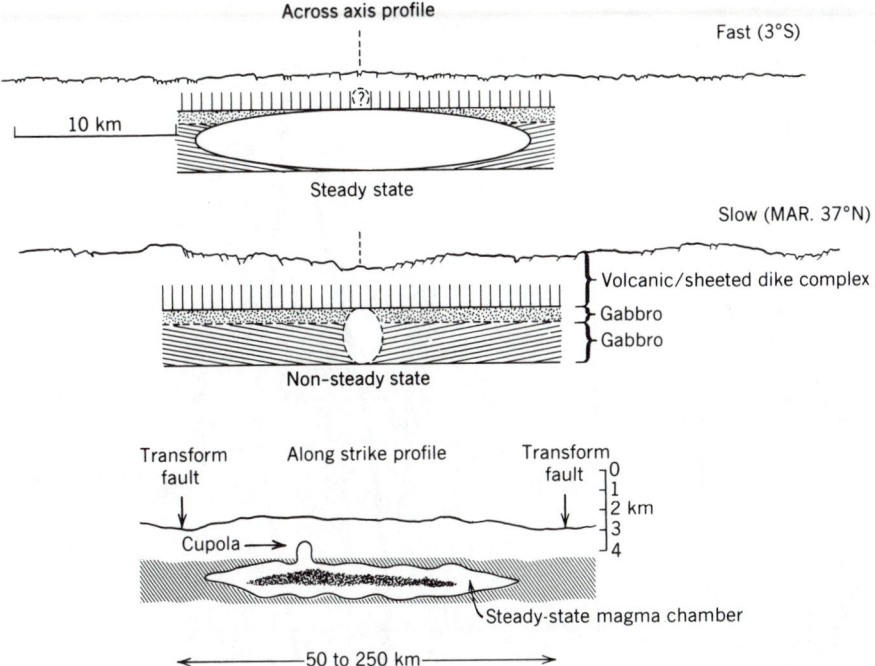

Figure 6-12. *(Top)* Cross sections across the fast and slow spreading ridges show the differences in surface topography and magma chamber extent, yet the layered structure produced as both freeze is virtually identical. *(Bottom)* Along-strike variation in structure on a fast-spreading ridge. Notice that the magma chamber must pinch out toward transform faults (from Macdonald, 1983).

spreading ridges, and therefore an understanding of them is critical to discovery of the mechanism by which plates pull apart. For example, the discovery of a bizarre pattern of transform faults, fracture zones, and ridge crests off the coast of Oregon has led to a significant new corollary to plate tectonics. In wax or on almost all spreading centers, the transform faults are exactly perpendicular to the spreading center. Why? Because Eulerian geometry forces them to be on small circles about the pole of rotation of the two plates pulling apart. The spreading centers naturally form on great circles because the lava always seeks the easiest path to the surface, and that is the place where the hottest rock is—along the ruler. What then of the peculiar z-shaped ridge and transform fault combinations found off Oregon (Figure 6-14)?

These turn out to be the ridge axes' response to changes in direction and rate of spreading of the two plates involved. We have seen that the plates move independently of ridge axis processes. Whatever is pushing or pulling

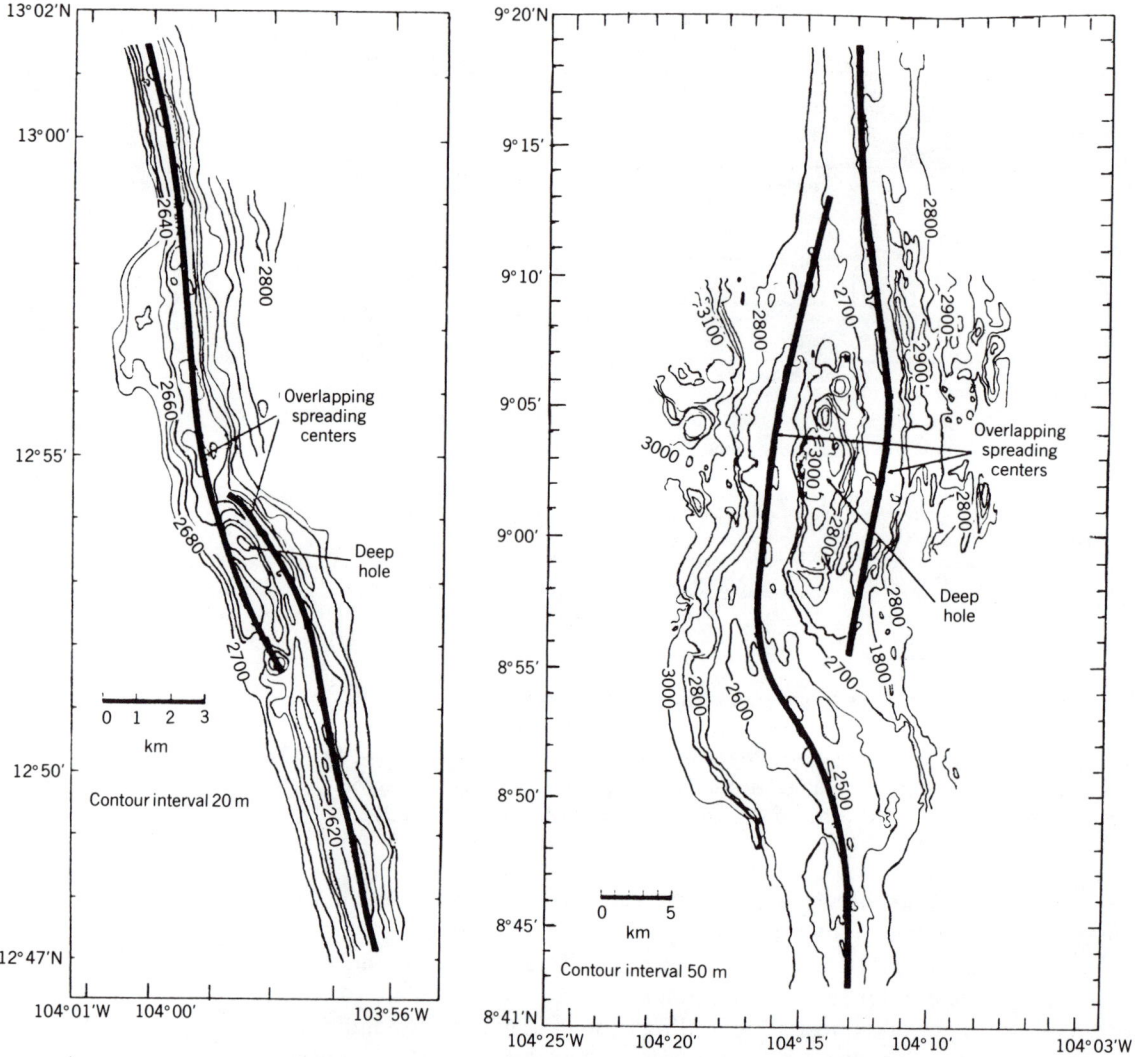

Figure 6-13. Mapping the detail of ridge axis–transform intersections on fast-spreading ridges, such as here on the East Pacific Rise, has turned up surprising complexity. One of the tenets of plate tectonics appears to be violated on a small scale. Two spreading centers exist across the same plate boundary (solid lines). These overlapping spreading centers occur at transform-fault intersections and result in complex fracture zone scars in old crust as one center survives and the other slowly freezes. Excessive heat in magma chambers perhaps causes them to overshoot as they are pinched out at transform faults. Alternatively, small adjustments in ridge strike as poles of rotation slowly move relative to each other cause the overlapping spreading centers. In any event, they are widespread on fast-spreading ridges (from Macdonald and Fox, 1981).

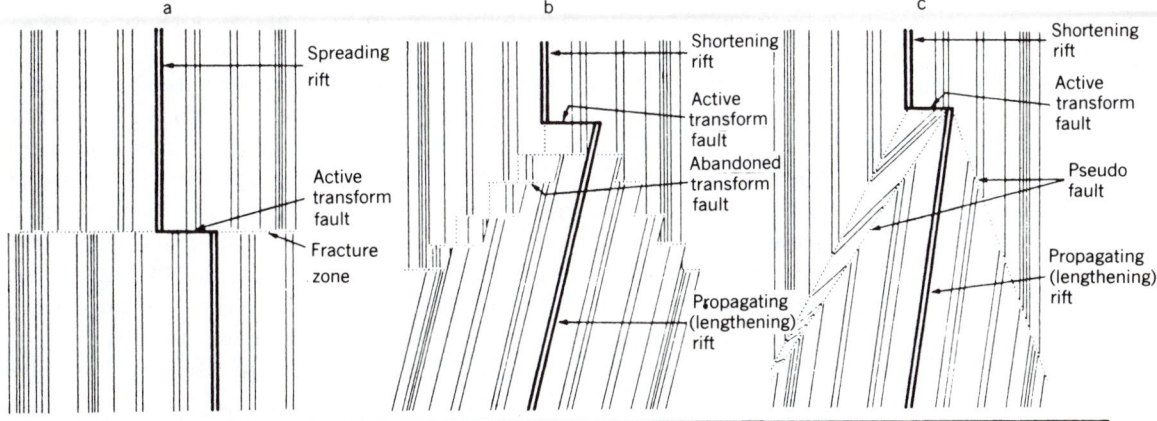

Figure 6-14. An even more extreme mode of plate–boundary reorganization is the propagating rift, where a change in pole positions causes a ridge axis (double lines) to change orientation by propagating the new axis across the old. A characteristic wedge-shaped zone of magnetic anomalies (stripes) is recognized to accompany ridge propagation (after Hey, 1982).

them around sometimes changes. In fact, Dick Hey of Scripps Institution of Oceanography found that the plates regularly rearrange their opening patterns. The ridge axis responds by **propagating** a rift or spreading center in the new, correct Eulerian direction through rock with the old direction preserved. This rearrangement often takes millions of years and produces completely new orientations and locations of spreading. Thus propagating rifts must also be understood if we are to know how oceanic lithosphere was formed.

Summary

If we see an ophiolite on land, can we tell if it was formed at a normal spreading center, at overlapping spreading centers, at a transform fault, or at a propagating rift? We do not know all the differences between these various systems yet, so interpretation of ophiolites in terms of ridge axis processes is still quite primitive.

However, an understanding of the volcanic control of the geology of midocean ridge spreading centers by magma chambers has gone a long way toward helping us understand how new ocean plate is formed. Far beyond that, some of the most awesome and unbelievable discoveries in the oceans have been found associated with these magma chambers. Hot springs spewing forth metal-laden waters over 800°F have been discovered at the ridge axis. To be exiting the sea floor at "firehose" velocities beneath 2 km of water is itself remarkable. This water column weighs over 200 atmospheres! But far beyond even this, the singular most remarkable ecological community on the Earth was discovered to be living off the geothermal heat from these **black smokers.** The existence of this biological community was not even discovered until 1977 by Jack Corliss of Oregon State and others. These animals are the major new discovery in marine biology in 100 years. Put another way, we thought we knew all the animal forms living in the oceans 100 years ago. Now scientists are beginning to speculate that this form of biological community might show us the key to how life itself began on the Earth.

Further Reading

Macdonald, K. C., 1983, Crustal processes at spreading centers: Reviews of Geophysics and Space Physics, v. 21, pp. 1441–1454.

Rona, P. A., Bostrum, K., Laubier, L., and Smith, K. L., 1983, Hydrothermal Processes at Sea Floor Spreading Centers: New York, Plenum.

Black Smokers and
Fantastic Organisms

S cientists are not as likely to talk in wondrous superlatives as, for example, stockbrokers or used car salespeople, so imagine the surprise in 1979
to hear the following reports coming over ship-to-shore radio from the *Alvin*
deep-diving submarine. The *Alvin* was working at the axial spreading center
of the East Pacific Rise just south of Baja California (The RISE Project Group,
Spiess et al., 1980). Here are some of the quotes from the *New York Times's*
coverage of the event:

It was like Pittsburgh in 1925, with all those blast-furnaces going full force.

*It was like seeing a 19th century steam locomotive going uphill, just pouring out
smoke.*

It was like a municipal fire hose going full blast.

Other newspaper headlines trumpeted:

  Sea-floor geysers may be key to ore deposits.

  Sea-floor oases of mineral-rich springs and amazing creatures fulfill
oceanographers' dreams.

  An eyewitness account of the discovery, written by Ken Macdonald and
Bruce Luyendyk of the University of California, Santa Barbara (1981)
follows:

It is difficult to convey the strange quality of such an experience. First one spends two hours or so in almost total darkness, dropping by gravity more than two and a half kilometers to the sea floor. Three people are huddled in the cold and cramped confines of the Alvin's pressurized spherical compartment, which is only two meters in diameter. On approaching the bottom, the submersible's running lights are turned on, and the illuminated water takes on a dim, greenish glow. Minutes later the sea floor is sighted. As soon as the Alvin has reached the bottom, the team reports its position to the control ship and is given a course to steer to a bottom target. Edging ahead slowly (at about half a kilometer per hour) over the glistening volcanic rock, the investigators peer through portholes, seeing only 10 or 15 meters into the darkness.

On the dive in question we were making gravity measurements in the volcanic zone (of the ridge axis) when we came on the hydrothermal field. The scene was like one out of an old horror movie. Shimmering water rose from between the basaltic pillows all along the axis of the neovolcanic zone. Large white clams as much as 30 centimeters long nestled between the black pillows [Figure 7-1, color insert]; white crabs scampered blindly across the volcanic terrain. Most dramatic of all were the clusters of giant tube worms, some of them as long as three meters. These weird creatures appeared to live in dense colonies surrounding the vents, in water ranging in temperature from 2 to 20 degrees C [Figure 7-2, color insert]. The worms, known as vestimentifera pogonophorans, *waved eerily in the hydrothermal currents, their bright red plumes extending well beyond their white protective tubes. (The red color of both the tube-worm plumes and the clam tissues results from the presence of oxygenated hemoglobin in their blood [Figure 7-3, color insert].) Occasionally a crab would climb the stalk of a tube worm, presumably to attack its plume.*

A subsequent Alvin dive was guided directly to another hydrothermal area identified by the Angus camera sled, southwest of the first vents we visited. The sight here was even more dramatic: extremely hot fluids, blackened by sulfide precipitates, were blasting upward through chimney-like vents as much as 10 meters tall and 40 centimeters wide. We named the vents "black smokers" [Figure 7-4, color insert]. The chimneys protruded in clusters from mounds of sulfide precipitates.

Our initial attempts to measure the temperature of the black fluids were unsuccessful. Until then the highest temperature record on the ocean floor was 21 degrees C., measured only two months earlier on the Galapagos spreading center. Our thermometer was calibrated to 32 degrees C.; when it was inserted into the first chimney, the reading immediately sailed off the scale. Moreover, when the probe was withdrawn, the plastic rod on which it was mounted showed signs of melting! [Figure 7-5] The temperature probe was hastily recalibrated at sea and measurements were made on several more dives; they indicated temperatures of at least 350 degrees C! [The location of these discoveries is shown in Figure 7-6.]

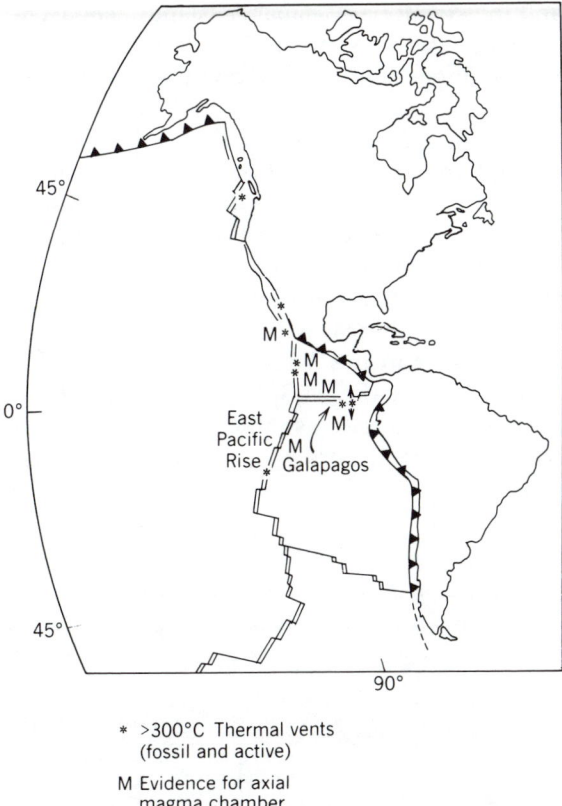

* >300°C Thermal vents
  (fossil and active)

M Evidence for axial
  magma chamber

Figure 7-6. Locations in the East Pacific where black smokers have been found. Recently Craig and others discovered black-smoker evidence in the western Pacific off Guam for the first time (from Macdonald, 1983). Double bars are spreading centers, single lines are transform faults and hatched lines are subduction zones.

Early Indirect Evidence

The excitement voiced by these accounts is better understood from a historical perspective. The hot spring activity seen from the viewing port of the *Alvin* had been predicted for more than twenty years (Bostrum, K., and Peterson, M. N. A., 1966), but because the prediction was based upon indirect, geophysical evidence, no one expected the visual verification to be so spectacular. The first evidence for the existence of hot springs above the axial magma chamber came from the discovery in the early 1960s of metal-rich sediments at the axis of the East Pacific Rise in one of the most remote locales from land in the world—15 degrees south and equidistant between

Peru, Tahiti, Easter Island, and the equatorial Galapagos Islands. The technique used to recover these samples was also one of the oldest, most primitive, yet still most effective in oceanography: a bucket dragged across the sea floor behind a ship. This dredge was first used on the original *Challenger* in the 1870s. When the modern drilling ship *Glomar Challenger* began consistently returning similar metalliferous sediments from the very deepest sediments it drilled just above rock, it became apparent that some form of hydrothermal or hot spring activity must be occurring at midocean ridges.

The decisive evidence came from the collection over the 1960s and 1970s of a worldwide set of heat-flow measurements on the sea floor. It quickly became clear that a great deal of heat was missing in young ocean crust on all spreading centers, whether in the Atlantic, Indian, or Pacific oceans. Work then centered upon the Galapagos Spreading Center in the eastern equatorial Pacific. This particular place was rather randomly chosen for its good weather and proximity to a good working port, Panama. Ocean-

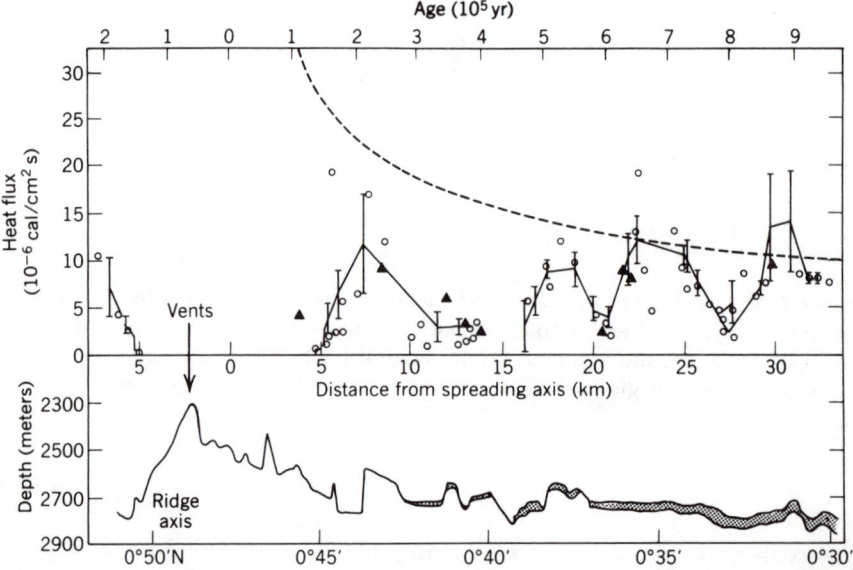

Figure 7-7. The black smokers are only the surface expression of well-developed convection cells that penetrate several kilometers into the crust at midocean ridges. The presence of convection cells can be mapped away from the axis using heat-flow measurements (open circles and black triangles). Vertical bars mark error bars for several points. The cyclical heat flow from cold to hot and back to cold again is characteristic of the top surface of convection cells. The dashed line is the heat flow expected to be present from plate tectonics. Topography is shown at bottom with the shading representing sediment thickness (from Williams et al., 1972).

ographic ships are constantly passing through the canal. It was on the Galapagos Spreading Center in 1972 that the first hints of hot springs were found.

Cyclical heat flow was measured away from the center of spreading (Figure 7-7). This could only be explained by the penetration of seawater into the volcanic rock at the spreading center in organized patterns called convection cells (Figure 7-8). Any liquid will convect when its buoyancy balance is upset (e.g., when heated unevenly from below). Patterns of upwelling hot liquid and downwelling cold fluid can develop in a porous medium such as the oceanic crust, just as easily as we saw it occurring in partially melted rock in the mantle, or in the outer core of the Earth. Only the scales are vastly different, with the distance between rising and sinking seawater reaching only a few kilometers on the ridge axis.

Towed thermometers held just above the ridge crest found hot water that was less than one degree above the temperatures that should have been measured at those depths. We were stumbling around in the dark in those

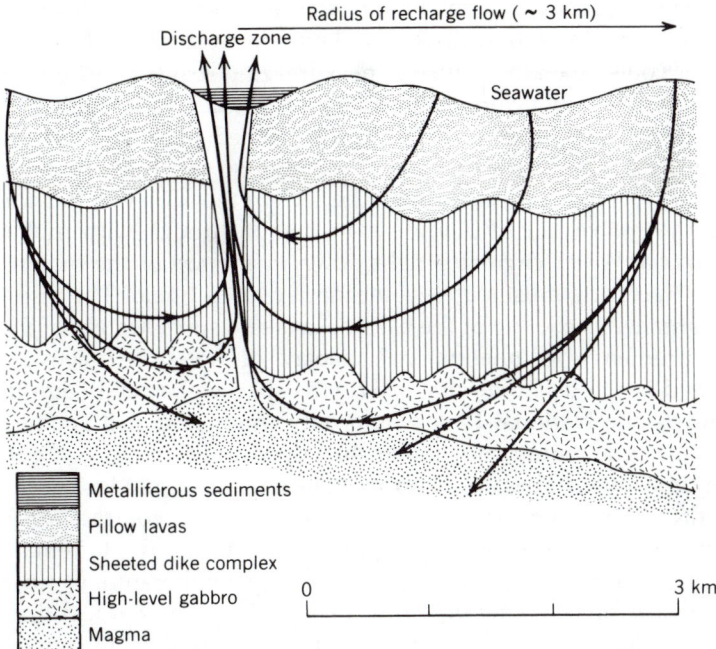

Vert. and horiz. scales approximately equal

Figure 7-8. Cold seawater penetrates downward toward the magma chamber, then rapid heating forces the buoyant hot water to the surface as a hydrothermal vent. If the hot water is not mixed below the surface, it exits as a black smoker (Bonatti, 1981).

days, yet even one degree too hot was significant enough to persuade the National Science Foundation to fund further exploration. There must be a significantly hotter source for even one-degree-hotter water because the volume of supercold water at the sea floor is so large that any heating at all is significant. That is the way American science works. The seed of an idea must be backed up with just enough hard evidence to spark the imaginations of colleagues to the point that they, as peer reviewers of your proposal to do follow-up work, will recommend to the National Science Foundation or Office of Naval Research that the project be funded. In the latter part of the 1970s, the Galapagos Spreading Center became the most heavily studied midocean ridge in the world, and the process of hydrothermal circulation discovered there has rewritten our understanding of how the oceanic lithosphere forms—because of a one-degree temperature anomaly!

Hydrothermal Convection

The remarkable process that seals the final fate of the oceanic lithosphere is called *hydrothermal circulation.* The new lava extruded from the axial magma chamber cools beneath 2 miles of near-freezing seawater. The lava fractures from the quick quenching caused when 1200°C lava impacts 2°C water. The water invades deep into the newly formed plumbing system above the magma chamber as the rock fractures. Some scientists say that this fracturing even travels like a wave through the rock in the form of a *fracture front.* Soon, the extrusive pile of pillow basalt is shot through with rubble zones called *breccia.* Water circulates right down to the top of the magma chamber where fracturing must stop—you cannot crack a liquid. The result is virtually instantaneous cooling of the basaltic lava and superheating of the water. The byproduct is a phenomenal display of hot-spring activity. Nowhere on land is the hydrothermal activity as spectacular. Old Faithful Geyser in Yellowstone National Park would only come close if it spouted water twice as hot and continuously rather than once an hour.

The ocean lithosphere's basaltic layer must be kept very cold by the circulation of hydrothermal fluid so that a strong temperature contrast exists between the pillows and dikes and the magma chamber. In order to remain partially molten, a magma body must have an average temperature of close to 1000°C. Cold seawater moving downward keeps the pillows at less than 50°C. When this cold downwelling water hits the top of the magma chamber, it heats up dramatically. But it cannot heat above about 400°C because of the remarkable buoyancy of hot water. Please don't ever try to prevent the steam from a boiling teapot from escaping. The greatest hazard during the days of steam-powered ferries was the occasional blocked smokestack. The result was an explosion that would leave hardly a trace of boat, or of the people aboard.

Metallogenesis

While the 2 miles of seawater pressing down on the ridge axis prevents steam from forming, the water becomes so buoyant at 350 to 400°C that it shoots directly up to the sea floor. The water that exits is hotter than any hot spring on land. The result is spectacular hot-spring activity at the ocean floor: white smokers and black smokers, as they are called. As water moves through basalt, it changes chemically, giving up its sodium and magnesium and taking up calcium and potassium. But superheated water also extracts copper, zinc, iron, silver, gold, and other precious metals and concentrates them into a supersaturated fluid. If the supersaturated fluid is cooled quickly, as when it escapes at the sea floor, it drops these metals into black, sootlike precipitates that form ore bodies. If this cooling occurs from mixing with ocean bottom water right at the sea floor, the ore bodies are formed by the accumulation of these chimneys, which emit the "black smoke." These chimneys form ore deposits called *massive sulfides* because the metals are in the form of sulfide minerals.

If mixing occurs *beneath* the sea floor in the pillow basalt rubble zone, the hot springs drop their black metals into veins and a *stockwork* forms beneath the sea floor. The hydrothermal water exiting the surface is then a cooler white smoker because it loses heat and color during the precipitation of the black metals. Massive sulfides dissolve in seawater, so volcanic eruptions must bury them quickly if an ore deposit, exploitable in the future, is to result.

That the black smokers are periodic and directly related to volcanic eruptions can be seen from several facts. First, they are only found within a few hundred meters of the exact axis of the spreading center. Like the dike intrusion, they form a straight line delineating the axis of the magma chamber. Second, they remove far too much heat to be continuous features. One single 350° C black smoker removes 1 million years worth of heat from the ridge axis in 1 year. So they must be periodic, or they would quickly freeze the magma chamber into solid rock (Macdonald, 1983).

Tube Worms and the Origin of Life

How then do we measure the duration of hot-spring activity at a ridge axis? One fascinating and beautiful byproduct of the hot springs is a biological community that lives in the vents and is like no other on the surface of the Earth. Using sulfur-eating bacteria as the basis of their food chain, giant tube worms, huge clams, and blind crabs live, not off the Sun's energy as does virtually every other known ecosystem on the Earth, but instead, off the thermal energy of the Earth. This power source is unique for such a biological community, and it wasn't even discovered until 1977. Now you see the excitement of working in a profession where so little is known that it is as much exploration as science.

The hot-spring organisms are oversized because of the plentiful food supply. Not unique to the vents, they live in smaller forms throughout the ocean. The tube worm, *pogonophoran* for example, is a larval, free-swimming worm that in other environments never attains enough size to be dissected except under a microscope. Yet in the vents, this worm grows a chitinous tube that is up to 10 m high and is attached to a rock. The worm itself is up to 18 inches long, has a bright, beautiful red color, and moves freely within its tube (Figure 7-2). Similarly, the clams are quahogs, eaten by many Cape Cod vacationers. Yet here they are 12 to 18 inches long, their meat is red like liver and they weigh up to a pound (Figure 7-3). You wouldn't want to eat them though; they ingest lethal quantities of metals such as mercury from the black smokers. Both the tube worms and the clams use hemoglobin, just as we do, to extract oxygen from the bottom water. They need more oxygen than their shallow-water cohorts because they metabolize hydrogen-sulfide-eating bacteria, which they use as an energy source. So they have magically turned on a genetic "hemoglobin switch." How they do this is still one of the great biological mysteries of these fascinating organisms.

There are many more remarkable features of these organisms. The tube worms have so much food available that they do not even need a stomach. They filter food in the smokers directly into their cell membranes. The crabs have eye sockets like their shallow-water cousins, but since no light at all ever filters down to these great depths, they have no eyes in their sockets. Instead, they appear to use the sockets to scrape bacteria off the worm tubes for food.

The clams grow about 10 times as fast as their shallow-water cousins. Karl Turekian of Yale and others have age-dated the clams using carbon isotopes and find them never to be older than 10 to 20 years. So the vents must be that age or less since a shallow-water clam lives much longer than that. Vast colonies of dead clams have been found just off the spreading axis, but since their calcium carbonate shells dissolve in seawater, the skeletons quickly disappear. They live and die with the hot-water source, and we have seen that the smokers can only last for a short time before they mine too much heat from the magma chamber. We can use the oldest clams to say that we have yet to find a black smoker older than 20 years. How then do the animal colonies survive through the millennia if their food source turns off after only 20 years in any one spot? Clams can hardly pick themselves up and walk over several miles of rocky terrain to the next vent. They survive by sending their young off as free-swimming larvae in search of new vents. The vent animals are therefore able to survive, and become part of the larger picture of periodicity of the volcanic process building new oceanic lithosphere.

Perhaps the most remarkable speculation to come from the finding of this, the first completely new ecosystem to be discovered by biologists in the last 100 years, is the hypothesis by Jack Corliss and others at Oregon State, in 1982, concerning the relationship between these hot-spring organisms and the origin of life on Earth. They reviewed the composition and form of the earliest rocks on the planet and the life forms found imbedded in them, and concluded that these sediments were formed by black smokers. Although not yet proven, their scenario for the earliest life is very different from the current dogma in the biological community. In their opinion, it is much more likely in a geological sense that the early Earth, rather than being covered with shallow seas so essential to the organic soup hypothesis for the origin of life, was instead, as today, encircled with ridge axes. The black smokers of today are like the black smokers of the distant past. Great heat is required to force amino acids into protein strings that accidentally string together into RNA and DNA to form life. But quick quenching is also required, or the newly formed organic chains will simply burn up. In the organic soup hypothesis, lightning is the source of this rapid heating followed quickly by cooling. In the black smoker hypothesis, the organic compounds form inside the chimneys in the 350° C water, then are dislodged by the firehose velocity water and carried out onto the cool sea floor. If the black smoker hypothesis is correct, an intriguing possibility is that life is continually formed at smokers, even today. If so, where is all that new life? Corliss et al. would say it is now eaten for food by the life already existing around the smokers. More traditional biologists would say the whole idea is ridiculous. At this early stage of investigation, anything is possible. Corliss et al. are to this day trying to find a way to scrape the inside walls of a smoker chimney to return traces of newly forming life to the laboratory.

Black Smokers and the Chemistry of the Oceans

The entire biological community exists at the ridge axis because of abundant sulfur, but where does the sulfur come from? The circulating sea water contains sulfate. This reduces to hydrogen sulfide during chemical reaction with basalt at high temperature, so the food source enters the rock from the ocean floor as inedible sulfate. The water heats up as it moves closer to the magma chamber, and the sulfate becomes hydrogen sulfide. Then as the water becomes superhot, it explodes upward toward the surface, where sulfur-eating bacteria are able to metabolize the hydrogen sulfide. These bacteria then themselves become the base of the food chain that fuels the oasis.

This gives us a hint of another important geological process accompanying this ridge axis hot-spring activity. The oceans circulate through basalt fast enough so that the crust "buffers" the composition of the entire ocean. That is, every single cubic centimeter of seawater moves through a hot spring once every 5 to 10 million years. So in the history of the oceans, their volume has been through the ridge axis hot springs hundreds of times. If there is too much magnesium or too little sodium, the basalt adds the missing ingredients back in, keeping the oceans at their constant composition. This flow rate is less than 1 percent of that of the world's rivers, the other major source of ocean chemical equilibrium. But because this system circulates at elevated temperatures, it is easily 100 times more active chemically, hence the buffering ability.

Yet other chemical tags come out at the ridge axis. One, helium and its isotopes, provides an excellent tracer for the flow of ocean currents since it is not manufactured anywhere but inside the earth. As it enters the ocean, one can trace its path around the globe, thus tracing the flow and interaction of ocean currents. We will discuss this example more fully in a later chapter.

Cold Hydrothermal Circulation

How do we estimate the quantity of chemical interchange that occurs in mid-ocean ridge hydrothermal systems? Exchange between seawater and basalt occurs not only in high-temperature hot springs on the axes of fast-spreading ridges such as the East Pacific Rise, but similar chemical changes accompany lower-temperature surface systems such as those at the medium-rate Galapagos Spreading Center. There, however, the water exiting at the surface is only 20°C, but these so-called "white smokers" clearly contain elements that require mixing of seawater with 350°C hot water—but *below* the sea floor instead of *at* the sea floor. In such cases, the metals are deposited within the oceanic crust instead of at the sea floor. White smokers may be even more important for ore generation than the spectacular black smokers, as we have been in the Troodos ophiolite. The *Glomar Challenger* has even drilled through a stockwork, or feeder channel, to a large subsurface sulfide ore deposit on the flank of the Galapagos Spreading Center (see Figure 7-9, color insert).

The chemical exchange between basalt and seawater continues onto the flanks of midocean ridges long after most of the heat has been lost from the hot springs. The magnitude of both hot- and cold-spring activity can only be estimated at this time by using heat-balance calculations to determine the magnitude of heat missing from hydrothermal circulation.

The axial heat flux can be estimated from thermal modeling, which assumes that all crustal basalt began as 1200°C magma. This obviously gives a maximum value for the amount of heat present at the axis. Of the maximum axial heat flux available of about 2×10^{19} cal/yr, Norman Sleep of

Stanford University has estimated that a limit of 0.2 to 0.5 $\times$ 10^{19} cal/yr can be removed by black smokers. If they absorbed any more the magma chambers would all freeze. Another estimate can be derived from the amount of helium that comes out with the hot water. Bill Jenkins of Woods Hole estimated that 6 $\times$ 10^{26} atoms of helium come out per year based upon the concentration of helium in the ocean water above ridge axes. But direct measurement of the black smokers only accounts for one-tenth of this total. Yet heat and helium can be directly linked, so the 6 $\times$ 10^{26} atoms per year converts to 0.5 $\times$ 10^{19} cal/yr of heat, almost exactly that calculated for ridge axes by Sleep. Where are the other five-sixths of the heat and helium coming out?

This leads to another remarkable result of hydrothermal circulation, that it is not confined just to the ridge axis and its magma chamber. While the extremely hot phase of water circulation is located only on the ridge axis, a cold-water or groundwater type of hydrological circulation continues on the flanks of midocean ridges for thousands of kilometers.

Looking first just off-axis, models of convection in a porous medium, the oceanic crust, yield fascinating results. Udo Fehn of Rochester University has shown that a convection cell of upwelling hot water and downwelling cold water (Figure 7-10) would be expected to remain fixed in space at a ridge axis because the volcanic center is essentially a line source of heat. The rock through which the water circulates spreads away from the axis, and therefore must pass through the various upwelling and downwelling phases of the convecting fluid. What this means is that all ocean basalt sees both hot and cold water during its history. Thus, much more mass is available to interchange chemically with seawater. Some distance off-axis the cell becomes locked into the rock through which it circulates. That is, upwelling and downwelling zones stay fixed within the rock, but the hydrothermal water does not stop flowing. It merely begins its long history of cooling.

Evidence for continued convection even in very old sea floor at far distances from the ridge axis comes from periodic variation in heat flow away from the spreading center. Such thermal behavior can only come from convective heat transfer. Even the sediments, which begin to form their thick blanket on rock just off the axis, are not spared. Convection in rock and sediment has been found in sea floor as old as 55 million years in the Indian Ocean (Figure 7-11), 80 million years in the Atlantic (Figure 7-12), and 25 million years in the Pacific (Figure 7-12).

When one looks for areas that have active circulation of seawater in basalt at the present time, at least half of the entire ocean floor is involved. What is the relative importance of ridge crest versus ridge flank chemical fluxes? Some controversy exists as to whether the net flux of some elements is into the oceans at the ridge axis or out of the oceans on the ridge flanks, but with other elements we have firm results.

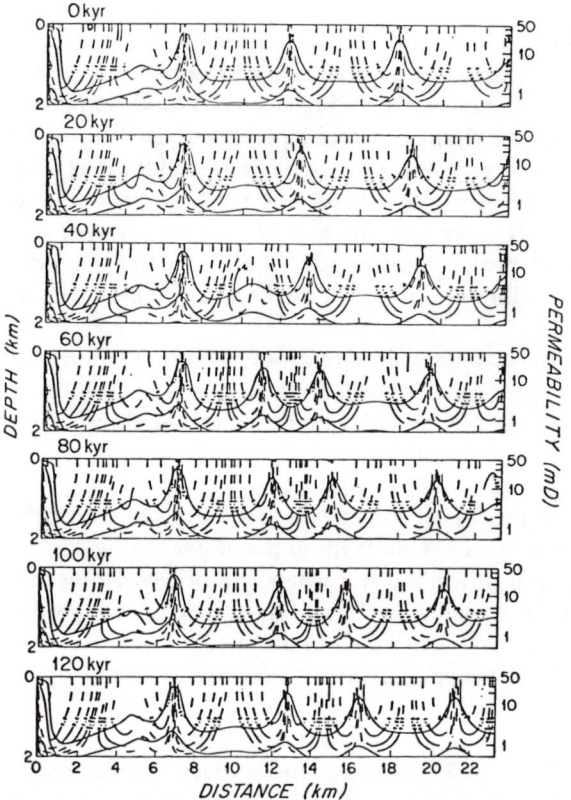

Figure 7-10. Computer model of convection cells and how they change with spreading away from the axis of a ridge. The black smokers would occur at the upper left. Then as the years go by, the axial rock spreads away from the ridge crest and actually moves through the first two convection cells shown by dashed lines. Temperatures shown by solid lines mark upwelling hot water by their peaks. By 120,000 years, (bottom) the rock that started at the upper left is now at the lower right at a distance of 22 km from the axis. The convection cell is now fixed within that rock, and it likely will continue as a progressively colder convection pattern for millions of years (from Fehn et al., 1983).

As John Edmond of MIT has shown, black smokers take magnesium and sulfate from the ocean and exchange them with basalt for lithium, potassium, and rubidium, which are added to the oceans. The quantity of alkalies and magnesium dumped into the ocean is greater than that input by rivers all over the world according to Edmond, but Sleep would estimate fluxes based upon his heat-balance calculations at only 10% of the river input. Stan Hart of MIT would further argue that ridge flank cold-water convection results in gross fluxes of potassium, rubidium, and cessium into rather than out of the basalt. He would say that 15, 75, and 95 percent of the entire river

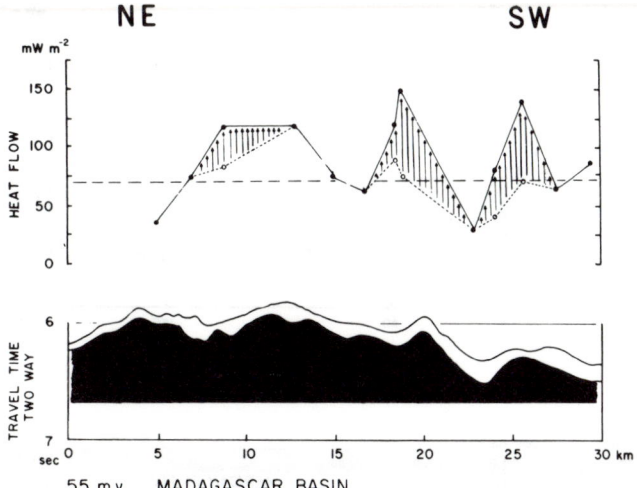

Figure 7-11. Convection patterns in surface heat flow have been mapped in oceanic crust as old as 55 million years in the Indian Ocean. Arrows estimate the amount of heat being carried by the convecting fluids as they move from the rock through the sediment covering this old sea floor into the ocean bottom water (from Anderson et al., 1979). Topography is displayed below with the double line representing sediment thickness.

input of these three elements, respectively, goes not into the ocean, but out of the ocean into the underlying basalt.

Summary

Convection is therefore an important chemical and physical process. For example, manganese nodules are accretions onto the sea floor caused by the supersaturation of ocean bottom water with manganese. Manganese is a prime product of the off-axis convection process. It is likely that this ground-water circulation is responsible for one of the bright hopes for a new mining source in the future, provided technology and politics allow it.

In the next chapter we look in more detail at the direct benefits to man of this convection process in the oceanic lithosphere; specifically, how, why, and where metals are concentrated on the sea floor. For the first time ever, we are able to watch this process in action. The hints that metallogenesis, as the formative process is called, will give us about where to look for as yet undiscovered deposits, and about how to process those metals once we find them, will go a long way in determining how much farther our great indus-trial society advances in the future.

at over $2 billion for one segment of the Galapagos Spreading Center alone, such estimates do not consider the cost of mining such deposits beneath two miles of water. Put another way, we are interested in what such metallogenesis tells us about ridge-axis processes rather than the economic value involved.

Metals are not formed by a geological process. They exist as primary elements present at the formation of the earth. Differentiation has redistributed most of the iron into the center of the earth. The remaining iron, along with copper, zinc, silver, gold, manganese, titanium, chromium, platinum, and other metals, has been distributed in rocks of the continents and ocean lithosphere and dissolved in the ocean water itself. The sources of metals in the ocean are from rocks via either weathering or volcanic activity. At the ridge axis, when seawater circulates downward into basalt as it heads toward the magma chamber, the metals undergo chemical reaction to form compounds with sulfides and to switch places from the basalt to the water. Their history is complex, however, because if they are deposited back onto the sea floor, the metal sulfides are unstable in the presence of oxygen and will dissolve back into the ocean water. Burial is required in order to preserve metals on the sea floor. But we are getting ahead of ourselves. Let's take a systematic look at metallogenesis in the ocean floor.

History

The first hard evidence of formation of metals beneath the sea comes from the original *Challenger* expedition reports from the 1870s. Manganese nodules were recovered by the *Challenger* with bottom dredges. A manganese nodule is a spherical accretion of heavy metals, predominantly manganese and iron, formed slowly around some seed. The seed actually is a catalyst allowing the metals to accrete to it from the ocean water. Shark's teeth often are found at the center of manganese nodules, for example.

In the science lounge of the now-retired drilling vessel *Glomar Challenger* there was a manganese nodule from the original *Challenger* expedition, presented to the new vessel by the British Museum. The original scientific report describes the recovery of this nodule from the North Pacific on July 2, 1885, enroute from Yokohoma to the Hawaiian Islands. The depth was 2740 fathoms (1 fathom is about 6 feet), and the deposit was described as "manganese about red clay with traces of carbonate of lime." Murray and Renard (1891) proposed three hypotheses for formation of these metal deposits:

1. By slow precipitation from seawater
2. By deposition from submarine volcanic activity
3. By diagenesis (remobilization) from sediments

Current ideas of the origin of metal deposits on the sea floor have not added to this list of three sources. In fact, virtually nothing was done about the origin of these deposits from the time of the original *Challenger* expedition until after World War II. Then, in the late 1950s, metal-rich sediments were first recovered along a midocean ridge. More recently, in the late 1960s the first observations of direct metal formation came from small enclosed ocean basins. Hot brines above metalliferous muds were found at the bottom of the Red Sea, then the Gulf of California, and now in the open ocean near the Galapagos Islands and along the East Pacific Rise south of Baja California.

Metal Deposits in Ocean Basins

Manganese nodules are accretions of heavy metals such as chromium, titanium, and predominantly manganese, which solidify out of seawater (within which they are supersaturated) when a catalyst is present. For some unknown reason, small round objects lying on the sea floor serve as the catalysts for manganese nodule formation. They form very slowly, over millions of years, off-axis, in deep water, and right at the sediment surface (Figure 8-1). Why are they round, and why aren't they found buried? These questions have been around since the first studies of nodule formation in the late 1950s. Bill Menard (1972) suggests a novel explanation for these quirks of nature. Bottom-dwelling biological life, such as worms, "roll around" the slowly forming nodules, keeping new surfaces pointed upward toward the precipitation source, and this rolling around prevents burial.

In any event, these nodules form because seawater becomes supersaturated with manganese (Figure 8-2). The sources of the ocean's supersaturation in manganese and other metals are river runoff, ridge-axis hot springs, and ridge-flank hydrothermal circulation. For example, the effluent from black smokers floats great distances off-axis where it gradually precipitates back onto the sea floor, preferring to accrete into spheres about some object lying on the bottom. A uniform pavement sometimes forms. These deposits cluster in basins near the most active spreading centers (Figure 8-3). Both the continuous pavements and the nodules are distinctly enriched in iron and manganese relative to deep-sea sediments in general, but the nodules have decidedly more nickel, cobalt, and copper than the hydrothermal pavements (Figures 8-4 and 8-5).

Mining of nodules with giant deep-sea vacuum cleaners is entirely possible from an engineering standpoint. Theoretically, barges could be filled with strategically important quantities of nickel, cobalt, copper, and manganese then towed to port. But this process is currently not economical given the low prices of metals on the world market.

Figure 8-1. The manganese nodule on the left is composed of 20 percent manganese, 15 percent iron, and significant traces of cobalt, copper, and nickel. There have been many serious plans to mine these nodules by sucking them off the sea floor with giant vacuum cleaners. The price of metals is too low today to be economical. The inside of the nodule on the right is a pebble. Nodules form by accretion about round objects. Even shark's teeth have been found inside manganese nodules (from Fyfe, 1981).

Metal Deposits at the Ridge Axis

Dredged rocks near fracture zones were the only proof that metals exist beneath the sea floor until the *Glomar Challenger* drilled into a stockwork of a massive sulfide deposit beneath 600 m of pillow basalts just off the flank

Figure 8-1. (*Continued*)

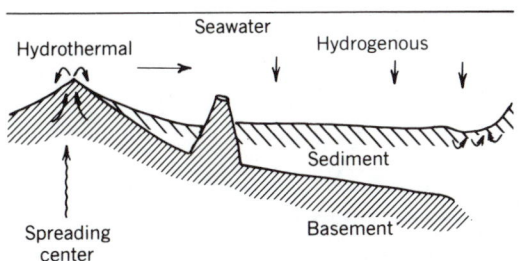

Figure 8-2. The likely source for the metals that fall gently to the sea floor to accrete into manganese nodules (called hydrogenous deposition) is the ridge-axis hydrothermal activity and the black smokers (from Bonatti, 1981).

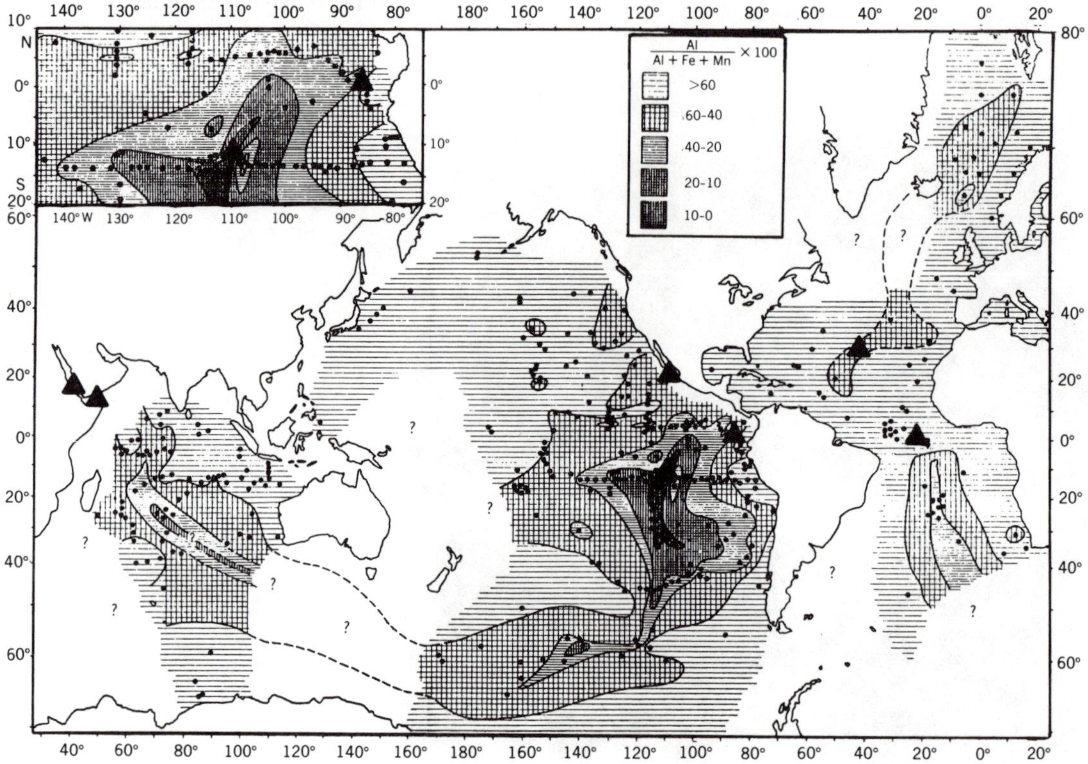

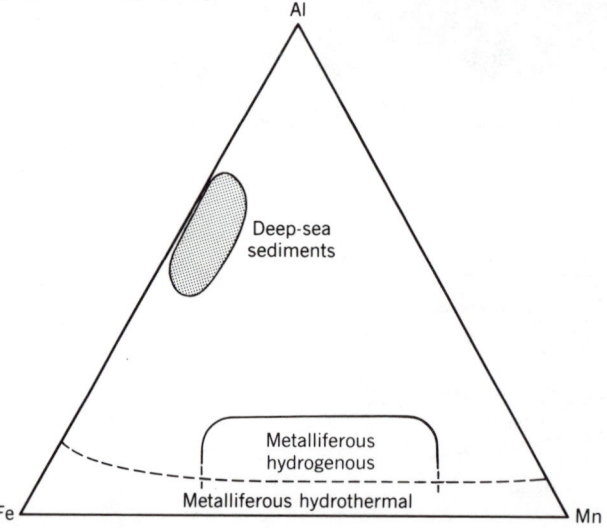

Figure 8-3. Location map of major manganese nodule deposition in the oceans (from Bonatti, 1981).

Figure 8-4. Three-axis chemical plot showing that manganese nodules have slightly higher aluminum contents than ridge-axis hydrothermal sediments. Normal deep-sea sediments have far more aluminum and much less iron and manganese than metalliferous sediments (from Bonatti, 1981).

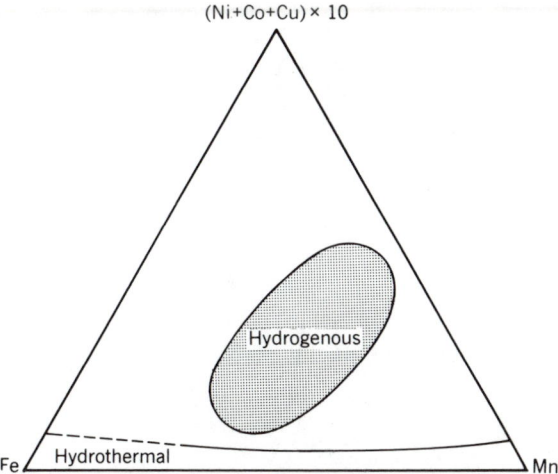

Figure 8-5. Manganese nodules have much more nickel, copper, and cobalt than ridge-axis hydrothermal sediments, probably because these elements are easily soluble in ocean water, and they dissolve at the axis only to be carried far away from the axis before being redeposited as manganese nodules (from Bonatti, 1981).

of the Galapagos Spreading Center, where the white-smoker hot springs are found.

Our study of the locations within ophiolites on land from which mining occurs suggests that massive sulfides are not formed at the sea floor but below it (Figure 8-6). The total metal content of the oceanic crust could be quite large if burial at the ridge crest preserves massive sulfides. Therefore, it is important to understand in detail the mechanism of formation of a massive sulfide.

Our observational bases are again ophiolites, black and white smokers, and a few drilled and dredged stockworks beneath the sea floor. First of all, the surface manifestation of ore genesis is of itself not very economical (Figure 8-7). A few hundred tons of copper, zinc, and iron ore surround each black smoker on the East Pacific Rise, whereas the land mining of ophiolites generally requires deposits of a few million tons to be economical. The big economic question, of course, is what is below the black smokers.

It is from the fluid exhaled at the sea floor that a good picture of the mechanism of sulfide metallogenesis emerges. Whether a smoker is black or white depends only upon whether mixing of the superheated hydrothermal fluid with cold seawater occurs at the sea floor or *below* it. If below, then all the black smoke is deposited in or below the pillow basalt layer. There, it is isolated from oxygenated seawater, and preservation of millions of tons of ore is possible. That this occurs is shown by the Galapagos white smokers, where mixing is clearly seen in the chemistry of white-smoker waters to be

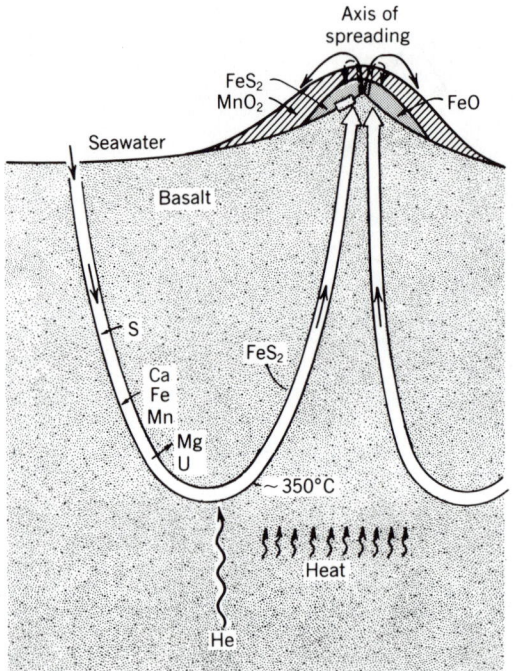

Figure 8-6. The pathway to a black smoker consists of a stockwork of feeder veins and fractures within which seawater leaches metals from basalt at the same time that tremendous heating is occurring (from Bonatti, 1981).

occurring *below* the sea floor. The elemental concentrations of the white-smoker effluents all point to a beginning fluid of high temperature and exactly the same composition as the fluid exiting the sea floor at black smokers.

Therefore at white smokers, ridge-axis massive sulfides are not exhaled at the sea floor, but instead are deposited within the rock as soon as cold downwelling water percolates into the permeable basalt to mix with the hot upwelling fluids. The deposition of metals can form throughout the upwelling vent, or metals can plate the walls of a chimney. This chimney can grow upward until it breaks the surface. The plating isolates the hot water from surrounding cold water and the black smoke can then break the surface without mixing. Such a case exists on the East Pacific Rise axis at the present time. But much more extensive deposits are likely to exist beneath the black smokers, since sulfide deposition was required to prevent mixing within the basalt in order to form a chimney in the first place.

The black-smoker chimney material at 21 degrees north on the East Pacific Rise axis contains up to 28 percent zinc, 43 percent iron, and 6 percent copper, but has no manganese. Manganese dominates the white smok-

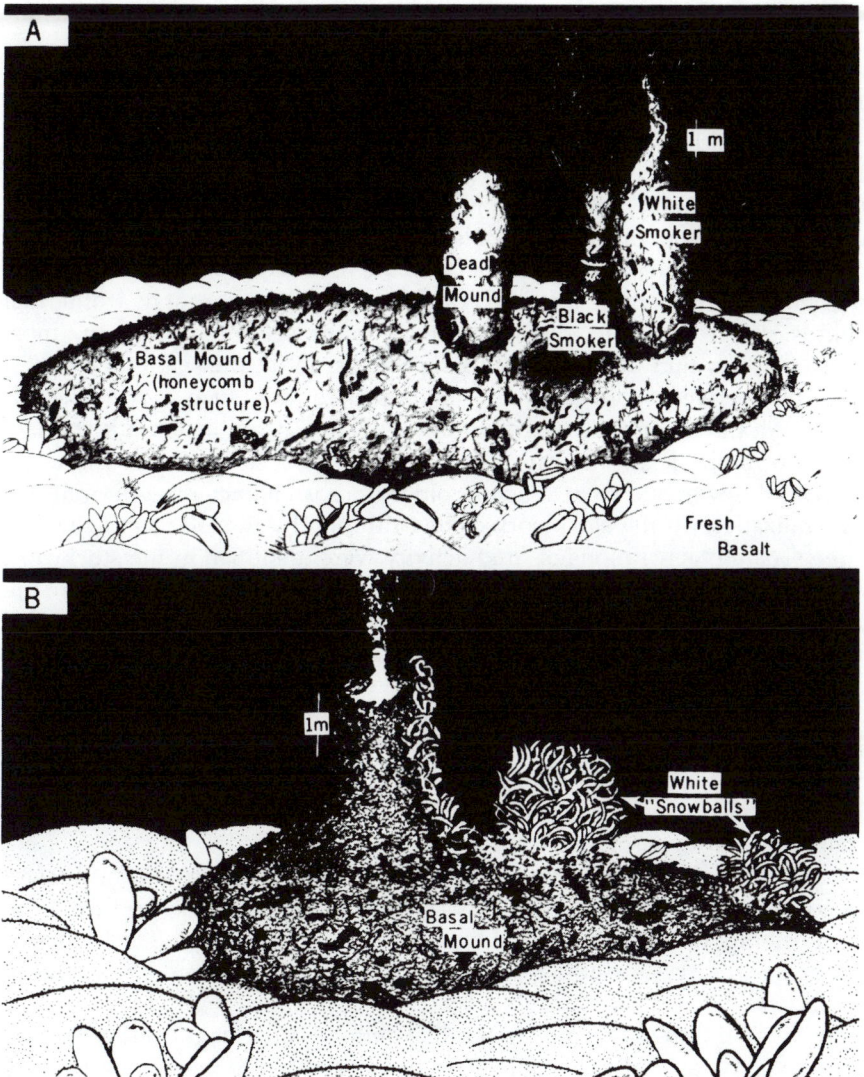

Figure 8-7. Schematic of black and white smokers with their surrounding organic community of giant tube worms and clams (from Bonatti, 1981).

ers, however. Where does it go? It stays in the water to very low temperatures, and so it precipitated only when the water cools below even white-smoker temperatures. It is not affected much by below-surface mixing. The manganese then moves upward into the water column at all smokers. There it floats far off-axis to eventually reprecipitate onto the sea floor as manganese nodules. We thus see a connection between all the different metallogenesis processes in the oceans and hot-spring activity.

A black smoker can evolve from and back to a white smoker during the brief volcanic history of a hot-spring event. Thus, the final form of the deposit depends not only upon the proximity to and magnitude of the heat source, the magma chamber, but also on the *permeability* of the plumbing system. Permeability depends on the interconnectedness of cracks and voids. The more permeable the pillow basalt layer, the deeper the penetration of cold seawater and the deeper into the rock the deposition of the massive sulfide. This depth marks the point at which the superhot hydrothermal fluid is mixed with cold, downward-penetrating seawater. Thus, the most likely place to find massive sulfide deposits is not at the sea floor but at a boundary between permeable and impermeable rock, such as the dike pillow basalt transition that separates layers 2B and 2C in the oceanic crust.

Also, multiple events can affect any given deposit; that is, the overgrowth of newer stockworks across older ones is characteristic of ophiolite mineralization. In the stockwork drilled-through by the *Glomar Challenger*, three separate generations of fluid activity were identified in the stockwork veins. These separate events were easy to identify because not only were the temperatures of the hydrothermal fluids each different, but different minerals were deposited in the veins as each event sent fluid gushing anew toward the sea floor. There was a first stage of relatively unaltered seawater that passed through this vein 600 m below the ocean floor 6 million years ago at 200 to 250°C. Then, cracks that were filled during the first stage were reopened by a metal- and silica-rich hydrothermal fluid circulating at 250 to 350°C. Finally, a magnesium-depleted and calcium-rich, relatively cool fluid sealed the cracks permanently at 135 to 220°C.

How can we know so much from observing mineral veins? The answer comes from the kind of minerals left behind to fill the cracks and from the compositions of microscopic bubbles of the original fluid left behind and trapped in the crystals filling the cracks. These inclusions are like chemical fossils.

One final note: The smokestack-like chimneys that sprout from the sea floor are gravitationally unstable and quickly break into metalliferous boulders. If a later lava flow should cover these boulder fields, a small ore body is made. Otherwise, the metals will dissolve back into seawater, float far away from the axis, and eventually be redeposited along with manganese in the form of nodules.

The Kuroko Massive Sulfide Deposits of Japan

Black smokers can vary in the amount of each metal present depending upon the composition of the country rock through which the hot fluid convects. As an excellent example of this, consider the Kuroko copper sulfides of southwest Honshu, Japan. Here is a Miocene (10 to 15 million years old) deep-sea metal sulfide deposit that was formed in the Philippine Sea and obducted as an ophiolite onto Japan during the subduction of that sea floor by the Nankai Trough along the southern boundary of Honshu (Figure 8-8).

This Kuroko deposit has been mined for several hundred years in Japan, but its origin had been unclear until the black smokers were discovered on an active spreading center. The deposit consists of banded ores of borax, lead, zinc, and copper grading to the center into a pyrite-rich core. The his-

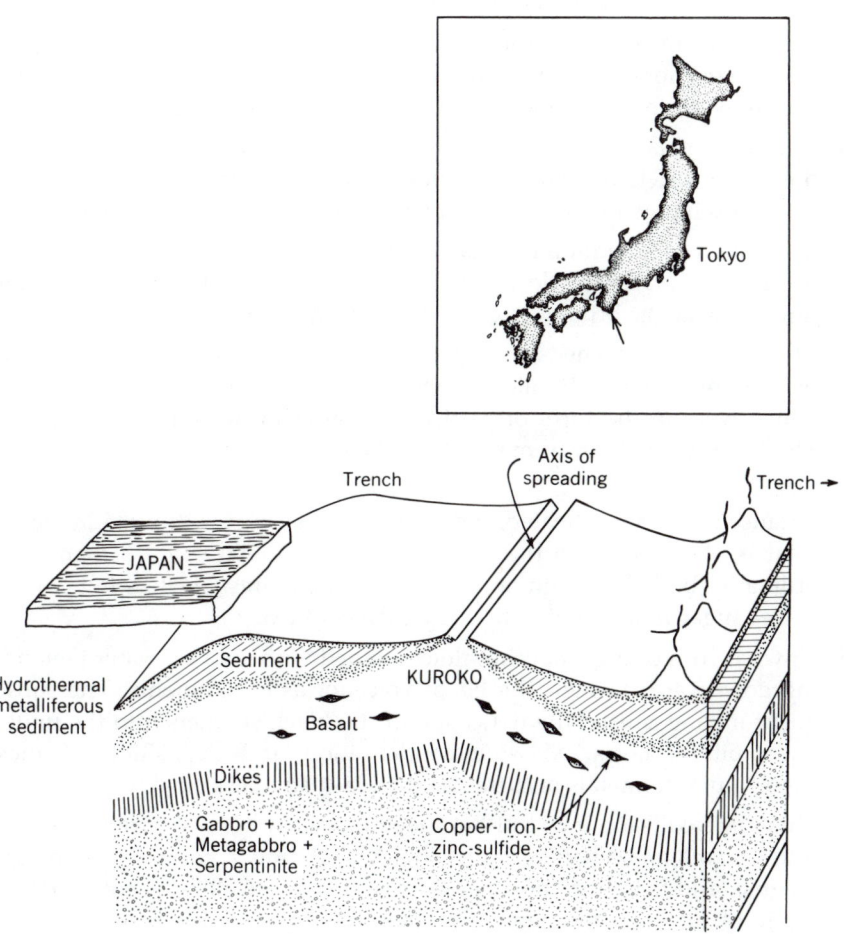

Figure 8-8. Schematic of the mode of generation of the Koroko metalliferous deposits now on Honshu, Japan. In this model, the Koroko were laid down at a ridge axis of a back-arc spreading center in the Pacific Ocean to the east of Japan. The sea-floor spreading system and the island arc to its east were both subsequently subducted at the Japan trench. The Koroko were obducted to form an ophiolite complex.

tory of this ore body might have been as follows (paraphrased from Dick Holland of Harvard University and an international team studying the deposits):

1. A mid-Miocene, deep-water, back-arc spreading center was being continuously buried by sediments coming off an adjoining volcanic land mass— an island arc similar to the Marianas of today.

2. Hot-spring activity was vigorous but was capped by this volcanoclastic sedimentary lid. Temperatures were still below 250°C, however.

3. Then a magma chamber formed with subsequent intrusion of more silicic lavas than those at 21°N on the East Pacific Rise. This magma forced its way upward into the newly formed sheeted dikes of the ridge-axis crust.

4. The volcanoclastic lid allowed infiltration of seawater downward to leach out sulfur, calcium, iron, manganese, and helium from the country rock and to exchange magnesium and uranium with the newly cooling crust.

5. Deposition of alteration minerals such as clay sealed some of the plumbing and channeled the flow into narrow plumes of hot (350°C) upwelling fluid. This acidic brine was quite different in composition from seawater.

6. The acid water leached large quantities of metals from the country rock by altering metal-rich silicates and oxides from the rock into sulfides, which were in the form of particulate matter in the superheated water. The sulfur came both from sulfate in the sea water and from sulfur in the magma.

7. Because it was superheated, the water was also supersaturated in metals. That is, dissolved into the water were more metal sulfides than could ordinarily be held in solution at cold temperatures—just as hot tea dissolves sugar much more efficiently than cold tea.

8. Upward convecting, superhot fluid collided with cold seawater penetrating downward through the lid of volcanoclastic sediments. The subsequent mixing caused the deflection of the black smokers into the underlying pillow lavas. Massive condensation and deposition of these supersaturated metals occurred as the black smokers quickly cooled.

9. This same collision event of hot meeting cold waters occurred time after time as magma chamber after magma chamber formed, discharged magma, and froze into new ocean crust. Each upwelling event deposited a pile of metals a few tens of meters thick, then subsequent hot-water pulses buried them one after another. Cooler edges collected copper and galena (lead) plus gold and silver.

10. Then the volcanic intrusion's heat sources died out, and the whole thing was buried by later volcanoclastic deposition from the adjoining island arc.

11. Cold-water circulation continued off-axis, moving manganese out of the rock and into the sedimentary layer. Thick deposits of manganese formed in this manner.

12. Subduction caught a sliver of this sea floor and cataclysmically thrust it upward onto the landmass of Japan.

13. Millions of years later, man stumbled into the Kuroko metal deposits completely by chance.

Summary

What lessons do the Kuroko metal deposits and other extinct black smokers tell us about exploring for new massive sulfides? For one thing, untold billions of dollars worth of metal deposits must exist beneath the sea floor. We will never run out of metals, if only we can develop ways of exploring for them and of drilling into them to extract the ores.

Drilling the stockwork on the flank of the Galapagos white smokers might have given a hint of how to find future buried deposits. A low seismic velocity zone was found to correspond to the stockwork deposits. If sophisticated seismic exploration techniques that are capable of seeing 100-m-thick low-velocity zones in the oceanic crust could be developed, perhaps we could find where to drill for the mother lode. It is just such great bonanzas that have driven people to the far reaches of the continents—to California and Alaska in United States history, for example. Might the next gold rush be to the ocean floor?

Further Readings

Bonatti, E., 1981, Metal deposits in the oceanic lithosphere, *in* C. Emiliani, ed., The Sea, vol. 7: New York, Wiley.

Hekinian, R., Renard, V., and Cheminee, J., 1983, Hydrothermal deposits on the East Pacific Rise, *in* P. Rona et al., eds., Hydrothermal Processes at Seafloor Spreading Centers: New York, Plenum.

9

Chemical Interchange
Between Ocean and Crust

Oceanography is not a science but a collection of scientific disciplines. Marine geology, one of those disciplines, contributes to understanding the *chemical oceanography* of the sea as well as the *physical oceanography* or physical movements of the water column. The geology of the sea floor cannot be separated from the evolution of the oceans above. Changes in character or distribution of the ocean basins affect both the composition of the oceans and the way in which the seawater circulates. These changes, in turn, affect the form and composition of sediments deposited on the sea floor. Therefore, the study of the sea floor is inextricably tied to the understanding of the oceans themselves.

Geology shows us that some quite remarkable events have occurred to the ocean, yet it seems to have a powerful ability to recover rather well from catastrophes. By studying the mode of recovery, we learn how the ocean itself works.

Consider, for example, the Mediterranean Sea. Deep-sea drilling has shown that 10 million years ago, the entire Mediterranean Basin became sealed to open circulation across Gibraltar and the whole sea evaporated (Figure 9-1). The result was a gigantic hole over 1 mile deep at the site of the present sea. At the bottom, salt deposits called evaporites formed. All the salt in the entire water column evaporated and was deposited on the sea floor. Then Gibraltar sank a little, the dam was broken, and the sea refilled. Subsequent sedimentation has buried trillions and trillions of tons of salt beneath younger sea-floor sediments.

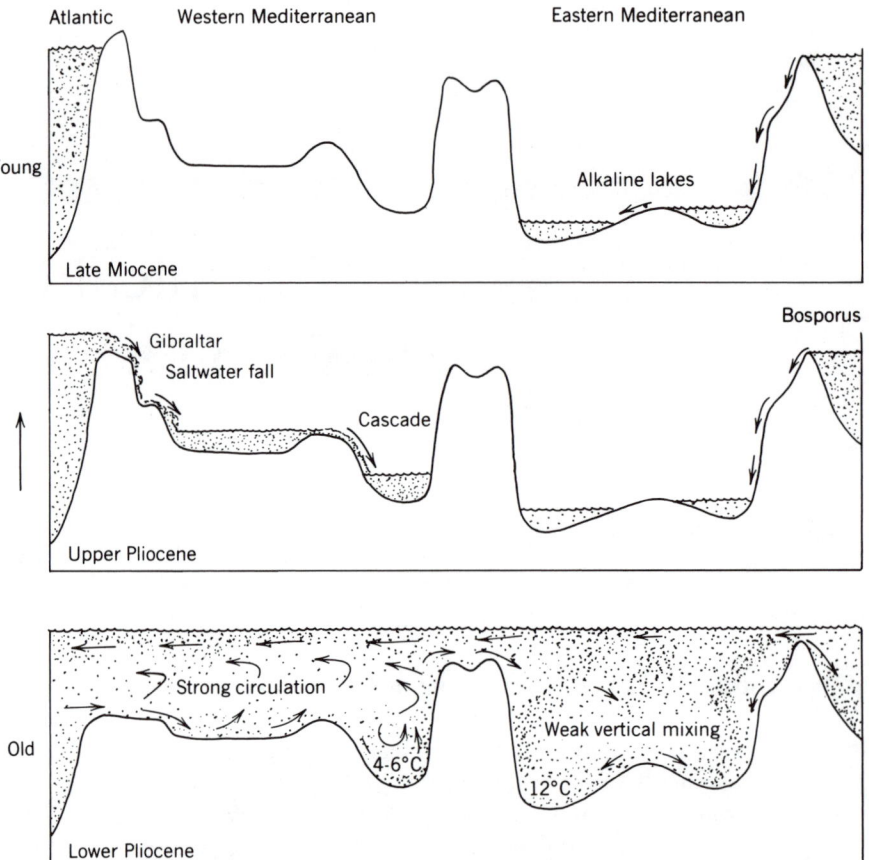

Figure 9-1. Dessication of the Mediterranean Sea about 10 million years ago. Note the great flood of the upper Pliocene period.

This dramatic event should have set off a salinity crisis within the oceans. Yet the whole ocean accommodated the removal of all this salt with virtually no change in its overall chemical composition. Furthermore, this evaporite event was not an isolated geological occurrence. The entire Gulf of Mexico was dry during the Jurassic period (140 million years ago). The Red Sea and the North Sea are also floored with the telltale signs of evaporation: thick layers of salt.

Perhaps the most astounding fact about the oceans is that they have had approximately the same chemical composition for the last 3.5 billion years, in spite of these catastrophic but localized events. The geology of the sea floor is responsible for this remarkable chemical stability, along with the input from rivers. Volcanism on midocean ridges adds not only major cations such as calcium, potassium, and manganese, but also trace elements, and even gases, such as helium and methane, which are needed to maintain a consistent composition for the entire ocean mass. This composition has remained essentially unchanged through more than half the history of the Earth. It is obvious that a powerful buffer must be acting to keep the chemical composition of the oceans constant.

For example, how does the sea replenish its supply of sodium and chlorine after a great salinity crisis? The evaporated water rains down again, quickly returning its volume of water to the oceans. The oceans, in turn, completely mix in 2000 years (we can age-date water just as we can Cro-Magnon man, by using radioactive carbon), so one would expect the salinity of the ocean to drop because of the dilution of the Mediterranean Sea. Yet it does not. And the rivers that carry the rainwater back to the ocean do not become salty for 2000 years and then become fresh again. Thus the ocean's response to salinity crises was indeed a scientific puzzle until the black- and white-smoker hot springs were discovered at the ridge axis. They provide an instantaneous source of not only sodium but also chlorine through the buffering effect of midocean-ridge volcanism on ocean water chemistry.

The salinity of the hydrothermal waters circulating in the ocean crust is measured by its chlorine content. And the fluid is naturally an acid brine; that is, it has a low pH and is salty. If the circulating fluid suddenly becomes fresher water, the amount of sodium absorbed from the volcanic rock by the fluid increases. The sodium in the fluid absorbs excessive chlorine from the rocks, making the fluid even more salty than usual—a heavier brine. The input of excess salt continues into the ocean until new seawater circulating downward into the oceanic crust returns to its natural salinity. The acidity of the fluid then returns to normal, and the crisis is overcome.

Sillenian Oceanography

The existence of a steady-state ocean presents a classic geochemical mass–balance problem. Just as rivers and winds constantly bring chemicals to the ocean as mud, biological activity such as shell-making removes dissolved material from the ocean as sea-floor sediments. All inputs must exactly balance all outputs for steady state to exist. L. G. Sillen in 1961 proposed that this balance occurred through a process he called "reverse weathering." Weathering is the breaking down of continental rocks by rainfall, ice, wind, and so on. These products of weathering are deposited into the oceans by the rivers. This weathering is counterbalanced in the oceans by sedimentation, which returns solids to the ocean and from there to the geological system. But the chemical reactions between rain and rocks are all a result of cation exchange from the rocks to water for which protons that replace the cations in the rock must be derived exclusively from reaction with carbonic acid in rainwater. Sillen suggested that this rain-produced weathering ends up in rivers. Then this cation-rich, proton-poor river product pours into the oceans, where somehow the proton–cation reactions are reversed—thus the name reverse weathering. Cations are deposited as sea-floor sediments, and protons are released in the form of carbon dioxide, which comes out of seawater during the formation of carbonate sediments or limestones. The carbon dioxide cycles back onto land during evaporation, only to weather once again in the form of rain.

The Sillen model is simple and elegant. It is a dynamic model that is in equilibrium, so changes in weathering from, for example, tectonics (Mediterranean example) or climate (ice ages) should result in an equal and opposite change in sedimentation (Figure 9-2). However, 20 years of looking at sediments could not find the cation–proton reverse weathering reactions occurring anywhere at the required rates or extent.

Then came the direct observational evidence for hot springs on mid-ocean ridges. John Edmond of MIT realized that reverse weathering was exactly what was occurring in the black smoker reactions of seawater with basalt in the oceanic crust above the magma chamber. Though hot springs circulate seawater through basalt at only one twohundredth of the rate that rivers deposit water into the ocean, the hot springs have a big chemical advantage over rivers—hot reaction temperatures. Easily 200 times more cation–proton exchange occurs with rock for every cubic centimeter of seawater at 300°C than at 20°C.

This is not to say that rivers are not as important as hot springs to the composition of the oceans. The Sillen model is actually completed by the Edmond model. The rivers deliver weathering products, and the hot springs reverse them on a one-for-one basis.

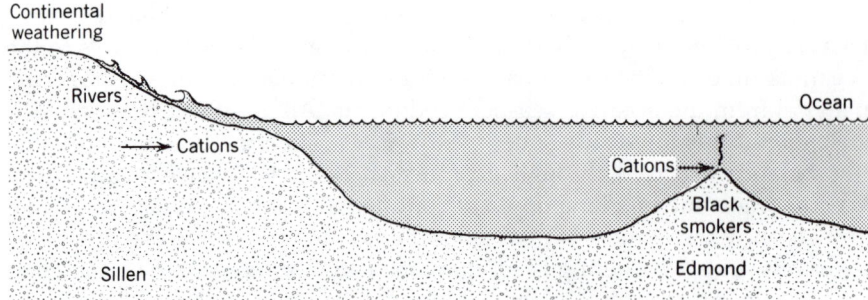

Figure 9-2. Schematic of the Sillien–Edmond model of the geochemical mass balance of cations in the oceans.

Chemical Tracers

The Edmond proposal was not immediately accepted by the vast majority of chemical oceanographers. He still had to prove that the few hot springs found to date on midocean ridges were not flukes. For the proof of the widespread occurrence of hot springs along ridge axes, geochemists turned to a gas that is escaping from our atmosphere so fast that the only source of heavy concentrations must be from primary mantle outgassing. Helium-3 is just such an isotope; one that must have an ocean-floor source, since all helium-3 in the atmosphere escapes within about 500,000 years of getting there, and all the helium-3 released into the ocean quickly makes its way into the atmosphere. The amount of helium-3 in the oceans is up to 50 percent higher directly above the ridge axes than in the atmosphere. The amount of helium-3 is so great that hot springs must be active over the entire 50,000-km length of the sea-floor spreading system in order to supply that much helium. Thus we have proof of the general applicability of the Sillen–Edmond mass–balance model for maintaining constant ocean chemistry.

But helium is even more useful. It has two stable isotopes, helium-3 and helium 4. Helium-4 is produced by radioactive decay of uranium and thorium, and therefore is quite abundant on Earth. Helium-3 was not even discovered until 1938. In actuality, helium-3 is made by cosmic ray bombardment of the atmosphere, but that flux is quickly lost back into space because both helium-3 and helium-4 have such low masses that they escape quickly. Because the vast majority of helium-3 is primordial (i.e., trapped inside the Earth since its original formation), any new melting of mantle material will release its trapped helium-3 to the surface. Thus, the ratio of helium-3 to helium-4 is a unique measure of mantle outgassing.

Two hundred and fifty meters above the black smokers at 21°N on the East Pacific Rise, a plume of helium-3 has stabilized and now extends 500 km to the west, marking the direction of flow of Pacific bottom water across the East Pacific Rise at this latitude (Figure 9-3).

But it is at 15°S that the true predictive power of the ratio of helium-3 to helium-4 can be seen. There, the East Pacific Rise spreads at the fastest rate in all the oceans, about 16 cm per year. Helium measured in the water column perpendicular to this ridge shows that the ratio of helium-3 to helium-4 is about 10 times greater than at 21°N, indicating even more vigorous hydrothermal activity than at 21°N. In fact, the plume can be traced to the west of the axis for thousands of kilometers, whereas only 300 km to the east of the axis no trace of excess helium-3 can be found. This plume does not show up in any traditional ocean current measurements such as temperature, salinity or silica content (Figure 9-4). Why to the west but not to the east? Because the ocean bottom water is flowing from east to west across the ridge axis at 15°S.

This helium-3 to helium-4 ratio is higher than anywhere else in the open

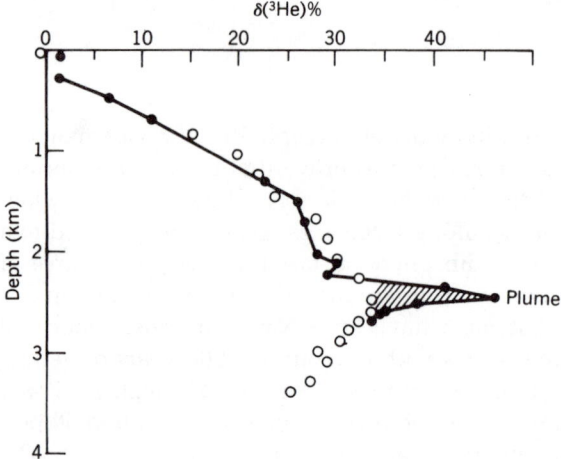

Figure 9-3. Helium-3 plume west of the East Pacific Rise axis at 21 degrees north (solid dots) compared to a nonridge profile at 23 degrees north (open circles) (from Lupton and Craig, 1981).

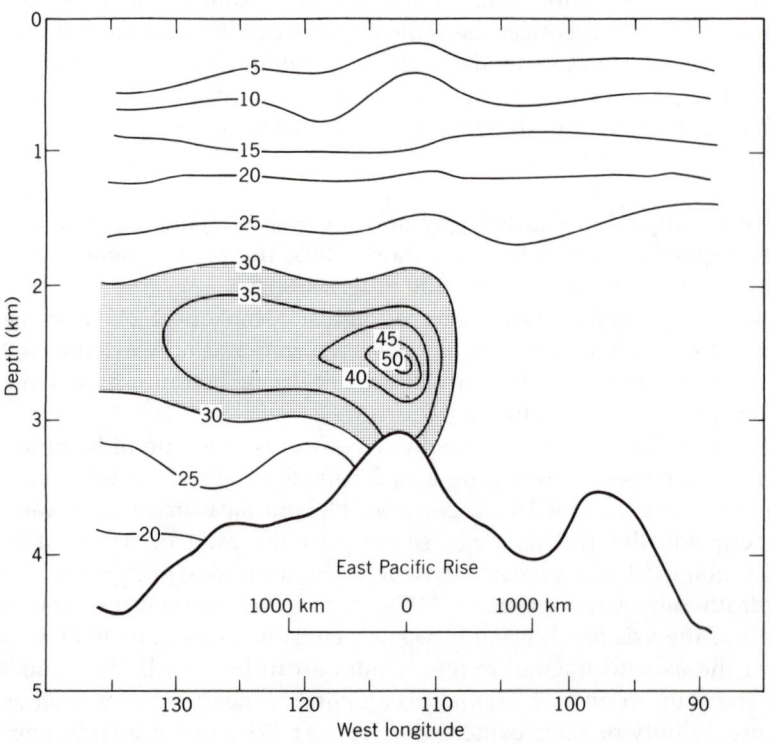

Figure 9-4. The helium-3 plume at 15 degrees south across the East Pacific Rise. Numbers are percent enrichment. The plume is huge and extends for thousands of kilometers west of the axis indicating that ocean currents flow from east to west across prolific black smoker fields at the axis (from Lupton and Craig, 1981).

ocean. Only in the Gulf of California and the Red Sea, where midocean ridges form the sea floor of small basins in which ocean circulation is highly restricted, are local values found that are as high as at 15°S.

One missing physical measurement is the flow velocity of the plume. But the recent discovery of mantle methane also exiting the black smokers may give a speedometer to the current measurements because methane is slowly "consumed" by bacteria in ocean-bottom water. The amount of methane remaining in a plume is therefore a function of the time since it was ejected into the water column.

The discovery of the helium-3 plume has already shown modern concepts of deep-ocean circulation to be slightly in error. Henry Stommel proposed in 1958 that major currents in the oceans were, quite logically, geostrophic. Geostrophic flow is horizontal flow driven principally by the Coriolis force from the earth's spin, which is balanced by horizontal pressure forces caused by temperature and salinity contrasts to cause motion in a liquid. The Coriolis force arises from rotation of the Earth and causes the great surface currents such as the Gulf Stream in the North Atlantic and the Kuroshio in the North Pacific, both of which flow clockwise. In the southern hemisphere the flow should be reversed, that is, counterclockwise, so that by 15°S in the eastern Pacific the flow should be toward the east and South America. Surface currents agree with this geostrophic model (Figure 9-5).

The helium-3 plume shows clearly that midlevel in the ocean column a countercurrent is flowing westward toward Tahiti in direct opposition to the geostrophic surface patterns. Some driving force other than geostrophic flow must be proposed for this midlevel westward flow. The helium plume has been shown to have no measurable temperature or salinity gradient within it, which further proves that geostrophic forces do not control this current. Some force must be pushing the current westward at about 0.1 cm/s against the geostrophic flow.

Here the vertical helium-3 variation enters the picture. Harmon Craig of the Scripps Institution of Oceanography, and John Lupton of the University of California at Santa Barbara noticed that the helium plume is not being mixed or dissipated but is being forced into a thinner and thinner horizontal plume to the west away from the ridge axis. Sharp density boundaries must exist on the top and bottom of the westward-flowing layer. Such a midwater layer of strong vertical density contrast is called a **benthic front**. A benthic front has interfaces that are turbulent mixing zones, which propagate something called **internal waves.** Internal waves move within the ocean at density boundaries in the same way that surface waves move (Figure 9-6). These waves mix water between the two layers along their interface and therefore exert a force on the two layers. The force would be directed toward the density anomaly driving deeper water flow. In this case, the Antarctic bottom water flowing up from the South Pacific is this deeper water current. Flow both from above and below this midwater plume is thus against the eastward flow. The surface and probably deep water layers both flow, as the

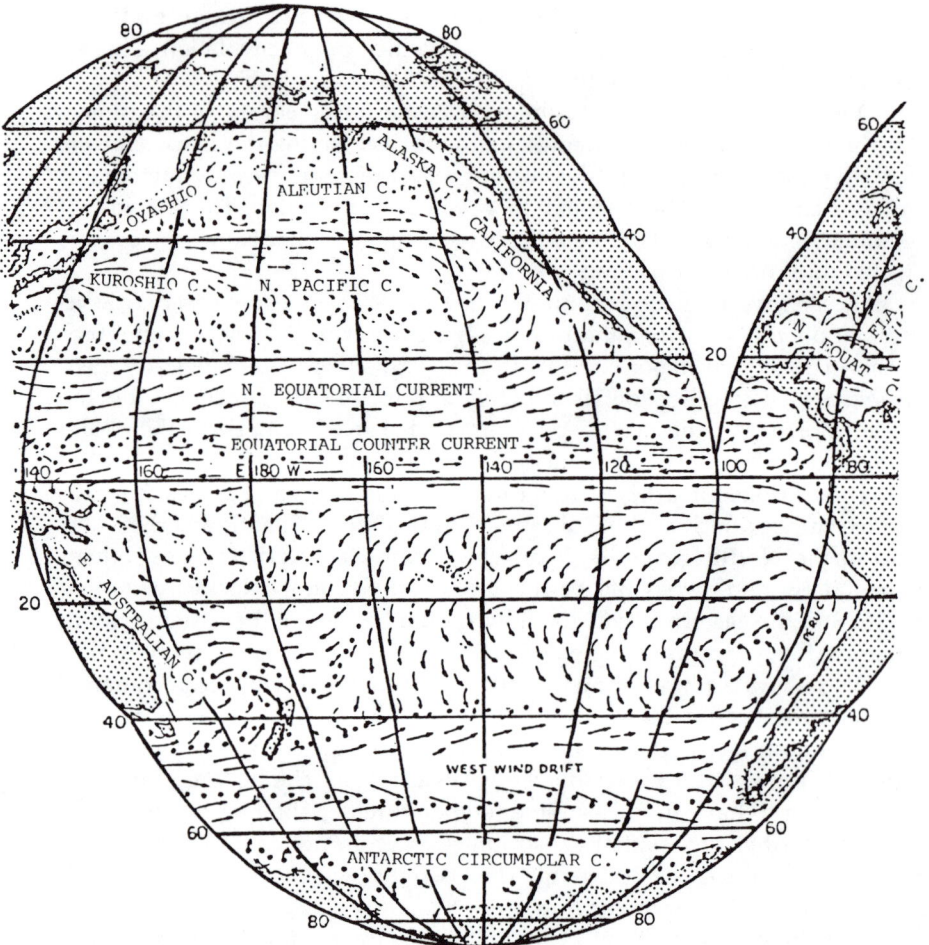

Figure 9-5. Current flow in the Pacific Ocean.

geostrophic model suggests, to the southeast. They then exert counterforces on the midwater current through the formation of internal waves at the contacts between the zones. The result is that the helium-3 plume flows to the west.

Thus we can use the chemical signature of volcanic input into the oceans from midocean ridges as tracers to monitor the behavior of the oceans themselves. The mapping of the locations of concentrations of some of the more exotic elements that neither mix with other chemical elements nor have any other sources than volcanism can be used as tracers for the flow of currents in the ocean. The directions and velocities of currents across the midocean ridges can be traced by measuring the dilution of these exotic elements as currents sweep them far away from the midocean ridges.

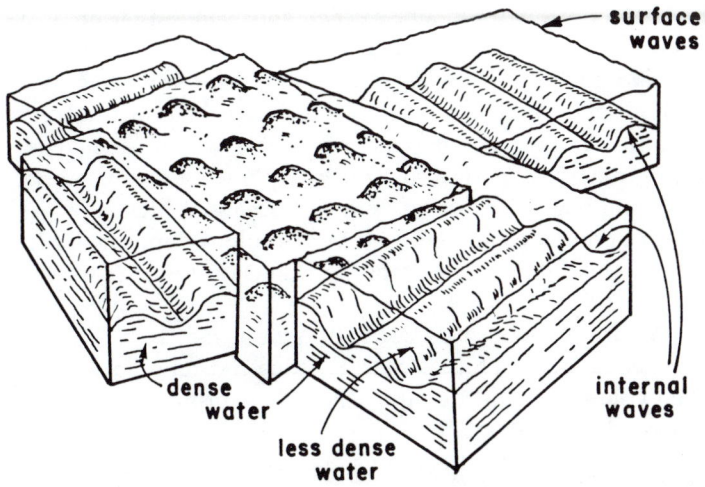

surface waves

dense water

less dense water

internal waves

Figure 9-6. Internal waves set up along planes of strong density contrast within the ocean. Motion can go counter to flow either above or below the boundary.

The Great Cretaceous Oxygen Shortage

We can use similar logic to deduce the chemical signature of past oceans by observing the chemistry of sediments deposited beneath past oceans. For example, the old salt basins such as the Gulf of Mexico, which we discussed earlier in the chapter, are prime locales for the production of hydrocarbons (oil and gas). Why does oil go along with salt? Oil is unoxidized organic material that is usually formed in sediments called black shales. The connection between salt and the formation of oil and black shale becomes obvious when you realize that all three accumulate where the resupply of oxygen to the water is restricted, such as near the Gibraltar or Bosporus straits. The sea evaporates, but long before all the water is gone all the oxygen in the water is used up, and black shales result. Oil forms millions of years later from the geological cooking of black shales. The Black Sea is the next prime candidate for evaporite formation. It may soon be a giant hole in the gound; it may already have been in the past.

We have seen what restricts circulation in the oceans, and we have attempted to understand how the ocean recovers from a salt crisis without much overall effect on its composition. But the ocean has not always been successful in coping with large changes in chemistry. There are isolated examples of long periods of disequilibrium.

A major exception to the constancy in the chemistry of the oceans occurred during the Cretaceous period, about 110 to 80 million years ago. It appears that the oceans suffered a major oxygen shortage at that time. We know this in the same way that we know from observation that the chemistry of sediments laid down over the last 600 million years was the same as the chemistry of those deposited now. This tells us that somehow the oceans had to have the same composition then as now. The anomalous chemistry that occurred during one small part of that record, in the Cretaceous period, tells us that something was very wrong with the oceans at that time. The sediments from that period are characterized by enormous deposits of black shales rather than by the dominance of more typical clays found before and after.

The black shales are black because decay of organic matter in the clays, which requires oxygen, has not fully occurred, thus indicating an oxygen deficiency. A large volume of existing oil reserves was formed during times of abundant black-shale formation.

What was different about the Cretaceous oceans that might account for this oxygen deficiency? In order to answer this question, we must develop the rationale for the study of past oceans, and that requires the understanding of the past geology of the sea floor. This study is called **paleoceanography,** or the attempt to understand the oceanography of past geological times when the continents and oceans were very different configurations from today.

As always, the simplest place to start is the present oceans, then we can work our way back in time. Black shales are now being deposited in the Black Sea. It is called that not because the water is black, but because the mud at the bottom is black. Chemical analysis of that mud shows that the dead organisms falling to the sea floor are not fully decaying. The reason is a lack of sufficient oxygen. The bottom of the Black Sea is anoxic because all the oxygenated waters entering the enclosed basin come from freshwater rivers. This water is lighter than the salt water at the bottom of the sea. It floats at the surface, then runs out at the Bosporus Straits into the Mediterranean Sea. The Bosporus is blocked by a solid rock sill that runs from the deep sea floor up to only a short distance below the surface, so the heavy and stagnant salt water of the Black Sea is trapped and cannot escape. Every few years, tremendous rains cause the incoming rivers to flood and overfill the Black Sea. The fresh waters reach deep into the sea and force an overturn of bottom waters to the surface, and fresh water moves to the bottom. A tremendous fish kill then follows as surface fish suffocate in the oxygen-starved salt water from the stagnant bottom of the sea. At first, this kind of event is a cause for celebration for local fishermen as they rush out to collect all the dead fish floating on the surface that they can grab. But there are always too many dead fish, and a terrible problem eventually arises on the beaches as dead fish pile up on shore and begin to decay.

The same thing happened during the Cretaceous period as the Atlantic Ocean was being formed from the rifting away of North and South America from Africa and Europe. Small enclosed basins with restricted circulation preserved oxygen-starved black shales as a reminder of past geological conditions. The Pacific Ocean, on the other hand, was not restricted from open circulation, and consequently no oxygen shortage at all is recorded during the Cretaceous period in that part of the world. This is an excellent example of the inextricable tie between the ocean floor and the water above.

Paleoceanography

We can learn even more from the Cretaceous black shales. We suspect them to be due to oxygen deficiency in the deep waters of the oceans, particularly in the Atlantic, where most of the Cretaceous black shales are found. The ultimate cause of the oxygen deficiency is thought to be from sea-floor topography that restricts free circulation of ocean water within the ocean basin in question. How then do we reconstruct the form of the ocean floor back in Cretaceous time? The sea-floor depth away from the spreading center can be described very exactly if we know its age because we have already

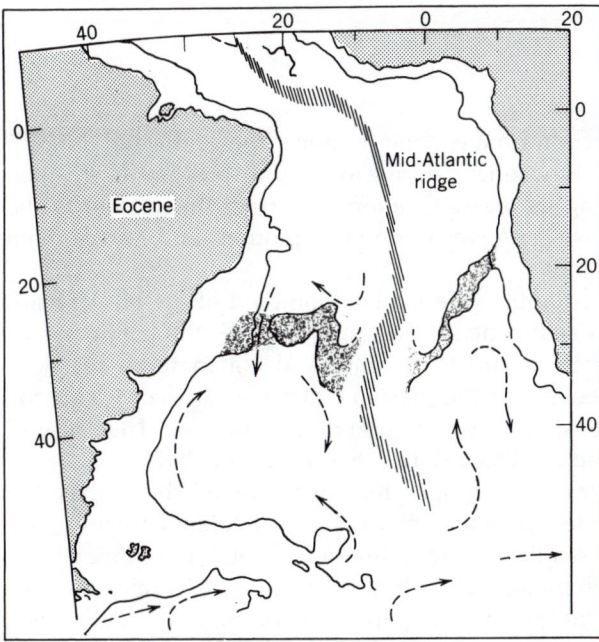

Figure 9-7. The Walvis and Rio Grande ridges (hatched above), now sunk deep beneath sea level, were above the surface, and they blocked circulation of ocean water in the Eocene. The South Atlantic then was similar to the Mediterranean now (from Kennett, 1982).

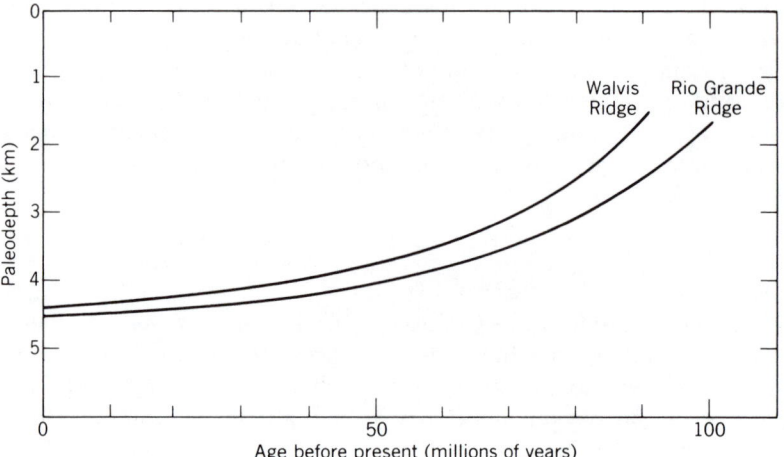

Figure 9-8. The Walvis and Rio Grande ridges subsided just like midocean ridges because of thermal contraction during cooling. The ridges became progressively deeper with time so that the water passages became deeper until the Atlantic was essentially open to circulation from other ocean water (from Kennett, 1982).

seen that thermal contraction from cooling produces the gentle and uniform subsidence of all ocean lithosphere during the aging process. If we then backtrack the ocean along its magnetic anomalies from the present to the desired age in the past, we can reverse the plate motions and restore them to any of their past positions.

Consider the South Atlantic, where a large amount of the black shales are found in Cretaceous sediments. If we can backtrack the continents of South America and Africa toward each other and eliminate all sea floor formed between Cretaceous and the present, then we can reconstruct the depth to sea floor in this smaller South Atlantic proto-ocean. The cause of the oxygen deficiency and the black shales then becomes obvious.

The key to this puzzle is a topographic barrier called the Walvis–Rio Grande Ridge. At the present time it is split by the mid-Atlantic ridge (Figure 9-7). This ridge, like the sea floor surrounding it, is likely of volcanic origin, so that its depth has been increasing with time just as with normal sea floor (Figure 9-8). How has the paleoceanography of the South Atlantic been affected by the closing of the ocean, its shallowing (because the ocean contains no old, and consequently no deep, basins), and the barrier posed by the Walvis–Rio Grande Ridge as we backtrack in time?

If we reconstruct the South Atlantic as outlined, we see quite a different

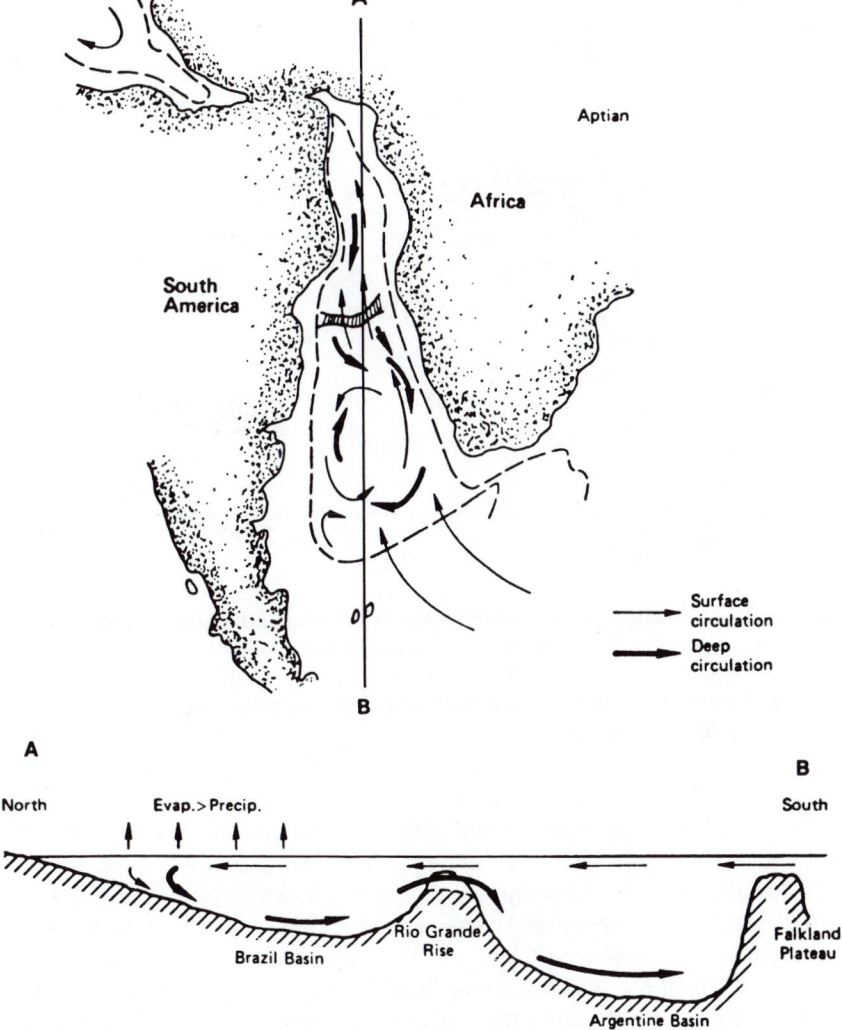

Figure 9-9. In Cretaceous time, the Rio Grande ridge was just below sea level, and restricted bottom water from flowing into the northern South Atlantic Ocean (from Kennett, 1982).

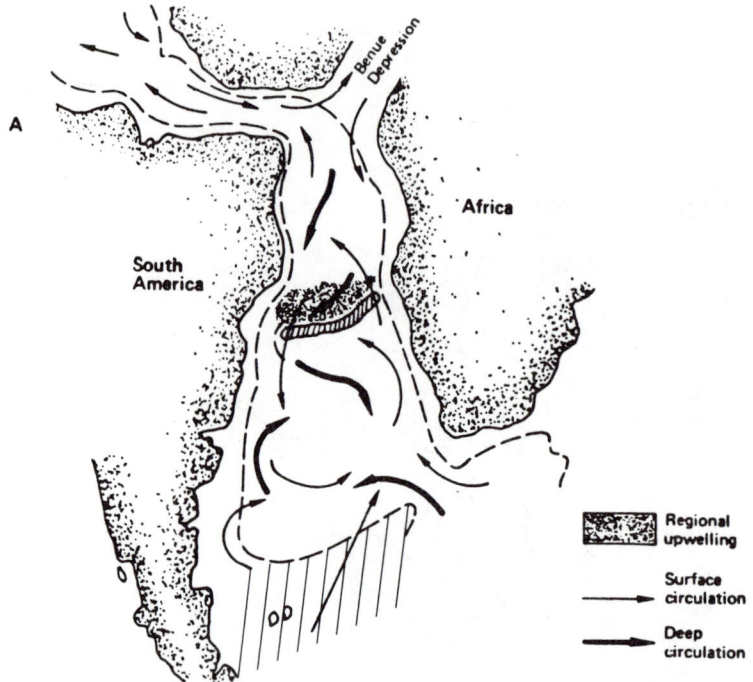

Figure 9-10. As South America moved away from Africa, the South Atlantic was only a small ocean blocked by an almost emergent Rio Grande ridge in late Cretaceous time. The dashed line indicates the extent of shallow continental shelf. The Falkland Plateau (hatched) completely blocked deep water from the South Atlantic at this time (from Kennett, 1982).

ocean during the Cretaceous period (Figure 9-9). The Walvis–Rio Grande Ridge was an effective barrier to the exchange of deep water between the South Atlantic and the Antarctic. To the north, the newly opening Brazil–Nigerian Straits also prevented deep-water exchange with the North Atlantic, particularly in the earliest part of the Cretaceous period (Figure 9-10). The deep waters of the South Atlantic quickly became stagnant. Anoxic conditions prevented the decay of dead organisms as they fell to the bottom of the ocean, and black shales resulted. The surface waters were recharged across the Walvis–Rio Grande Ridge, so abundant life existed in the surface waters and evaporation to form salt deposits was prevented. These hotter and lighter surface waters were density stratified, and therefore could not mix with the deep, oxygen-starved waters. The South Atlantic proto-ocean must have been similar to the present-day Black Sea, except that there were no fishermen to rush after dead fish, only dinosaurs.

Summary

One final example of using chemistry to measure water flow (again using helium concentration ratios) forms an excellent introduction into the next section—the study of the sedimentary column. Recall that heat-flow measurements predict convection on the flanks of ridges (cold-water) as well as at the axis (hot water). The outgassing of primordial helium-3 occurs only at the ridge hot springs where the volcanic source is active. The measurement of the ratio of helium-3 to helium-4 in sediments on the flank of a ridge should show the presence or absence of convection through the sediments and into the ocean water. This does *not* show up as an increase in helium-3, which would be long gone from the flanks, but as an increase of helium-4, which is generated by the decay of uranium and thorium. Fred Sayles and Bill Jenkins (1982) of Woods Hole Oceanographic Institution provide proof of convection through old sediments of the Guatemala Basin on the flank of the East Pacific Rise. An observed curvature of the helium-4 to helium-3 ratio, with decreasing gradient toward the basalt under the sediments, indicates convection or flow of water is occurring through the pore spaces of the sediment. They measure a rate of 20 cm/yr for the velocity of hydrothermal

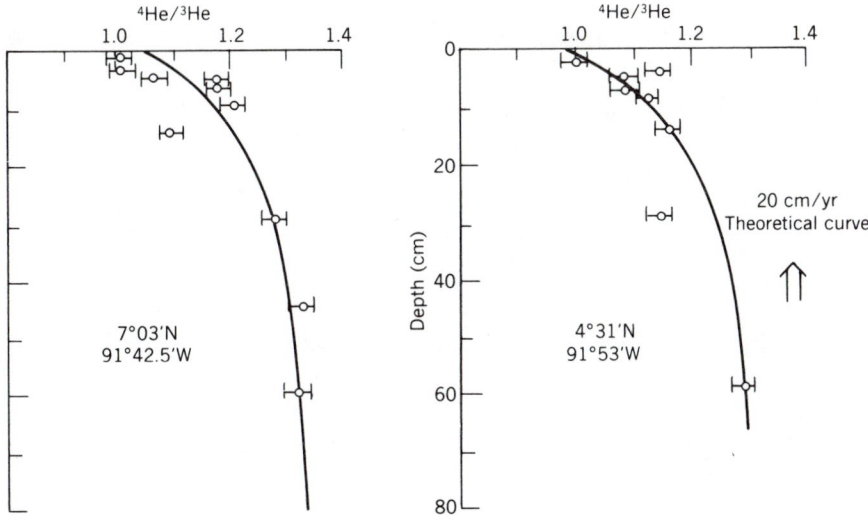

Figure 9-11. Helium-4 to helium-3 ratio in surface sediments of the Guatemala Basin 500 km east of the East Pacific Rise axis. The curvature indicates that convection of hydrothermal fluids is occurring upward from the basalt, through the sediment, and into the ocean bottom water at a rate of approximately 20 cm/yr (Sayles and Jenkins, 1982).

fluid flowing upward from basalt (where helium-4 is picked up), through the porous sediments to the sea floor (where helium-4 is dumped into the water column) (Figure 9-11). Thus the sediment column is an active chemical system like the rock system, and both are inextricably interconnected to the oceans. To understand the physics of the oceans and sea floor, we must understand their chemistry as well.

Further Reading

Craig, H., and Lupton, J. E., 1981, Helium-3 and mantle volatiles in the ocean and the oceanic crust, *in* The Sea, v. 7: New York, Wiley, pp. 391–428.

10

Marine Stratigraphy and Sedimentation

One aim of this book is to understand the continents on which we live, but in order to do so, we must first decipher the ocean floor. First of all, the oceans are a much simpler geological system than the continents. The main reason for this is that the continents are made of buoyant, light rock and therefore are difficult if not impossible to subduct back into the mantle. Although the oceans record only a short period in the Earth's history, the continents record collison after collison of the great plates. The way the continents record the long-ago past of long-gone plates is through the preservation of sedimentary rocks which were once deposited under oceans. These sedimentary rocks, in turn, preserve not only a history of animal and plant life that lived in the oceans of the past, but they also yield records of massive volcanic eruptions and great floods.

Sedimentary rocks are those that are deposited (usually slowly) from above onto the floor of the ocean or other bodies of water. Like a slow but continuous rain, the debris suspended in the ocean slowly settles to the sea floor and over millions of years forms massive layers of rock. These sedimentary rocks then are scraped off the oceanic plates at subduction zones and are plastered onto the continents, or they pile up along the shores of continents until they extend the shoreline out to sea. Either way, the continents end up being composed mostly of sedimentary rock or the metamorphosed remains of sedimentary rock. Because major constituents of the debris are the skeletal remains of animals and plants, these sediments form the single most important record of the geological past of the planet.

The sedimentary record on continents becomes very complex quickly, as rocks scraped off one plate are intermixed with the river-carried remains from erosion of the existing continents, both soon to be buried by the scraped-off sediments from still another plate. In fact, continents are built from the center out because most plate interactions occur along continental margins. Yet the continents are torn down from the top, since erosion is continually trying to break down anything standing above sea level.

In contrast, the oceanic sediments form in a very systematic and simple way, layer-caking themselves onto the flanks of midocean ridges and piling up as cones at the mouths of the great rivers of the Earth (Figure 10-1). There are major gaps in the preserved history of this sedimentary record, however. Unconformities are the boundaries where gaps in the normal time sequence of sedimentary rocks are formed by forces such as erosion and nondeposition. In general, however, the sedimentary record is so complete that these unconformities are extremely useful indicators of anomalous behavior of sea level, of mountain-building, or of other geological forces.

Our method in this chapter, as in the book, is to proceed systematically from the simple to the complex. Therefore, we begin with the first sediments deposited on the newest sea floor at midocean ridges and proceed to those accumulating on ridge flanks as the oceanic plates slowly cool and subside. In subsequent chapters we discuss the continental margins, and see that two types of sedimentary deposition are possible. First, the continent and ocean

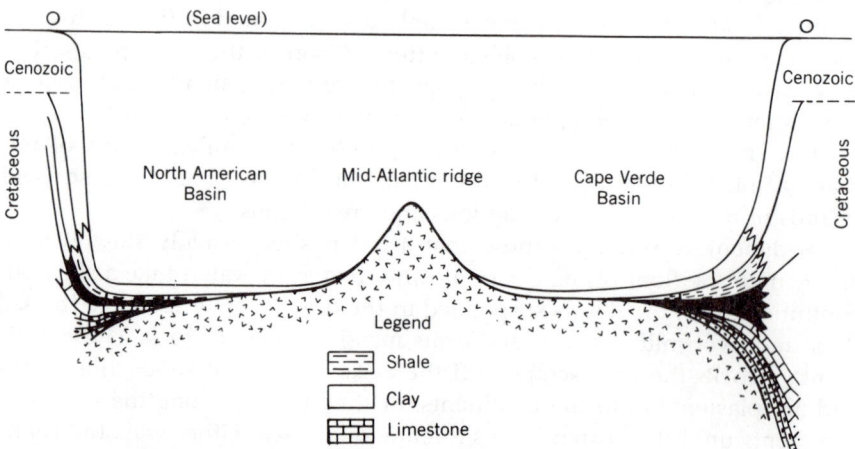

Figure 10-1. Schematic of the lithology of the North American and African sides of the Atlantic. The black is salt marking the opening of the Atlantic with barriers to open circulation (from Kennett, 1982).

collide with the light and fluffy oceanic sediments being scraped off the ocean plate and onto the continental margin. Second, the passive accumulation of sediment occurs in basins at the continental margins that have been newly fragmented by the rifting apart of a continent. We will see that the oceanic domain is one of slow, gentle deposition controlled by chemical composition, physical chemistry, upwelling, and biological activity in the ocean, whereas the continental domain is dominated by more vigorous geological forces such as flooding, collision, accretion, ice, and winds.

These domains represent the three possible plate boundaries (extension, shear, and collision). If, for example, a continental margin is involved in transform fault movement, significant sedimentary accumulations are possible. Such was the case off the shore of California 10 million years ago. These deposits produced thick but areally limited sedimentary basins within which much oil and gas are now being discovered. Santa Barbara and Santa Maria are two such basins. But let us first understand marine sediments deposited on the deep ocean floor before we return to the deposition of deep basins along continental margins and how they relate to oil and gas formation.

Marine Stratigraphy

As the sea floor spreads away from the midocean ridge, the oceanic lithosphere cools and subsides, increasing the depth of water above succeedingly older plate. This subsiding conveyor belt is slowly covered by a blanket of sediment as it ages. Consequently, the first sediment to fall onto the sea floor is also the oldest. The youngest is the last to be deposited and therefore is on top (Figure 10-2). Very simply, this sequencing of sedimentary layering

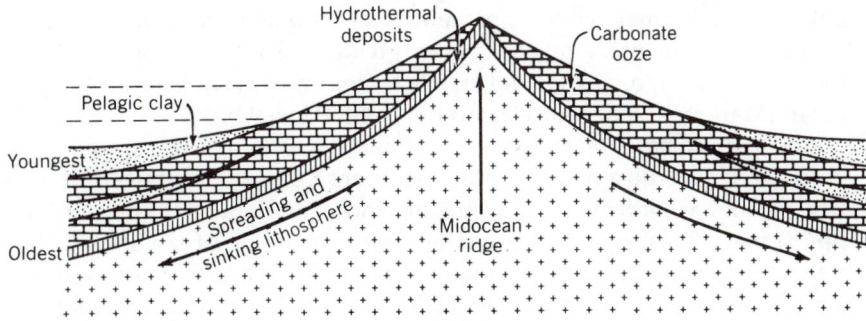

Figure 10-2. Limestones are first laid down near the ridge axis only to be buried later on the flanks by clay deposition as the lithosphere sinks deeper than the CCD (carbonate compensation depth) (dashed line). Variations in the CCD depth with time can cause interfingering of carbonates and clays as shown in the figure (from Kennett, 1982).

is called **stratigraphy.** More properly, the understanding of the history of layers of sedimentary rock deposited on the sea floor is maring stratigraphy. Because of some great upheaval experienced in the past by these layers, the oldest rock may be found at the top of the pile. If we encounter such a disruption, then we ask, how did such a thing happen? The study of the stratigraphic history of the layers may offer clues, but we have to know what to look for.

The sedimentary record is best studied using a drill bit. The *Glomar Challenger* has now drilled over 600 holes through the sedimentary layers above the oceanic crustal basalts. By cutting cores, or round cylinders through the sediments and returning them to the surface for laboratory study the *Challenger* has rewritten our knowledge of how the sediments form on the sea floor. For one thing, no record of sediments older than 160 million years has been found from those 600 cores. This fact, combined with proof that the farther from the ridge axis one drills, the older the sediments found at the sediment–basement rock interface, has confirmed the validity of the plate-tectonic hypothesis. However, the chemical composition of the sediment was also found to vary depending upon the distance from the ridge axis and the depth of the drill's penetration into the sedimentary pile.

The deepest sediments cored by the *Challenger* drill bit were consistently red and rusty looking. Analyses back at the lab showed them to be metalliferous deposits which settled back to the sea floor from the ridge-axis black-and white-smoker hot springs. These hydrothermal deposits vary in thickness away from the axis, and between sea floor of the same age but from different oceans, proving that the output from black smokers not only varies from ocean to ocean but from time to time at the same ridge axis. A recent line of *Challenger* boreholes from 30-million-year-old plate near Tahiti to the ridge axis of the East Pacific Rise off Peru showed that although that spot on the midocean ridge system is spreading at the fastest rate of new plate generation in the world at this time (and presumably, at the fastest rate of black-smoker hydrothermal activity), metalliferous sediment accumulation at the base of the sedimentary pile was even greater 4.5 to 8 million and 21 to 25 million years ago. Black smokers back then must have been truly spectacular! (Margaret Leinen and David Rea, DSDP Leg 92).

Above these basal metalliferous sediments, a form of sandy ooze is usually found. If you rub a handful of the sediment through your fingers, it feels gritty as sand would. But if you put the individual grains under a microscope, a marvelous sight appears. The sand is made up of sea shells! They are the microscopic remains of small animals that live at the surface of the sea and make a calcium carbonate shell, which, though similar to that of a nautilus, is in fact much more ornate and very tiny (Figure 10-3). These microorganisms are **foraminifera,** or forams, and we are exceedingly lucky for their existence. Although they look like a fragile puff of glass fibers when alive (Figure 10-4), they leave behind the most important of all fossil remains on Earth. Far exceeding the dinosaur in importance to either evo-

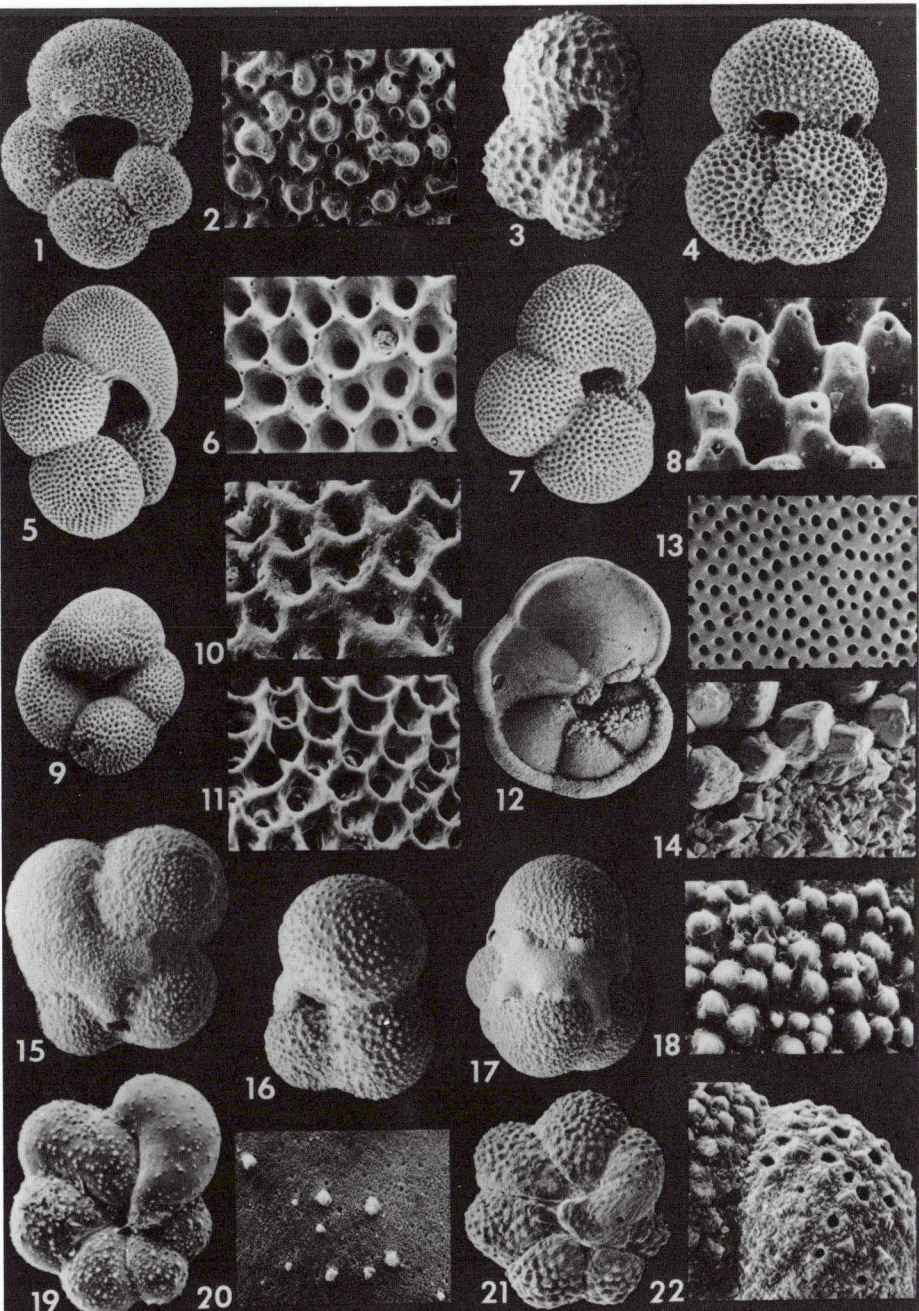

Figure 10-3. Deep-water foraminifera shells photographed by a scanning electron microscope (blow-ups). These shells make up carbonate limestone sediments (Vincent and Berger, 1981).

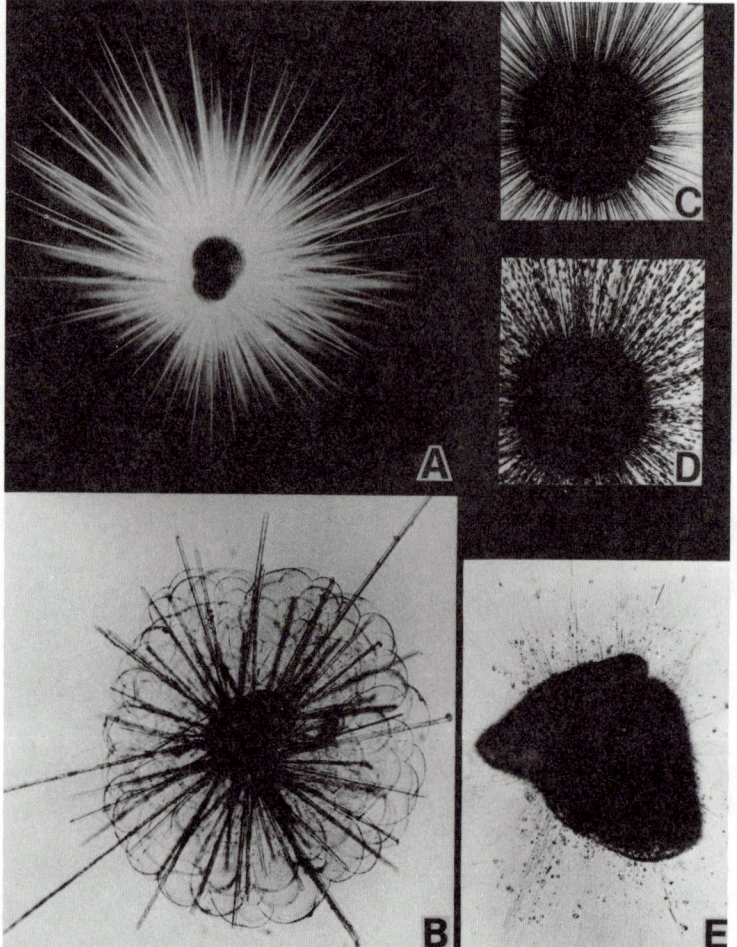

Figure 10-4. Living foraminifera cover the intricate shells with beautiful spires. (Vincent and Berger, 1981).

lutionary theory or to geology, forams and other micro-organism shells form the basis of an extremely detailed age-identification scale. It seems that the shell of the foram has evolved a varied and complex set of chambers and lobes to its shell over the millennia (Figure 10-5). Identification of a particular stage of shell development in forams from a particular sedimentary core

Figure 10-5. Evolution added complexity to the foram shell structure so that if we recover fossil shells as part of marine cores, we can date the sediment from the evolutionary stage of the foram shells (Vincent and Berger, 1981).

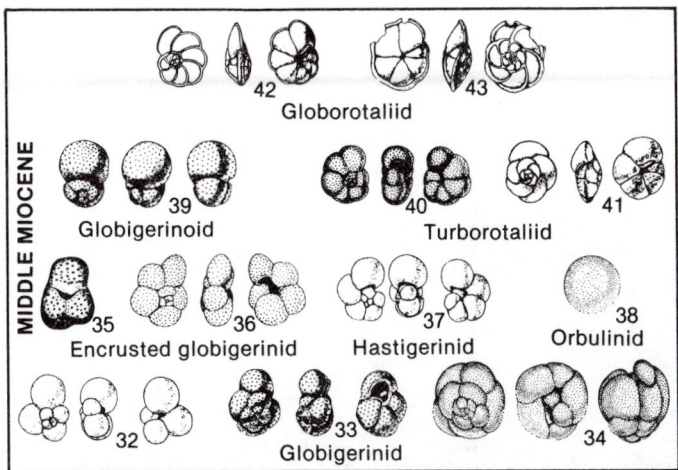

MIDDLE MIOCENE

Globorotaliid 42 43

Globigerinoid 39 Turborotaliid 40 41

Encrusted globigerinid 35 36 Hastigerinid 37 Orbulinid 38

32 Globigerinid 33 34

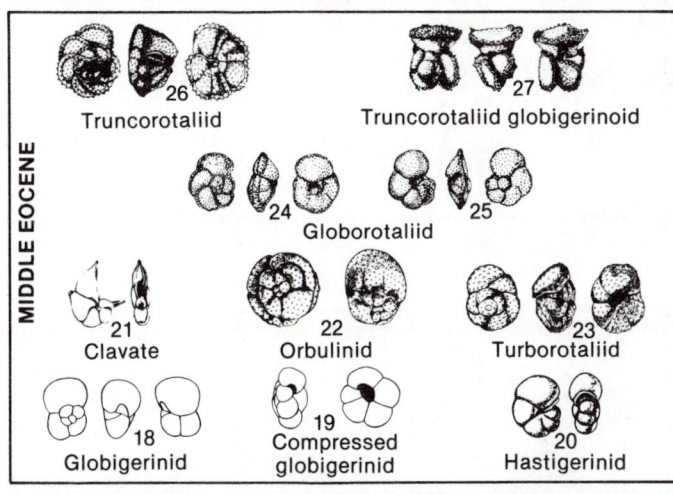

MIDDLE EOCENE

Truncorotaliid 26 Truncorotaliid globigerinoid 27

Globorotaliid 24 25

Clavate 21 Orbulinid 22 Turborotaliid 23

Globigerinid 18 Compressed globigerinid 19 Hastigerinid 20

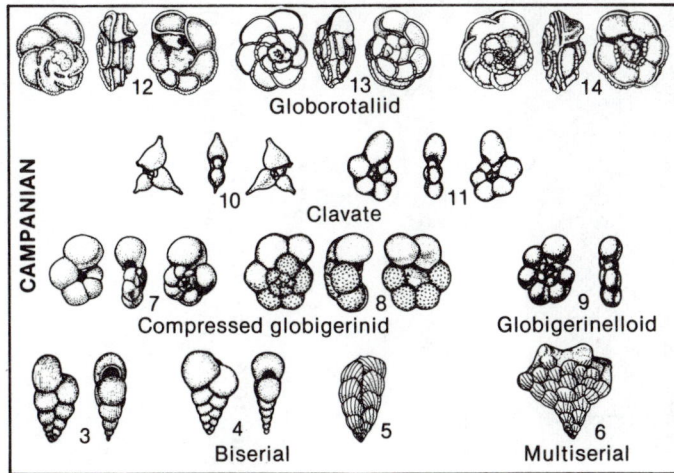

CAMPANIAN

Globorotaliid 12 13 14

Clavate 10 11

Compressed globigerinid 7 8 Globigerinelloid 9

Biserial 3 4 5 Multiserial 6

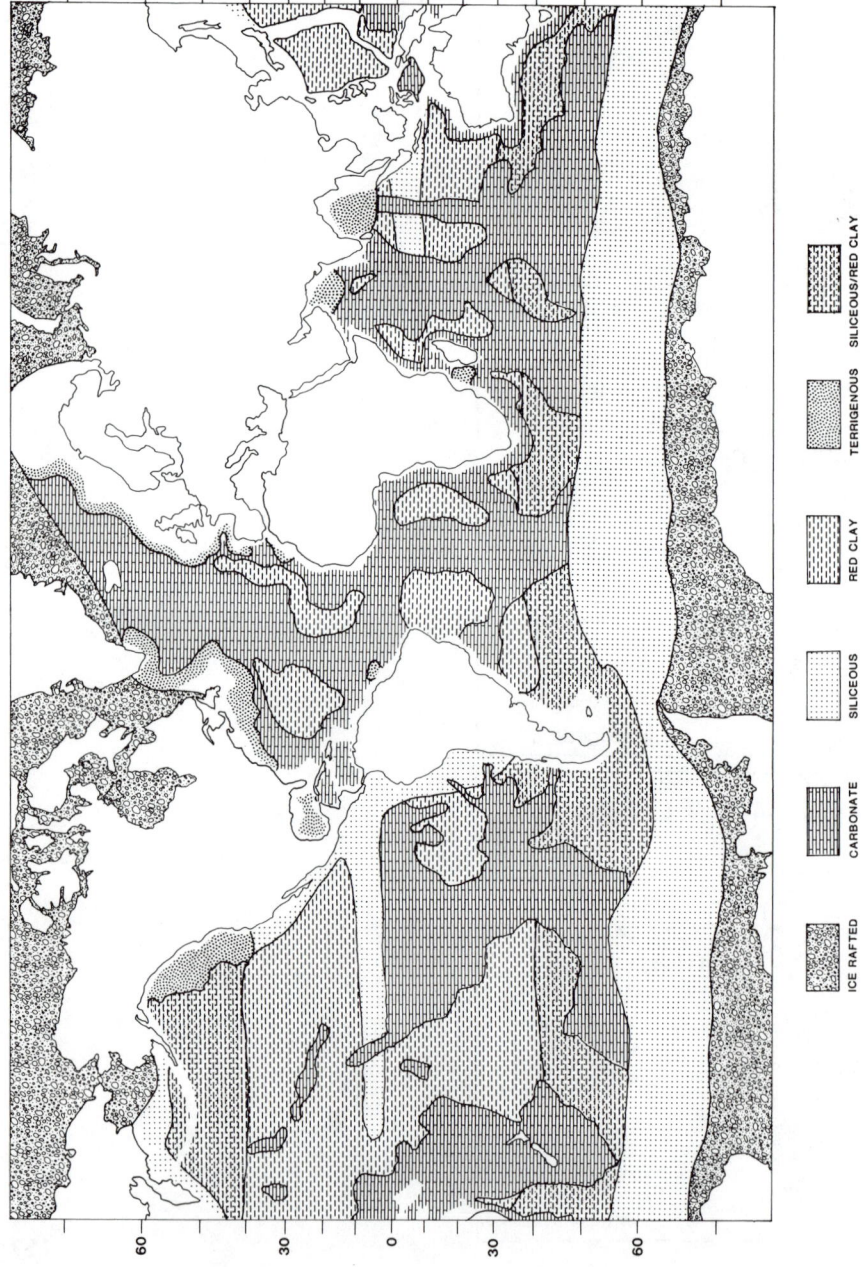

Figure 10-6. The present surface of the ocean floor is covered by a variety of sediment types (Barron and Whitman, 1981).

allows one to date precisely the age of that sediment. We will discuss this in more detail later.

If you examine the latest sediment to fall on the ocean floor worldwide, a curious fact becomes apparent (Figure 10-6): calcium carbonate oozes make up far less than half of all surface sediments. That is not because forams live only in certain climates, for they are found alive all over the oceans. Instead, they dissolve if they fall to levels deeper than what has come to be called the calcium-carbonate-compensation depth, or CCD. This rather curious behavior is thermodynamically controlled; that is, it depends upon the pressure and temperature of the water, which in turn determines the solubility of calcium carbonate. When seawater is oversaturated in calcium carbonate, foram shells settle peacefully to the sea floor and reside there for millions of years. If undersaturated, the seawater is chemically deficient in calcium carbonate and a foram shell will dissolve back into the water column. This happens so quickly that a dead foram will dissolve even before it falls to the sea bottom if it passes through the CCD. An example of similar behavior is sugar in a glass of tea. If the tea is hot, all the sugar will dissolve quickly. If iced, however, it is difficult to force all the sugar to dissolve.

In addition to this chemical control of the dissolution of carbonate shells, other organic factors influence the distribution of sediments in the oceans. The Atlantic sea floor is predominantly carbonate, whereas the Pacific floor has mostly siliceous sediments with little carbonate preserved (Table 10-1). The circulation of ocean waters controls this variation in addition to pressure and temperature changes. The Atlantic is close to new bottom-water supplies from the Arctic and Antarctic oceans. There, ice formation leaves behind very heavy water full of nutrients, oxygen, and carbon dioxide. This heavy water slides into the middle latitudes. Whereas access of bottom water to the Atlantic is relatively unimpeded, its access to the Pacific from the north is blocked by the Aleutian trench. Also, the Pacific is twice as large as the Atlantic. Cold bottom water enters the Atlantic Ocean and makes its way slowly around the globe, with much of it welling up toward the surface in the Pacific. Upwelling of nutrient-rich deep waters promotes biological activity, most of which is dominated by silica-producing organisms. So whereas forams can be found throughout the oceans, silica-producing microorganisms flourish most notably in the zones of upwelling of nutrient-rich bottom water. Ocean currents rather than geochemistry control silica sediment production. The past locations of continents relative to the polar bottom-water currents influenced where carbonate versus silica sediments were deposited in past ocean basins. By studying the distribution of these sediment types, we can decipher the past circulation patterns of the oceans.

For example, consider the variations in the CCD in the past. Even though the CCD varies from ocean basin to basin and has fluctuated by almost 2 km in the past 150 million years (Figure 10-7), the general observation holds that sea floor with calcium carbonate surface sediments is shal-

Table 10-1 Percentage of Pelagic Sediment Coverage in the World Oceans

	Atlantic	Pacific	Indian	Total
Foraminiferal ooze	65	36	54	47
Diatom ooze	7	10	20	12
Radiolarian ooze	—	5	0.5	3
Brown clay	26	49	25	38
Relative size of ocean (%)	23	53	24	100

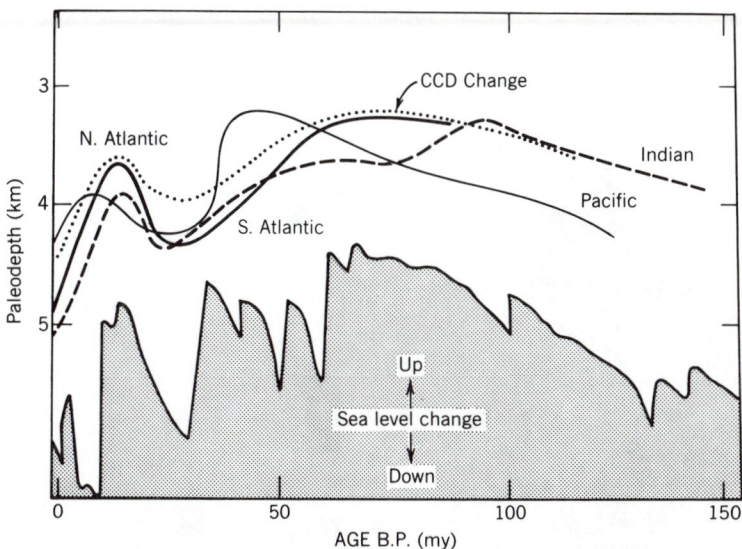

Figure 10-7. Past depths of the CCD plotted versus time in the different oceans *(above).* Note the crude similarity of CCD fluctuations and the variation of the sea-level changes (after Kennett, 1982, and van Andel, 1979).

lower than the CCD, whereas sea floor with no calcium carbonate in the surface sediments is deeper than the CCD. Since the sea-floor depth is controlled by a physical process that is completely independent of the CCD, the geographic distribution of carbonate sediments is controlled only by how young, and therefore, how shallow is the sea floor of an ocean. The Pacific has a greater volume of old, deep sea floor than the Atlantic, and so it has much less carbonate sedimentation.

What the physical and chemical processes are that actually control variations in the CCD are poorly understood at this time. Though the depth to the CCD is clearly related to sea-level changes in some way, global temperature fluctuations, which control polar ice volume and subsequent changes in sea levels, cannot explain 2-km variations in the depth of the CCD. The temperatures at 3 or 4 km in the ocean hardly change during a glacial event on land. Sea level can also rise if sea-floor spreading rates suddenly accelerate, because of the existence of much more young sea floor around the world. This literally raises the bottom of the ocean, producing more shallow seas. Since the volume of the oceans has remained approximately constant, sea level must go up. An indirect result of such rises in sea level would be an invasion of the continental flatlands by a rising ocean. These marine transgressions have been numerous in the past. The result of more shallow seas is a shift of the primary deposition site of carbonates from the deep sea to the shelves. The much more rapid removal of carbonate in fertile and

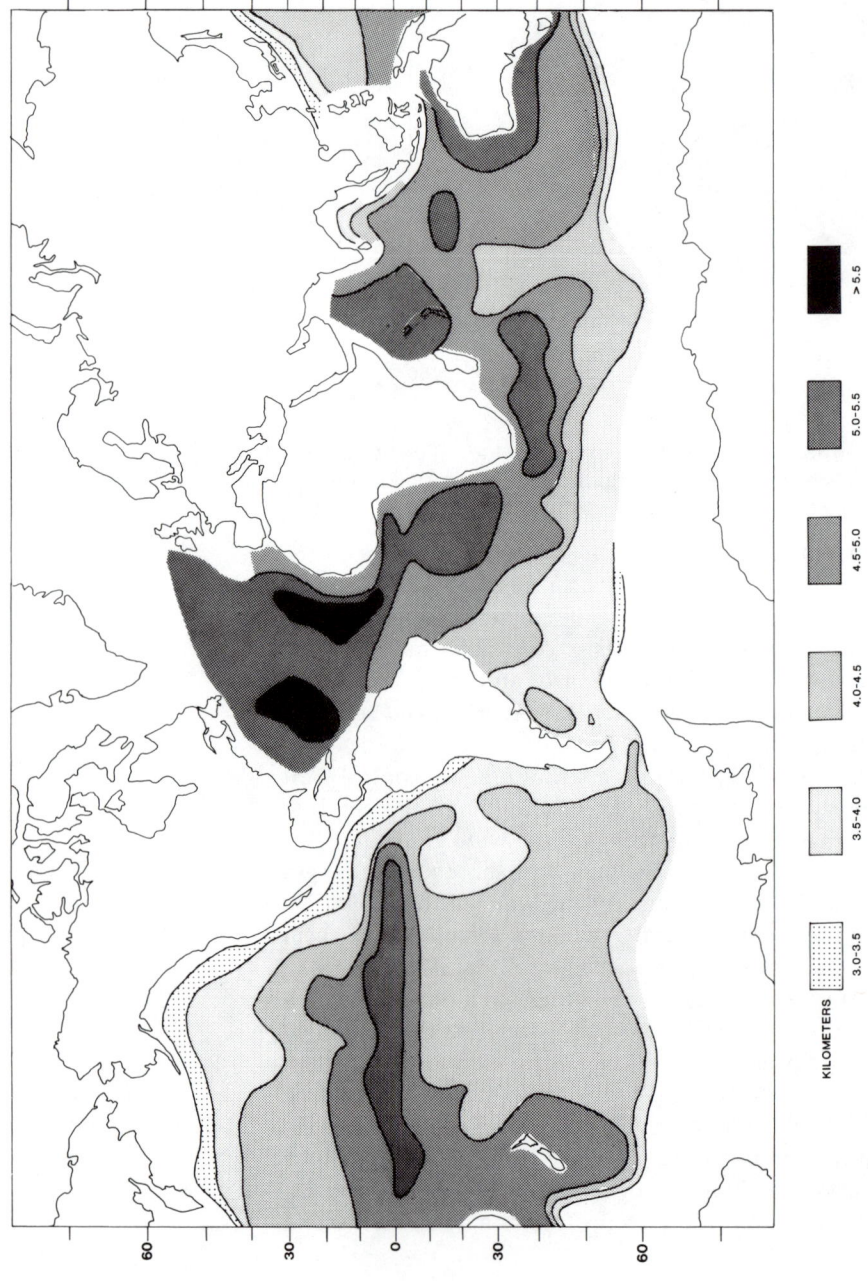

Figure 10-8. Variation in the CCD in the different oceans (from Barron and Whitman, 1981, Berger, 1974).

productive shallow waters would leave the deep sea undersaturated in carbonate. The result would be to dissolve shells much more rapidly and consequently at a shallower depth as the ocean tried to compensate for the tremendous removal rate occurring with the more abundant life of the shallow transgressive seas. When sea-floor spreading slowed down or glaciers grew, sea level dropped and the sea subsided. This marine regression would have

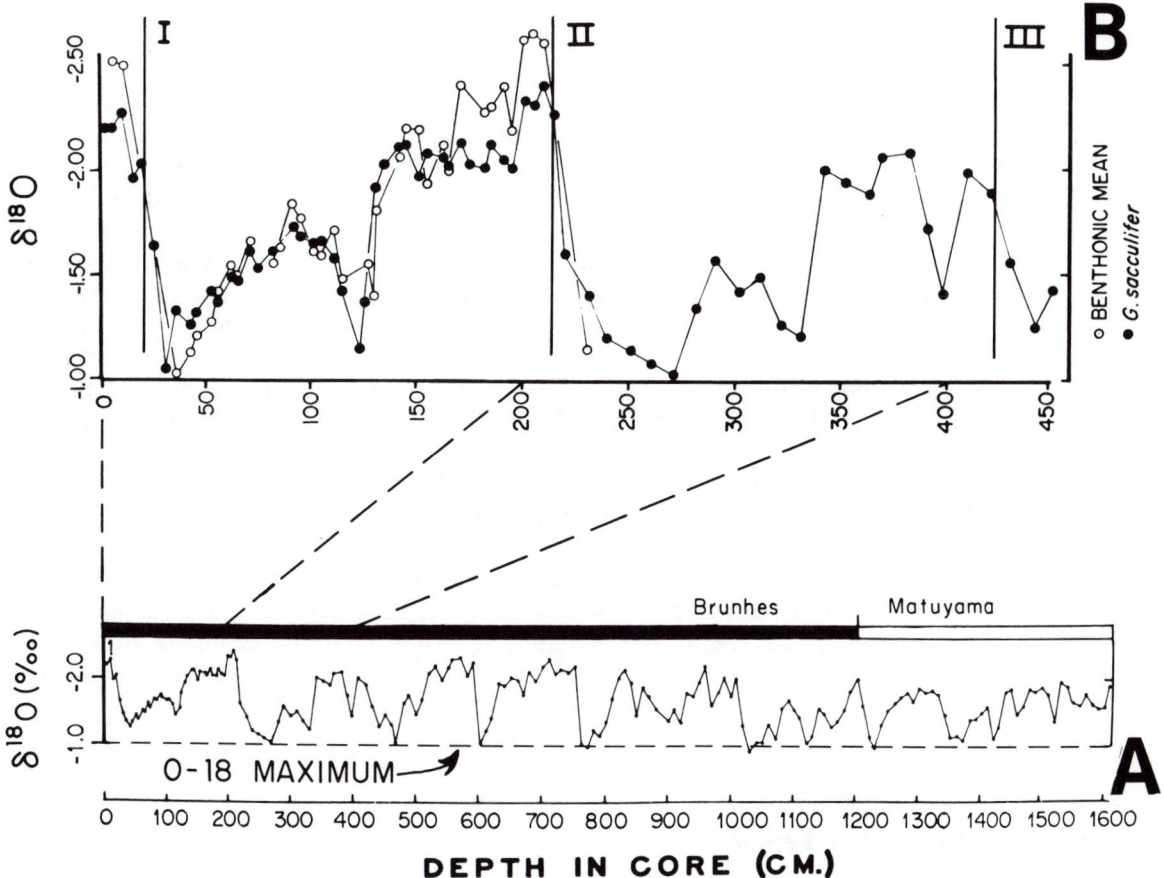

Figure 10-9. Bottom: Oxygen-18 isotope variations versus depth in a sedimentary core from the western equatorial Pacific with troughs representing cold water and peaks, warmer water. Glacials happened during the troughs. Top: A blow-up 0 to 450 cm below the surface. The vertical line I was the last glacial 12,000 years ago. II was the hugh glacial at 127,000 years ago. III was another glacial at 250,000 years ago (from Thompson, 1976, and Kennett, 1982).

the opposite effect. Little carbonate would be removed on the shelves, so the ocean would be saturated and the CCD would become deeper. Such an explanation does not explain basin-to-basin fluctuations such as those shown in Figure 10-8. As mentioned earlier, other influences such as circulation patterns and proximity to cold Antarctic bottom water must also play some role.

If temperature-related phenomena can be extracted from the carbonate sediments, an important geological record of the past climate of the Earth can be determined. One way to do this is to measure the variation of oxygen isotopic ratios in the foram shells. In cold water, the amount of oxygen-18 relative to the standard oxygen-16 is at a maximum, whereas in warmer water there is less oxygen-18. The reason for this is that at cold temperatures, oxygen-18 reactions occur at thermodynamic equilibrium (at maximum efficiency), whereas at higher temperatures, equilibrium is not achieved (less efficient reactions). The last three deglaciations on the Earth show up as rapid drops in oxygen-18 ratios in forams in the deep sea (Figure 10-9). Presumably, the entire ocean became slightly warmer as the ice sheets melted.

However, complications to this simple thermodynamic picture arise from other chemical influences on carbonate dissolution. Nutrient-rich waters also carry abundant phosphates, for example, and these are kinetic inhibitors to carbonate dissolution. Shells from temperature environments that would not ordinarily be preserved are found in sediments deposited under upwelling zones rich in phosphates. In contrast, some organisms make silicic rather than carbonate shells, and these dissolve in shallow rather than in deep water. The silicic-based shells then become the primary constituents of sediments deposited in very deep water, but not on continental shelves.

We begin to see the importance of deep-sea sediments as record-carriers from the Earth's past. There are actually three types of deep-sea sediments: *terrigenous*, or those originating from the land; *authigenic*, or those from metallogenesis and metamorphism on the sea floor; and *biogenic*, or fossil shells from organisms.

Budgets of the Different Sedimentary Types

Before we discuss each sedimentary type, we should consider the relative importance of each. Calcium carbonate covers 50 percent of the present sea floor. Siliceous sediments are second in importance, covering about 30 percent of the present-day ocean floor. Most production of carbonates is among the rapidly circulating ocean waters near the continental margins. The Atlantic Ocean has a much larger percentage of such water than the huge Pacific.

Terrigenous sediments are those originating on land. Proximity to glaciers, deserts, rivers, volcanoes, or mountain belts determines the amount of terrigenous sediment a given ocean basin receives. The Atlantic again receives far more than the Pacific. One reason has to do with trenches. The Pacific basin is surrounded by subduction zones. The deep troughs formed by the trenches prevent much of the terrigenous material from reaching the deep Pacific sea floor. The Atlantic, by contrast, does not have trenches to provide barriers to terrigenous deposition. In general, the Indian Ocean is between the Atlantic and Pacific extremes, lest you think we have forgotten one quarter of the ocean floor in the world.

Biogenic sediments are controlled by nutrient supply, temperature, salinity, oxygen, carbon dioxide content, and the pH or acidity of the surface waters of the ocean. These same factors influence the deep waters as well through their control of the CCD. The physical and chemical oceanographic factors are in turn influenced by the positions of the continents relative to the major climatic belts of the planet. The Sahara Desert, for example, is now a major producer of windblown sedimentation in the central Atlantic. But the Sahara also shows clear scars from massive glaciers that covered it hundreds of millions of years ago when the Sahara was at the South Pole. Then she was a major supplier of terrigenous sedimentation through ice-rafting and other forms of glacier-controlled sedimentation.

The locations of major circulation currents such as the Gulf Stream and the Kuroshio are just as clearly tied to the locations of the continents as are the locations of glaciers to the poles, so biogenic sediments follow drifting continents in a similar manner.

Authigenic sediments are controlled by the locations and extent of black-smoker activity on the ridge axes, by where upwelling zones are found, and by super-slow processes that only produce abundant sediment if all other types are essentially nonexistent. Weathering of basalt produces zeolite sedimentation for, example, but only far away from the more rapid sedimentary processes such as river input, biological productivity, or ice rafting. We then find such sedimentation only in the stagnant centers of vast ocean circulation systems far from land. The Sargasso Sea, in the Bermuda Triangle of the western North Atlantic, is one such place.

Terrigenous Sedimentation

The forces of erosion that constantly scour the surface of the Earth attempt to wear down any protrusion above the lowest point on the surface. The powers of wind and water to accomplish this goal are well known to us all. What is not so well known is that similar forces of undersea currents, driven by gravity's inexorable pull, continue to erode the continental shelves and slopes underwater, forcing the debris from the eroding continents deeper and deeper into the open sea. Consequently, one of the dominant forms of sedimentation in the oceans is from this **terrigenous** deposition. Everything from windblown dust called **loess** to sand and cobbles from floods ends up on the shelf and slope of the continents. How far each particle is carried to sea before it reaches a resting place is largely controlled by its size and weight. The heaviest grains of eroded rock form sands, the lightest form clays and their rock equivalent, shale.

The major rivers all pour debris into the ocean and onto piles called **deltas** or cones for their slightly conical shape (with the point at the river mouth). However, none of these rivers stops at the ocean boundary. They continue hundreds of miles out to sea as subsurface rivers of erosional slurry traveling down **submarine canyons** (Figure 10-10).

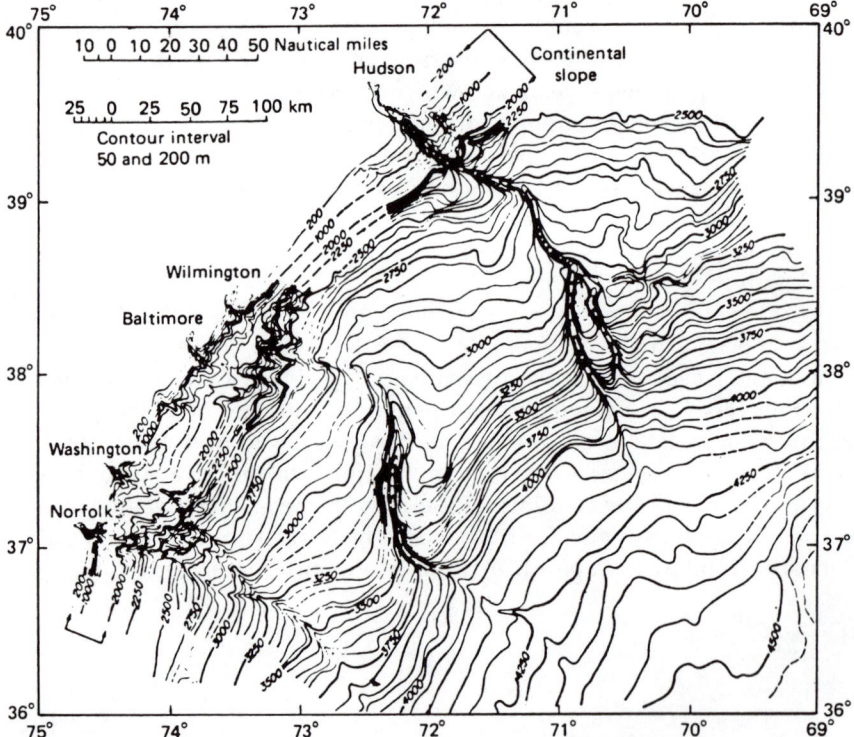

Figure 10-10. Bathymetry shows that the deep canyons offshore the east coast of the United States were cut by rivers when the shelf was exposed. The fall in sea level was caused by the removal of huge volumes of water into glaciers (from Kennett, 1982).

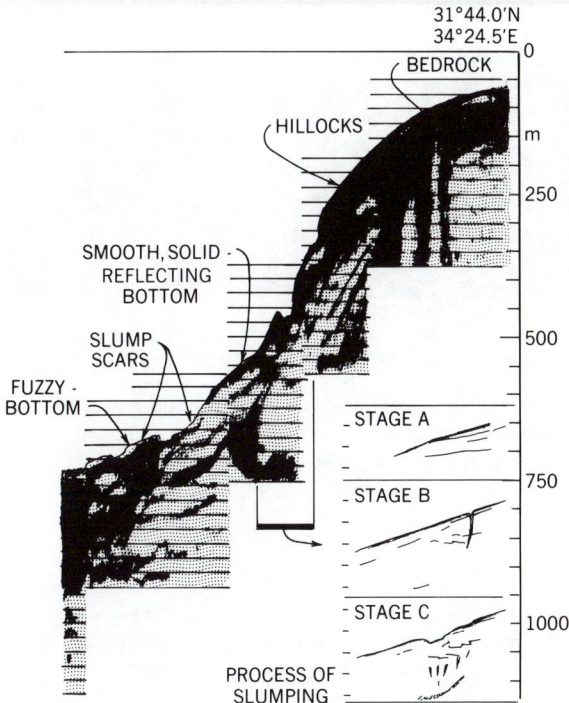

31°44.0'N
34°24.5'E

BEDROCK

HILLOCKS

SMOOTH, SOLID
REFLECTING
BOTTOM

SLUMP
SCARS

FUZZY
BOTTOM

STAGE A

STAGE B

STAGE C

PROCESS OF
SLUMPING

Figure 10-11. Slumps of sediment often slide down the steep slopes of continental margins. Such slumps often set off Tsunamis and send debris thousands of miles across the sea floor (from Kennett, 1982).

Often movements offshore from the shallow, flat **continental shelf** down the steep **continental slope** to the ocean **basin** occur as the underwater equivalent of landslides, called **slumps.** These in turn generate flow that often travels up to 1000 miles over exceedingly gentle slopes as **turbidity** currents. These slurries travel over such gentle slopes because they have virtually no frictional resistance to sliding. They accomplish this because they are composed of up to 90 percent water (Figure 10-11). The deposits from such slides are called **turbidites,** and they can be found over much of the deep sea floor of the world's oceans (Figure 10-12).

It is interesting that the great rivers of the world do not deliver similar sediment compositions or volumes to the ocean. The geology through which they flow is quite different, and consequently, the erosional products carried by each river are unique. A river's sedimentary load is not necessarily a function of how much rainwater it carries either (Figure 10-13). The Rio Grande

DEEP SEA DRILLING PROJECT

96 62/ 33-2   0-38 cm

Figure 10-12. Turbidites are debris from slumps which are liquefied and glide literally thousands of miles over very gentle slopes into the deep-sea basins. Here is a core from the Gulf of Mexico with such a turbidite flow. The layering is characteristic of multiple slumps (from Suzanne O'Connell, Lamont-Doherty Geological Observatory).

in the United States carries as much sediment into the ocean as the Rhine in Europe, even though its annual rainfall runoff is more than 100 times less. Its thunderstorms are more effective eroders of a less-well eroded country-side than the Rhine Valley's gentle rains. Each river is chemically different as well. The Amazon carries very little magnesium, but is plentiful in calcium, potassium, and quartz (Figure 10-13), whereas the Uruguay river carries abundant magnesium, potassium, and quartz but little calcium. This is an obvious reflection of changes in the chemistry of rock eroded within the drainage basin of each river.

Rivers form deltas as their waters reach the ocean and sedimentary deltas are built. Because of the difference in scale between river flooding cycles and geologic time, a cone will be built from the constantly shifting mouth of a river in a manner analogous to the shaking of a loose waterhose. Sediment at any one location within the cone will form into a complex interlayering of sandstone when the river is close by to shale, and the even more gentle deposition from calcium carbonate shells when the river mouth is far off. The latter sediments form limestones with compaction and time.

Remember that the great rivers of today were not necessarily producing any sedimentary accumulation in the past. The Theyes River is the ancestor to the Mississippi. Yet it flowed east to west across North America and deposited its delta into the plains of the central United States 200 million years ago. Before that, the entire center of the country was a shallow sea with no great rivers flowing into it at all. In contrast, the Appalachian Moun-

DEEP SEA DRILLING PROJECT

96 622 18-3 110-140 cm

Figure 10-12. (*Continued*) The turbidite grades into finer and finer sediments. Here, sediment from the Gulf of Mexico exhibits very fine layering (black streaks).

tains once were larger than the Rockies. The higher the land mass, the greater the erosion from the rivers that drain it.

Another form of terrigenous deposition is not important so much for its volume as for the geological record it recalls. Volcanic ash from great eruptions in the long-ago past are recorded in the deep sea as ash beds. These can be dated and chemically traced to their source to provide information about volcanic cycles from millions of years ago. It is not exactly correct to say that the volume of ash flows has been small, just that the preserved record of those eruptions is small. Bioturbation, mixing, and chemical alteration have altered much of the record.

The predominant deep-sea terrigenous sediment, however, is clay. Fully one-third of the ocean floor is covered by this river-derived sediment. It travels the ocean currents in suspension, falling to the sea floor at a much slower rate than organic remains. But in very deep water, all the calcium carbonate shells have dissolved away, and clay is often the only accumulating sediment. There are vast expanses of the western Pacific that are over 100 million years old but that, because of their isolation from any river input from land masses or biologically rich currents, have only a few tens of meters of clay resting above crustal basalts.

Eolian, or wind-carried, sediments are also predominantly clay depositors because in the thousands of miles that the dust must travel, all the heavy sands have long since settled back to land. These deposits are extremely important, again not for their abundance but for their location, since they determine for us the past locations of deserts. Paleoclimate is tightly constrained by the locations of deserts in the past.

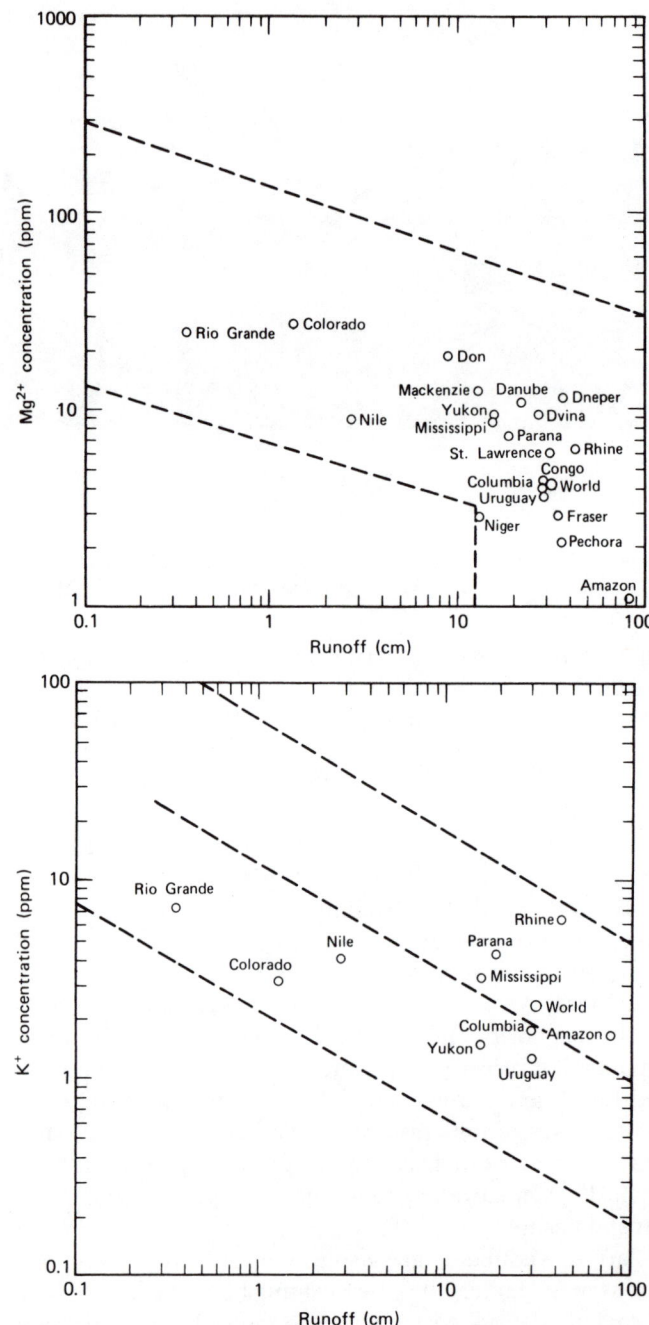

Figure 10-13. Different rivers have different concentrations of magnesium (top, left), calcium (top, right), potassium (bottom, left) and silica (bottom, right) depending upon the chemistry and weatherability of the rock through which the river runs. The Rio Grande carries much more of each than the mighty Amazon (from Holland, 1981).

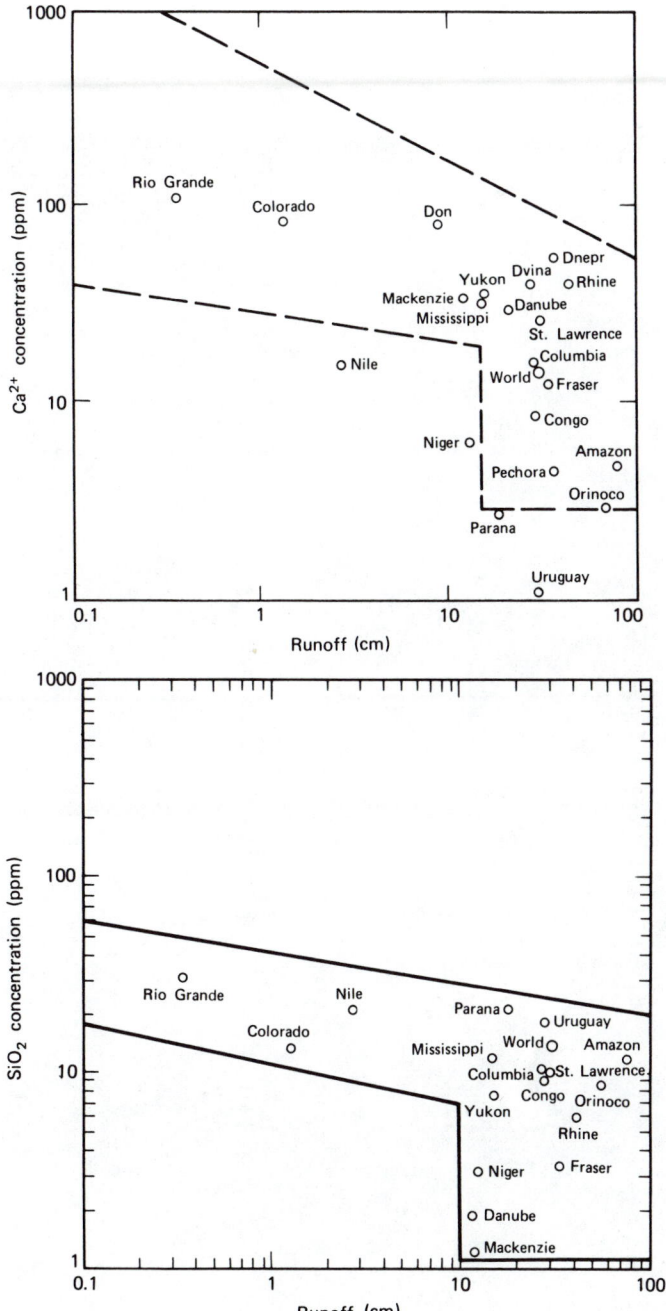

Figure 10-13. (*Continued*)

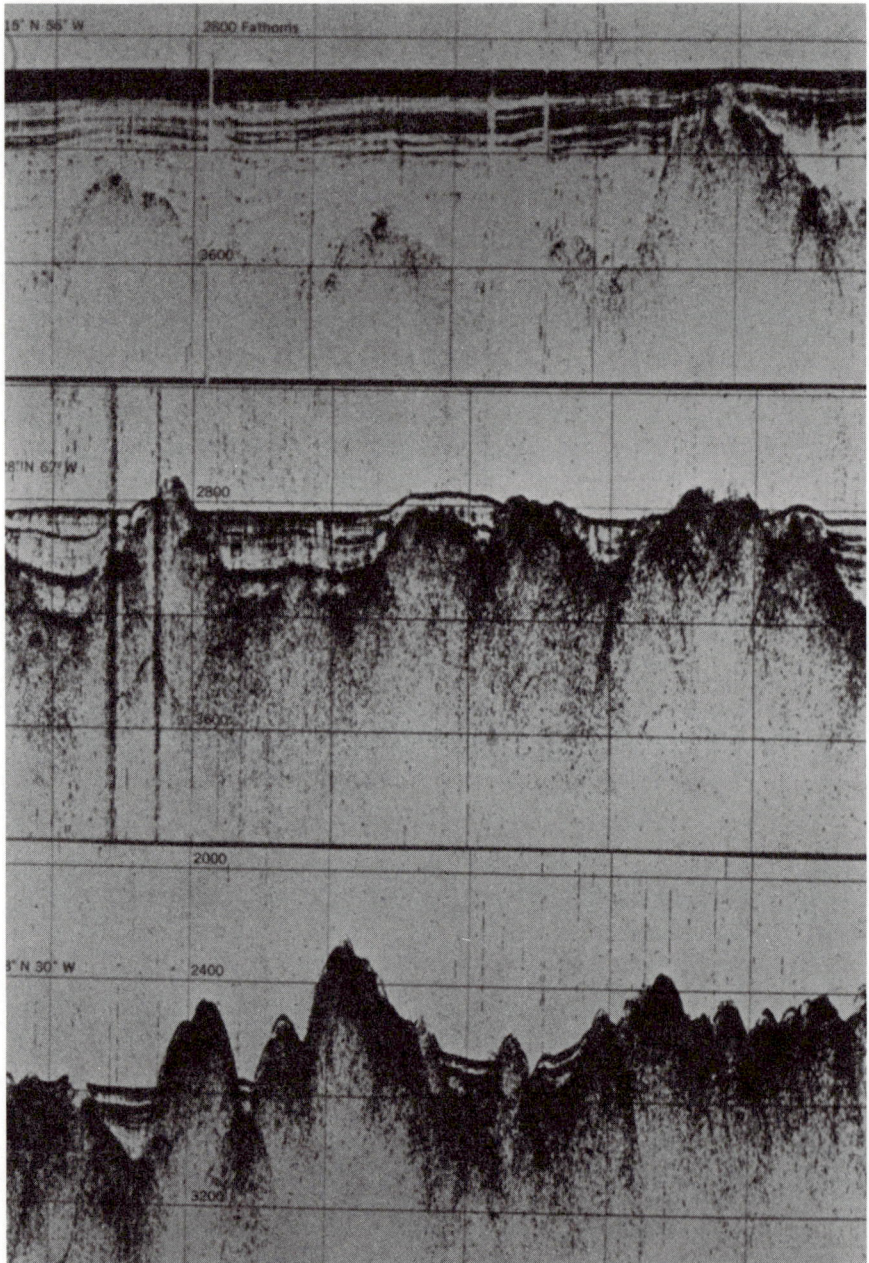

Figure 10-14. Rough basalts of the ridge axis *(bottom)* are progressively covered by sediments *(middle)* as the lithosphere ages until the sediment cover provides a smooth floor to ocean basins *(top)*.

Authigenic Sedimentation

Other clays form not from terrigenous sources but from chemical weathering of the basalts of the oceanic crust (as well as from ashes of volcanic eruptions). These differ from black-smoker metalliferous sediments, which are also authigenic, in that they are from cold-water chemical reactions that occur very slowly over millions of years on the flanks of ridges. Their locations are often controlled by rock outcrops called **scarps.** These fault-controlled cliffs are the last basement topography to be covered by sediment on the flanks of midocean ridges (Figure 10-14). Fractured basalt is many orders of magnitude more permeable to hydrothermal convection than mud, so the sedimentary blanket gradually forms a hydraulic seal to prevent the exchange of convecting fluids between the ocean and the crustal basalts. Before this seal occurs, however, millions of years' worth of weathering and subsequent chemical exchange can occur along these scarps.

Other authigenic sediments such as phosphorites are located under zones of upwelling nutrient-rich waters. The three principal nutrients are phosphorous, silica, and carbon. The sediments deposited under these upwelling waters reflect these chemical predominances.

Another dominant authigenic sedimentation process is manganese formation. This in turn is controlled by the degree of supersaturation of the water column in heavy metals from black-smoker activity. Again you can see the usefulness of the study of sediments for the determination of the past geology of the planet, continents as well as oceans. A manganese layer found on land might indicate that this rock was once deep beneath the ocean floor in the long-ago past.

Biogenic Sedimentation

In addition to forams discussed earlier, other marine biota contribute shells that form significant thicknesses of biogenic sediment. Other calcium carbonate shell formers are nannofossils (Figure 10-15), pteropods, and coccoliths (Figure 10-16). These combine to form carbonate oozes which, when cemented together into rock, form limestone. At least two different depth boundaries for dissolution of carbonate shells can be defined in the ocean. Shallower than the previously discussed CCD (which is the depth below which no carbonate sediment is deposited), the **lysocline** is the depth at which dissolution of carbonates first begins. Sediments deposited on sea floor at depths between the CCD and the lysocline are made up of partially decomposed carbonate shells.

Below the CCD are deposited siliceous oozes that are made from **diatoms** (Figure 10-17), and **radiolaria** (Figure 10-18) (or rads). Diatoms make up about 70 percent of silicic sedimentation with rads making up most of the rest. Both siliceous animals live in the upper 150 m of the water column, preferring deep, open ocean rather than shallow continental shelves.

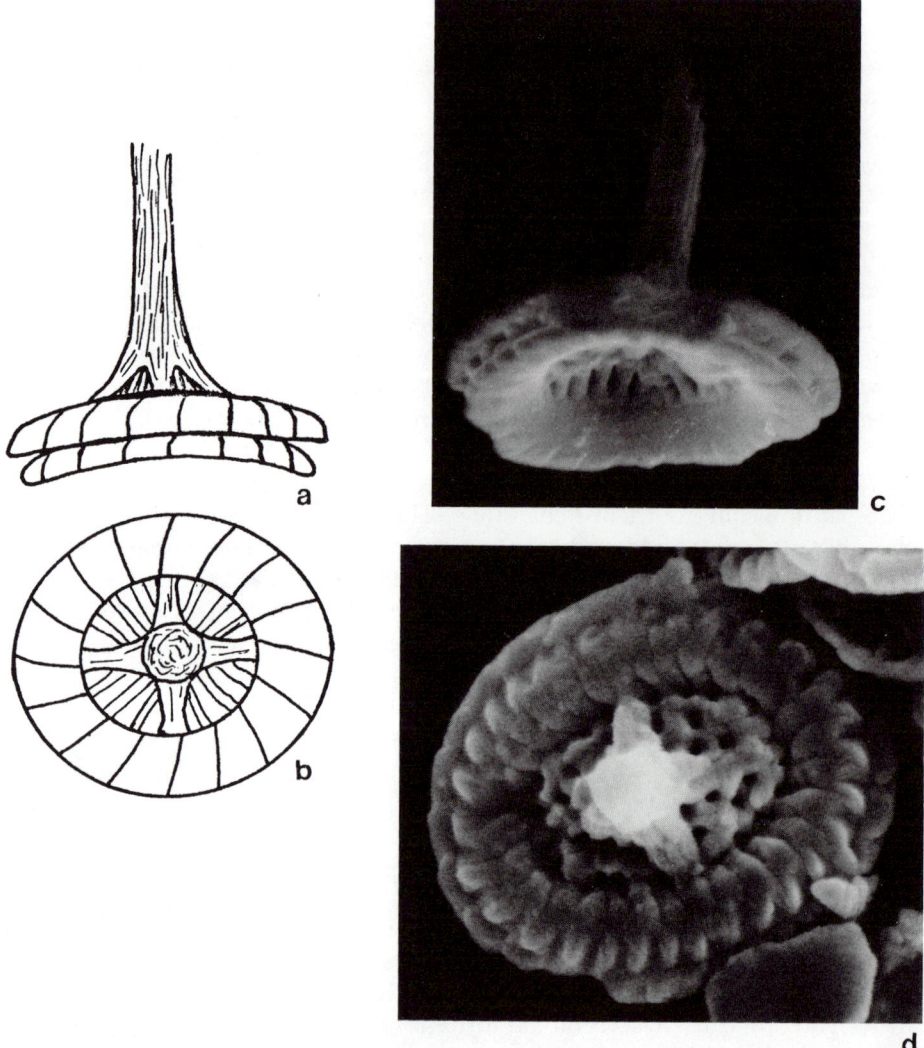

Figure 10-15. Nannofossil shell that forms part of carbonate sediments (Gartner, 1981).

With time and heating, siliceous sediments gradually transform to a rock that was extremely important to the survival of *Homo sapiens* in his early developmental years. **Cherts,** or flintstones, were used for weapons and arrowheads. Because sediments begin at the sea floor and from then on are buried deeper and deeper, they heat up with time. Heat passing out of the plates as they cool and subside conducts through the sedimentary layer

Figure 10-16. Photomicrograph of calcareous microfossil called a coccolith (Gartner, 1981).

which acts as an insulating blanket. The basalt is always hotter than the surface sediment, and the deeper any layer of mud is buried by subsequent sedimentation, the hotter it becomes as it moves up the geothermal gradient between the cold sea floor and the hot basalt. This allows chemical reactions to gradually transform siliceous ooze into chert (Figure 10-19). This thermodynamic process is called **diagenesis.**

Calcareous sediments also undergo diagenesis, and transform from soft mud to hard rock. First chalk, then limestone forms from carbonate ooze. Pressure and temperature make these reactions happen, so the white cliffs of Dover represent chalk sediments that were heated enough to transform ooze to chalk but the rock never became hot enough to transform into limestone.

Paleoenvironment

Age dating by identifying the specific shape-changes in fossils is widely known. For example, these techniques were used by Louis Leakey for tracking the development of fossil man in the Olduvai Gorge in Tanzania. Similar

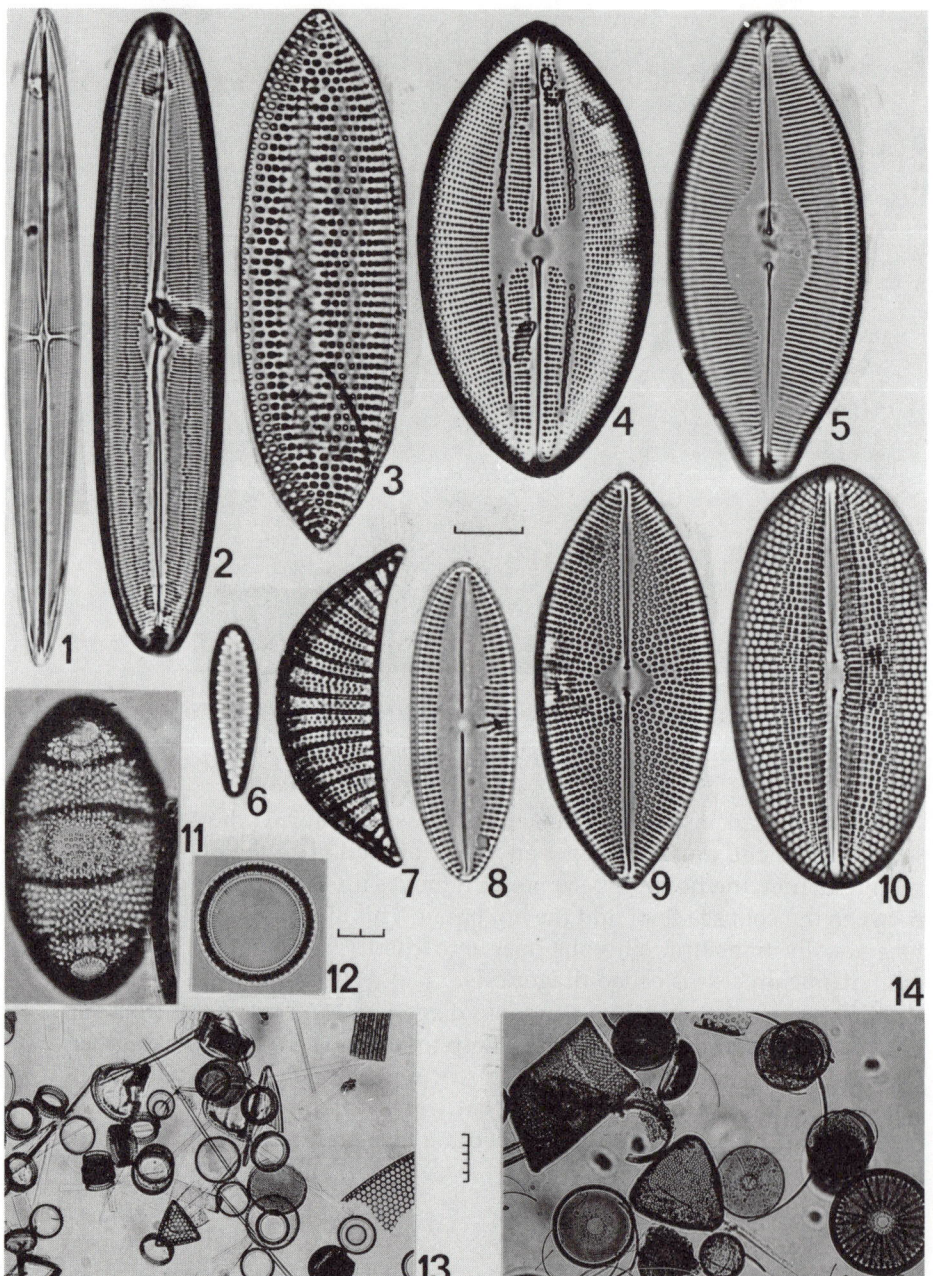

Figure 10-17. Siliceous diatoms are not dissolved below the CCD, so they make up a significant portion of deep-water siliceous sedimentation (from Schrader and Schuette, 1981).

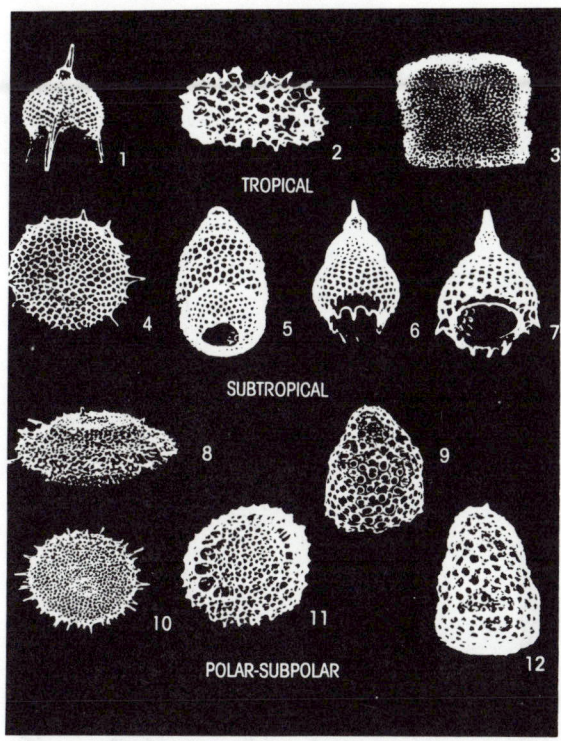

Figure 10-18. Siliceous radiolaria are even more numerous than diatoms in the fossil record. They form an alternative evolutionary sequence to forams for dating siliceous sediments. They also indicate the temperature of the water in which they lived (Kennett, 1982).

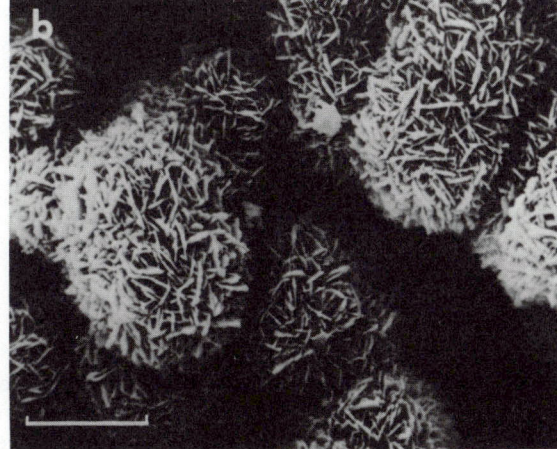

Figure 10-19. Photomicrographs of authogenic siliceous sediments. These are crystals of opal (from Kastner, 1981).

analyses can easily discriminate dates for sedimentary layers in the ocean using the evolutionary changes in the biogenic microfossils. But the changes in form and composition of microfossil shells from past oceans tell far more than just ages. Consider the differences in appearance between tropical and

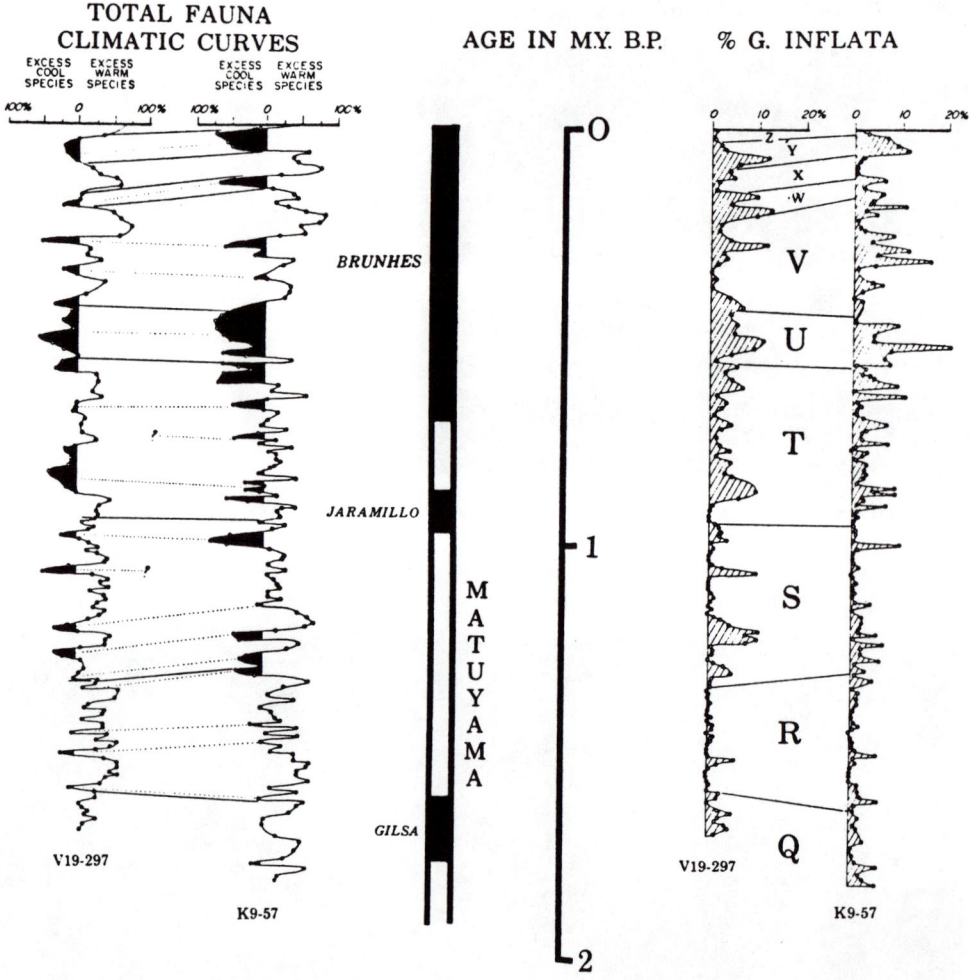

Figure 10-20. Hot and cold water in the oceans of the past can be determined from fossils as well as from oxygen-18 content (*left*). The ratio of warm to cold water species of foraminifera from a core in the South Atlantic (*right*) was correlated with time by dating the foram mud layers by magnetic reversals (*middle*). The total percent of one species (in this case the Globogerina inflata, a cold-water animal) also reflects the same temperature variations that the ratio technique does. Temperature changes of only a few degrees can change the depositional pattern of entire species in any given ocean (from Shackleton and Opdyke, 1973).

polar rads in Figure 10-18. By correlating rads, one can tell the proximity to the pole of that part of the oceanic plate upon which the sediment was deposited. By doing this worldwide, beginning with today's climate and meticulously stepping back into the past, the changes in climate can be reconstructed.

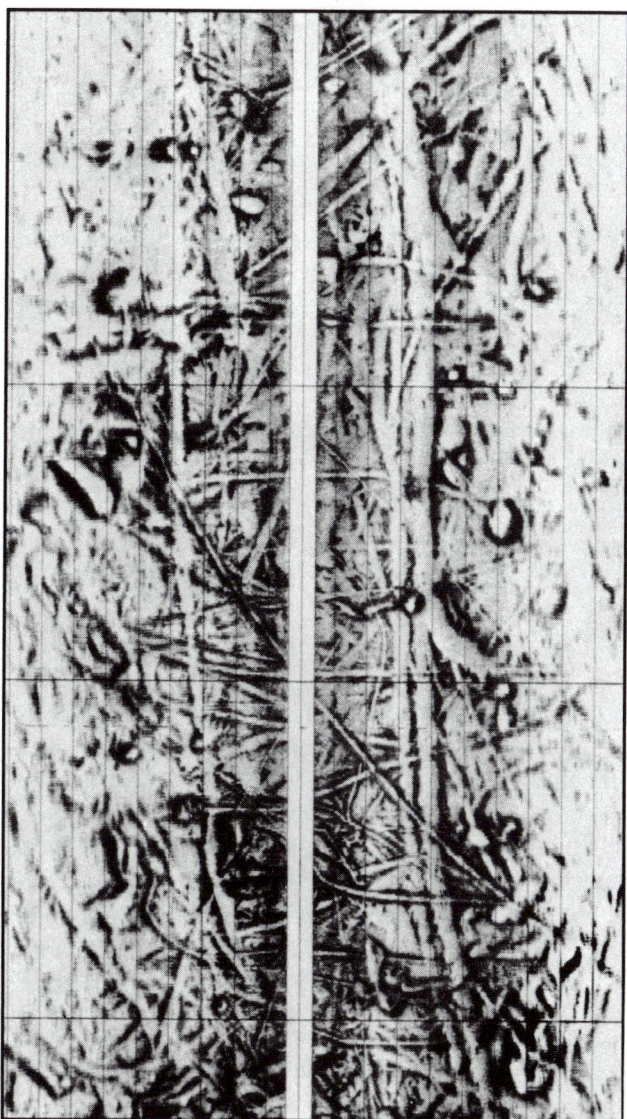

Figure 10-21. Acoustic images of the seafloor of the continental margin off Cape Code appear as if from Mars (from Farr and Ryan, 1982). In this case the deep scars were made by passing icebergs dragging erratically across the sea floor.

By using **paleomagnetic** reversals of the Earth's pole also recorded in the same sediments as an independent check for age progression, the cooling and heating of the last 2 million years have been determined. Both the variations in percent of particular species of forams in the sediment (which are very sensitive to cold) and oxygen isotope measurements on the shells (which we have already seen can be related directly to temperatures of past oceans) have been used to determine the paleoclimate over this interval (Figure 10-20).

Glaciation events have dominated the paleoclimatic history of North America over this period of time. Repeatedly, glaciers charged to the south, only to melt back again. The terrain of most of New England, for example, is dominated by the scraping and gouging of these glaciers of the past. Cape Cod and Long Island are both rubble heaps of rock left behind by the melting of past glaciers. Surprisingly, even the continental shelf offshore is still scraped and gouged from the countless icebergs that drifted to the south after the last glacial event (Figure 10-21). Although a great deal of publicity has been generated by the supposed extraterrestrial appearance of the "landing strips" on the Nazca plain of Peru, these iceberg tracks have produced the most extraterrestrial-like terrain on the Earth. In Figure 10-22, Bill Rudiman (1982) of Lamont traces the path of the last deglaciation of the North American continent. Remember, we are only in an interglacial cycle at the present time. It is likely that the ice will invade the United States again in the next few tens of thousands of years.

The mechanism that causes the cycles relating to glacial maxima and minima is one of the great mysteries of the geological past. What causes extensive glaciers to form, then just as mysteriously melt back into the ocean? The correlation to past climates is obvious. When the globe heats, the glaciers melt, and vice versa. By determining the pattern of cycles in the past heating and cooling events from microfossils (Figure 10-23), a pattern has been discovered that correlates directly to the changes in the orbit of the Earth in the past (Figure 10-24).

Milankovitch (1941) calculated these past orbital perturbations based on precisely known astrophysical parameters controlling the orbit of the Earth. The Earth wobbles on its axis with several different frequencies (Figure 10-23). These wobbles appear to force the climate on the Earth's surface to heat and cool because the amount of solar radiation hitting the Earth's atmosphere changes as the axis wobbles. There is naturally some time lag in the glacial response function. The major shifts of the orbit at 24,000 and 43,000 years ago resulted in glacial–interglacial boundaries at 23,000 and 41,000 years ago, respectively. Figure 10-22 traces the melting of that last glacial invasion from 18,000 years ago until the present.

These wobbles of the Earth's axis have occurred throughout the planet's past, yet glaciers have been much more periodical than that. The movement of the plates must place continents at the poles in order to produce extensive

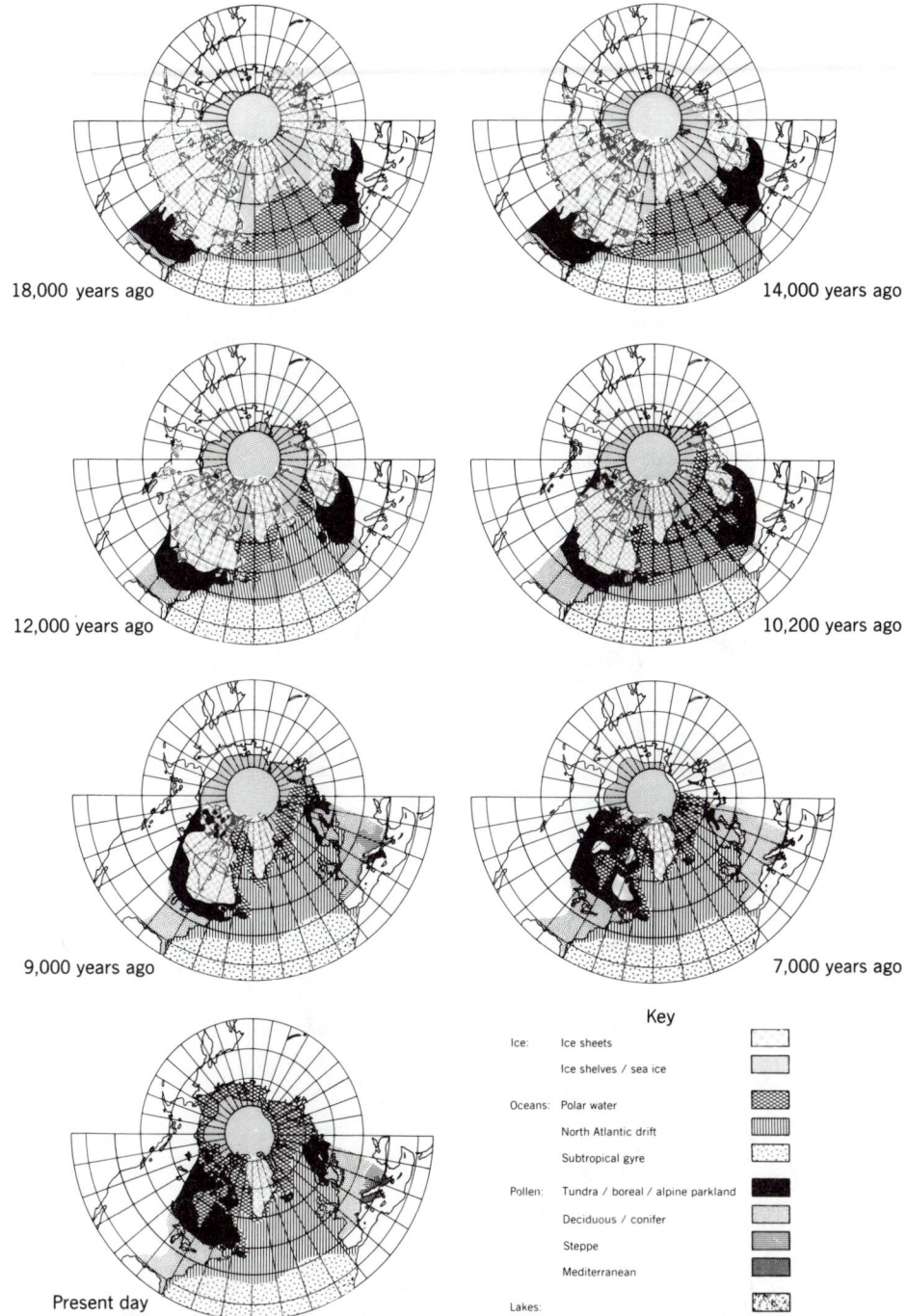

Figure 10-22. Major changes in glaciation over the last 18,000 years (from Ruddiman, 1982).

Key

Ice:	Ice sheets
	Ice shelves / sea ice
Oceans:	Polar water
	North Atlantic drift
	Subtropical gyre
Pollen:	Tundra / boreal / alpine parkland
	Deciduous / conifer
	Steppe
	Mediterranean
Lakes:	

18,000 years ago

14,000 years ago

12,000 years ago

10,200 years ago

9,000 years ago

7,000 years ago

Present day

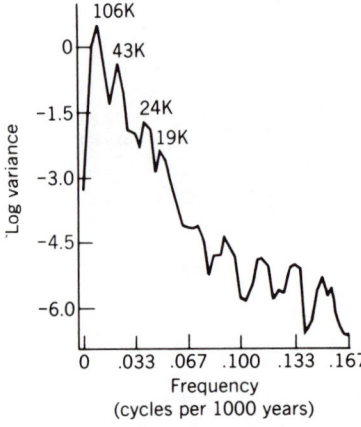

Figure 10-23. A power spectrum of the change in climate from oxygen-18 changes plotted against the frequency of occurrence. Peaks in power at 106,000, 43,000 and 24,000 years mean that glacial events occur with a high likelihood at periods of these three times. That is, every 106,000 years, etc. Thus, glaciers are not random events (from Hays et al., 1976).

Ice-growth orbital configuration

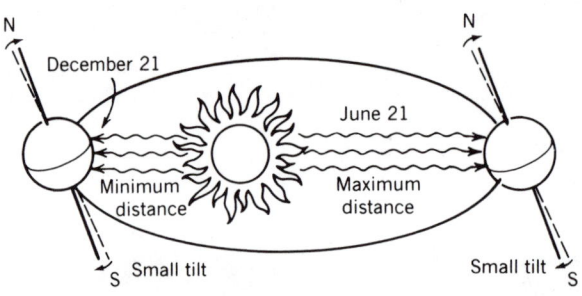

Ice-decay orbital configuration

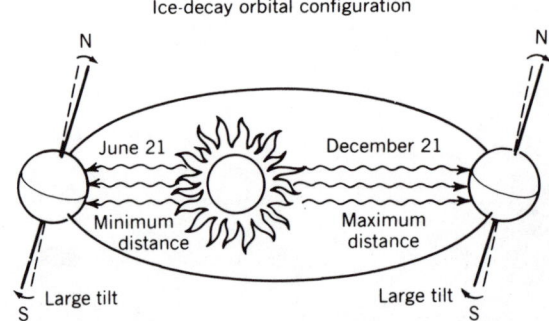

Figure 10-24. The change in orbital configurations of the Earth-Sun alternately grow ice and melt it. Milankovich calculated cyclicity of the Earth's orbital changes which match the periodicity of glaciers over the last few hundred thousand years. There is a delay between changes in the orbit and the onset of glaciation which would be expected (Kennett, 1982, from Ruddiman and McIntyre, 1978)

glaciation. Ocean water does not support extensive ice formation because it cannot become as cold as land. Also important is the ocean circulation pattern around the poles. Open circulation keeps the pole relatively ice-free by delivering warm water to the poles. Another goelogical control to glaciation is the total area of land exposed. If there are few giant mountain ranges being made from collision near the poles, then glaciers do not easily form and expand. So we see both extraterrestrial and geological processes must both be right in order for the planet to be plunged into an ice age.

Extinctions and the Sedimentary Record

One of the most remarkable events to continually reappear in the fossil record in sedimentary rocks is the repeated extinctions of vast numbers of organisms from the surface of the planet. The most robust and plentiful species die off as readily as the tiniest of microorganisms during these extinction events. Dinosaurs are the most famous example; they all died out at the Cretaceous–Tertiary boundary 65 million years ago. But there are other extinctions as well. For example, trilobites dominated the ocean floor prior to their extinction 500 million years ago.

What killed off such prolific organisms? The mechanism for mass extinctions has been a controversial topic of geologic speculation for over 100 years. Disease, overspecialization, dramatic climate changes, magnetic pole reversals, and extraterrestrial interference have all been extensively discussed. Recent dramatic improvements in analytical precison have allowed geochemists to measure the concentrations of rare earth elements to accuracies of one part per billion. The measurement of significant quantities of one of these elements has sent lightning bolts through the community of scientists who study extinctions.

Walter Alvarez and his colleagues at the University of California at Berkeley have been studying one outcropping exposure of the Cretaceous–Tertiary boundary at Gubbio, Italy, for over 10 years. There are no dinosaur fossils at Gubbio. The limestones of Gubbio were deposited in a deep sea that existed 65 million years ago between Europe and Africa. With the subsequent closing of the Mediterranean Sea, the Gubbio limestones were accreted onto Italy.

The exposure of the Cretaceous–Tertiary boundary at Gubbio is particularly well preserved. In 5 cm of rock, the secret to the extinction of the dinosaurs was unlocked (Figure 10-25). Walter's father, Luis Alvarez, a Nobel laureate in nuclear physics also at Berkeley, measured the content of rare earth elements in the Gubbio limestones sampled by Walter. He found not the usual 10 parts per billion of iridium, but 10,000 parts per billion. These high concentrations were found only at the Cretaceous–Tertiary

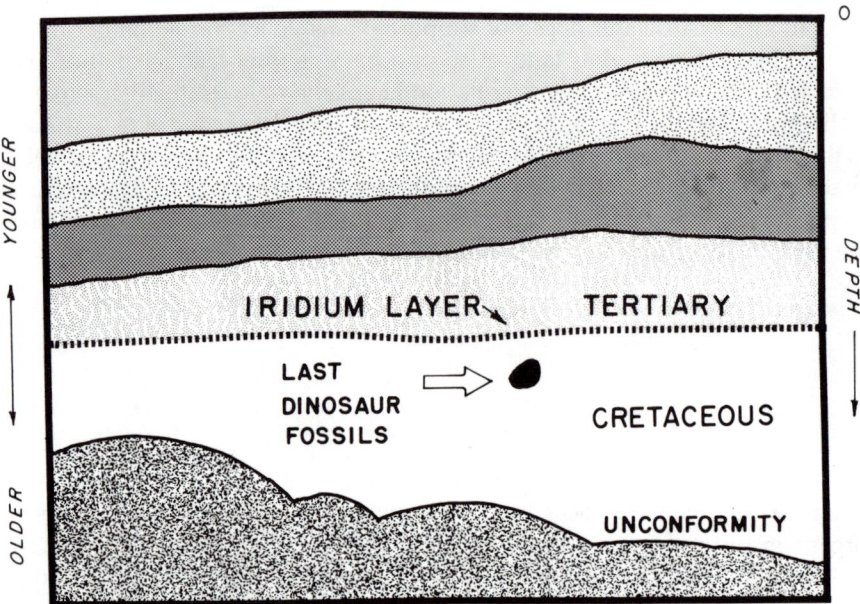

Figure 10-25. The rock strata in Wyoming from which iridium-rich soil was recovered at the Cretaceous–Tertiary boundary. The last dinosaur fossils are found below this iridium layer.

boundary, and neither above nor below it. The only major source for large concentrations of iridium is not the Earth, but space!

Meteorites, asteroids, and comets release iridium during collision with the earth, whereas rocks on the Earth's surface do not have any appreciable concentration. The Alvarezes proposed that a large meteor impacting the earth caused the extinction of the dinosaurs. The meteor (10 km across) would have kicked so much dust into the atmosphere that the climate of the surface would have been changed for tens of years.

This excessive iridium anomaly has since been found in over 60 other locations of Cretaceous–Tertiary boundaries worldwide. For example, near Trinidad, Colorado, the iridium anomaly is accompanied by dramatic changes in plant spores, which tell us how the dinosaurs actually died (Figure 10-26). Fern spores show a dramatic increase, indicating that most other biota were killed off by the same event that produced so much iridium. Ferns can only compete sucessfully for space with other very primitive plants. Throughout geological history, ferns disappear whenever higher forms of plants are abundant. The dinosaurs starved to death.

The extraterrestrial impact theory is not without controversy, however.

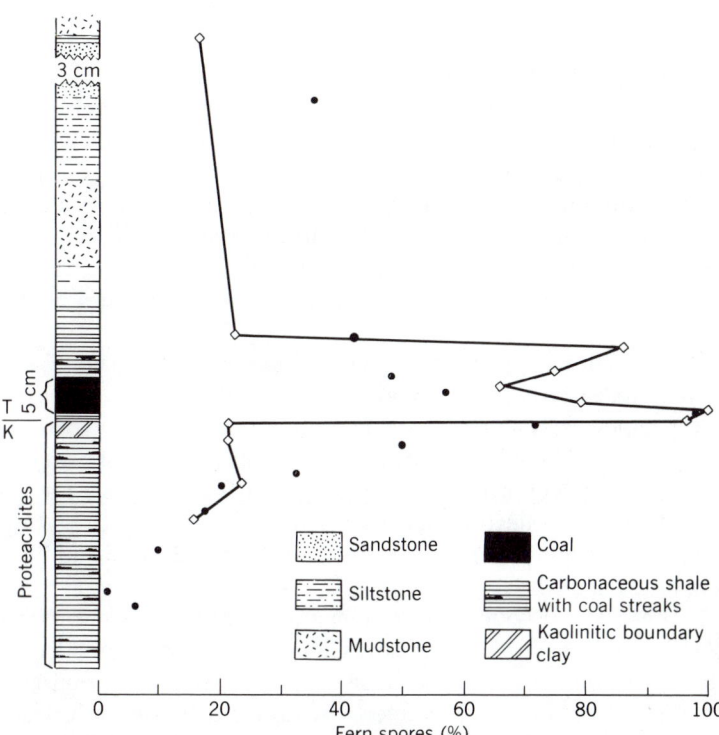

Figure 10-26. The Cretaceous (K)–Tertiary (T) boundary in Trinidad, Colorado, is also rich in iridium (black dots). The solid line (diamonds) shows that fern spores are also enriched in this narrow zone. Fern are very primitive and do not compete successfully with higher plants. This abundance is taken to indicate that the more advanced plants were significantly curtailed at this boundary as well. A type of "nuclear winter" caused the extinction of the dinosaurs and the severe disruption of higher plants. The impact of a large meteorite or the explosion of many huge volcanoes must have filled the atmosphere with iridium-rich dust for thousands of years (from Tschudy, 1984).

United States Geological Survey scientists recently found high iridium contents in gases spewing out of Kilauea volcano on Hawaii. These gases come from deep within the Earth's mantle. Could the extinctions have come from massive volcanic eruptions instead of from a meteorite impact? We know that Mount St. Helens darkened the northwestern sky for days after it erupted. The largest volcanic eruption in recorded history, Krakatoa, in Indonesia, darkened the sky for weeks—in New England.

Whatever the cause of the climate change, it has profound implications for our existence as a species. The biological implications of catastrophic extinctions are to free up niches that were once dominated by one species for exploitation by other species. Thus, mammals inherited the kingdom of the dinosaur. The biological consequences of the iridium anomaly were caused by a disruption of the climate of the entire planet by dust entering the atmosphere and staying for years. Sound familiar? The **nuclear winter** scenario for what might happen after a nuclear war is no far-fetched scientific guess; it has happened repeatedly in the natural evolution of planet Earth. This is not an untested hypothesis. Dust in the atmosphere, whether from meteorite impacts or from volcanic eruptions, has killed more than 50 percent of all living things on the planet not once but several times in the past already.

In fact, mass extinctions appear to be regularly spaced in the past. Every 26 to 30 million years or so, an extinction event can be found in the fossil record, which corresponds to a periodicity in crater impacts on the Earth as well. This has led to an extremely controversial speculation that our Sun has a companion star, called **Nemesis.** It is hypothesized that Nemesis travels through the Oort Cloud (a collection of comets and stellar debris), triggering a shower of comets and meteors that hits the Earth every 26 to 30 million years. No such Nemesis has yet been found by astronomers, however. An alternative hypothesis is that our solar system travels periodically through the galactic plane, itself perturbing the Oort Cloud. It is harder to conceive of a periodicity in volcanic eruptions because they relate to plate–boundary interactions than of some orbital parameter that brings us close to destruction every 26 million years. No periodicity to plate tectonics has yet been found.

Don't fret for our place in nature, however. The last extinction event on earth happened about 13 million years ago. If we do not bring extinction upon ourselves through a nuclear holocaust we have another 13 million years to prepare for the next geological extinction winter.

Summary

Now that we have seen how the sediments form on the passive, gentle flanks of midocean ridges and margins of continents, we must move to the more violent interactions that characterize the collision of two plates, particularly at a more violent form of continental edges. Massive offscraping and underthrusting of oceanic sediments occur at subduction zones. Our plan is to discuss the geology of subduction, with its accompanying volcanic and earthquake activity. Then we will return to the fate of sediments caught up in this major mechanism by which continents are formed. We will then finally be prepared to move directly onto the continents to see how they have formed and rifted apart in the past. We will expand our interest in massive sedimentary accumulations to deep basins and the oil and gas that forms in these basins. Our final topic will be the great unanswered question that has interested us since Wegener's time: What is the driving mechansim of plate tectonics that causes all these remarkable surface processes to occur?

Further Reading

Kennett, J., 1982, Marine Geology, Englewood Cliffs, N.J., Prentice-Hall.

11

Subduction Zones

S urrounding the Pacific Ocean is a line of volcanoes often called the "ring of fire." Coincidentally, most of the violent earthquakes occurring in the Pacific region are also located along this ring of fire. Why is there so much geological activity along the boundaries of the Pacific Ocean? A visual inspection of the distribution of earthquakes around the margins of the Pacific hints at the explanation. Consider Japan and Kamchatka, for example (Figure 11-1, color insert), and the area between Tonga and New Zealand in the South Pacific (Figure 11-2, color insert). In each, red denotes the locations of earthquakes shallower than 200 km, those occurring from 200- to 400-km depth are in green, and those deeper than 400 km are in blue. In both the examples, each color clusters into a separate region or band. Why? In each case the red earthquakes are located closest to the deepest topographic depressions in all the oceans (called trenches), the blue are located the farthest from each trench, and the green are in the middle. If one can visualize the three-dimensional image required by these earthquakes, a plane appears to dip from the sea floor at the trench, deep into the mantle at the blue earthquake clusters. These planes define parts of the Pacific lithospheric plate being subducted back into the mantle at the other end of the plate-tectonic conveyor belt from the midocean ridges.

From the Aleutians in the north to Kamchatka, Japan, and the Marianas on the west to New Guinea, the New Hebrides, and Tonga in the south, and Peru and Chile, Central America, and the Cascades in the East, the Pacific Ocean is rimmed by subduction zones. For some yet unexplained reason, most of the plates surrounding the Pacific are converging on its borders. The result is that Pacific oceanic lithosphere is being overridden by the surround-

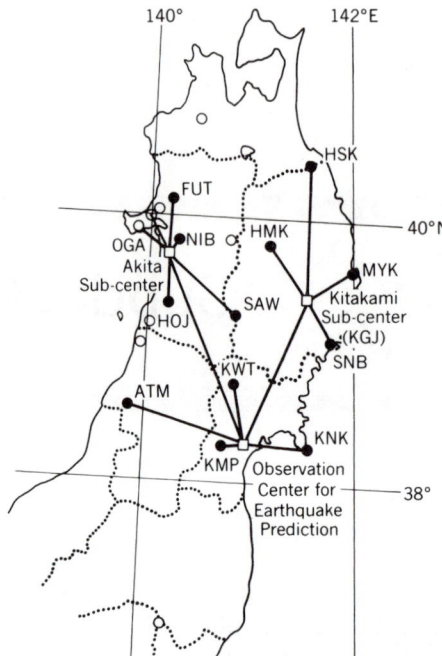

Figure 11-3. Location of observation stations to Tohoku seismic network (open circles show cooperating observation stations with other networks).

ing plates, forcing its edges downward, deep into the mantle. The edges of the oceanic plates are literally hanging beneath Alaska, Japan, the Andes, and western United States. The evidence is incontrovertible that these catastrophic events definitely occur; that is, the underthrusting of oceanic plates back into the mantle from which they ultimately came. We can see the slabs hanging beneath the subduction zones by looking for the earthquakes and volcanoes that occur during this violent underthrusting event.

Why subduction is located where it is and what processes control the physical and chemical dissemination of the lithosphere back into the asthenosphere are less clearly understood. Our interest in this phenomenal event is required, however, because most of the geological violence that affects our daily lives occurs along these subduction zones. Until we understand them better, we stand little chance of controlling the destructive forces of earthquakes and volcanoes, or of ever successfully predicting their fickle outbursts.

The Downgoing Slab Beneath Japan

Perhaps the best-described subduction zone in the world is beneath Japan. Because the Japanese people suffer over 3000 earthquakes per year (mostly

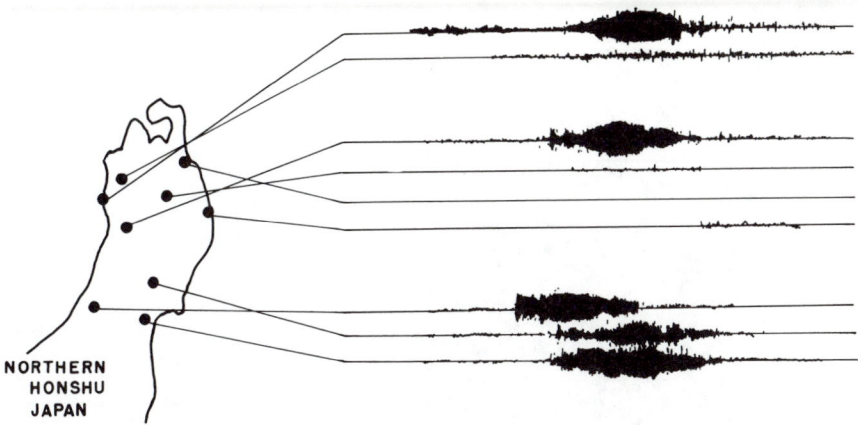

Figure 11-4. On the left are some station locations from Tohoku (Fig 11-3), and on the right the seismograms from one earthquake which is obviously closer to stations on the west coast than to those on the east coast (from Hasegawa, Takagi et al., 1978).

small), the government has funded extensive networks of earthquake sensing stations. Over the years, these seismic stations have recorded and located enough earthquakes to clearly define the Pacific plate that is being underthrust beneath Japan. For example, Tohoku University in Sendai, northern Honshu, operates a network of 14 observatories equipped to detect even the smallest events (Figures 11-3 and 11-4). To appreciate the level of earthquake activity beneath Japan, consider the July 1975 to June 1976 time period (Figures 11-5 and 11-6).

But why are so many earthquakes occurring beneath Japan? The exact location of an earthquake within the earth is called its **hypocenter,** the projection of that point to the surface is called the more familiar **epicenter.** If one plots in cross section across Japan from the Pacific to Asia the hypocenters of all these earthquakes, the cause of the events becomes obvious, (Figure 11-7). Silhouetted by the earthquakes is the Pacific plate hanging at a 45-degree angle from the deep trough just seaward of eastern Japan (called the Japan Trench), toward the west. Several observations about this hanging slab are remarkable. First, there are two planes of earthquake activity, each dipping at a 45-degree angle and parallel to each other. These are the top and bottom, respectively, of the rigid part of the Pacific plate. Remember that earthquakes are caused by breakage of solid rock along a fault. The rigid part of the plate is the only rock capable of supporting faulting. The deeper and hotter plastic part of the lithosphere will creep instead of breaking. We see then the outline of the most solid part of the plate, which must break if forced to bend by a 45-degree angle. It is not so remarkable that the plate is

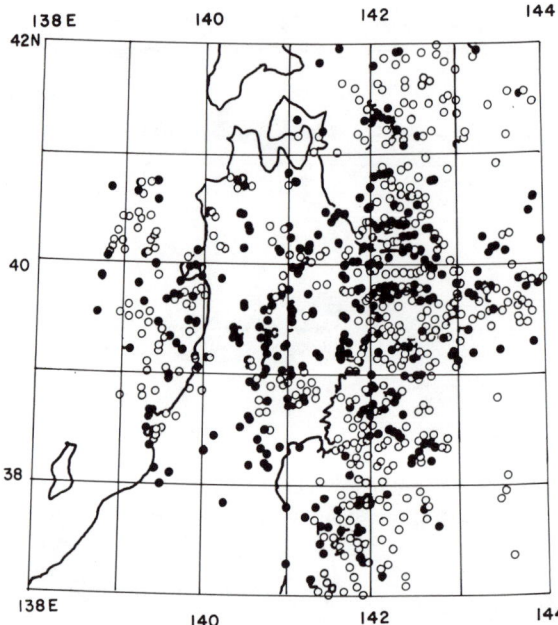

Figure 11-5. Shallow events less than 100 km deep recorded by the Tohoku network during July 1975 to June 1976 (from Takagi, Hasegawa et al., 1978). Black dots are events of magnitude >3.0.

outlined by earthquakes as it is that the plate can be forced to bend at a 45-degree angle!

Next, how do we know which direction the Pacific plate is moving beneath Japan? Is it moving to the west deeper into the mantle or to the east toward the Pacific Ocean? Perhaps it is being pulled out of the mantle from beneath Japan. From the Tohoku network, one is able to discriminate that the earthquakes are occurring along faults parallel to the dipping slab of Pacific plate, and that the fault motion is downward toward the mantle.

Notice that there are two seismic planes, a top and bottom of the rigid part of the plate, and at about 150 km below Japan the two planes appear to merge into one. What is happening here? The cold and solid Pacific plate is being thrust downward into the hot and partially molten asthenosphere. The cold plate must warm up just as the hot mantle must cool down. As the plate heats up, less and less of it is left rigid as more and more becomes plastic from the increased heat. The brittle earthquake zone therefore moves from the heated surface of the plate inward into the cooler center of the plate.

If we change our perspective and dive to the tip of the subducting slab

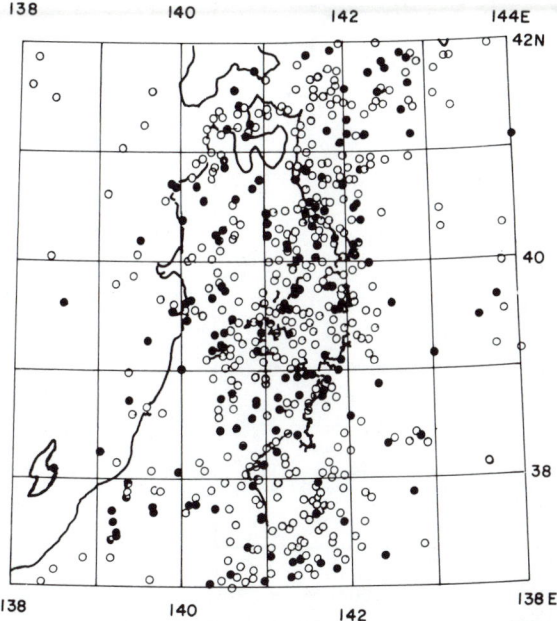

Figure 11-6. The earthquakes that occurred deeper than 100 km between July 1975 to June 1976 (from Takagi, Hasegawa et al., 1978). Note the shift from east of Japan (Fig 11-5) to under Japan (Fig 11-6) as we move from shallow to deep earthquakes.

then look back upward toward the surface (Figure 11-8), we see that the earthquake activity outlines a boundary with quite different seismicity on either side of the trench axis. Landward, there is a gap, called the **aseismic front,** where no earthquakes at all occur. Then still farther landward, the earthquakes appear to cluster into clumps. If one were to examine the geology of Japan, one would find that volcanoes are centered above these clumps. Seaward, the activity is much more diffuse.

Looking straight up the plane of subduction (Figure 11-9), we can clearly see the separation between the upper and lower planes. Although all the material between these planes is solid, only the edges appear to crack when the plate is bent.

The exact location where the plate leaves the surface and plunges deep into the mantle is always marked by the deepest depths of the oceans. These trenches reach 10 km below sea level and are a characteristic of subduction zones (Figure 11-10). The deep depths are caused by the bending of the subducting plate. The trenches mark the exact line along which the two colliding

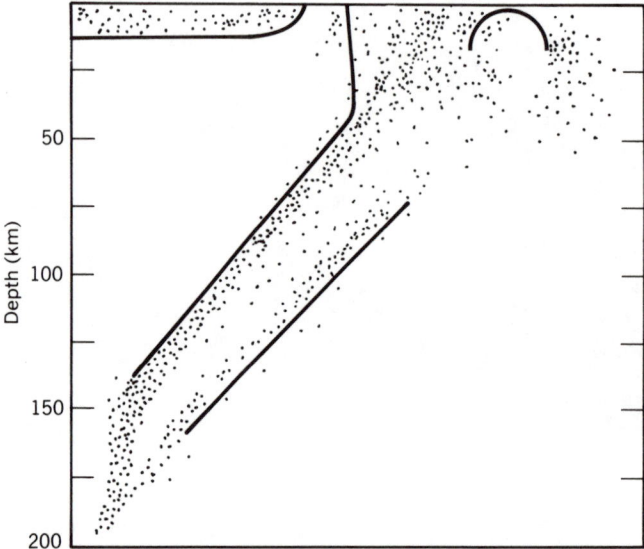

Figure 11-7. Three-dimensional view of earthquakes recorded below Honshu by the Tohoku network. This cross-sectional view is from the south. The island earthquakes are at the surface, the double plane of activity on the Pacific plate being subducted beneath Japan can be seen angled downward at 45 degrees, and the seaward bulge where the Pacific plate bends downward has earthquake activity surrounding a bending area parallel to the trench which is aseismic (half circle). (From Hasegawa, Takagi, 1978).

plates are in contact. The only thing that prevents the trenches from being even deeper is that soft sediment from the subducting plate is scraped off by the overriding plate and accreted or plastered onto the trench wall. Thus, trenches where subduction of plates upon which thick sedimentary piles reside are much shallower than those where the subducting plate has little sediment at all on the plate. That is, the deep trough in the sea floor, which is called the trench, is actually deeper if not filled with sediments scraped off from the subducting plate. The latter accounts for the deepest trench located in the Marianas, where the sediment-starved Pacific plate is being sub-ducted. The former phenomenon can be seen in seismic reflection profiles across subduction zones where large volumes of sediment are being scraped off. One can easily see that the mud is being removed from the subducting plate as if by a knife blade (Figure 11-11).

The slabs themselves often have ripples in them, caused by their uneven subduction into the mantle (Figure 11-12). Think of a towel laid carefully onto the surface of a water-filled tub. If you then touch ever so gently one

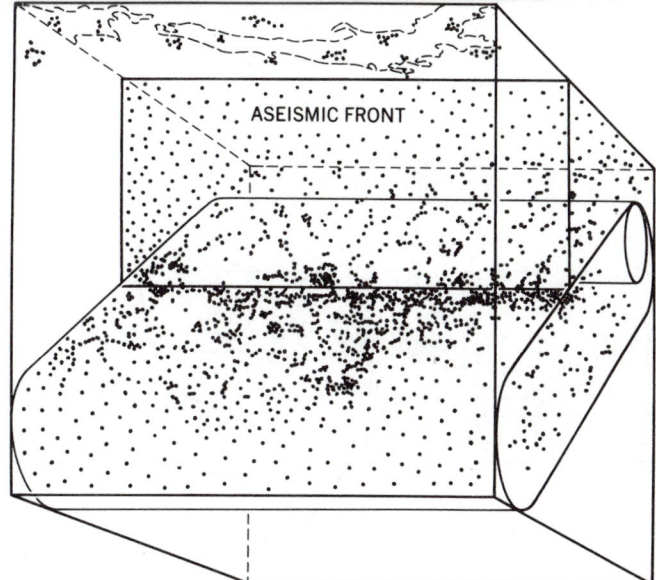

ASEISMIC FRONT

Figure 11-8. Three-dimensional view upward along the 45-degree planes of seismic activity seen in Figure 11-5 and 11-6.

corner of the towel, it will subduct into the water. Why? Because it is heavier than the water. The fact that it floats at all is because of the surface tension of the water. If that is disturbed, the towel plunges to where its weight dictates it should reside—at the bottom of the tub. The plates form hot at the ridge axis. When they are hot, they are lighter than the mantle. But as they age, they cool and become heavier than the mantle. Collisions with other plates allow the plate with the lesser buoyancy to sink back into the mantle. The heavier ocean lithospheres will sink back into the mantle, but their paths to the bottom will often contain ripples just as with the towel.

In fact, ripples can be seen not only in the subducting plate, but also on the overriding plate, in this case, on Japan itself (Figure 11-13). These ripples are caused by collision with the Pacific plate at the trench, and they propagate across the surface of Japan. But don't put off your Japanese holiday yet, because the height of the ripples totals only a few centimeters. They must be detected by sensitive leveling meters, which are like supersensitive altimeters. These instruments are also operated by Tohoku University, giving that university perhaps the best and most sensitive earth-motion detection network in the world.

Looking in detail at the double-planed subduction zone beneath Japan,

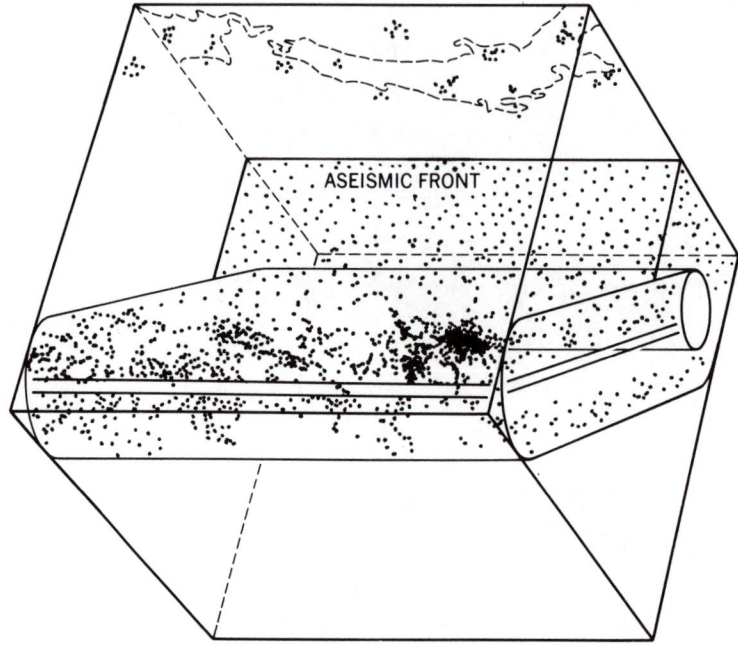

Figure 11-9. Slightly different three-dimensional view, this time directly up the aseismic front which is between the subducting slab of the Pacific plate and Honshu. The big concentration of earthquakes at the right are not all together but are distributed through 150 km of length within the Pacific plate. Note the double line of no earthquakes between the upper and lower planes of the subducting Pacific plate.

we see that each plane is absolutely straight (Figure 11-14). The lower plane does not begin, however, until a depth of about 75 km, and from there to over 100 km only small earthquakes of magnitude less than 3.0 are found. Additionally, small events predominate in the upper plane in the 75- to 100-km region as well. We will discuss this later.

A profile of only those events larger than magnitude 3.0 (Figure 11-15) shows a seaward bulge beginning at greater than 50-km depth in the Pacific and becoming shallower toward the trench. This seismic bulge does not correspond to the topographic bulge seen seaward of the trench in Figure 11-10 but rather, is 100 to 300 km farther from Japan. The topographic bulge is the surface manifestation of bending, but the earthquake bulge is showing us where within the plate the bending forces result in breakage of rock. It is clear that this energy is released considerably farther from the collision boundary than the overall surface deformation would indicate.

The shoaling of the earthquake bulge as one approaches the trench produces an aseismic zone running parallel to, but considerably landward of, the topographic trench. The exact center of the aseismic zone is 10 km below

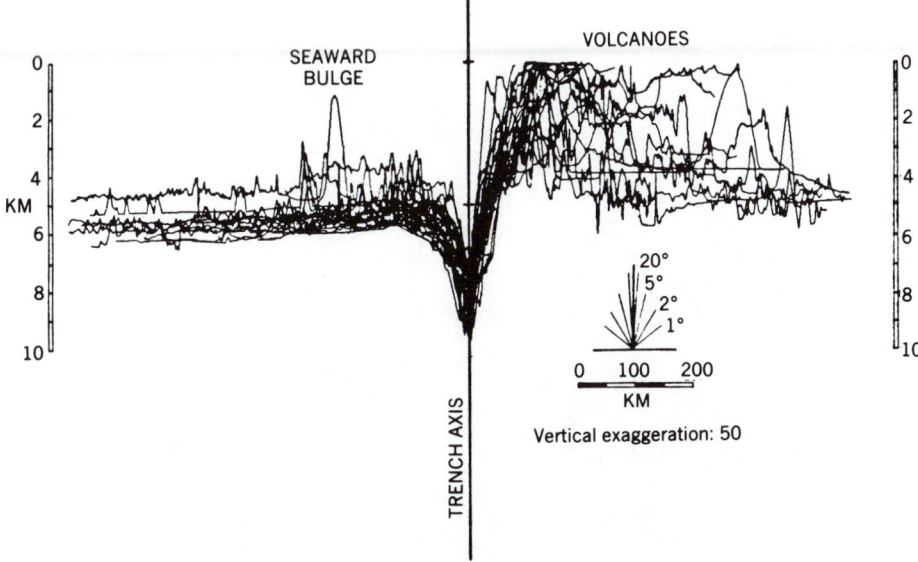

Figure 11-10. A superimposition of the topographic profiles across 35 different trenches in the world. All have a deep trench where the subducting plate departs from the surface, and a seaward bulge where the plate bends before plunging back toward the mantle. Behind the trench, all subduction zones have volcanic island arcs or mountain ranges where the melted subducting plate produces volcanic activity at the surface (from Hayes and Ewing, 1970).

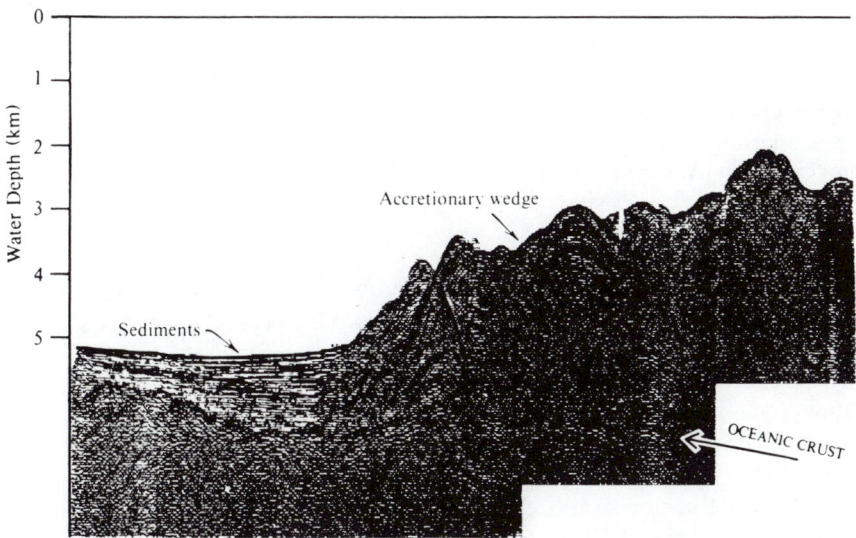

Figure 11-11. The subducting plate and the offscraping sediments of the accretionary wedge can be seen by seismic reflection profiling (from Moore, 1982).

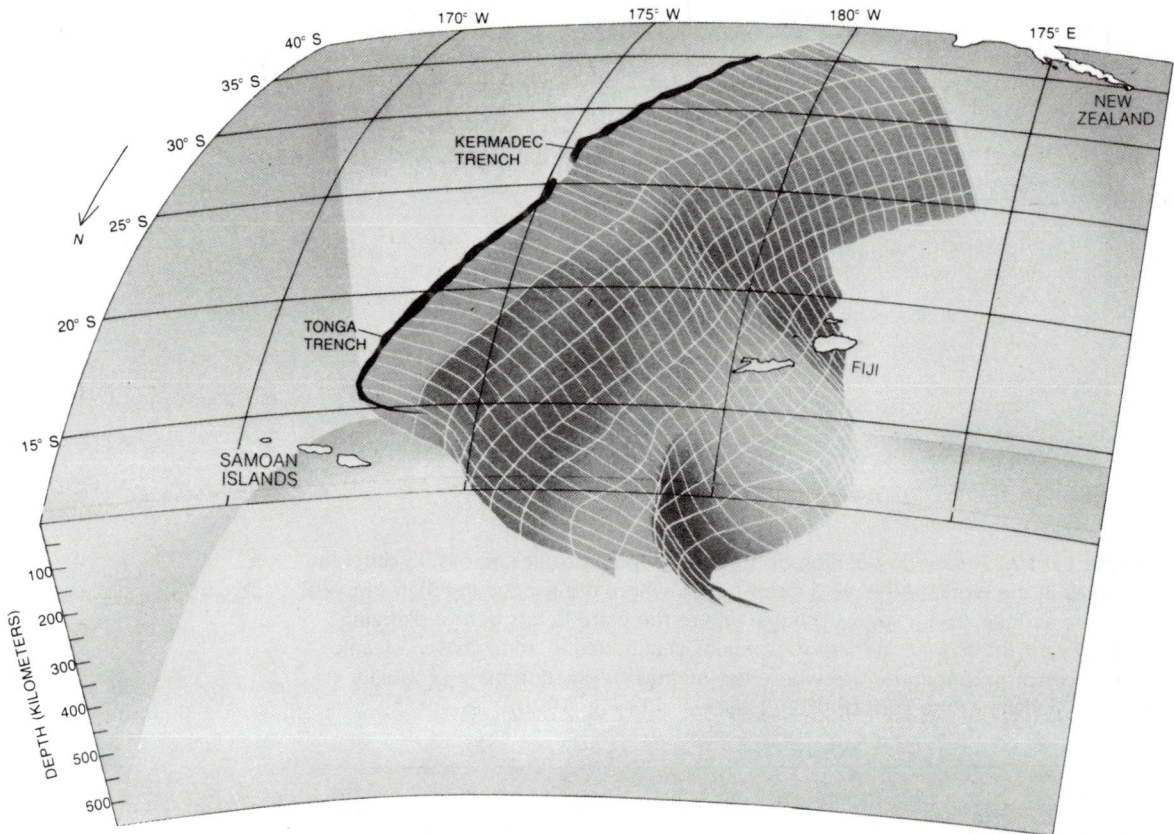

Figure 11-12. Three-dimensional planar view of the Tonga trench with a ripple in the subducting Pacific plate caused by slight irregularities in the subduction process (from McKenzie, 1984).

the surface and inside the Pacific plate (Figure 11-15). This zone likely marks the true place where the plate bends over from horizontal to plunge at a 45-degree angle beneath Japan.

The rate of subduction of the Pacific plate beneath Japan can be calculated from the energy release and amount of slip on earthquakes beneath Japan each year. Alternatively, plate motions between the Pacific plate, Asian plate (on which Japan sits), and Philippine plate (directly south of Japan) can be vector-summed to derive a subduction rate. Both techniques predict rates of about 10 cm/yr. Subduction to the 200-km depth shown in Figures 11-14, 15 took about 2 million years to accomplish. That is, the subducted slab of Pacific plate residing 200 km beneath Japan today was at the surface of the trench about 2 million years ago, and the present trench floor

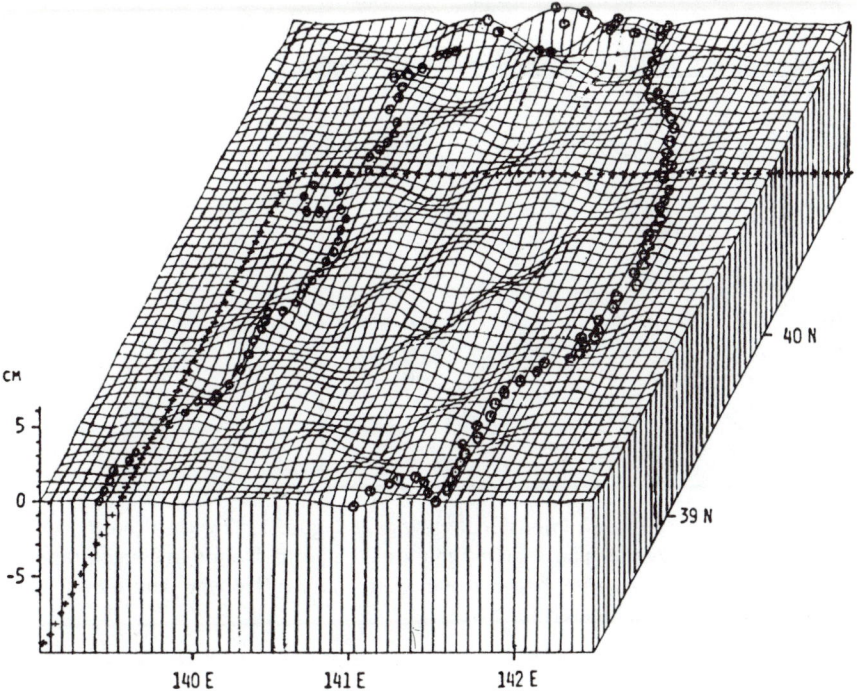

Figure 11-13. Ripples in the surface of Japan caused by the collision of the Pacific plate against the Eurasian plate upon which Japan resides. These remarkable data come from leveling measurements made at hundreds of sites in Japan from 1956 to 1966. The ripples move across Honshu, but have a height of only a few centimeters (Iida, 1985).

will be at 200-km depth in another 2 million years, if forces acting on the plates today remain the same. We thus have a window into millions of years of ocean lithosphere which has long since disappeared from the surface of the planet.

Over the geological times involved in subduction, earthquakes will occur all along both planes of the subducting slab. If we find a hole in the present-day activity, you can bet that earthquakes will occur there in the geological future. The holes in such **seismic doughnuts** are particularly likely locales for future dangerous earthquakes, and as such are watched very carefully by the Japanese. One such doughnut can be seen off the coast of Sendai when looking upward from below the double plane, (Figure 11-16). It is, in fact, a blank figure eight. Part of the double doughnut was recently filled by the magnitude 7 Sendai earthquake of June 6, 1978. The fore- and aftershocks from this event filled only one lobe of the figure-eight shape, however, and the likelihood of future events is still quite high.

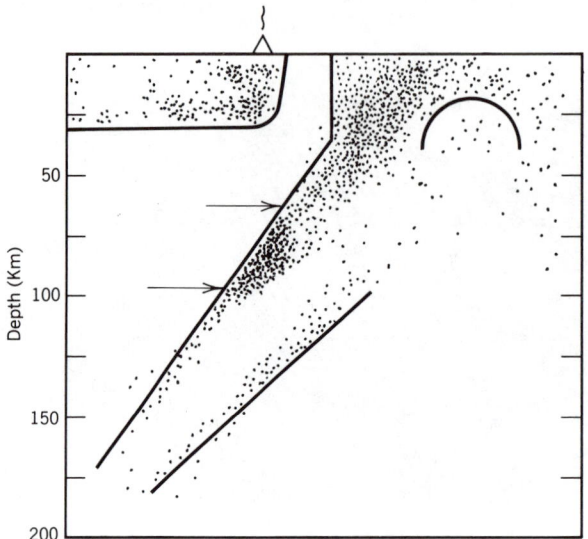

Figure 11-14. Same three-dimensional view as in Figure 11-7 except only displaying earthquakes smaller than magnitude 3.5. Note change in concentration of small events in slab directly below the eastern shore of Honshu where the active volcanoes are all located (arrows).

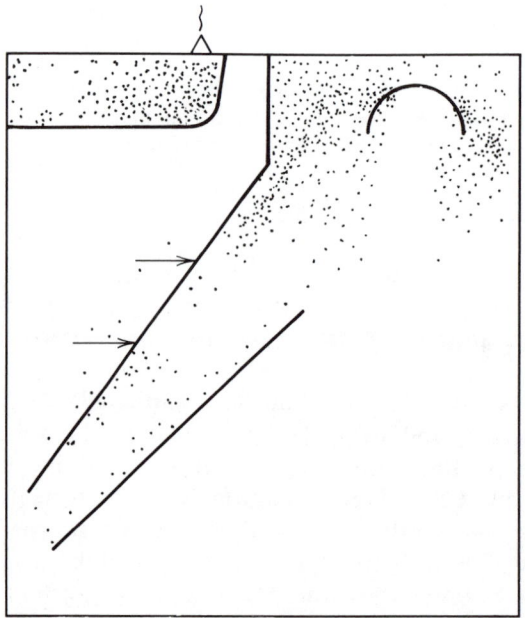

Figure 11-15. Same three-dimensional view as 11-12 except displaying only earthquakes greater than magnitude 3.5. There are few large events beneath eastern Honshu volcanoes.

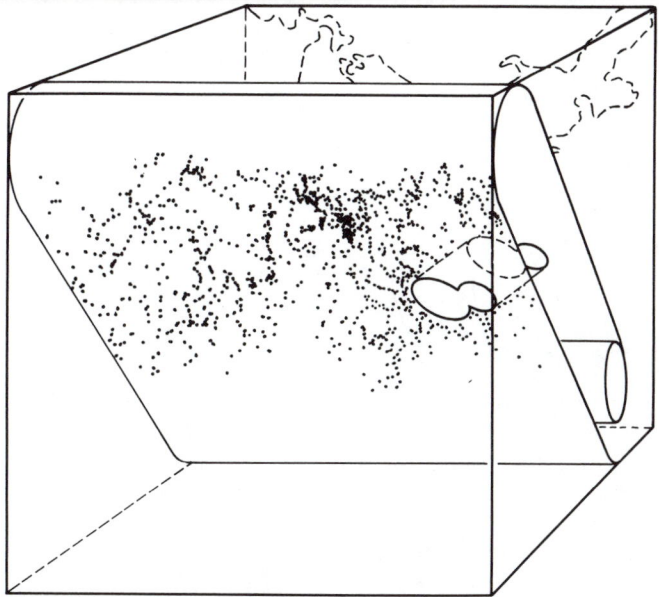

Figure 11-16. Upward view from underside of the Honshu subduction zone with the dangerous figure-eight area where no earthquakes have occurred during the recording period of the network (1975–1977). Since then, a large earthquake of magnitude 7 filled the small loop in 1978 offshore Sendai, Japan. Great earthquake danger still exists off Sendai, but then again, 3000 earthquakes occur beneath Japan every year.

The physical difficulty of subducting a planar object as large as the edge of the Pacific plate into the Earth's mantle produces some interesting differences from the ideal case described in Chapter 3. As seen earlier in Tonga, there is a ripple in the Pacific plate about 200 km beneath Japan (Figure 11-17). The rates of subduction on a spherical surface vary smoothly with latitude, and if the slab of rock is too stiff to accommodate this constant rate change, ripples can develop. Again the wet towel can be forced into ripples by slowing the rate of sinking of one end relative to the other.

In northern Japan, even more severe problems are encountered when the subduction zone takes an abrupt 30-degree turn from Hokkaido, Japan, to the Russian Kurile Islands. Here, the Pacific plate is actually torn at the trench so that two slabs subduct at the Kuriles and Hokkaido and diverge as they penetrate into the mantle at different angles. But they begin as the same Pacific plate to the east of the trench. Earthquakes show that the tearing forces actually begin hundreds of miles offshore from the trench axis, however, and deep within the plate. A cone-like shape of the seismic activity that accompanies this tear can be seen in the earthquake distribution with

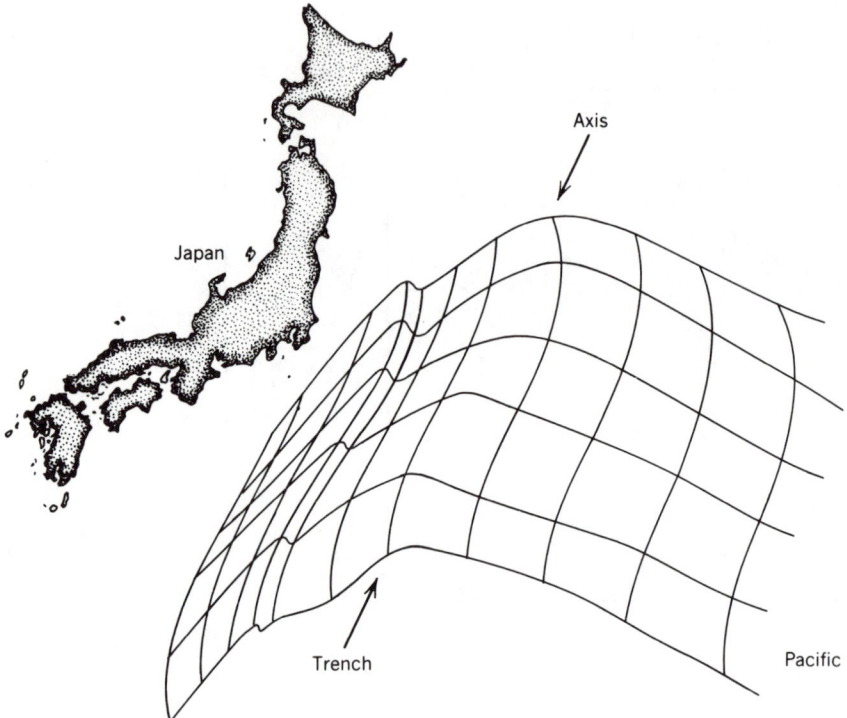

Figure 11-17. Japan subduction zone also shows a ripple in the Pacific plate (from Yoshii, 1978).

the tip pointing downward at an angle of about 45 degrees to the east from the point where the tear in the two trenches originates (Figure 11-18). The tip of the seismic cone is where the tearing is beginning, and this point is easily deeper than 50 km into the Pacific plate.

Another locale beneath Japan where reality complicates simplistic theory is south of Tokyo. Here, the Pacific plate is being subducted from east to west at a 45-degree angle. But to the south, the Philippine plate is being subducted from the south to the north at about a 30-degree angle. The tip of the Philippine plate is just now beginning to gouge into the top of the subducting Pacific plate (Figure 11-19); that is, they are colliding beneath Japan. Something will have to change. One or both of the massive plates will have to be deflected because of this collision. Luckily for the people of Japan, this subsurface collision will not reach crisis proportions for another hundred thousand years or so.

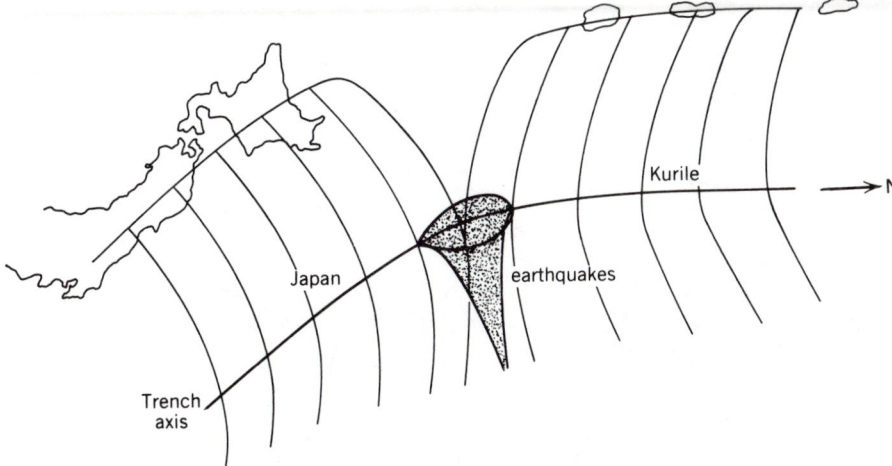

Figure 11-18. To the north, the Pacific plate is ripped into northern and southern subduction zones which plunge under the Kurile Islands and Hokaido, Japan respectively. Seaward of the rip, a downward pointing cone of earthquake shows how the tear in the plate extends into new lithosphere as subduction proceeds (stipled). The force originates at the collision zone and propogates progressively deeper to the east and into the interior of the Pacific plate.

Other Subduction Zones of the Earth

The subduction zones of the world underthrust at many different angles and at many different rates. Most begin shallow then steepen their angle of descent below about 50 km as the weight of the slab hanging into the light mantle begins to overpower the surface forces of collision (Figure 11-20 from the Aleutians of Alaska, for example). Some, like the Peru–Chile trench, stay at a shallow 30 degrees, whereas the Marianas and New Hebrides end up almost vertical (Figure 11-21). Again the wet towel provides a reasonable analogy. If the towel is stationary in the water, it usually takes a 45-degree angle of descent, but if the towel is sinking along the water surface and away from the corner touched, the angle of descent will be shallow. If, however, the towel is pulled along the water's surface toward the corner touched, the angle of descent will be steep as the towel remaining at the surface overtakes the descending slab. The relative angle of the subducting plate relative to the mantle into which it plunges thus has a lot to do with the stress regime in and around the slab (Figure 11-21).

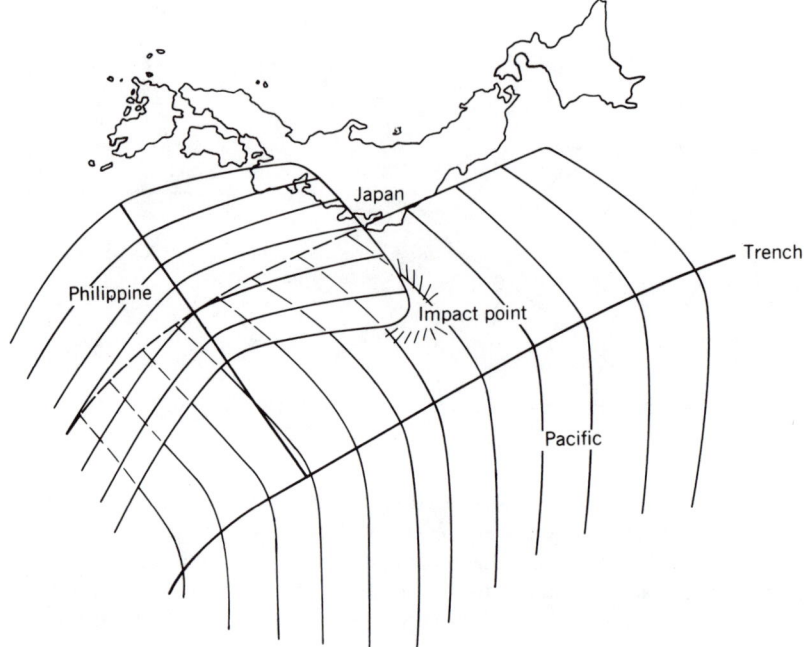

Figure 11-19. Future havoc is promised within the next 100,000 years beneath Japan where the subducting Pacific plate is colliding with the subducting Philippine Plate about 50 km beneath Tokyo. Something must give, with a plate direction change of one or both plates most likely.

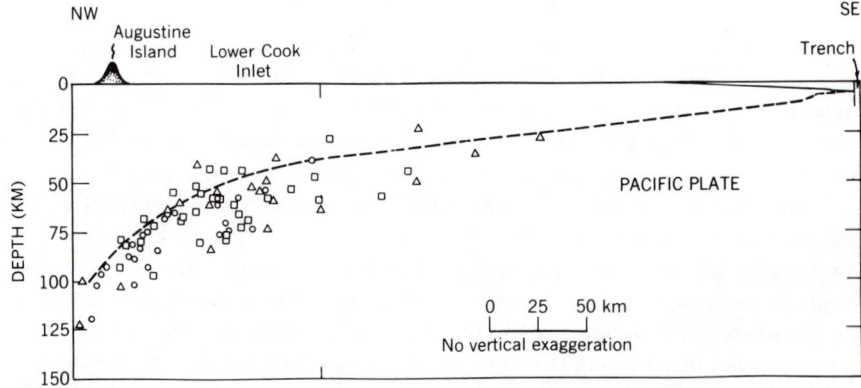

Figure 11-20. Cross section of subduction zone beneath the Aleutian trench of Alaska. Subduction is initially shallow, then steepens at 40-km depth, which is over 250-km inland from the trench axis (dashed line is top of subducting Pacific Plate) (from Fisher, 1983). Symbols are earthquake locations.

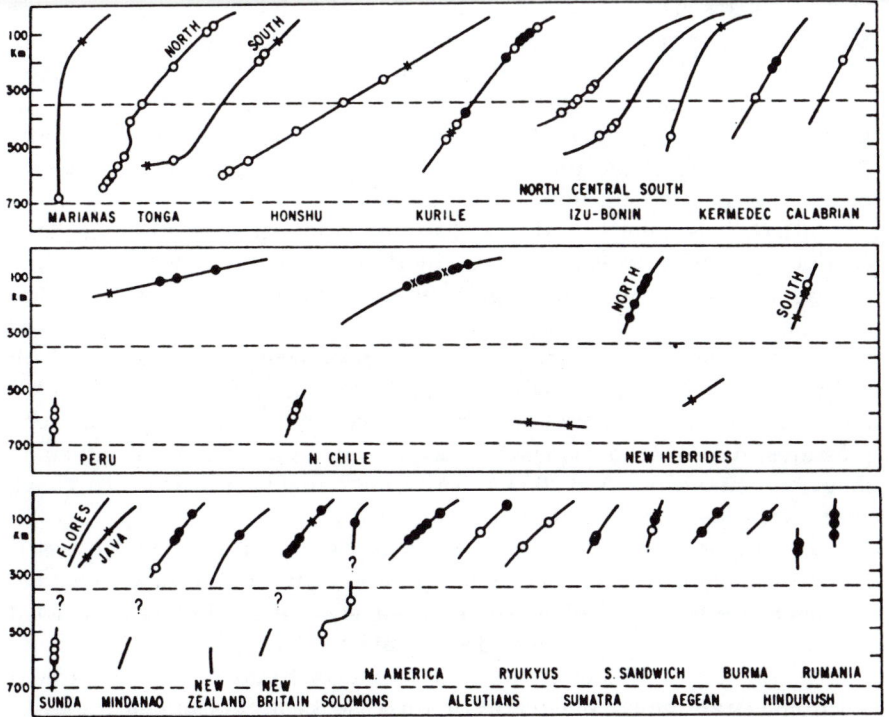

Figure 11-21. Shape and state of stress of many subduction zones of the world. Solid lines are cross-sectional shapes of downgoing slabs. Open circles indicate where earthquakes are compressional or thrust in the direction of subduction. Solid dots are where earthquakes are in tension or normal in the direction of subduction. Note that many of the deepest subducting slabs are compressional throughout their length whereas many of the zones with only shallow slabs hanging into the mantle are in tension. This difference could be from whether the subducting plate is also moving toward the landward plate (compression) or away from the colliding plate (tensional) (from Isacks and Molnar, 1971).

Most other subduction zones do not have the observational seismic network of Japan to define in much detail the structure of the downgoing slab, and certainly not like that seen by the Tohoku network. At only three other trenches, for example, have double seismic planes been detected so far (Peru–Chile, New Hebides and Aleutian trenches). However, in every locale where a sufficiently sensitive seismic network has been set up, a double plane has been discovered. We have every reason to believe that such is the standard form for all subduction zones.

In addition to a variable angle of subduction, each convergence zone involves plates moving at different rates toward each other. For example, the Marianas trench marks the convergence of the Pacific plate into the Philippine plate at 10 cm/yr, whereas the southern Chile trench is the site of Antarctic plate subduction beneath South America at only 2 cm/yr. The combination of different angles of subduction and variable rates of convergence gives us a strong hint of the causal mechanism for the occurrence of earthquakes along the subduction zones.

In fact, it is quite remarkable that any earthquakes at all occur along subduction zones. An earthquake is by definition caused by brittle failure along a fault zone. Such breakage requires solid, rigid rock, which in turn must be cold to remain brittle. How then can a plate that is being subducted back into the hot mantle continue to have earthquakes occurring along fault zones down to 700 km below the surface? After all, the pressure at 700 km is over 210,000 atmospheres. How could a fault zone move at all under such pressures? And once earthquakes are explained at such depths, why then do they not occur deeper than 700 km worldwide? That is, no earthquakes have ever been known to occur deeper than 700 km.

As with most geological processes we have studied so far, the answer is found by applying physics and chemistry to the problem. Thermodynamics defines phase boundaries between successively more and more compacted crystal structures as rock moves deeper into the Earth. But such structural changes in the lattice, or framework of the rock, do not occur without absorbing large amounts of energy; in this case, heat. So a subducting plate must increase in depth to undergo such phase changes. Why is this relevant to earthquakes? It is significant because the same composition rock may become more rigid if its structure is more tightly packed. So we would then find the unusual physical event that rock that gets hotter becomes harder instead of softer. The phase changes themselves may initiate the earthquakes because the volume of rock shrinks as the structure becomes more tightly packed. No space may exist at these pressures, so faulting might close the spaces.

Thermodynamics describes phase boundaries in pressure–temperature space. If we know the subduction angle and rate of a plate, we can draw such a phase-change diagram custom-made to each subducting plate by plotting pressure as depth and temperature as time since the slab was at the surface of the Earth. The assumption is that the subducting plate heats up at a constant rate by conduction of heat from the surrounding mantle into the plate (Figure 11-22). We see that by placing laboratory-determined phase changes onto this plot, we can explain the gross differences between earthquake patterns of most of the world's subduction zones. For example, the Marianas trench is both a fast-rate subduction zone and a steeply dipping one as well. Therefore, the Pacific plate reaches from the surface to 700-km depths faster than at any other trench; that is, in less than 6 million years. It is therefore colder by about 500°C at that depth than a slowly subducting

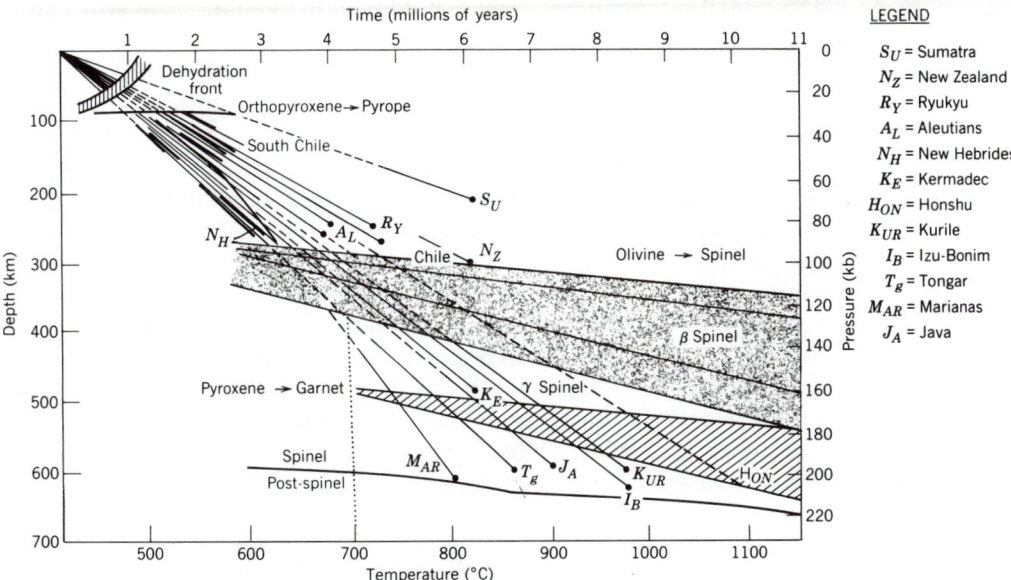

Figure 11-22. Deep earthquakes perhaps are caused by phase changes deep within the subducting plates, since it is not easy to break rock under high temperatures and hundreds of thousands of atmospheres of pressure. Perhaps the spinel–post-spinel phase change ends all earthquake activity at 700 km subsurface. Alternatively, the post-spinel phase change is an inpenetrable boundary to subduction. Initials on solid lines are portions of subduction zones with large earthquake activity. Dashed lines indicate no earthquakes along that portion of the slab. The β-spinel zone appears to have little earthquake activity in the 300 to 400 km depth range.

Chile trench, which is underthrusting at a much shallower angle and slower rate (Figure 11-22).

The major phase changes that occur in the slab are three successively more compacted structures of magnesium silicate called olivine. These are called the beta-spinel, gamma-spinel, and post-spinel phases of olivine. One quick conclusion from Figure 11-22 is that the beta-spinel phase appears to be less brittle than olivine because, worldwide, when any subduction zone is within the beta-spinel region, few earthquakes appear to occur. This produces the clear separation between blue and green earthquakes, which we noticed in Figures 11-1 and 11-2 (color inserts). However, when in the gamma-spinel region, earthquakes reappear.

The post-spinel phase change may again turn off earthquakes at 700-km depth (Figure 11-22). All the subduction zones either reach the post-spinel phase boundary at 600 to 700 km, or they reach melting temperatures of

1000 to 1200°C at that depth. This is not the only hypothesis for why earthquakes stop at 700 km, though. Alternatively, the slabs hit an impenetrable boundary and are deflected to a horizontal trajectory at this depth. The post-spinel phase boundary in the surrounding mantle is coincidentally at this same depth as well. So, while thermodynamics provides an explanation for deep earthquakes, its rules are such that unique explanations are not always possible. To clarify this point further, we still have very little knowledge of what processes are actually occurring as the slab reaches 700-km depths in the mantle. Either it keeps going right through the post-spinel phase change but with earthquake activity no longer possible or it hits an impenetrable boundary, the post-spinel phase change, and is deflected along this boundary. Some slabs may be deflected and some may penetrate. This is one of the great avenues for research in the earth sciences at the present moment.

In any event, we must learn more of the thermal changes that happen as the plate is reassimilated into the mantle if we are to make much further progress in understanding the processes occurring at subduction zones.

The Thermal Structure of Subduction

One of the great paradoxes of this planet is the correspondence between volcanic activity which occurs directly above the one locale on the earth where cold surface rock is being thrust into hot mantle. Physics tells us that because the plate must heat up, the mantle must cool down. How is it then that in a subduction zone where the mantle must be **colder than normal mantle,** enough heat is generated to produce most of the volcanoes on the Earth?

Obviously, melting must occur at depth below volcanoes. Peculiarities, such as how colder-than-normal mantle melts, are in fact excellent indicators of what is happening inside the Earth. The volcanism must be intimately related to the subducting plates, although the underthrusting of a cold plate into a hot mantle would not normally be considered a favorable environment for the generation of melts or magma.

We start by building a geophysical model of an ideal subduction zone, where we can describe the heating process by equations that govern heat transfer. We then see what additions to the basic equations must be made to produce the appropriate pressures and temperatures for melting to occur. Thermodynamics again will tell us precisely when melting will happen.

We must begin by constraining our model. We know that the plate remains rigid to great depths since earthquakes are present. The only heat-transfer mechanism possible between the mantle and the plate is **thermal conduction,** or the transfer of heat by vibration of a solid matrix. The mantle however, can transfer heat by **thermal convection,** or the transfer of heat by mass (fluid) flow, because we have already seen that partial melt exists in the asthenosphere below the plates. If we force a rigid plate into a liquid, the liquid will convect around the motion of the solid body (Figure 11-25), but heat will be transferred into the solid only by conduction.

What other evidence do we have with which to constrain our model? When rock pushes past rock, frictional heat is generated. Maybe that is the source of the extra heat required to produce volcanoes in an otherwise cooling process. We quickly run up against another observation that constrains the amount of heating allowed by friction along a subduction zone. If there were large amounts of heat generated by friction as the two plates slide across each other, that heat would eventually produce high heat flow at the surface, since the heat must flow upward. In fact, however, low surface heat flow is found between the trench and the volcanoes above subduction zones (Figure 11-26). This is exactly the area that should have high heat flow if friction alone is producing melting conditions along the subduction zone. Again, we are not certain at the present time if the low heat flow landward of trenches is from lack of heat due to friction, or whether this heat is present, but carried like a ghost to the ocean by hydrothermal waters released by the squeezing of sediments being scraped off by the subduction process.

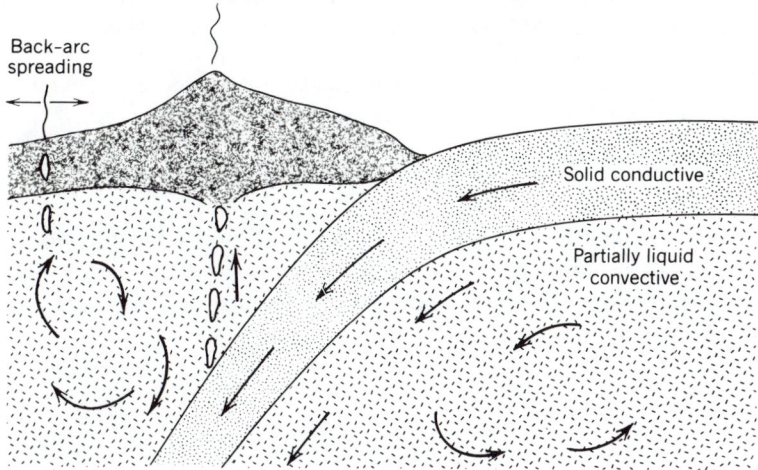

Figure 11-25. The solid plate subducting deep into the mantle diverts the convective pattern of the mantle to produce downwelling flow above and below the slab. Upwelling within the mantle farther landward of the volcanic arc is thought to cause back-arc spreading, (a sea-floor spreading system which produces new sea floor behind the island arc).

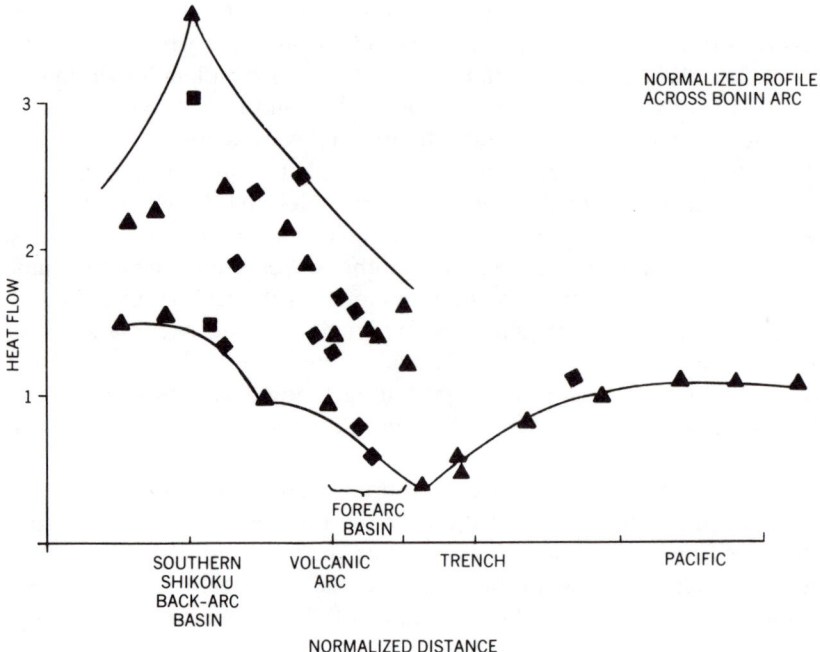

Figure 11-26. Heat flow shows the same general pattern as topography across a trench—low at the trench axis, high at the landward volcanic arc, and normal over the seaward bulge. The heat flow between the arc and trench is held low possibly by dewatering of the sediments that are subducted. In any event, no large heat source from friction between the plates during subduction is evident in the heat-flow pattern. Symbols are different quality measurements with the triangles best.

We turn then to another source of information about what physics is happening at depth in subduction zones: the chemistry of lavas from the volcanoes. After all, these magmas come to the surface directly from the zone of interest. Perhaps they bring clues with them.

Volcanology

Volcanologists study the details of volcanic eruptions. Because of human nature, it is very difficult to keep volcanologists away from erupting volcanoes. Consequently, it is a risky profession. The geological news magazine *Geotimes* recently ran an advertisement for a job as chief volcanologist for the government of Papua, New Guinea: excellent pay, good fringe benefits, liberal vacation time, etc. On the very next page was the obituary for the last chief volcanologist of Papua, New Guinea. He had ventured too close to an eruption. So volcanic samples are not always easy to obtain, especially if the gases and volatiles of an erupting volcano must be sampled!

Several volcanologists were killed during the eruption of Mt. St. Helens. Yet we are entertained often by beautiful pictures of lava flowing as rivers down the slopes of Kilauea Volcano in Hawaii. There are even tourist look-outs at the National Volcano Observatory on the big island of Hawaii so that eruptions can be witnessed first-hand. Understanding the dangers involved in some but not all volcanoes gives us a grand hint at processes that are active beneath volcanoes in a subduction zone. What makes volcanoes like Mt. St. Helen's or those on Papua, New Guinea, so dangerous compared to a passive eruption such as on Hawaii?

The Japanese classify their volcanoes according to what they call the E-factor, which rates the violence of the eruption. For one extreme Vesuvius erupted, killing the residents of Pompeii as they slept. They did not even have time to be awakened by the noise of the eruption. How can this be? How can a volcano kill so quickly? Here is an eye-witness account of the eruption in 1902 of Mt. Pelée on Martinique reprinted from Press and Siever (1978):

I saw St. Pierre destroyed. The city was blotted out by one great flash of fire. Nearly 40,000 people were killed at once. Of eighteen vessels lying in the roads, (harbor) only one, the British steamer, Roddam escaped and she, I hear, lost more than half of those on board. It was a dying crew that took her out. Our boat, the Roraima, arrived at St. Pierre early that morning. For hours before entering the roadstead we could see flames and smoke rising from Mt. Pelée. No one on board had any idea of danger. Captain Muggah was on the bridge, and all hands got on deck to see the show. The spectacle was magnificent. As we approached St. Pierre we could distinguish the rolling and leaping of red flames that belched from the mountain in huge volumes and gushed into the sky. Enormous clouds of black smoke hung over the volcano.... There was a constant muffled roar. It was like the biggest oil refinery in the world burning up on the mountain top. There was a tremendous explosion about 7:45, soon after we got in. The mountain was blown to pieces. There was no warning. The side of the volcano was ripped out and there was hurled straight toward us a solid wall of flame. It sounded like a thousand cannons.

The wave of fire was on us and over us like a flash of lightning. It was like a hurricane of fire. I saw it strike the cable steamship Grappler broadside on, and capsize her. From end to end she burst into flames and then sank. The fire rolled in mass straight down upon St. Pierre and the shipping. The town vanished before our eyes.

The air grew stifling hot and we were in the thick of it. Wherever the mass of fire struck the sea, the water boiled and sent up vast columns of steam. The sea was torn into huge whirlpools that careened toward the open sea. One of these horrible, hot whirlpools swung under the Roraima and pulled her down on her beam end with the suction. She careened way over to port, and then the fire hurricane from the volcano smashed her, and over she went on the opposite side. The fire wave swept off the masts and smokestacks as if they were cut by a knife.

Captain Muggah was the only one on the deck not killed outright. he was caught by the fire wave and was terribly burned. He yelled to get up the anchor, but before two fathoms were heaved-in, the Roraima was almost upset by the boiling whirlpool and the fire wave had thrown her down on her beam ends to starboard. Captain Muggah was overcome by the flames. He fell unconscious from the bridge and overboard. The blast of fire from the volcano lasted only a few minutes. It shriveled and set fire to everything it touched. Thousands of casks of rum were stored in St. Pierre, and these were exploded by the terrific heat. The burning rum ran in streams down every street and out into the sea. This blazing rum set fire to the Roraima several times.

Before the volcano burst, the landings of St. Pierre were covered with people. After the explosion, not one living soul was seen on the land. Only twenty-five of those on board were left after the first blast.

The French cruiser Suchet came in and took us off at 2 P.M. She remained near by, helping all she could, until 5 o'clock, then went to Port de France with all the people she had rescued. At the time it looked as if the entire north end of the island was on fire.

On the other hand, the entire country of Iceland lives on active volcanoes. Icelanders even produce their electricity from hot springs on the flanks of these volcanoes. An occasional eruption threatens to direct rivers of lava into one of their towns, but only rarely is anyone killed by an eruption.

What is different about Iceland that allows volcanologists to sit calmly at the crest watching lava bubble up (Figure 11-23, color insert) or that allows visitors to Hawaii to have cocktails at the famous Volcano House, which is the only resort hotel on the crest of an active volcano in the world; whereas their colleagues risk death even approaching an eruption off the coast of Japan or in Papua, New Guinea (Figure 11-24, color insert).

The E-factor measures the explosivity of a volcano. Mt. St. Helens exploded, as did Vesuvius and Mt. Pelée. Why? Poisonous gases killed the people of Pompei. Where did the gases come from?

Plate tectonics provides an answer to this interesting paradox. Explosive volcanoes are erupting above subduction zones, whereas passive volcanoes are located great distances from subduction zones. Iceland is on the crest of the mid-Atlantic ridge, for example, and Hawaii is an isolated hot-spot tapping deep mantle magmas far from any plate boundary.

The volcanoes above subduction zones are explosive because they contain large quantities of volatile compounds such as steam, carbon dioxide, and hydrogen sulfide. These do not come from the mantle directly, or all volcanoes would be explosive. Most of the mantle's gases have been lost to the oceans and atmosphere long ago. Explosions occur when volatiles such as water come up entrapped in the lava as liquid. As they approach the surface, water flashes to steam, and we have a pressure cooker. Any small breach of the cooker walls and the steam explodes out, often taking entire sides of a volcano with it.

What is the source of the water and other volatiles? The subducted oceanic crust is the prime candidate. Notice how plate tectonics has a way of tying world-encompassing events into one another. Here is a case where, if it were not for ridge-axis black smokers and pervasive hydrothermal circulation of seawater that becomes locked into newly forming ocean crust at the start of a plate's traverse along the conveyor belt, there would be no volcanoes at the other end of the conveyor belt, because, we will see, this same water causes volcanoes above the subduction zone.

Water is captured in the structure of alteration minerals within the basaltic crust of the oceanic plate. Perhaps 5 percent by weight of the rock of the upper 2 or 3 km of the plate is water locked into the mineral structure of clays as hydroxyls. This altered rock passively rides the plates until subduction.

Water, that is, free water, is extremely buoyant, and therefore cannot be subducted with the plate. It must force itself upward to the surface. One way this occurs is along shallow dipping faults made in the soft sediment being accreted onto the landward plate. The combination of soft mud and buoyant water trying to escape provides liquid surfaces for the sediments to scrape off the downgoing slab and accrete onto the overlying plate. Similar décollement surfaces are seen as nappe structures in old collision zones such as the Alps (Figure 11-27). These low-angle thrust sheets produce great quantities of oil and gas in the United States as large slabs of rock slide many tens of miles over the top of younger rock.

The *Glomar Challenger* drilled into such a fault zone off Barbados and accidentally provided graphic proof of the existence of free water along such décollement faults in accretionary wedges. The drill string became stuck in the fault zone. When that occurs, dynamite must be used to shoot-off the stuck pipe, thus freeing the boat itself from the anchorage in the rock. During the 12 hours it took to dynamite off the pipe, water began backflowing onto the rig floor at rates of hundreds of gallons an hour. In order to push water in a reverse direction to gravity and up the pipe, pressures in the fault zone must overcome the hydrostatic weight of the entire column of water standing in the pipe. The water depth alone was 6 km. Pressures 5 percent over hydrostatic, or the weight of the column of water, were required. Such pressures must be from the free water in the crust and sediments trying to force its way back to the surface.

But chemically bound water does not have the buoyant force of free water, since it is trapped within the lattice structure of the minerals themselves. Bound water will subduct to great depths until it is cooked out of the

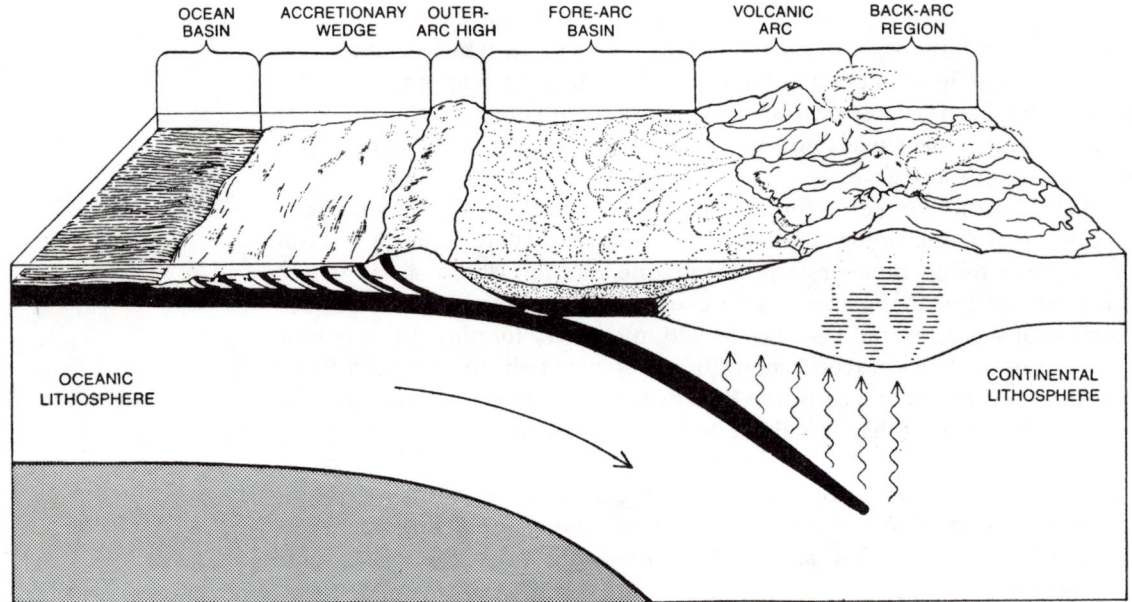

Figure 11-27. The structure of all subduction zones is generally the same, with an accretionary wedge of sediment coming from the deep ocean basin being offscraped onto the landward plate. A fore-arc basin forms when sediments from off the island arc are ponded between the accretionary wedge and the island arc. Décollement faults are found within the accretionary wedge (heavy black lines) (from Birchfiel, 1983).

mineral lattices. Sound familiar? Here again we encounter the rock kiln. As the oceanic rock is heated by friction and the heat flow from the surrounding hot mantle, dehydration eventually occurs. The water is suddenly freed. This newly freed water is restored to a buoyant fluid. As it forces itself into the overlying mantle, melting occurs in the cooled-off mantle, in rock that would not ordinarily melt at those temperatures. Water acts as a catalyst, allowing rock to melt at cooler temperatures than normally would be possible.

Melting is the breaking down of the rigid lattice structure of solid rock into liquid. It requires heat because this breakdown is accomplished by excessive vibration of the molecules. Water acts as a catalyst to melting because it is highly soluble, both into the solid and liquid structure of the rock. It penetrates between individual molecules and separates them. Less energy is then required to raise each individual molecule to the vibration state required to produce breakdown of the structural bonds into liquid. Being less tightly interconnected, individual vibration states are lower and

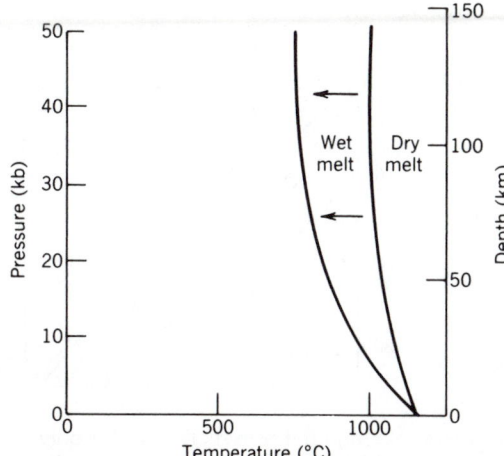

Figure 11-28. A plot of the melting relation of mantle rocks as a function of pressure and temperature shows how magma can form in the cold environment above a downgoing slab. Water, released by dehydration of the slab, lowers the melting temperature of mantle rocks.

closer to breakdown; that is, the melting temperature is lower in wet mantle than in dry mantle (Figure 11-28).

Temperatures in a Subduction Zone

We are now prepared to make a thermal model that takes normal mantle temperatures at the onset of subduction and, using basic physical equations of heat and mass transfer, predicts the thermal structure of a downgoing slab and the mantle surrounding it after subduction has been going on for millions of years. Chemical constraints can then be applied to such a temperature structure to ask when and where melting will occur. In such a way, volcanoes above subduction zones can be explained (Figure 11-29). Once liquid rock and free water exist at great depth, the buoyant forces of these fluids drive them to the surface at a rapid rate as diapirs of magma, and volcanoes result.

Such models can even account for the differences in chemistry seen between volcanoes that penetrate overlying ocean plate, such as in the Marianas, and those that come up through overlying continental material such as volcanoes in Mexico and Central America. The former melt only iron- and magnesium-rich mantle material and come up as island-arc tholeiite, of sim-

GEOLOGICAL NOTES

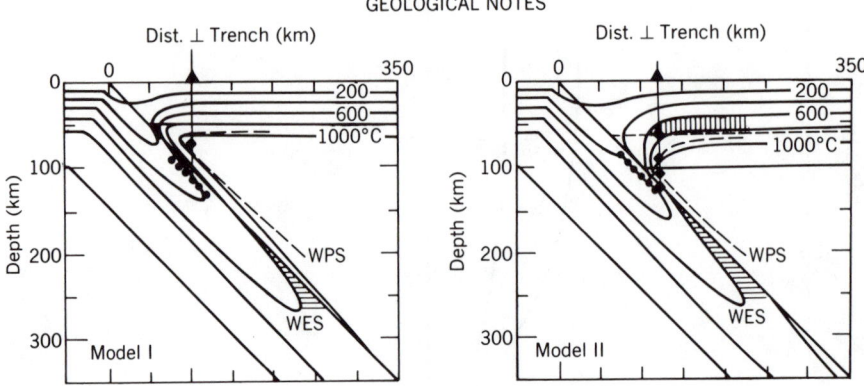

Figure 11-29. Melting temperatures are attained in the presence of water only in the mantle above the subducting plate when the landward plate is oceanic (left). When the landward plate is a continent with its thick crust, however, melting can occur in either the mantle or continental crust (black diamonds). Magmas on land are correspondingly more complex and more alkalic than island-arc basaltic magmas. WES is wet eclogite (basalt) solidus. WPS is wet peridotite (mantle) solidus. Hatching is area of melting of oceanic and continental crusts. Black dots are where dehydration and water release occur.

ilar composition to midocean ridge basalts, except with many more volatiles present. The latter melt continental material on their way up, resulting in lighter lavas made of more calcium, sodium, and potassium than their island counterparts. They are called calc-alkaline rocks. (Figure 11-29).

It is not enough to produce a theoretical model for the effects of dehydrated water on melting deep within the subduction zone. One must then seek observational proof that the model is producing reliable predictions. One item of proof is the existence of water vapor in erupting lavas at the surface. But there are ways of seeing into the subduction zone by remote means as well. Take for example the recording of earthquakes beneath Japan. Can the Tohoku seismic network record information from below Japan that sees the kiln in action?

Probably the single, easiest observation to make about earthquakes is their b-value. A plot of the frequency of earthquakes occurring at all magnitudes in a given area falls along a straight line on a log– plot of the number of earthquakes occurring at each magnitude or size. There are always more small earthquakes than large ones (Figure 11-31). The slope of such a plot is called the b-value of a group of earthquakes, and it varies from locale to locale. Some places have many large earthquakes; others have only a few large earthquakes and many more small ones. While we do not fully understand the physical basis of why earthquakes are always distributed linearly on such a plot, we can still use such an observation to classify different earth-

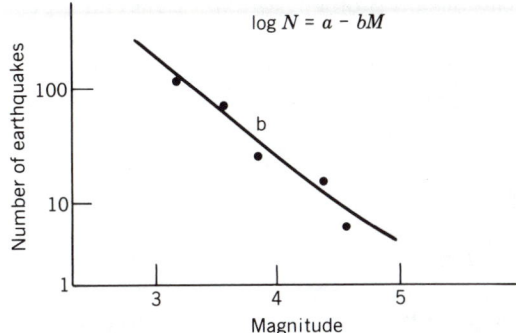

$$\log N = a - bM$$

Figure 11-31. The water coming off the slab during dehydration causes the occurrence of many small earthquakes in the slab directly below the volcanos. This change from a few large earthquakes to many small earthquakes can be noticed from a b-value plot. Number of earthquakes plotted versus magnitude shows a linear relationship. Normally, the slope of this line is 0.7 (the b-value). When water is present as in a slab at dehydration depths, the b-value goes up to 1.0, and many more small earthquakes are recorded by a network such as Tohoku.

quake provinces. The name b-value comes from the equation of a linear relationship: $y = a + bx$, where b is the slope. What would you guess the effects of water would be on the b-value?

Water lubricates a fault, so there are more, but smaller, earthquakes in a wet rock environment than in one that is dry. The slope of the b-value trend then steepens, and the b-value itself increases if water is present along a fault zone. This has been proved in cases where humans have altered the water pressure inside the earth artificially. Near Rangely, Colorado, in 1967, liquid was being pumped into deep wells when suddenly earthquakes began to occur beneath nearby Denver. Since no previous earthquake activity had been recorded in the Denver area, the pumping was stopped. The earthquakes stopped. A series of pump tests were then undertaken in 1968 by Barry Raleigh, now director of Lamont, in which the b-value beneath Rangely was controlled by the pump rate of water into the wells: The higher the water pressure was, the larger the number of small earthquakes recorded. The good news for Denver is that when pumping stopped, the earthquakes stopped. The bad news is that the b-value returned to its normal low value, indicating that there will be very few earthquakes, but they will be larger than if pumping had continued.

Another example of human intervention resulting in b-value changes occurs beneath large water reservoirs. The empoundment of millions of gallons of water weighing countless tons into a new reservoir forces some of that water deep into the rock beneath the dam. The b-value increases with the added water content of the rock, and many small earthquakes begin to occur. While this is an unfortunate design problem for dam builders, it provides an excellent empirical framework from which to test for water release beneath Japan along the subduction zone. We can actually see the increased occurrence of small earthquakes beneath Japan as the water is being released by activation of the kiln in the subducted oceanic crust.

Looking down the upper plane of seismic activity along the subducted plate beneath Japan, we first see high b-values from the escape of free water in the shallow accretionary wedge near the trench (Figure 11-32). Surprisingly, it appears to take 50 km of depth to squeeze all the free water out of the subduction zone. Then a dry zone is encountered from 50 to about 100 km as seen from low b-values. A dramatic increase in b-value occurs at the proper depth for dehydration reactions to be occurring in the upper seismic plane (Figure 11-32). This change in seismic activity exactly corresponds to the depth predicted for dehydration by the subduction model. We can believe the results of these thermal models a little more strongly as a result. We can see the effect of released water not only in seismicity but in the subsequent volcanoes that are caused as well.

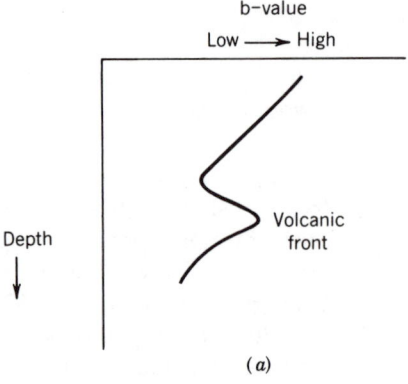

(a)

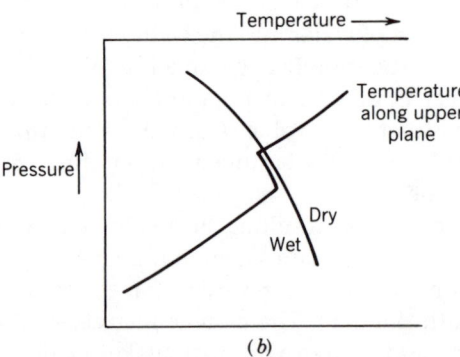

(b)

Figure 11-32. The b-value along the subducting slab is initially high from water coming out of sediments. Then the b-value returns to the dry 0.7 value until the depth below the volcanic front shows an increase in b-value due to dehydration. The slab also becomes colder during this dehydration making melting of the slab rock itself difficult at this depth. Volcanic magmas must utilize water from the slab mixing with mantle above the slab to produce magma.

Island Arcs, Accretion, and Back-arc Spreading

Most of the activity that affects man in a subduction zone occurs landward of the trench axis. Volcanoes made from dewatering of the downgoing slab come to the surface in either newly formed mountains or in an island arc, both on the landward side. Whether the volcanoes form islands or become part of a large mountain range has to do with the previous geological history of the plate margin that is colliding with the subducting plate. If it is continental, a mountain range will be formed because all the volcanic activity from subduction will be piled on top of an already emergent coastline. Examples are the Andes of South America and the volcanoes of Central America. If however, the overriding plate is oceanic, new volcanoes must begin by piling lavas onto the sea floor. They emerge as islands only after they have flowed enough magma to build a pyramid tall enough to break the sea surface.

Several new islands have formed on the earth's surface within the last 20 years. In the early 1960s, an airplane pilot reported seeing steam billowing out of the open ocean south of Japan. Search vessels were sent to the scene expecting to find a ship in distress. Instead, they witnessed the birth of an island (Figures 11-30*a*–11-30*d*, color insert). However, this volcano had been active for thousands of years before it produced enough lava to break the surface.

Island arcs are the early beginnings of a continent. They are arcuate (curved) because the subducting slab is a plane penetrating into a sphere. The surface expressions of volcanic plumes moving directly to the surface from such a plane define an arc. Volcanoes appear at the surface spaced about 100 km apart. That is the segregation distance for the production of enough magma along the slab to produce individual lava diapirs, which then congeal and move upward to the surface. If volcanism continues, enough rock is extruded to completely fill the space between individual volcanoes to the point that sea level is exceeded even between volcanoes. Then an island arc becomes a single large island (Figure 11-30*d*, color insert). Japan is only partly made from that process, however. Most of Japan is continental Asia, which was rifted away from Korea long before subduction of the Pacific plate involved Japan.

More often than not, collision with a different plate occurs before the late stages of island arc formation are concluded. This results in the accretion of the island arc onto the colliding continent. Southern Chile was made in this manner.

There are two other processes active above the subduction zone that add rock onto the island arc to fatten it into a small continent. First, soft sediment and volcanic seamounts on the subducting plate are often scraped off onto the overriding plate to form the accretionary wedge. Second, a remarkable

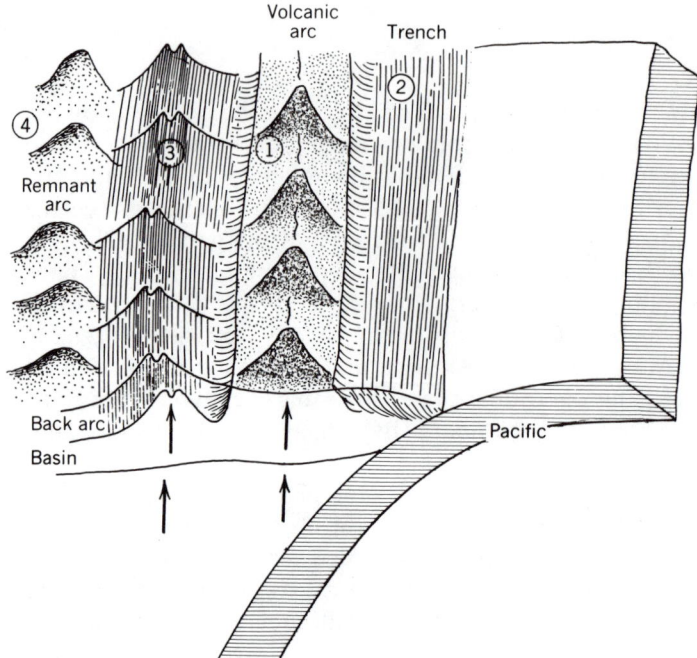

Figure 11-33. During the evolution of an island arc, first subduction occurs, then dewatering promotes melting and diapirism, and an island arc soon forms, (1). Accretion scrapes sediments off, (2) and convection in the mantle soon causes sea-floor spreading to form a ridge system back-arc of the volcanic arc, (3). **Bold** arrows are magma path to surface. Remnant arc (4) is spread by new sea floor (3) away from presently active, new volcanic arc (1).

phenomenon occurs even farther landward from the trench than the volcanic arc. Sea-floor spreading often occurs landward of the volcanic arc and is called back-arc spreading. The forces involved must be extensional since the process is virtually identical to midocean-ridge volcanism. They also must be related to the slab's interaction with the overriding plate. But we often call the subduction process collision, so how can tension result in the back arc? One scenario is that the subducting plate falls into the mantle like our wet towel example, with one end tied to the edge of the tub. This results in a trench that migrates seaward with time pulling the volcanic arc away from the overriding plate. Whenever tension opens rifts in the surface of the planet, mantle magma comes passively to the surface as a sea-floor spreading system. Just as on the mid-Atlantic ridge, new material is accreted to the back of the volcanic arc.

Summary

Examples of back-arc spreading are the Mariana Trough behind Guam in the western Pacific, and closer to home, the Basin-and-Range province of the western United States (Figure 11-33). Here, tension within the continent is left over from the Pacific plate's subduction beneath the Sierra Nevada range. This tension is pulling California to the west relative to Colorado. The result is faulting, which produces a series of north–south-aligned basins separated by ridges; thus the name Basin and Range. The geological term for such extensional features is horst and graben topography. Extension is still only occurring along faults today; that is, no actual gaps have appeared along which mantle lavas can reach the surface in large quantities—yet. The whole basin is hot, with high heat flow at the surface indicating that the molten mantle is working its way closer and closer to the surface. Eventually, the continent could split apart, separating California from the eastern United States.

This is one example of how we are beginning to understand more and more of the continent as we study the ocean floor. It is now time to turn our full attention to the remarkable rafts upon which we live.

Further Reading

Uyeda, S. , 1984, Subduction zones: Their diversity, mechanism and human impact: Geojournal, v. 8.4.

12

Continental Formation and Deformation

The geology that has the most visible effect on our daily lives is that which occurs on the continents. Volcanoes such as Mt. St. Helens kill scores of people, disrupt thousands of lives, and even change the weather. Earthquakes such as that in the San Fernando Valley of suburban Los Angeles in 1973 destroy billions of dollars worth of property and threaten thousands of lives. Yet we have seen that many more volcanoes erupt below the sea than above it, and many more earthquakes occur each year below the ocean. Plate boundary events, which happen repeatedly over millions of years, are the building blocks from which the continents have been made. The continents are much more complex than the ocean floor because they have existed at the Earth's surface 20 times longer than the oldest sea floor. They are like buoyant logs in a flood: they crash and collide, smash together, and rip apart only to remain as debris for years after the last waters have receded. The prime reason for this is that continents are very difficult to force down into the mantle because the rock from which they are made is just too lightweight.

The continents record most of the Earth's history not simply because they are older than sea floor, but also because they are built from old oceans. It is not altogether correct to state that the oldest ocean floor is 160 million years old. The oldest rock currently under water is that age. In fact, the oldest rock on the planet is a piece of 3.7-billion-year-old sea floor, which long ago was forced onto land, probably at a subduction zone. This rock now forms the core of the Australian continent. We know this rock was formed deep below the ocean because it is sedimentary in origin; because its chemical composition is not too different from that of present marine sedimentary rocks; and for certain proof, because there are fossils of the earliest sea creatures buried within it.

In this chapter we ask how a continent forms, then observe the modifications, additions, and subtractions that occur as the continent deforms while it rafts back and forth on the plates of the earth's surface. We will see that plate tectonics not only explains how the ocean floor evolves, but also how the continents rift apart, collide together, slide across each other, or ride passively in the center of plates during their long evolution. Remember that a continent is not synonymous with a plate. A continent's boundary need not be the edge of a plate. North America, for example, is not one large plate. In fact, the boundary of two plates runs through the middle of California, as we will soon see.

The same three plate-boundary processes affect continents when their fate brings them to a plate's edge: subduction, spreading or transform faulting. There is, however, one major exception: Continents are not subducted back into the mantle. Although continents are correspondingly more complex, it is all the more important to understand the geology of continents because the histories of all those long-ago events are recorded in the rocks of the continents, and nowhere else.

Formation and Deformation of California and the Western North American Continent

Continents generally have an old core called a **craton,** which is ringed by sequentially younger and younger rock as one proceeds from the center toward the coasts. This is because the continents are continually accreting new terrains, or pieces of other continents or sea floor during plate-boundary interactions.

It is perhaps wiser to begin at the edge of a continent and try to understand the geology there before we move toward the center. In this manner we can begin with current tectonic activity and work our way backward in time. In order to understand what happened to a continent, we must infer the relative interaction of plate boundaries in the past. This is no small task, especially when we realize that the continent is being degraded continually by a powerful but relatively unrelated force, **erosion,** which is attempting to wipe clean any record of the past that stands above sea level. The western coast of North America is an excellent place to begin because in the recent past, all three forms of plate boundary have interacted with the continent along this coast.

The Present
Geology of California

California is a truly spectacular state geographically, as anyone who has flown across it on a clear day will attest. Running down the center of the state is a great valley or basin (Figure 12-1). It is here that the produce for most of the nation is grown. Surrounding the great valley are mountains on all sides. To the north are the southern Cascades, with Mt. Shasta, an active sister volcano to the more famous Mts. Rainier, Hood, and St. Helens. To the west, the Klamath mountains grade into the Diablos. Then the San Gabriel and San Jacinto mountains of the Transverse Range are found to the south. On the east are the magnificent Sierra Nevadas (Figure 12-1).

Figure 12-1. Physiographic map of California and Nevada. The San Andreas Fault is the linear, northwest–southeast striking feature separating the great valley of central California from the coast (dashed line). The Sierra Nevada mountains separate most of California from the stark Basin and Range topography of eastern California and all of Nevada.

When one flies from west to east across the Sierras, one makes a truly impressive observation. From a take off in San Francisco, the airplane struggles to gain enough altitude to climb above the Sierras, but after passing the crest of the mountains, the ground does not fall off very much at all. It is as if the mountains were a great dam holding back the deserts of Nevada and eastern California from spilling into the Pacific Ocean. The elevation of the state of Nevada is almost as high as the Sierras themselves.

Nevada and eastern California are magnificent in their own right, and are more beautiful in many ways than the fertile and green western California. The topography consists of a spectacular series of north–south trending ridges and basins (Figure 12-1). Called the Basin and Range, this arid region looks as if great fingers have scratched the surface of the planet. The ranges are almost as high as the Sierras but the basins, or valleys, can reach to below sea level. In fact, Death Valley is the lowest point in the entire United States (282 feet below sea level).

What forces have shaped such a dramatic terrain? The western edge of the North American plate *and* the eastern edge of the Pacific plate are both in California. That boundary is the San Andreas Fault, which is why most of the earthquake activity in the United States is centered there. To the north are the Cascades and Mount St. Helens, part of a volcanic arc resulting from the subduction of Pacific Ocean floor under Washington, Oregon, and northern California. And to the south, the Imperial Valley is the northern extremity of the Gulf of California, a sea-floor spreading center currently rifting Baja California away from Sonora, Mexico. All three types of plate boundary can be found within the borders of California. We can learn a great deal about how a continent is made by deciphering how the interaction of these plate boundaries has formed California.

Plate Boundary Changes in California over the Last 80 Million Years

Off the shore of California, magnetic anomalies can be identified for only the western half of a great spreading center that has produced all the sea floor from California to Hawaii in the last 80 million years; a similar volume of sea floor is missing. The entire eastern limb of that sea-floor spreading system is gone from the surface (Figure 12-2). If we look closely, we can find the final remnant of this once huge Farallon plate within a small triangle offshore Washington and Oregon. The spreading center seperating this Juan de Fuca plate from the Pacific plate used to be connected to the East Pacific Rise, which now ends in the Gulf of California.

What happened? As one might guess, the North American plate overran

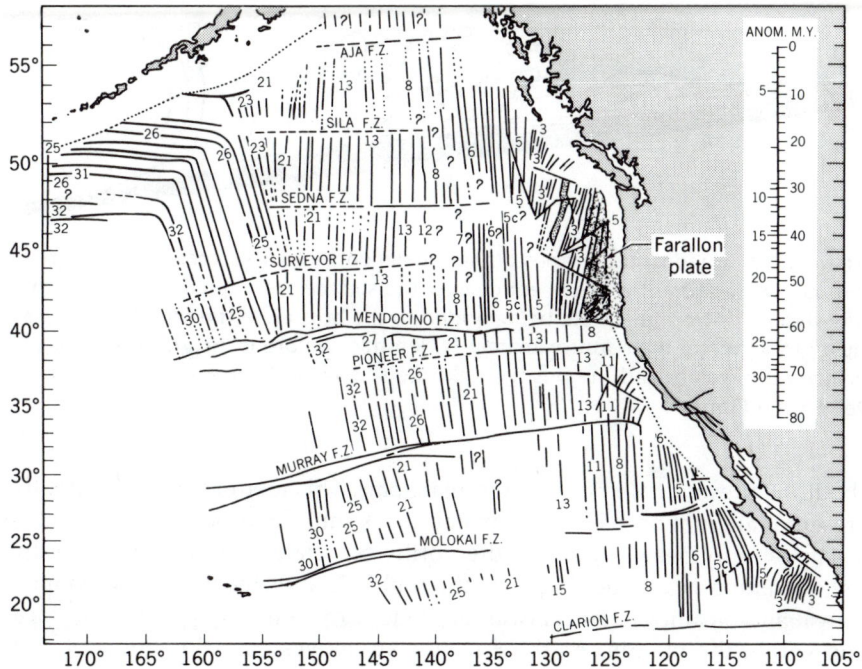

Figure 12-2. The tiny little triangle of plate being underthrust beneath Washington and Oregon is all that remains of the great Farallon plate which once covered half of the Pacific. Though small now, the Farallon is still responsible for volcanic eruptions such as Mt. St. Helens along the coast. Solid lines are magnetic anomalies of the present Pacific plate (magnetic anomaly numbers are proportional to age). The bend in the upper left is the only evidence still on the surface of the planet of the great Kula plate which was subducted beneath Alaska (from Atwater and Menard, 1970)

the Farallon plate, subducting almost all of it back into the mantle. Not all was subducted though, because some was scraped off to form the coastal mountains of western California (Figure 12-3). The remnants of the Farallon plate form the Franciscan formation, upon which the city of San Francisco was built. This process is called **accretion,** which is analogous to snow being shoved out of the way of a snowplow. That is, the softest top of the Farallon plate was scraped off during subduction onto the edge of the North American plate. This soft rock contains the fossil record of the animals that lived and died over the last 80 million years on the Farallon plate. So if you wish to study the history of Farallon, go to the northern coast of California

The history of this collision event can be traced by backtracking the motion of the three plates involved: Pacific, Farallon, and North America. Backtracking is accomplished by rotation of each plate backwards in time

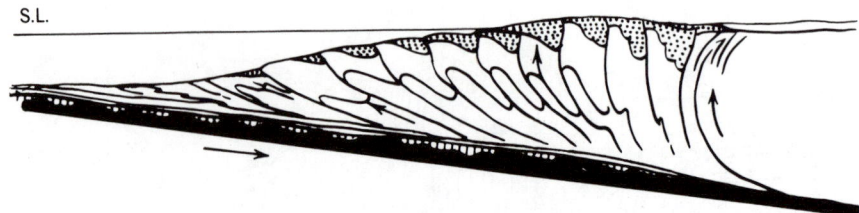

Figure 12-3. Subduction scrapes off soft sediments into an accretionary wedge of unusual stratigraphy. The sediment nearest the surface are often the oldest, with new sediments from the plate being added to the bottom of the pile. The wedge must grow greater than approximately 30 km thick before its height overcomes its increased weight and the prism breaks the surface and becomes land (from Dewey and Pitman).

about the present pole of each two-plate pair. This method assumes that the present plate motion has been constant back into the past. The Pacific plate has apparently been moving to the northwest relative to the mantle for the last 40 million years, judging from the trail of islands leading away from the Hawaiian volcanic center. Hawaii is thought to be a hot-spot fixed in location within the mantle. As the Pacific plate moves over this hot-spot, volcanoes cook their way through the plate to form islands at the surface. A trail of old islands to the northwest shows that the Pacific plate has been moving steadily in that direction for a long time into the past.

Relative motion of the other two plates about the Pacific plate is the relevant movement in this case, so we can assume the Pacific plate is fixed and ask how the others move relative to it. We can then convert the other plate motions to a reference frame fixed in the mantle, if necessary, because we know the Pacific-mantle movement.

The Farallon–Pacific motion is recorded in the direction of fracture zones frozen into the Pacific plate between Hawaii and California. Since these are almost straight lines, the assumption of constant Pacific–Farallon motion appears justified. North America–Farallon is more difficult, however. No fracture zones remain to record this motion. The San Andreas Fault is a transform fault that faithfully records the recent relative motion direction of the North America–Pacific plates, not North America–Farallon plate motion.

North American plate motion over the last tens of millions of years can be estimated either relative to a fixed volcanic center located within the plate (i.e., relative to the mantle) or relative to the Farallon plate if fracture zones can be found across a series of plate boundaries beginning with Farallon and ending at North America. For example, Yellowstone National Park in Wyoming is the latest volcanic center of a trail of lava extending across Idaho and into western Washington. This trail is a relatively straight line, so we might assume that North America has not changed motion by much in the period of time between the ages of Washington lavas (40 million years old) and Yellowstone lavas (recent). This direction for North America relative to the mantle is not relevant to the Farallon plate interaction so unless we can find a Farallon-mantle hot spot, we must deal in relative motions among surface plates.

For relative motion determinations of North America–Farallon plate motion, we must measure relative motion across fracture zones of the following plate pairs: Farallon–Pacific, Pacific–Antarctica, Antarctica–South America, and South America–North America. We find that again North American plate motion has been constant over the last 40 million years, moving southwestward and overriding Farallon (Figure 12-4).

The spreading center forming new Pacific and Farallon plates collided with North America about 30 million years ago just south of San Diego. From then until now, the San Andreas Fault has been gradually lengthening as the Farallon spreading center has been progressively subducted to the northwest (Figure 12-4). About 10 million years ago, the San Andreas Fault reached San Francisco, and now it extends some distance into the Pacific Ocean off Cape Mendicino north of San Francisco. As the spreading center was subducted, motion instantly changed from Pacific–Farallon and Farallon–North American plate motion to Pacific–North American motion at each point up the coast from San Diego through San Francisco. That change was from extension (Pacific–Farallon) and subduction (Farallon–North America) to transform fault motion (Pacific–North America).

To the south, the East Pacific Rise collided with Mexico, and rather than forming a transform fault like the San Andreas, North America–Pacific motion was slightly divergent instead of exactly across each other. The Gulf of California spreading center resulted. Transform motion is rather coincidental in California in that the plate boundary just happens to fall along a small circle about the Pacific–North American pole of rotation. To the south, the motion of the two plates is slightly away from each other. This results in continued sea-floor spreading, but at Pacific–North American divergence direction and rate instead of the previous Pacific–Farallon direction and rate at the East Pacific Rise. The resulting spreading center formed the Gulf of California as all of California west of the San Andreas Fault was rifted away from Sonora, Mexico, and onto the Pacific plate. These rocks are far from new. Some are hundreds of millions of years old. But now they ride on the Pacific plate. They were literally transferred from one plate to another as a piece of North America tore away and accreted to the Pacific plate—yet these are still part of North America, west of the San Andreas Fault.

Such an event is hard to believe, but the facts are incontrovertible. For example, you can pick up rocks on the beaches of southern California that have been polished by wave action to a brilliant red color. The exact same rocks can only be found in one other locale in the North American continent: Sonora, Mexico, hundreds of miles to the southeast.

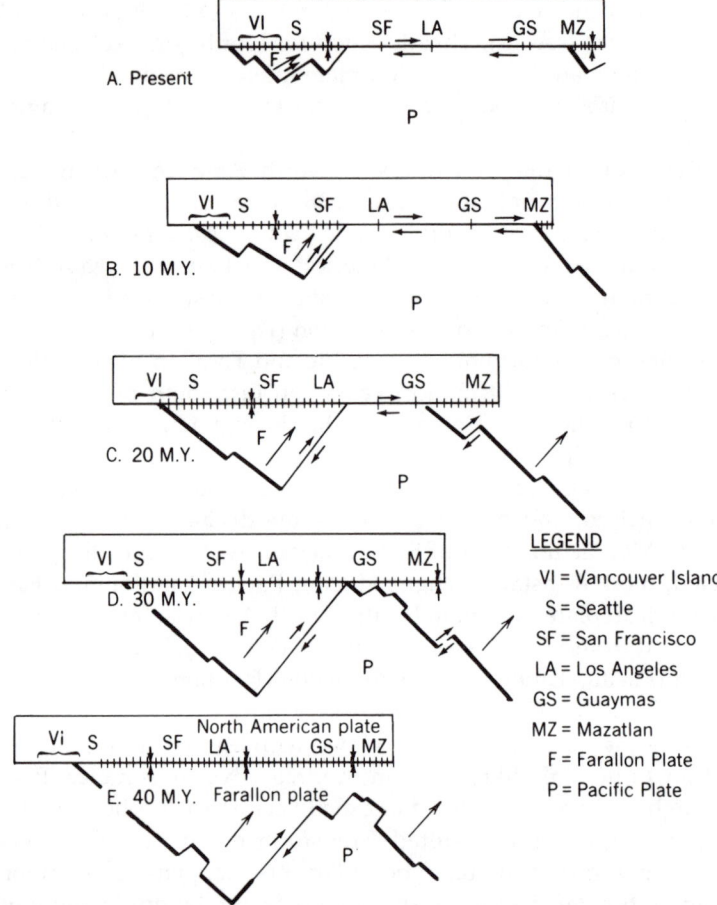

Figure 12-4. From bottom to top, the Farallon plate is being progressively shortened by subduction (railroad track symbols) under California. The Sierra Nevada mountains were formed at this time. Gradually, the East Pacific Rise was subducted as entire pieces of the Farallon plate disappeared (center). When the ridge axis was subducted, the plate-boundary motions along the California coast switched from North America–Farallon pole to North America–Pacific pole of rotation and the San Andreas Fault was born (horizontal arrows) (from Atwater, 1970).

California over the Next 50 Million Years

We can learn further how continents evolve if we assume that relative plate motions over the next 50 million years will remain as they are now. Then we can predict the evolution of the Pacific–North American plate boundary over that length of time. What will happen to California? Will it fall into the sea? Joe Curray of the Scripps Institution of Oceanography has constructed the following scenario based upon plate tectonic rules and regulations:

Five million years from now, Los Angeles will have ridden so far to the north that it will be across the fault from Berkeley (Figure 12-5). San Francisco, along with Palo Alto and Santa Cruz, will likely be under water.

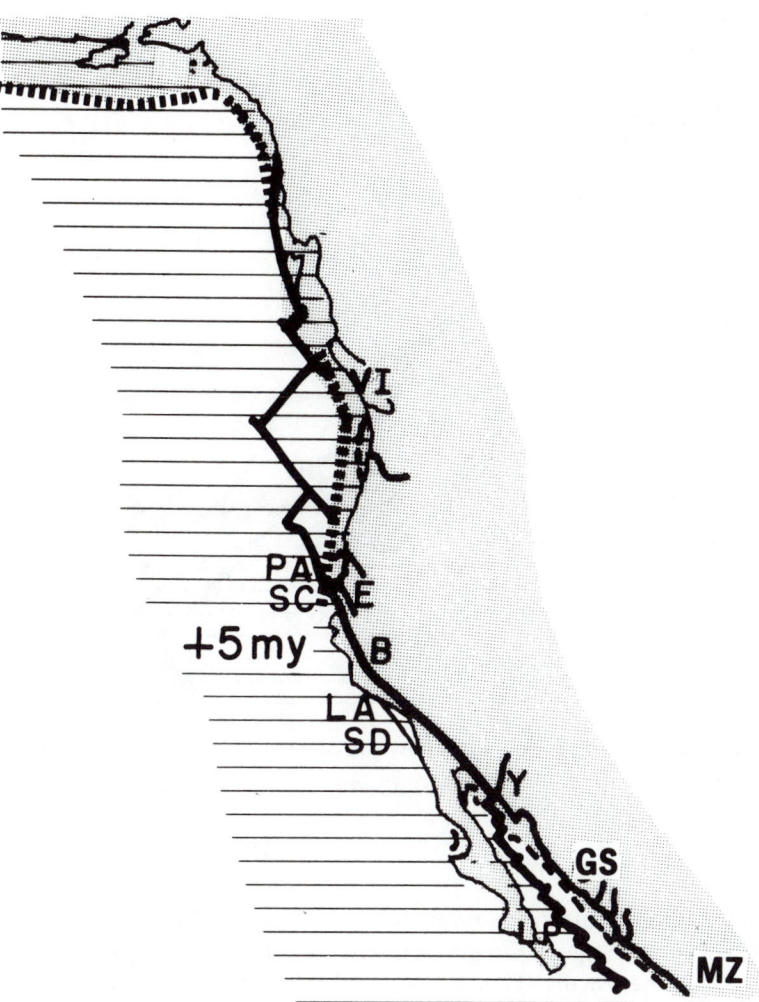

Figure 12-5. We can extrapolate the North American–Pacific plate boundary far into the future, though we will never know if these motions ever take place. Heavy solid lines are ridge and transform, heavy dashed lines are trench, stipled is land, and horizontal lines represent ocean. SD = San Diego, LA = Los Angeles, Y = Yuma, Arizona, GS = Guymas, LP = La Paz, B = Berkeley, SC = Santa Cruz, PA = Palo Alto, E = Eugene, Oregon, VI = Vancouver, MZ = Mazatlan (from J. Curray).

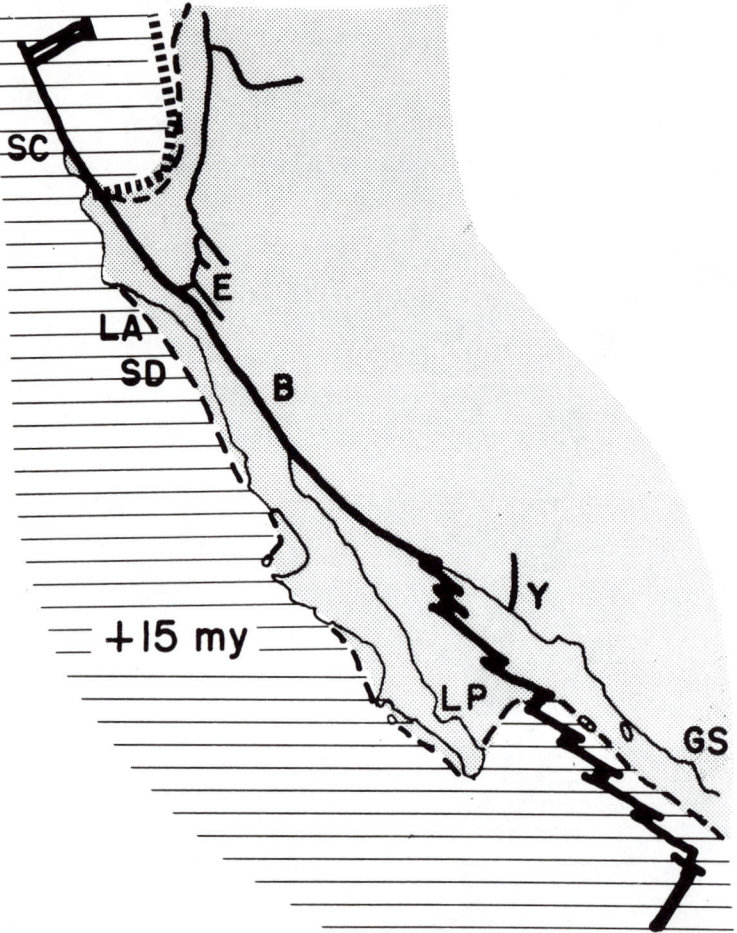

Figure 12-6. Fifteen million years from now the plates will be far displaced from the present locations (from J. Curray).

Fifteen million years from now, Los Angeles will be across the San Andreas Fault from Eugene, Oregon, but will be on a new peninsula of land protruding into the Pacific (Figure 12-6). Why will San Francisco sink but Los Angeles float? Because the rocks surrounding Los Angeles are hundreds of millions of years old and granitic (very lightweight), whereas those around San Francisco are soft, and only recently resident on the sea floor. The soft rock erodes easily, but not the granite.

The peninsula of Los Angeles will probably fill in with the deltaic outpouring of the Columbia River, producing a fertile valley. An even more fertile valley will by this time occupy the Gulf of California.

By 40 million years from now, a great inland sea will be almost sealed off from the Pacific by peninsular California (Figure 12-7). A huge river many times larger than the Mississippi will likely drain the fast-eroding Sierras and Cascades into this sea. Such an inland sea once covered most of mid-America 200 to 600 million years ago.

Fifty million years from now, peninsular California will collide with

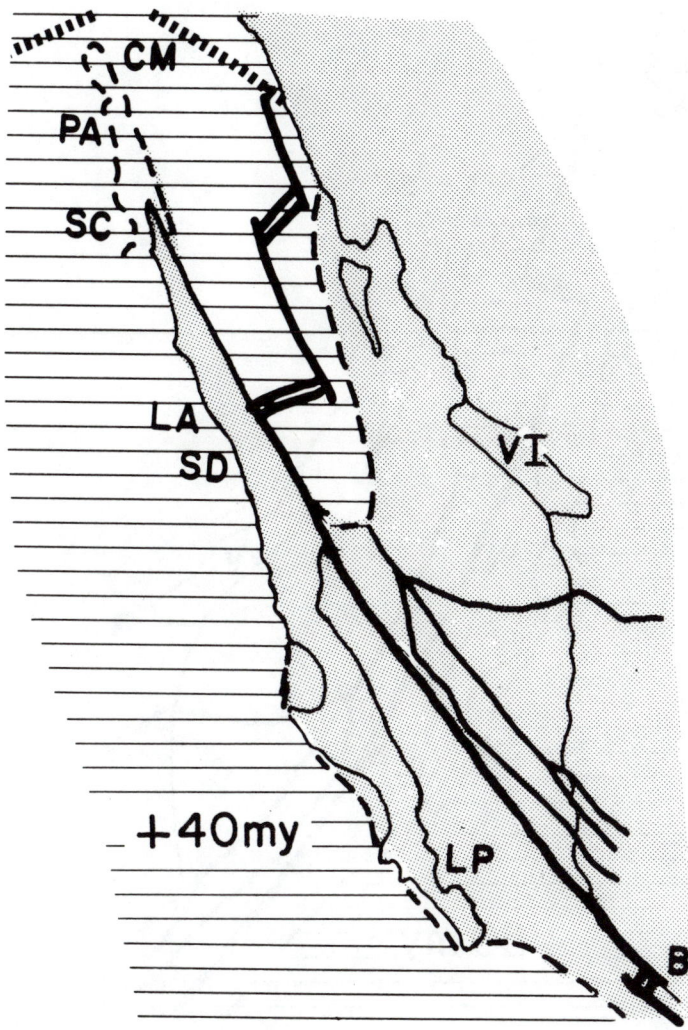

Figure 12-7. Forty million years from now, Baja California will be far north of Berkeley (from J. Curray).

Alaska. When continent meets continent, little is subducted; instead a new mountain range is formed from the collision (Figure 12-8). The remains of all the cities of western California will be incorporated into these mountains. If you wish to hunt for fossils from our civilization, southern Alaska will be the place to look. Behind the newly forming mountains, an inland sea which has been sealed from the Pacific is fast evaporating, leaving behind a vast salt lake about the size and depth of a dried-up Mediterranean Sea.

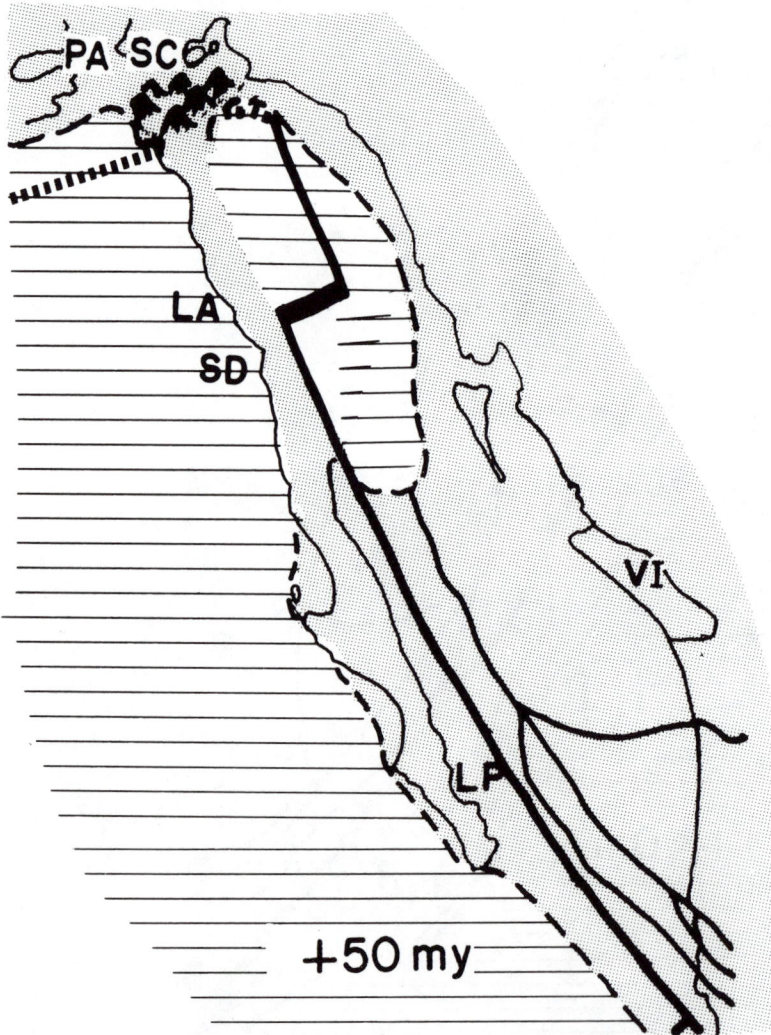

Figure 12-8. Fifty million years from now, fossils of life in San Francisco will have to be found among the mountains of southern Alaska (from J. Curray).

Are these predictions outlandish? Although we will never know whether Pacific–North American motion remains constant for the next 50 million years, we can say that each of the specific geological events described has happened elsewhere on the planet. The mountains of San Francisco will be small compared to the present Himalayas, which resulted from the collision of India and Asia. The Mediterranean Sea was indeed completely dry, only 10 million years ago as a result of the sealing of the Straits of Gibraltar. A great river, the Theyes, many times the size of the Mississippi, once crossed Ohio, Indiana, and Illinois from east to west.

Western North America 40 to 80 Million Years Ago

Back to the present and past of California, we still have not touched upon the origin of the two most striking features of the state, the Sierra Nevada Mountains and the Basin and Range. The Sierras are the volcanic pile left from millions and millions of years of subduction of Farallon ocean floor beneath the edge of the North American continent. The Farallon plate sank into the mantle, dehydrated, and then melted not only the surrounding mantle but also the bottom of the North American continent as the magma struggled to reach the surface. Granitic plutons, or remelted continent, were pushed to the surface along with basaltic magmas that had high concentrations of the light elements calcium and the alkalies. This volcanism formed

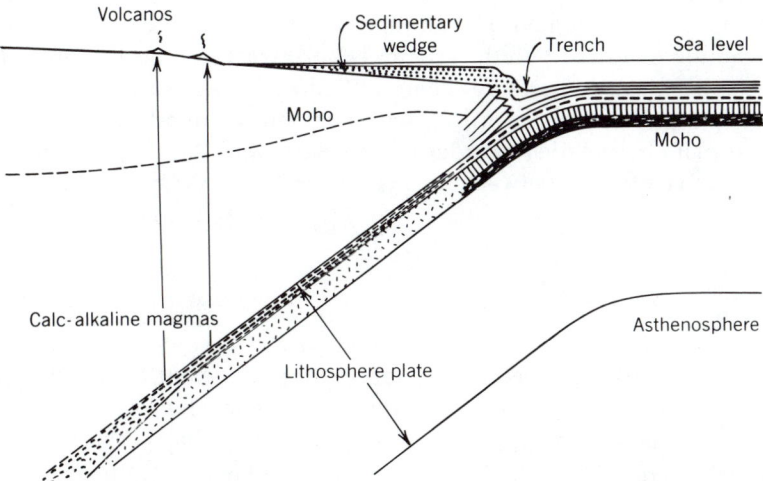

Figure 12-9. The detailed structure of a subduction complex (from Dewey and Pitman).

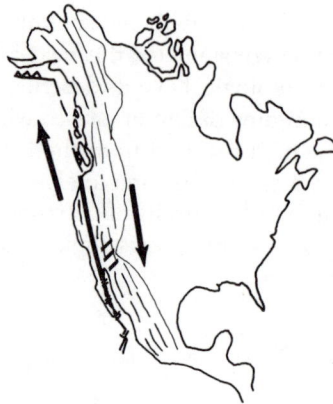

Figure 12-10. The bold arrows show the directions of relative motion between North America and Pacific plates. The major tectonic faults along the coast align with this direction, but the major faults of the Basin and Range are more oblique to this direction. The parallel faults are all strike-slip, and those that are oblique have a component of extension.

a buoyant pile of rocks that intermixed with accretion products to form a large mountain range, the Sierra Nevadas (Figure 12-9).

Considering all of western North America, the Sierra Nevadas were forming about the same time as the Rocky Mountains of New Mexico, Colorado, Wyoming, and Montana. The Rockies are an even larger mountain range that connects to the north with the Canadian Rockies. The Andes in South America are contemporaneous with the Rockies and the Sierra Nevadas. There must have been another plate between the Sierras and the Rockies whose underthrusting produced the **Laramide orogeny,** or the mountain-building episode responsible for the Rockies.

If we look between the Sierras and the Rockies today, we find the Basin and Range. The Basin and Range are a series of extensional basins behind the volcanic arc (the Sierras). The faulting direction is northeast–southwest, but the motion of Pacific–North America is northwest–southeast (Figure 12-10). These basins are, therefore, being pulled apart. As with any back-arc basin, coupling forces between the two plates must extend far away from the actual plate boundaries in order for the Basin and Range to be affected at all by relative motions between the plate boundary 1000 miles to the west.

The Evolution of Continents

The preceding examples illustrate an important point about plate-boundary interactions on continents: They generally involve a much broader area with more diffuse effects than oceanic plate interactions. Perhaps this is because of the much more substantial thickness of crust and mantle in the continental versus oceanic lithosphere. The Moho on continents is 30 to 40 km below the surface, and the root of the continent extends greater than 200 km into the mantle, in contrast to a Moho depth of 7 km and a lithospheric thickness of less than 100 km for the oceans.

There are only three ways a continent can be formed: collision, accretion, and volcanism. Each of these mechanisms results in the emplacement of large volumes of light rock (relative to ocean lithospheric rock) onto the continent. Most of that volume sinks below the surface, much the same as a block of floating wood, or better yet, an iceberg. If the continental rock is at equilibrium with gravity, then we call it **isostatically** compensated. If a mountain range both is made of lighter rock than the surrounding ocean floor and sticks upwards to much higher elevations, then it also must have a deeper root, or base, than oceanic rock. Indeed, we can measure the thickness of the continental plate by mapping seismic discontinuities caused by the partial melting of mantle rock at about 1300°C. Such partial melting slows down seismic waves, and the velocity anomaly can then be used to map the depth to the 1300°C isotherm under continents. Such seismic discontinuities are invariably deeper under continents, more than 200 km, compared to less than 100 km under oceans.

Once a continental fragment has been made, there are only three ways in which deformation can occur, and each affects the depth to the base of the continental lithosphere. First, rifting can occur. We can piece together the continents in much the way Wegener did by fitting the coastlines back together like one large jigsaw puzzle (Figure 12-11). Of course, we now can refit the continents in a more scientific way by backtracking along magnetic anomalies, using plate-tectonic geometries, and employing a whole suite of geological tools such as the dates of evolutionary branchings and geographical isolation of biota. We are certain that 200 million years ago North America, South America, Africa, Australia, India, and Eurasia were together as one large supercontinent we call Gondwanaland (Figure 12-11). The continents of today rifted away from the megacontinent and drifted on various plates to their present locations. This rifting or extensional event resulted in the stretching and thinning of continental crust along the margins of the present continents. We will look more closely at this process in the next chapter on the formation of sedimentary basins. It is along these stretched margins that most of the world's oil and gas were formed.

A second process that results in the deformation of the continents is, of course, collision. If oceanic and continental plates collide, an Andean-type mountain range forms from the melting of the subducting oceanic plate. But if two continents collide neither can underthrust and they accrete to each other. The increased volume forces the base of the continent to deepen under such a mountain range, and the land rises as a result of isostasy to form some of the highest elevations on the planet. Tibet and the Himalayas are the result of collision between India and Eurasia.

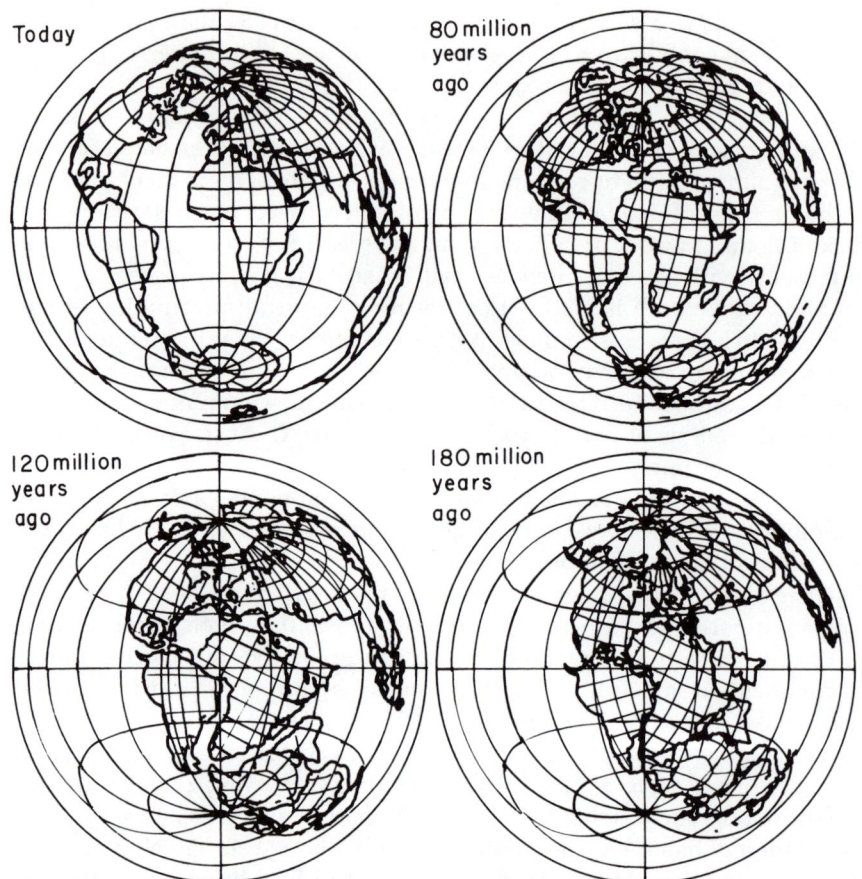

Figure 12-11. Paleomagnetism allows us to reconstruct the positions of the continents relative to the north pole, here shown from 200 million years ago to present. The present is the only time for which we know longitude, however (from Maxwell, 1985).

The third form of deformation of a continent occurs when a large weight is loaded onto the plate. Flexure of the plate occurs as the continent seeks isostatic equilibrium again. Deepening of the base of the plate results. Think of loading one corner of a block of wood floating in water. Not only will the base of the loaded corner sink deeper, but the whole block will tilt. The other edge of the block will actually rise out of the water to a higher altitude. These tiltings and horizontal compensations to loading are called **epirogeny,** as opposed to vertical motions from processes such as mountain-building which are called **orogeny.** One can see that the emplacement of any large load results in flexure as well as the more traditional plate-tectonic processes such as rifting or collision. Examples of emplacement of such loads are deep

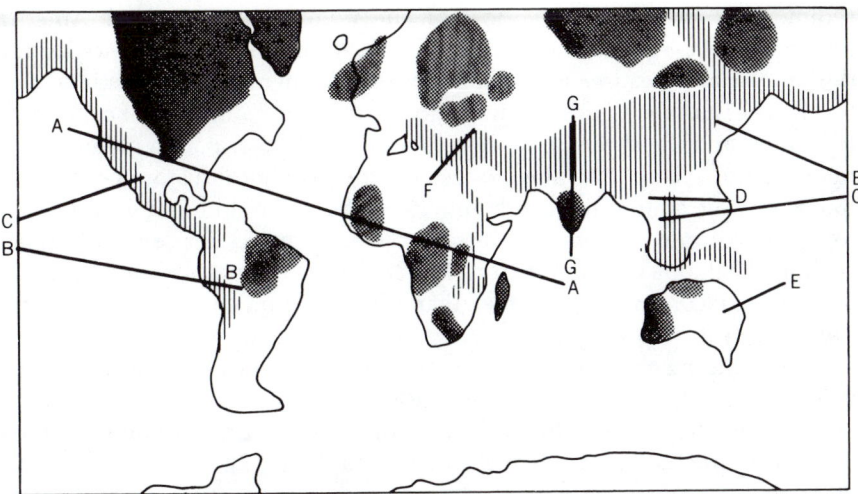

Figure 12-12. Center of continental cratons indicated by shading. Hatching locates mountain belts of the world. Cross sections indicated by lines and letters are shown in Figure 12-13.

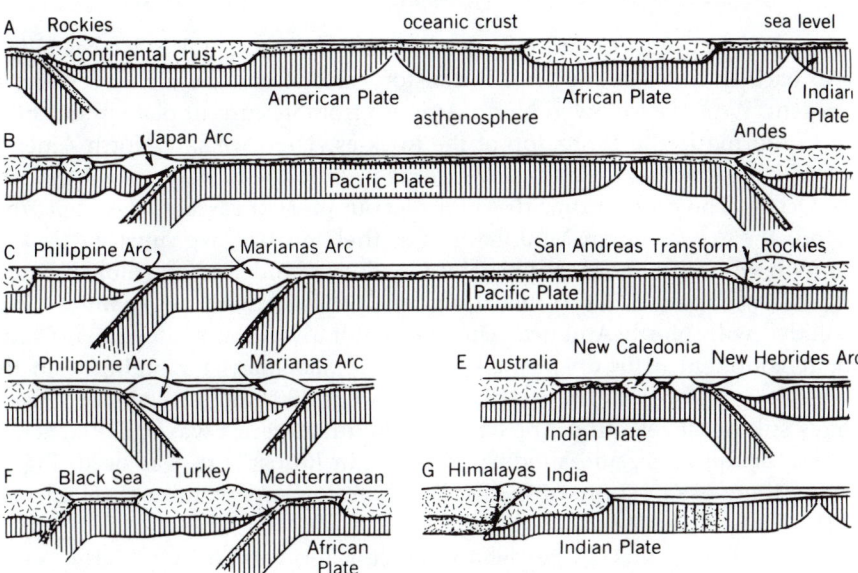

Figure 12-13. Cross sections along various transects of Figure 12-12 (from Dewey, 1972).

sedimentary basins, such as those off the shore of eastern North America, and river deltas such as the Gulf of Mexico. As another example, ice loading during glaciation causes major epirogenic movements within continents.

If we can understand the interaction of the three processes of continental formation and the three processes of continental deformation on any continent, then we should be able to describe the geological history of that continent. If we examine the continents as a whole, we find that each has one to several central cratons that have survived tectonics for several hundred million to billions of years (Figure 12-12). These are the remnants from the formation of continents after the great differentiation event that formed the Earth's core (Chapter 1).

Surrounding these cratons are successive histories of collision, rifting, volcanism, and/or flexure. At the present time, large areas of North and South America, Eurasia, India, and Southeast Asia are experiencing these formation and deformation processes (Figure 12-12). Slices through the lithosphere across several of these continental deformation zones illustrate the various formational and deformational processes in action today around the globe (Figure 12-13).

The Geological History of an Exemplar Continent: North America

It is perhaps useful to end our introduction of continental processes with a trip back through as much of the history of one continent as we know at present. We have followed North America from its current plate interactions in California to the formation of the Rockies. Then we saw North America could be reattached to Africa and Europe prior to the formation of the Atlantic Ocean. The rifting from Africa formed our present eastern coast, but what about the Appalachian Mountains? For their history, we must go back in time to when the megacontinent of Gondwanaland was assembled, before it was torn apart. Prior to the rifting event that formed the Atlantic, Africa collided with North America. They were not always stuck together. Continent–continent collision pushed up the Appalachians far higher than the present-day Rockies. They were so high that 300 million years of erosion have still not leveled the Appalachians. South America was still attached to Africa at this time, and subduction of ocean lithosphere was occurring all along the western shore of the newly reforming supercontinent (Figure 12-14).

Even before this, in Permian time, collision was closing a large ocean that was even bigger than the Pacific at one time. This Tethys ocean floor was accreted onto the North American continent and into a mountain

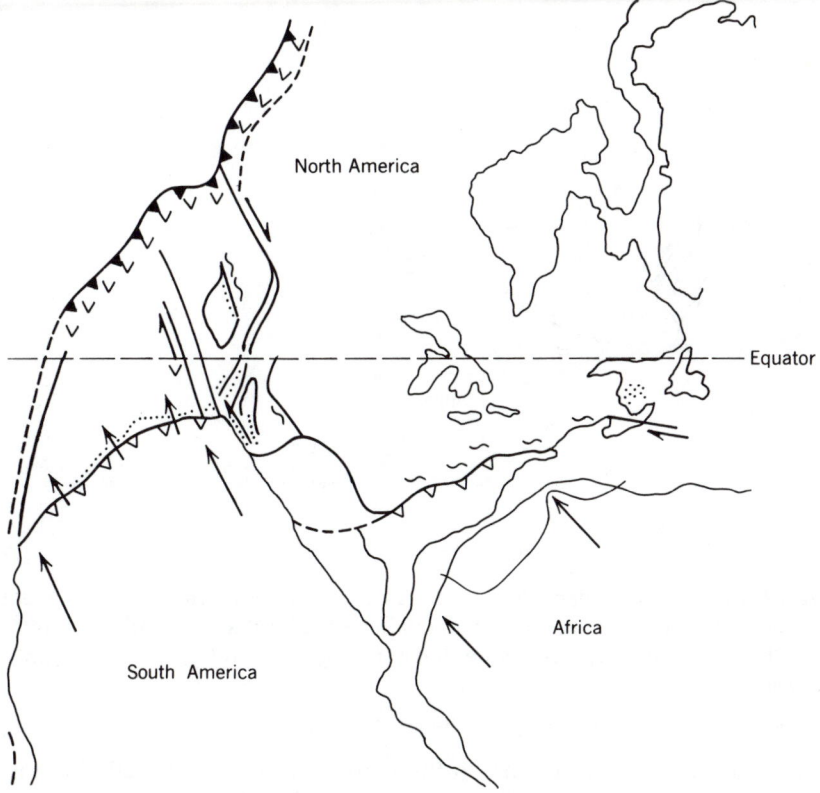

Figure 12-14. Plate boundaries about 300 million years ago (from Dewey and Pitman). Solid hatching is active subduction. Open hatching represents fossil subduction or collision zones. V's are volcanoes.

range of which only a few hills remain today. Yet this mountain range must have towered over the continent in its day. The traces of its remains are the Wichita and Arbuckle Mountains of Oklahoma and the Quachitas of Arkansas. It is hard to visualize these states as the mountain resort centers of that time. Other parts of this mountain range are now in the Yucatan of Mexico and in the country of Mauritania in western Africa (Figure 12-15).

Before the closing of the Tethys, a sea lane extended across central America connecting what is now the Atlantic with the Pacific. The closing of this passageway isolated an inland sea which dried up to form massive salt layers. These were subsequently buried with a hugh pile of organic-rich sediments. Millions of years of burial cooked the organic material into oil, and the weight of the overlying mud pushed the salt to the surface in the form of diapirs, called salt domes. These diapirs collected the oil into traps

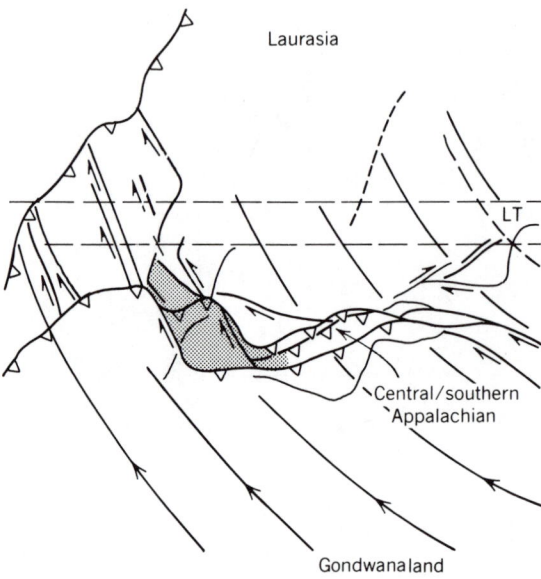

Figure 12-15. Plate boundary along the southern edge of the United States about 400 million years ago. A great mountain range far higher than the Rockies stood where Oklahoma, Arkansas, Tennessee, and Kentucky stand today (shading) (from Dewey and Pitman).

on their way to the surface, and so the Gulf of Mexico eventually became the center of the United States' production of oil and other hydrocarbons. We will see in the next chapter how this process occurs in detail, but it is important to realize that an understanding of the geology of the continents and how they interact with the oceans is essential to the discovery of new oil reserves in the world. After all, most of the professional employees of the huge oil companies of the world are geologists. That is why geology is the third highest paying profession today, behind doctors and lawyers.

Summary

We see why a course in marine geology must end on the continents, where all the old ocean floor resides on the planet. An understanding of the continents requires that the history of plate-tectonic interactions be understood

understood well into the geological past. And that requires a detailed knowledge of the history of the ocean basins. We always work from the relatively simple to the complex, and a cursory glimpse of Figure 12-15 shows how much more complicated the continents are than the oceans.

It is ironic that the profession of geology began with the study of the continents. The great intellectual leaps in our understanding of how the planet works came only after we understood the oceans. We are just now prepared to attack the original problem with new gusto, but the continents are so much more complicated than the oceans that many years of investigation are still ahead of us. For example, we still know most of our information about the continents from measurements made at the surface. Only in the sedimentary basins have we drilled deep into the interior to provide ground-truth observations to test our theories. We are just beginning to drill into the deep continents for scientific, rather than economic, purposes. New understandings to rival those from the oceans promise to follow the drill bit's progress deep inside the Earth.

Further Reading

Burchfiel, B. C., 1983, The continental crust: Scientific American, v. 249, pp. 130–145.

Woodcock, N. H., 1981, The deformation of rocks, *in* D. G. Smith, ed., Cambridge Encyclopedia of Earth Sciences: New York, Crown/Cambridge University Press.

Rifting of Continents, Sedimentary Basins, and the Formation Of Oil and Gas

We have seen how continents form and deform, but one of the first recognized observations about the continents was that they fit back together like a jigsaw puzzle. Wegener would have probably released his imagination on some other science during those long winters of physical isolation on the Greenland ice sheet if it hadn't been for the remarkable "coincidence" that scissors could easily reunite South America with Africa on the map. The actual process that caused the rifting apart of those great continents produced a legacy that affects our daily lives more than any other natural phenomenon. More than earthquakes shake and destroy, more than volcanoes billow and burn, more than hurricanes and tornadoes kill and terrify, hydrocarbons (oil, gas, and coal) govern our modern existence. Fertilizers feed our masses, gasoline powers our engines of war and peace, plastics form our consumer products, gas heats our homes, and coal makes our electricity. Believe it or not, all these things come from the past rifting and colliding of continents.

It requires a stretch of the imagination to believe that these things we see and use every day are the result of a monumental event that happened millions and millions of years ago. But did you ever wonder where oil and gas come from? Or why they are often found just offshore on the continental margins? Or why Oklahoma and Texas have an abundance of oil but New

Jersey has little? In this chapter we will use the example of the formation of hydrocarbons to illustrate the broader processes that occur before, during, and after continents rift apart.

The Rifting of South America Away from Africa

To begin to understand the process of rifting, consider the most famous continental fit: South America and Africa. First of all, do they really fit back together? Not as well if you cut along the present coastline as if you cut at the edge of the continental shelf. The shallow water of the continental shelf often extends for a hundred miles or more away from the coast. Then there is an abrupt deepening toward the deep sea called the continental slope.

The reason the continental shelf must be included in the continental fit is that the present-day sea level is really quite a tenuous place upon which to stake a claim. It has varied by up to 300 m in the last 100 million years. Sea level is partially controlled by how much water is in the oceans versus in the glaciers of the ice caps. It is easy to see that if the Earth were in the midst of an ice age, as it was only a million or so years ago, the oceans would be at a low point. Just that long ago, the New York and New Jersey coast extended 150 miles out to sea. Manhattan was merely a hill among many on the edge of the Hudson River. The Texas and Louisiana coast was 100 miles to sea from the present coast. Why? Because the shelves of the continents are very shallow, and they extend for long distances offshore. The Falkland Islands are 500 miles offshore of Argentina, for example, but the water is never deeper than a few hundred meters between the two. If the climate chills just a little bit, then the polar ice sheets expand at the expense of water in the oceans, and the sea level recedes.

Consider now the opposite case. We hear a great deal about the carbon dioxide problem: The burning of so much fossil fuel will fill our atmosphere with carbon dioxide and the greenhouse effect will increase the temperature of the surface by a couple of degrees. A greenhouse is transparent to light entering, even in the winter. But the light hits the floor and splits into all the wavelengths of the spectrum. The infrared portion of the spectrum tries to bounce back out the greenhouse walls, but the humid atmosphere trapped within the greenhouse is opaque to infrared light, and those wavelengths are trapped inside. This energy is retained as heat because the infrared energy bounces around the room ricocheting off the countless water and carbon dioxide molecules in the attempt to escape. The opaqueness of the atmosphere causes many collisions, and the collisions heat up the atmosphere.

If we continue to pump more carbon dioxide into the atmosphere, thus increasing its opaqueness, the result will be an increase in the planet's average temperature. An increase of just a couple of degrees will cause enough ice to melt to flood all of the great port cities of the world. Texas, for instance, would have new port cities of Austin, San Antonio, and Dallas. Florida would have no cities above water.

Sea level is also controlled by an equally powerful force, a rather subtle change that can occur in the elevation of the bottom of the sea. The volume of ocean water is fixed at any one time depending upon how much ice is in glaciers. If the spreading rate of midocean ridges suddenly increases (e.g., from 1 to 10 cm/yr), then the slope of the sea floor away from the ridge crest and toward the deep ocean basins will become more gentle (less steep). The slope changes because the elevation of the oceanic lithosphere is not controlled by the distance of any given piece of rock from the ridge crest but by its age, since it has been cooling at a uniform rate ever since it was extruded volcanically onto the plate. The cooling of the plate is age-dependent. If the spreading rate is 10 times as fast, then there is 10 times more young rock on the newly accreting edge of the oceanic lithosphere. Then the elevation of the sea floor is higher than at the slower spreading rate because the hot rock stands higher. The ocean is a fixed volume, so the water level is forced upward and must go somewhere. The lithosphere literally pushes the sea level higher, flooding the edges of the continents. This phenomenon is analogous to the rise in water level in a bathtub when you submerge all of your body versus half of it. The constant volume of water must go somewhere, and you have occupied more of the bottom space in the tub. Obviously, the spreading rate could just as easily slow down, forcing the sea level down and exposing most of the present continental margin to the forces of erosion. Then the port cities of Texas would be 100 miles seaward of Galveston or Corpus Christi.

All this past movement of sea level points to why geologists consider the edge of the continental shelf the true boundary of the continents. This is why if you cut South America along the edge of the continental margin, a better fit to Africa results (see Chapter 3, Figure 3-2). But is such a fit substantial proof that the two continents were indeed once together? If so, Wegener would have had much more success in convincing his colleagues of the truth to continental drift. Cut the eastern edge of Australia and place it against Chile. A reasonable fit results, yet we have no evidence that those two continents were ever together along those coasts. That fit is fortuitous.

Instead, the geological scars from the rifting event must match on the two sides of the ocean. Not only must the geography fit, but the geological similarity must be present as well. Remember the red rocks of southern California versus those of Sonora, Mexico. By examining that geological evidence, we will learn not only how continents came to separate, but also why countries that were once together along the coasts, such as Nigeria and Brazil, are blessed with some of the world's largest hydrocarbon reserves.

Rifting of Continents

The great Amazon River does not flow where it does randomly. It chooses the easiest path from the Andes Mountains down to the ocean. That easiest of paths is a large, gently sloping valley over 200 miles wide, which is the remnant of the rifting of South America from Africa (Figure 13-1). It connects directly into the Benue rift valley of Nigeria (Figure 13-2), and represents the failed arm of a network of rift valleys, which eventually succeeded in splitting a huge continent in two.

We know how these great rift valleys worked their magic, but we are not sure why. In the next and last chapter, we will discuss the driving force of not only continental rifting, but of all the motions of the plates. From among those forces, a pulling-apart within a continent originates. Such a force began in the Jurassic period more than 160 million years ago, along what was to become the east coast of South America and the west coast of Africa. The pulling apart "stretched" the continent. Since the surface rocks were too brittle to stretch, faulting occurred, and **Grabens** were formed. A

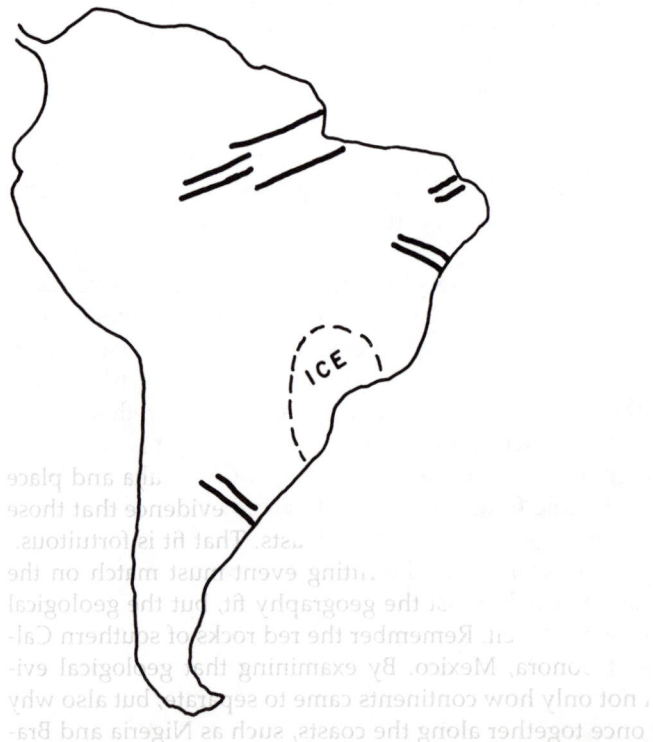

Figure 13-1. The major rift valleys of South America are shown by hatchered bars (from Windley, 1984). Ice indicates location of past glaciation.

Figure 13-2. Corresponding plot for Africa shows rift valley of Amazon extends into Nigeria (from Windley, 1984). Notice also fit of region of past glaciation into that in South America.

graben is a faulted valley where both sides are normal faults sloping away from the center. As stretching occurs, faults break and the center block of rock falls down into the space left from the stretching-apart (Figure 13-3). An analogous condition can be formed by pulling apart a Milky Way candy bar. The center is soft and stretches, but the brittle chocolate outer coating

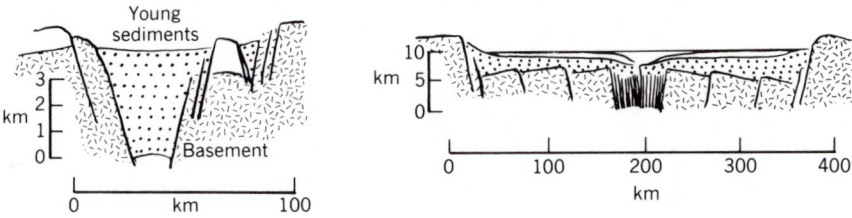

Figure 13-3. *(Left)* Syn-rift sediments are deposited into newly forming basin which is caused by stretching of continental crust. *(Right)* Post-rift sediments are deposited into new ocean basin as extension by sea-floor spreading takes over after continental stretching is completed (from Dewey and Pitman). Syn-rift sediments are buried by these new oceanic sediments.

breaks apart and forms many grabens. If you continue to pull, two smaller chocolate bars result.

A present-day example of such a graben is the East African Rift Valley, where eastern Africa is currently trying to rift away from western Africa (Figure 13-4). It has succeeded partially in the Red Sea, where ocean has invaded the graben, and Saudi Arabia is clearly split away from Egypt. Millions of years from now, East Africa will be in the middle of the Indian Ocean with a thousand miles of ocean separating it from western Africa.

The form of either the Red Sea or the East African Rift hints at the process that is actively rifting the continent apart. To get to either valley, you must negotiate mountains that flank both rift valleys. The rifting mechanism must produce uplifting of the graben edges as well as stretching within the valley, since mountains invariably surround such rift valleys. We have seen many times already on the planet that uplift often means that excess heat is present, and this example is no exception. The stretching produces faulting in the brittle continental crust, but the more ductile mantle below the Moho can thin like taffy that has been stretched. This thinning results in the upwelling of hot asthenosphere to fill the new gap. This hot material pro-

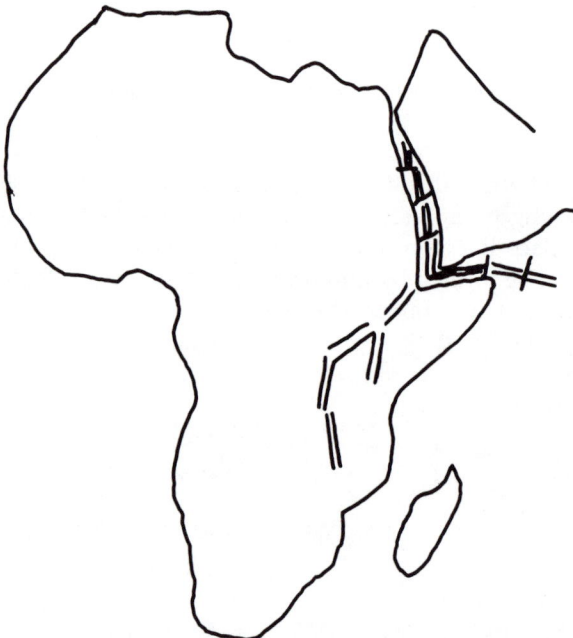

Figure 13-4. Rift valleys of Africa that are currently in the process of splitting eastern Africa away from the rest of the continent (from Windley, 1984).

duces uplift on the valley walls by thermal expansion just as the midocean ridges are elevated above the ocean basins by the same process.

As stretching continues, a crack is gradually made in the continental crust within the rift valley, and asthenosphere wells up to form volcanoes at the surface. As the stretching continues, volcanoes soon become continuous along the valley floor and ocean floor is made. It is ocean floor not because it is under water, necessarily, but because the rock is black, heavy basalt, which has only enough hydraulic head to rise to a mile or so below sea level. Remember that the surrounding continental mountains are composed of light-colored and lightweight granites, which are much more buoyant than basalt (Figure 13-5).

A long, linear valley full of erupting volcanoes a mile below sea level cannot help but eventually be flooded by the ocean. If we again look at the East African Rift and the Red Sea, we see that the former is not ocean, but the latter is. The Red Sea is a little wider and farther along toward the later stages of stretching than are the rifts. Yet even there, the ocean is beginning

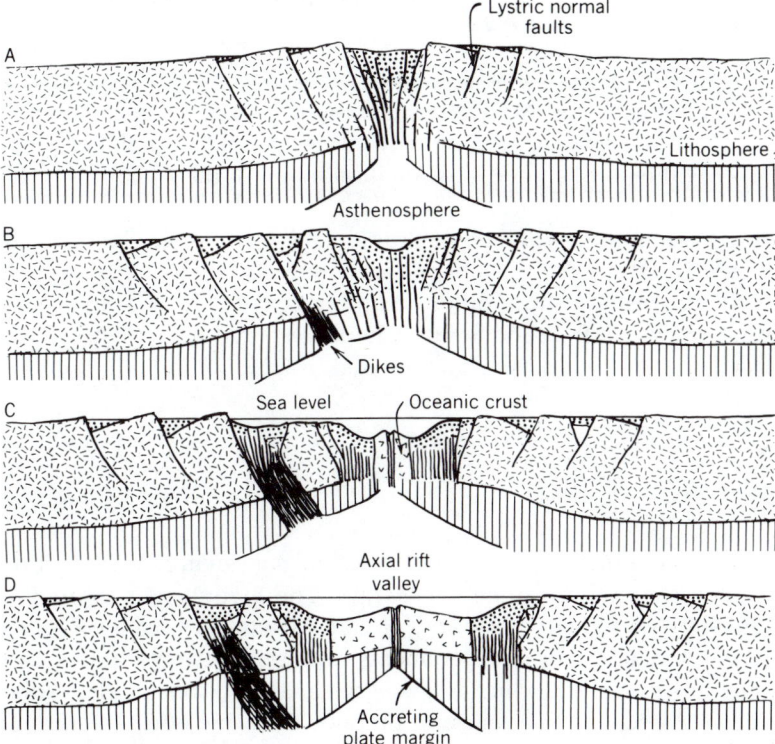

Figure 13-5. A through D carry us through the sequence of continental rifting. Note that the asthenosphere rises toward the surface as the lithosphere thins (from Dewey and Pitman).

Figure 13-6. View looking along the axis of a sea floor spreading center. The photo was taken from 155 m *below* sea level on the shore of Lake Asal, looking east toward the Gulf of Aden in Ethiopia. The central rift valley is surrounded by faulted blocks of progressively older and older rock. The Gulf of Aden will soon break through to annex the lake, and this will all be part of the Indian Ocean (from Courtillot, *Scientific American*, 1983).

to infringe. In Ethiopia, the Afar Desert is basaltic "sea floor" resting below sea level, with the ocean held back by only one remaining natural dike. Soon this last dike will be broken and ocean will flood all of the Afar (Figure 13-6).

As rifting continues beyond this volcanic stage, normal sea-floor spreading takes over and the new lithosphere added to the two sides of the original valley is indistinguishable from other ocean lithosphere. The present center of spreading between Africa and South America, the mid-Atlantic ridge, was once at the center of a sea as small as the Red Sea.

The Formation of Sedimentary Basins

After initial rifting comes erosion, deposition, and subsidence, as these three processes then shape the continental margin. The mountains surrounding the rift valley are slowly but inexorably eroded back toward sea level by the forces of ice, wind, and rain. The sediments from this erosion are deposited in the newly formed valley, which is below sea level. Erosion and deposition act in opposite directions to attempt to produce the same effect—returning the surface to sea level. Erosion tears down anything above sea level and deposition fills up any depressions below sea level.

The continental margins become sedimentary basins because the subsidence of the rift valley floor continues long after the continents have drifted away from the spreading center. Just as with normal ocean lithosphere, the continent that has been stretched has had heat added to it. The rock subsides slowly with time as it conductively cools and contracts. However, the crust contracts to a deeper level than before rifting because it has been stretched and thinned so that it is not as thick as it used to be. It is below sea level even at its most heated stage because uplift from thermal expansion is offset by stretching. Cooling then results in even deeper subsidence. Rivers deliver sediments from erosion to fill the subsiding continental margin and force it even deeper with the added weight they bring (Figure 13-5). Therefore, all the post-rift forces act to deepen the pile of sediments accumulating along the rifted continental margin, and a sedimentary basin is born.

The Deposition of Salt at the Bottom of Sedimentary Basins

Before we establish the proof that these processes really exist, we must discuss one final event that often occurs within the newly forming rift valley and that will have profound effects on oil and gas accumulation in later geological history. Have you ever wondered why oil and gas are often associated with salt domes?

Our concerns are (1) where the salt comes from and (2) why oil is found near salt. In the early days of formation of the new ocean within a rift valley, the graben is repeatedly flooded with seawater. Episodes of flooding begin at intervals spaced far enough apart for the new ocean to dry up between floods, with all the water evaporating to leave only its salt behind. Flooding events gradually increase in regularity until an ocean finally appears permanently. The Red Sea is now at that stage. But left behind at the very bottom of the valley are thick layers of salt. The Red Sea has almost 1 km of salt at its bottom. Other major oil-producing basins such as the North Sea, the Persian Gulf, and the Gulf of Mexico all have salt at the bottom of their considerable piles of sediment. Whether a basin has salt at its base is simply a matter of circumstance. If a newly forming proto-ocean is sealed off by dikes, then evaporation can occur. If it is open at one or both ends, no salt will form because the seawater will be well flushed.

The salt is not stable at the bottom of a large pile of sediment because it is much lighter than mud. With time, it squeezes its way toward the surface as diapirs called salt domes. Salt flows very easily while still remaining solid, so the weight of rock above it forces plumes of salt to rise up through the overlying sedimentary pile. Oil that has formed above then flows, or migrates, to the edges of the salt domes because they provide a pathway for the equally buoyant oil to rise. The salt blocks its further progress toward the surface, and a trap of oil and/or gas forms. We'll return to this later.

The secret to salt formation is the existence of rock barriers to the intrud-

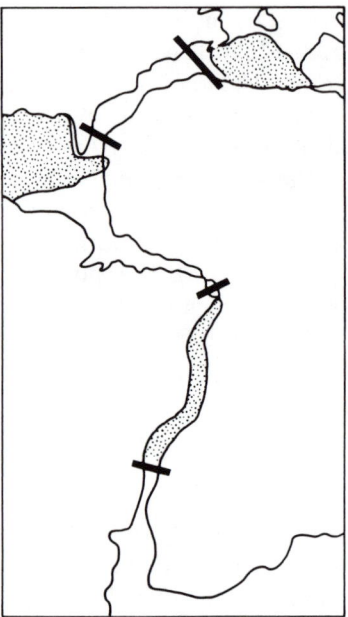

Figure 13-7. Salt deposits (stipled) formed in the small ocean basins which were blocked from general ocean water circulation by "Gibraltar-like" obstructions (from Dewey and Pitman).

ing ocean. The observation that repeated flooding occurs then requires that these barriers periodically build up in height only to be later broken back down. Erosion alone is not enough because no mechanism for buildup exists. Volcanicity appears necessary. For example, volcanic ridges across the southern, central, and northern proto-south Atlantic Ocean at the Rio Grande–Walvis ridges in the south, the Cabo ridge in the center, and the Bahamas–Canary ridge in the north isolated the Brazilian and Gabon margins, the Nigerian margin, and the Gulf of Mexico to form the mother salt that today traps oil in each of these basins (Figure 13-7).

Backstripping a Sedimentary Basin

Now for the proof that sedimentary basins form by stretching of continental crust, then subside as they cool, and are filled by sediments eroded from the surrounding mountains and deposited into the new depression. Most of what we know about sedimentary basins comes from the drill bit. When an oil well penetrates into the depths of a basin, we benefit from the knowledge returned to the surface by cuttings of rock or that detected in situ by a widely used technique called wireline logging. In logging, a nuclear, sonic, or electrical source is lowered into the well, and a geiger counter, transducer, or electrode records the response of the rock to nuclear particle bombardment, sound energy, or electric current. The type of rock, its porosity, and whether oil, gas, or water fill the pore spaces can be determined from these records, called **logs.** Literally hundreds of thousands of oil wells have been attempted in sedimentary basins by now, and although only one in ten finds commercial quantities of oil or gas, ten in ten yield useful geological information.

As the bit drills deeper into a basin, the rock becomes older, but it also becomes more compacted from the weight of the overburden above. By measuring the density of this sedimentary pile, we determine the magnitude of one of the dominant forces that causes the basin to subside. Loading bends the lithosphere as if it were a beam of wood. Flexure of the lithosphere upon which a basin sits produces not only subsidence at the center of the basin, but the edges actually bulge to a slightly higher elevation than if unbent (Figure 13-8). The bulge will be quickly eroded, exposing older rocks on the edge of a basin.

The other forces causing subsidence of the basin can be determined only after removal of the load-induced subsidence from the total depth of the basin. Consider one well in the center of a basin. It may hit basement after drilling through 10 km of sediments. The density of the sediment produces a load on the lithosphere which can account for some 50 percent of that 10-km depression in the solid basement rock under the basin. That is, the sheer

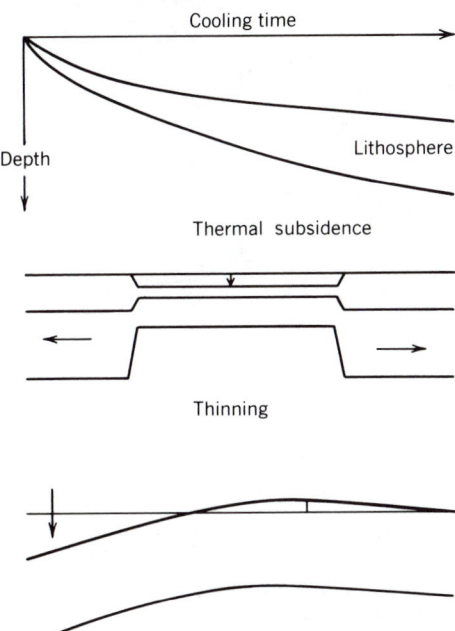

Figure 13-8. Three principal modes of lithospheric subsidence are thermal cooling, thinning, and emplacement of a load (from Watts).

weight of all that mud can account for 5 km of the depth of the basin. But it cannot account for all the sinking that is observed. A technique called **back-stripping** is used to calculate how much subsidence is due to the weight of the sediment, and how much is left over from tectonic causes.

Consider now a well that has been drilled off the shore of New Jersey. By dating the rock cuttings as they come to the surface, the total thickness of sediment accumulated over time can be determined. For example, 20-million-year-old fossils are encountered 1 km below the surface, 40-million-year-old bugs are found at 1.5 km, 100-million-year-old rock at 2.5 km depth and the oldest sediments are found just above basement. They are 140 million years old and 5 km below the surface. But the logs show that the density of that column of sediment is sufficient to produce a load capable of bending the lithosphere to only 3.5 km of the present total depth of 5 km. Backstripping determines the amount of subsidence caused by sediment weight at 20, 40, 100, and 140 million years ago by calculating a load from the thickness and density of sediment older than each of those ages (Figure 13-9). A curve of subsidence versus time caused by sediment loading is back-stripped off the total subsidence of the rock which is its actual depth in the well. The rock is consistently too deep for the sedimentary load. This extra subsidence is caused by the two tectonic forces acting to push the basin

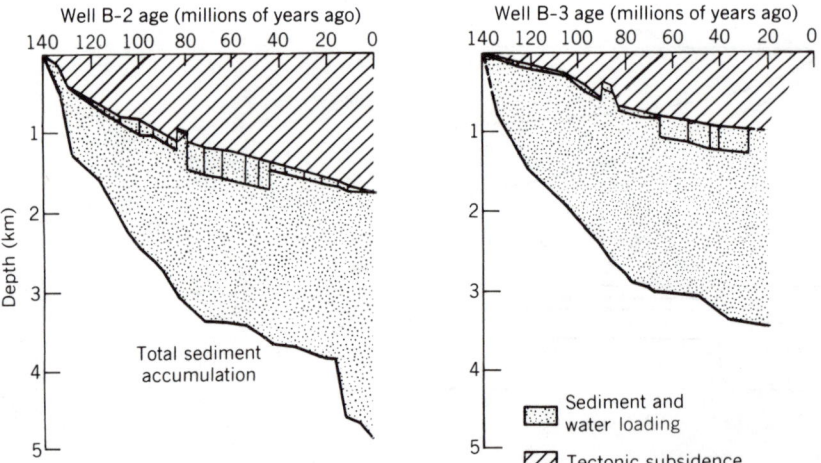

Figure 13-9. Total subsidence at two deep wells drilled off the east coast of the United States. The total subsidence is made up of three principal components, sedimentary load-induced *(stippled)*, thermal or tectonic cooling *(hatched)*, and minor sea-level changes (*vertical hatching*). Removing loading and sea-level effects from total subsidence to leave tectonic subsidence is called "backstripping" (from Watts and Steckler).

downward (thermal contraction and flexure). Backstripping allows us to isolate the form of these forces. We can then recognize their origin.

The subsidence not caused by loading is characterized by an exponential decay from the time of first rifting of the basin (Figure 13-10). That is, most of the sinking occurs just after rifting, and the subsidence slows progressively with time after that initial rapid pulse. Norman Sleep (1971) of Stanford University was the first to notice that the form of the subsidence curve is exactly that of the cooling of lithosphere away from midoceanic ridges. Therefore, we believe this subsidence force originates from cooling of the

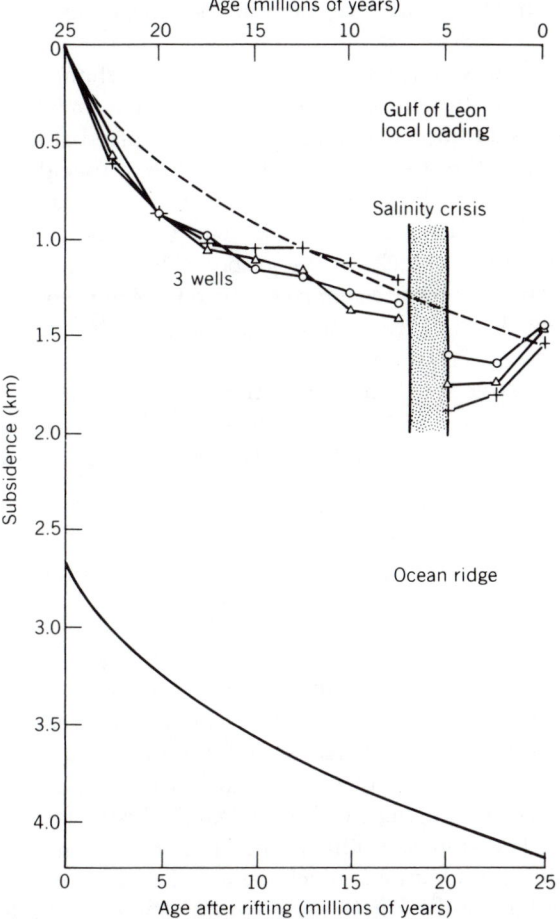

Figure 13-10. The tectonic subsidence left after backstripping (above) closely resembles oceanic lithosphere subsidence curves (below) that are caused by cooling after rifting. Here, a Mediterranean drill hole in the Gulf of Leon (*top*) exhibits such thermal-cooling induced subsidence after backstripping (*bottom*) (from Steckler and Watts, 1978).

newly stretched and heated continental basement beneath the basin. Cooling causes thermal contraction, which in turn forces the basin to deepen.

We can remove or backstrip the sediment from another basin and we should see the same exponential decay versus age after rifting if thermal subsidence is a dominant force. The Gulf of Lion is a very young margin along the Riviera of southern France. This gulf was formed by the rifting of Corsica and Sardinia away from Europe 25 million years ago. Since most of the thermal heating has cooled by about 50 million years after rifting, such a young margin should be dominated by thermal rather than load-induced subsidence. The backstripped form of tectonic subsidence in the Gulf of Lion has exactly that same exponential shape as ridge-flank subsidence, as expected (Figure 13-10).

Backstripping plus thermal subsidence usually account for the change in depth of the basin with time, but often the overall depth of the basement is still deeper than predicted. This additional sinking probably occurred at the time of rifting, and was caused by the stretching event itself. We can see that the very first sediments deposited in the basin were the salt and/or sands from the adjacent mountains, which fill not the entire basin, but only the vee-shaped valleys between the fault blocks of the graben. The very act of pulling apart the rift valley causes some subsidence because the fault blocks fall downward into the depression left from stretching. These fault blocks have a characteristic shape, called **lystric**, from this form of faulting. Note in Figure 13-5 that the faults have curved surfaces that are steep at the surface and become shallower at depth. Stretching produces these lystric faults as the basement blocks slide into the basin and are tilted as well.

The Evolution of the Eastern United States Margin after Rifting Away from Africa

Other than from drilling, most of our information about what resides beneath the sea floor under continental margins comes from seismic reflection profiling. As we saw earlier for the deep sea, sound energy is bounced off layers within the crust to return a map of the geological formations beneath the surface. Profiles like that in Figure 13-11 reveal the lystric faults cutting continental basement. The more smoothly draped post-rift sediments bury the syn-rift muds that fill the tilted fault-block valleys. On either margin of the Atlantic, only one half of the rift valley is found. The other half has been carried completely across the ocean to the other margin. For example, the rifted blocks of the shore of Morocco (Figure 13-11), and those buried deep beneath New Jersey (Figure 13-12) were each tilted away from the mid-Atlantic Ridge, and together they once formed a rift valley only 20 km wide separating North America from Africa.

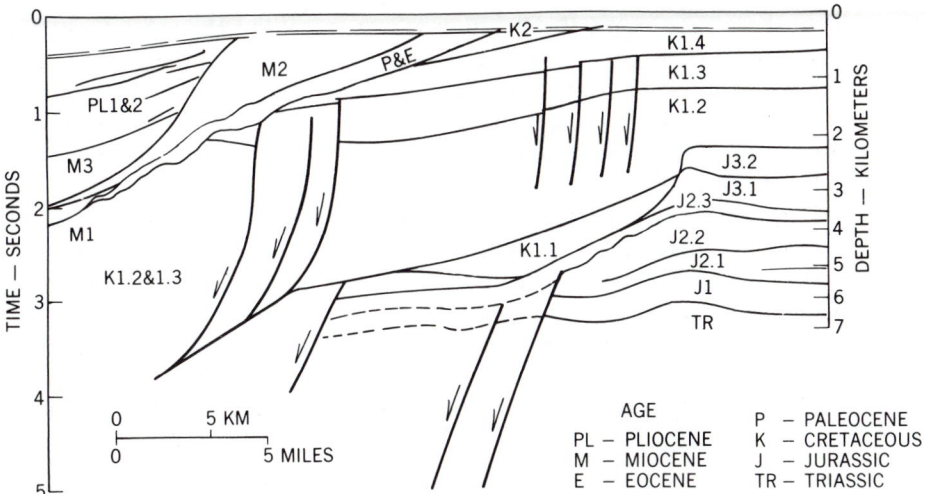

Figure 13-11. Line drawing of a seismic profile of the ancient rifted margin of western Africa. Stretched blocks can still be seen buried under more recent sedimentation (from Mitchum, et al, 1977). Arrows represent depositional (double-edged) and fault (single-edged) directions.

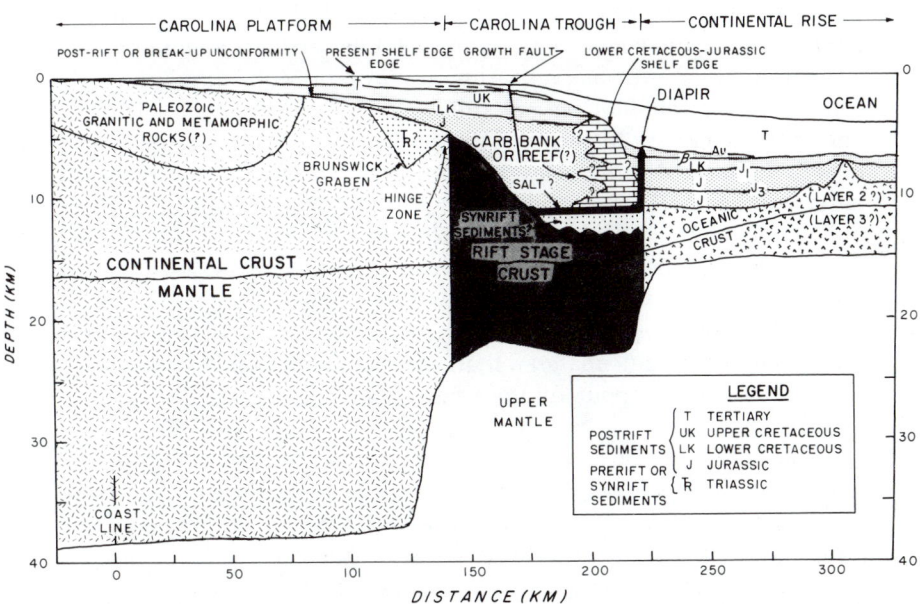

Figure 13-12. The corresponding rifted margin of North America has over 10 km of sediment. The outward growing reef at the continent–ocean boundary also tells a tale of the changes in the edge of the continent with time (from Hutchinson, et al, 1972).

At the present time, the Baltimore Canyon off the U.S. east coast contains over 10 km of sediment. There is even a large reef buried just beneath the slope break, the remnant of abundant coral life that ended about 80 million years ago. The reef, salt diapirs, and what are thought to be granitic domes add a variety of structures to the margin and make it an interesting locale for future oil and gas exploration.

If we backstrip the Baltimore Canyon sediments, we find that the sedimentary pile increased from about 8 km thick 100 million years ago to 12 km thick now. Thermal subsidence caused most of this deepening to occur between the time of initial rifting 140 million years ago and 100 million years ago. By then, most of the heat from stretching had been lost. The sinking from 100 million years ago until now was caused mostly by the sediment load. So during the lifetime of a margin, different subsidence processes dominate at different times.

The Maturation of Hydrocarbons

Did you ever wonder how old the gasoline is that you now have in your car's fuel tank? Different brands of gasoline are likely to be of significantly different ages. Chevron gasoline, for example, will be about 10 million years old if it came from California. Arco gas will be perhaps 50 million years old if it is from the North Slope of Alaska. Exxon or Mobil gasolines will likely come from the Middle East and will be 150 million years old. Texaco gasoline from the Gulf of Mexico will be about the same age, but it did not move near to the surface until the last million years or so. Shell gasoline from Indonesia will be about 60 million years old, and BP gas will be perhaps 200 million years old if it is from the North Sea.

But do not change from your favorite brand because of its age; new oil burns just as well as old. In fact, why does gasoline burn at all? In order to answer that, we must know how it is made. The ages we just discussed were the ages of the organic material that, after burial, became hydrocarbons. But what is so special about hydrocarbons that allow us to get energy from them?

The carburetor of a car mixes gasoline and oxygen together so that a spark from the spark plug can ignite the mixture. The fire causes the expansion of gases and the release of heat and power, which are converted into push on the wheels of the vehicle. But how is it that gasoline burns?

Organic material decays and decay is oxidation. Only so much energy is available from any organic compound for release during decay. Such reactions are called exothermic because they give off heat. If the organism dies in an oxygen-rich environment, then decay will immediately release all this energy harmlessly to the atmosphere. Only a fixed amount of total energy is released per decaying organism, so in order for gasoline to burn in your car, it cannot have been previously burned completely in nature. Hydrocarbons are nothing but undecomposed organic matter. If the organisms are small marine animals, then oil and gas form. If instead the organic material is from plants, then coal forms. But the rigid requirement is that the material has not totally decayed yet. The geological conditions that inhibit decay are rapid burial after death or deposition in an anoxic, or oxygen depleted, environment so that not enough oxygen is present to decompose the organic material fully.

We then think of the geological environments that promote rapid burial or oxygen-free conditions. River deltas, continental margins, flood plains, and the deep sea come to mind (the latter because there is little oxygen in the bottom waters of the oceans).

Plate tectonics can help us find many terrains where these conditions were met in the past. Thus, we begin to see the preponderance of geologists working for oil companies. But burial before oxidation is not enough by itself to make oil. It must be cooked, but not too much, or all that pent-up energy will be lost. We call this process **maturation** of hydrocarbons. Oil and gas must be matured in a pressure cooker. Pressure, and more importantly, temperature, must chemically alter the organic hydrocarbons. Just as with a kitchen pressure cooker, you can cook either fast or slow with essentially the same result. If fast, then the stove must be on high heat; if slow, then on low heat.

The way in which hydrocarbons are cooked depends on the depositional environment in which they happen to have come to rest. But, as with food, hydrocarbons can be overcooked; gas is the result. Then gas can be overcooked, and sour gas, heavy in sulfur and other undesirable chemicals, results. If, on the other hand, the hydrocarbons are not heated enough, the organic material remains immature and useless to man.

The evolution of a sedimentary basin presents the broad spectrum of pressure–temperature conditions. When and where within a basin oil or gas is found depends upon when the organic-rich source material was deposited into the basin. If it was early in the stretching stages of rift-valley formation, then the environment is hot and the hydrocarbons mature very quickly. This is why Chevron found 10-million-year-old oil in the Santa Barbara rift basin off the shore of California.

If instead the organic-rich material is not buried until long after the hot stage of rifting, then it will take millions and millions of years to mature into hydrocarbons. The rate or speed of formation of hydrocarbons doubles for each 10°C increase in temperature. But again like the pressure cooker, the heat must be sustained. You do not cook food by turning a blowtorch on it for 15 milliseconds.

The time versus temperature trade-off for maturation is called the time–temperature window (Figure 13-13). If an organic-rich sediment is held at

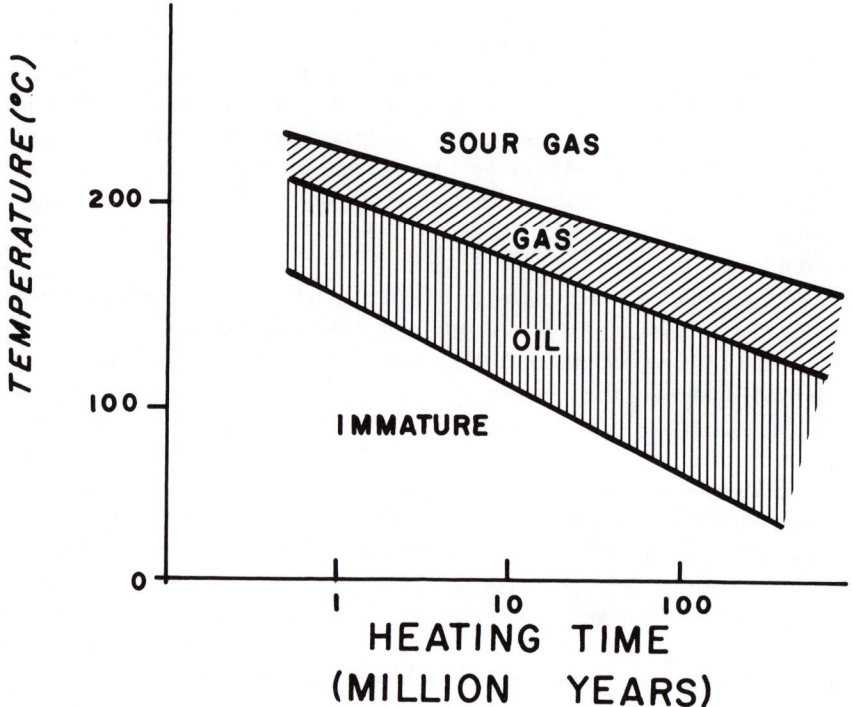

Figure 13-13. The generation of hydrocarbons in sedimentary basins is purely a matter of thermodynamics. The organic matter cannot have been heated too much for too long a time or first natural gas then sour gas would have been formed. Correspondingly, it could not have remained too cold either. Oil and gas do not form by luck; therefore we must look for sedimentary piles which were sufficiently heated in the past. Vertical hatching is oil-formation window; diagonal is for gas.

150 to 200° C for 1 million years, then oil will be formed. If the temperature exceeds 200°C, gas will form; but if the temperature becomes hotter than that, sour gas will ruin future prospects of ever producing energy from this formation. If, however, the same organic-rich source beds are only at 100°C, then it takes 100 million years to mature them into hydrocarbons (Figure 13-13).

The Beta-Value and Different Stretching Rates for Different Margins

We could predict the likelihood for maturation of hydrocarbons in any basin if we could predict the temperature history of the sediments in that basin from the time of initial rifting to the present. But that temperature history has been changing with time as the basin first became hot during rifting, then cooled as it subsided and filled with sediments. A rifted margin can be opened initially to varying extents. The continental crust can be stretched to two, three, or four times its previously undisturbed length. Hot asthenosphere fills the void left from stretching, so that the more the crust is thinned initially, the hotter is the beginning temperature structure of the margin. A basin that has been stretched significantly will heat sediments that fill its broad rift valley to much higher temperatures than will an only slightly stretched basin. We measure the extent of stretching of a rifted continental margin by its **beta-value.**

We can backtrack from the tectonic subsidence history of a basin after backstripping to determine its beta-value because the higher the beta, the higher the initial temperature, and consequently the steeper the cooling-induced subsidence after rifting. Obviously, a basin with a high beta-value will subside more than one with a small beta-value, since more initial heat enters a basin stretched to a higher beta-value.

The maturation level of a basin can be calculated as follows. First, determine the beta stretching value for the basin from tectonic subsidence curves after the sediments have been backstripped. For the New Jersey coast, beta-values of 3 to 4 fit the subsidence data best (Figure 13-14). A beta-value of 2 represents stretching or rifting of the continental crust to twice its original width (100 percent). Beta-values of 3 to 4 represent stretching of 200 to 300 percent. A beta of infinity would equal sea-floor spreading where no continental crust remains at all in the rift valley floor. The history of any continental margin that resulted from the complete splitting of a continent will

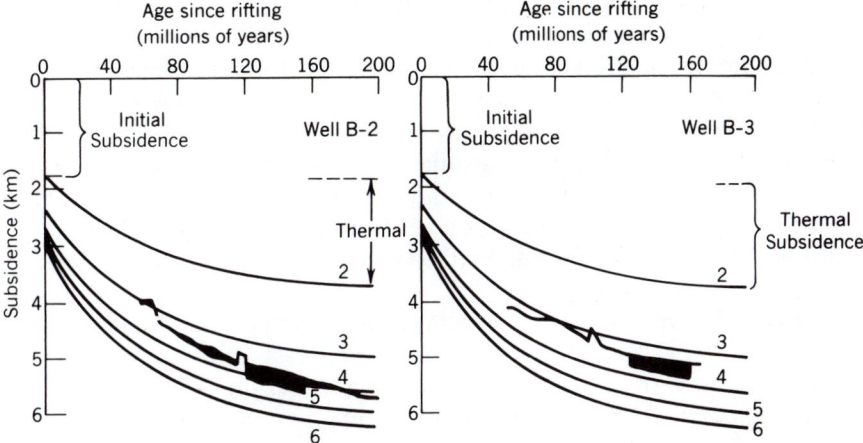

Figure 13-14. The amount of stretching during initial continental rifting controls the amount of heat that a basin saw during its cooling process. Here, backstripping was used to identify 200 to 300 percent (β = 3 to 4), stretching offshore New Jersey (Steckler and Watts, 1978). Beta values of 2 to 6 are shown.

require beta-values that may be small near shore but that must increase to infinity as soon as oceanic crust is formed. So the beta-value can increase across the margin, with the smallest value usually found closest to shore (defined here as unstretched continental crust).

The magnitude of the stretching event is calculated assuming crustal thinning and graben formation happened instantaneously. But in reality, the initial rifting stage might take several million years. Even so, almost all of the heat entering the base of the continental crust is still diffusing its way upward toward the surface by the time stretching is completed. So the instantaneous assumption, which depends upon the retention of all this heat, is still valid. Another simplifying assumption is that the continental lithosphere all stretches to the same degree. In reality, the brittle crust is harder to stretch than the more ductile continental mantle below the Moho. The stretching factor can actually be larger for the mantle than for the faulted crust at any given location on the margin. This condition is duplicated by the stretched Milky Way chocolate bar. We often ignore these complications when demonstrating the concept of margin rifting and basin formation and assume one constant beta-value over an entire margin.

After estimating the beta-value stretching factor for a basin, the time–temperature history of given sedimentary source beds can then be calculated. For the New Jersey coast, we can assume an even hotter beta-value of 5 for illustration purposes. Rifting began 170 million years ago, and the sediments in the rift valley have been steadily buried to deeper and deeper levels ever since deposition. We calculate two independent parameters of age and depth in the basin, then overlay them. First we calculate the temperature of the basin versus time and depth from the cooling at a given beta-value (Figure 13-15). We see that the sediment, which is at 8-km depth now, or 170 million years after rifting began, should be at 175°C.

Accurate information about the variation of thermal conductivity versus depth from the porosity changes of the sediment is required to produce this temperature curve from the cooling of the basin. We are fortunate that most thermal conductivity changes in sediments are caused by dewatering during compaction. Porosity determined from the geophysical logs accurately measures this effect. It isn't as complicated as it sounds because the physics controls the chemistry of oil formation (thermodynamics again), and the physics is simple heating and cooling.

Separately, we must calculate from backstripping the depth–time history of the particular sedimentary source layer of interest. The basal sediment is now 8 km below the surface. Sediment laid down at the top of the basin 30 million years after rifting is now about 4 km below the surface (Figure 13-15). We then predict from the combination of these two independent calculations that the basal sediment entered the beginning of the oil time–temperature window (Figure 13-16) at about 90°C, 10 million years after deposition, and has been maturing ever since.

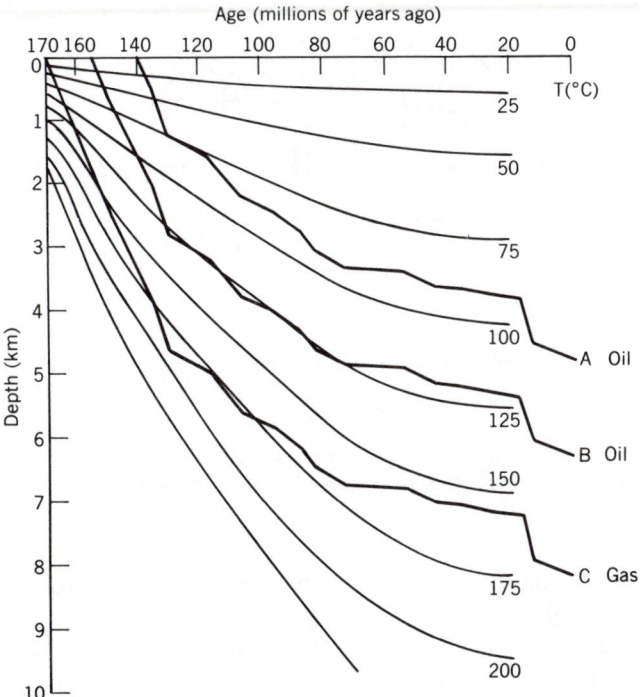

Figure 13-15. Isotherms of temperatures versus time (light lines) show that sediments at three depths in the present wells, 4.5, 6.5, and 8 km had thermal histories (bold lines) that indicate they have been eventually heated to 100 degrees, 125 and 150 degrees Celsius, respectively, during their residence on the continental shelf off New Jersey. Looking to hydrocarbon generation (fig. 13-16), oil should have been generated in sediments at 4.5 and 6.5 km, but 8-km source rocks become so hot that gas likely formed (from Dewey and Pitman).

Note that the sediment increases in temperature steadily with time in any basin. From about 110 million years ago until now, Horizon C has been too hot for oil to form. Fifty million years at 100 to 150°C would have been just long enough to mature oil in the basal sediments (Figure 13-16). Unfortunately, we were not around then to take advantage of this abundant oil. Now we predict only gas is left at the deepest depths off the New Jersey coast because it was too hot for too long (Curve C of Figs. 13-15 and 13-16). Any residual organic material is now gas after 110 million years in residence at over 150°C. Whether we are right depends upon the accuracy of our estimated beta-value of rifting. Only drilling will tell what is really offshore New Jersey.

We do predict something interesting about New Jersey oil prospects, however, the younger sediment did not reach the beginning of the oil maturation window at about 90°C until 70 million years ago at the earliest. We

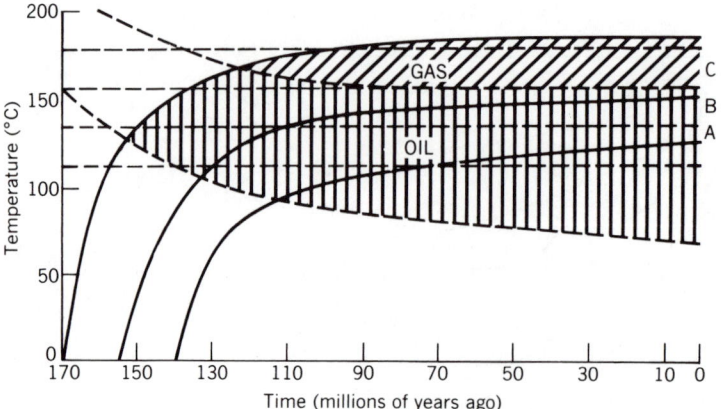

Figure 13-16. Time-temperature history of sedimentary layers A-C of Figure 13-15 traced through the maturation window of Figure 13-13 (from Dewey and Pitman). Oil (vertical hatching) and gas (diagonal).

predict that oil is just now maturing at about 4 km below the surface (Curve A of Figs. 13-15 and 13-16).

An oil company can now plan its exploration campaign offshore New Jersey. Remember that maturation alone does not make an oil well. The oil is not recovered from the source beds. It must **migrate** over millions of years to **a trap** of permeable rock underlying impermeable cap rock. Oil and gas are so buoyant that they will escape completely to the surface otherwise. So source beds only now maturing cannot become drilling targets. Structures that are seen on seismic reflection profiles at deeper depths, which might be traps, must be drilled. Depths of 6 to 8 km are reasonable targets for the New Jersey coast. Such wells are very expensive, so the oil companies will begin cautiously, probing the shallower, cheaper depths for oil that has migrated from source beds deeper in the basin. Only if these wells are dry will the companies eventually drill the deeper prospects. When economically feasible, oil and gas will inevitably be produced offshore New Jersey. The questions are, how much and when?

The Migration of Hydrocarbons

Once an oil company has determined that a particular basin is likely to have mature source beds, the problem shifts to the determination of likely trap structures for capture of the migrating hydrocarbons. The driving force of this migration is buoyancy. Oil, being lighter than water, tries to force its way to the surface. Much of it succeeds and is lost to the oceans and atmosphere. An interesting new exploration technique is the sniffer, a chemical analyzer that is towed above the surface to detect the occurrence of abnormally high hydrocarbon concentrations in the ocean bottom water or in the atmosphere. Such might indicate the locations of hydrocarbon seepage into the ocean.

The need for a lid to keep hydrocarbons trapped was painfully revealed to the oil companies recently when the massive structure that was to have succeeded the North Slope as Alaska's next great oil discovery was drilled. Mukluk, as it is called, is in the Beaufort Sea off the northern coast of Alaska. Sohio oil company had to build an entire island to drill the first well into Mukluk. The island and well cost over $2 billion. More than 5000 feet of producing sandstones were drilled through, but no oil was found. Instead, abundant evidence was found that oil once resided in the sandstones, but it is now all gone. It was not trapped successfully, and all escaped to the surface long ago.

Permeability is the key to the migration of oil and gas into traps. The more permeable a rock is, the easier it is for fluids to move through it. Unfortunately, there is no technique that detects permeability from the surface. Permeability depends not only on the porosity of the rock (which is easy to determine), but also on the pathway between pore spaces that the fluid must travel through. How tortuous the path determines how easy it is for hydrocarbons to migrate through any rock. The permeability pathway is thus called **tortuosity.**

A trap forms when gravitational buoyancy forces oil or gas upward into a dead-end permeability alley. A cap of impermeable rock must sit on top of a highly permeable structure. The oil then migrates through the permeable pore spaces until it is trapped by the impermeable cap rock. It will then remain there until some industrious drilling crew stumbles upon it by penetrating the cap with the drill bit. The gushers of olden days would then result from the overpressures of the trapped oil and gas. Now, we cannot waste the overpressures that blew out the early wells. Instead, we capture these excess pressures and use them to force the oil and gas from the ground naturally.

Are We Running Out of Hydrocarbons?

Any study of the geology of oil and gas must end with an inquiry into when we will run out of the commodity that seems so essential to our daily living. Obviously, we must run out; the question is when. Here is a little-known fact from the past: Europe ran out of wood in the 1600s. It was only then that coal began to be used extensively. The result of burning so much wood in Europe was to strip away all the forests. From coal usage came the famous pea-soup fogs of London. There are no longer such fogs in England because the pollution level has dropped since oil and gas replaced coal as the energy source for the Industrial Revolution.

We would certainly miss hydrocarbons if we ran out of them, but the loss of gasoline and plastics would be felt less acutely than the loss of fertilizers. The "Green Revolution"" of the last 50 years has allowed us to gain in the battle of food production versus the consumption requirements of the global population. This revolution in agriculture has largely succeeded because of ammonium nitrate and other fertilizers made exclusively from hydrocarbons. Long after we are no longer allowed to fill our cars with gasoline, fertilizers will still be made.

But don't sell your internal combustion car for solar cells just yet. There is still plenty of oil inside the earth. Our main problem now is how to find it and get it out of the ground. Bill Menard, recently director of the U.S. Geological Survey, once showed that the discovery rate of new oil and gas reserves was equivalent to what it would be if the wells had all been drilled completely randomly. He pointed out that this was true because the increase in technology for finding oil is just barely keeping up with the increased difficulty in finding the smaller and smaller oil fields left undiscovered. If it were not for this increase in technology, we would not be succeeding as well as randomly.

Once a large oil field is discovered, the hydrocarbons must be pumped to the surface. The very act of removing fluid from the pore spaces between rock causes the rock to collapse, destroying the high permeability vital to the recovery of oil. So we can only get about 40 percent of the oil out of any given field. Sixty percent of all the oil ever found is still in these old fields! As the commodity becomes more and more expensive, the technology for extracting this leftover oil will steadily improve. We are already doing some extraordinary things underground. A fire has been burning for five years inside the earth in Bulgaria to force oil out of the ground. Oxygen is pumped down to burn the deepest oil right in the formation 2 km below the surface, producing heat to force heavy, syrupy oil to flow from the shallower levels of the field. Otherwise, earthquakes are artificially caused in oil fields to provide new pathways of permeability along faults for oil to get to the well (hydraulic fracturing). Steam, acid, carbon dioxide, water, and nitrogen are pumped down old wells to improve their permeability and increase production.

Summary

In addition, several large geographical frontiers remain unexplored. The Arctic and Antarctica, China, the Falklands, and the coasts of Africa are all hot prospects at the moment. We will probably make it through the twenty-first century before oil and gas are replaced as our primary energy source on the planet. Some forecasts push that date forward by as much as 100 years, but the truth is that there are enormous quantities of oil and gas still underground. As the price soars, the uses of the commodity will become more and more efficient, and the incentive to find even more will increase.

Then there is all that coal. Coal does not burn as efficiently as oil, but at the present time there is roughly 100 times more of it. As liquefacation and gasification technologies improve, pipelines will begin to transport coal to electricity plants with regularity by the end of this century.

Eventually, we will run out of oil and gas. But by understanding how our planet works, we will uncover more and more exotic places to look for hydrocarbons. Before plate tectonics, it would have been heresy to suggest that oil could be found on the North Slope of Alaska. It was only after we understood that Alaska once was near the equator that the possibility that organic-rich source regions are now at the poles led us to explore above the Arctic Circle.

One outstanding problem that remains unsolved promises to lead us to further exotic terrains. By understanding what pushes and pulls the plates around, we may uncover further massive accumulations of hydrocarbons. The forces are clearly thermal, and where there is heat there is oil. To prove the point, consider the black smokers at the ridge axis. In the Gulf of California, these 350°C hot springs are covered by new sediments from the Colorado River. While exploring for metal deposits associated with these hot springs, scientists recently recovered brand new oil and gas in the sediments of the gulf. A core returned to the surface had diesel oil as its pore fluid. Age dating of the diesel revealed that it had been made within the last few years in the sediments above the black smokers. Where there are both new heat sources and concentrations of organic matter to be found, there are more hydrocarbons to be discovered as well.

Further Reading

Kennett, J., 1982, Marine Geology: Englewood Cliffs, N. J., Prentice-Hall.

The Driving Force of the Lithospheric Plates

We now return to the one outstanding problem that we delayed discussing until the complete framework of the surface had been laid out. Even the continents, with all their complexity, are simple compared to the workings of the mantle. The physics and chemistry are not complex, but the detection of geological facts is more difficult the farther from the surface you venture. We depend exclusively upon geophysical and geochemical measurements made at the surface to tell us what is happening in the mantle beneath the plates. We have left this to the end because an understanding of the surface does not require the deciphering of deeper processes, and because it is more complex.

Alfred Wegener (1915) ran up against one major stumbling block to widespread acceptance of his concept of continental drift: What drives continents to split apart and drift halfway across the globe? Even now that seafloor spreading and plate tectonics are accepted models for how the Earth's outer shell works, planet Earth's internal workings remain something of a puzzle. We now know that somehow the surface plates respond to the pushes and pulls of **mantle convection,** or fluid motion of partially molten asthenosphere caused by density and temperature anomalies. Had Wegener even the rudiments of this concept, his treatise might have gained widespread acceptance. Arthur Holmes, a renowned and respected geologist of Wegener's time, added convection to continental drift and produced a theory in the early 1930s for how the planet works, but he too suffered from little data with which to prove his hypotheses. It was not until after World War

II and the acquisition of new knowledge of the geology of the sea floor that the concept of large-scale horizontal motions of a dynamic earth could no longer be denied, even if the driving force of these motions was still obscure. In fact, understanding the driving mechanism is completely unnecessary to the tenets of plate tectonics. The theory of plate tectonics provides a geometric framework for understanding the causes and locations of earthquakes, volcanoes, continental drift, marine magnetic anomalies, sea-floor depth, heat flow, and the like without identifying what is pushing or pulling the plates around.

Yet the driving mechanism is the fundamental force of plate tectonics, and as such, an understanding of mantle convection is necessary to an understanding of how the oceanic and continental lithospheres work. Many observations on the surface of the lithosphere are completely explained by plate evolution and interaction, but they say nothing about what is going on beneath the lithosphere. The state of stress within the stable plate, deviations in depth and heat flow from that expected from the plate model, deep seismic velocity anomalies, and long-wavelength gravity anomalies measured principally by satellites are geophysical data sets that speak directly about motions deep in the asthenosphere. In addition, our understanding of processes active in the mantle has been greatly enhanced recently by numerical and laboratory modeling of convection, which has been constrained by, and designed to reproduce, these observations affected by the mantle.

The Observational Constraints

Most fundamentally, mantle convection must produce the forces that account for both directions and magnitudes of plate motions. Bernard Minster and Tom Jordan, while they were at Cal Tech, began the compilation of a self-consistent, world plate motion data set for the last 5 million years (Figure 14-1). These relative plate motions are derived from fixing one plate and looking at the velocities and directions of motion of surrounding plates relative to that fixed plate. We saw earlier how this was done across the San Andreas Fault between the Pacific and North American plates. Movement away is tensional and results in spreading centers and marine magnetic anomalies. Thus the *rate* can be derived from these magnetic stripes. The *direction* of motion comes from transform faults where, by definition, two plates slide across each other.

It is harder to get a rate and direction for convergence because a subduction zone can collide at an oblique angle to the surface manifestation of that collision, the trench floor. But a worldwide data set is obtainable by crossing only tensional and shear boundaries to derive relative directions among all the major plates in a roundabout way. For example, the Nazca and South American plates are completely separated by a subduction zone.

.EURA — Eurasian plate;
INDI — Indian plate;
ARAB — Arabian plate;
ANTA — Antarctic plate;
AFRC — African plate;
NOAM — North American plate;
SOAM — South American plate;
COCO — Cocos plate;
NAZC — Nazca plate;
PCFC — Pacific plate

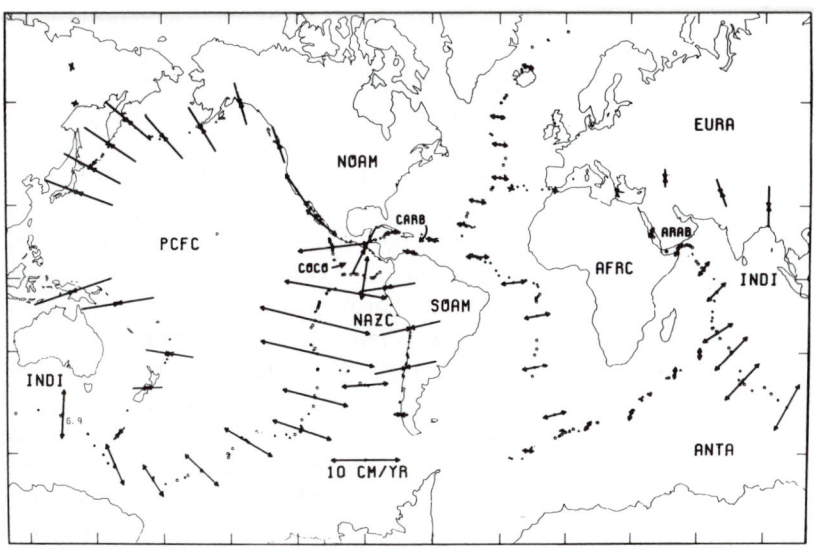

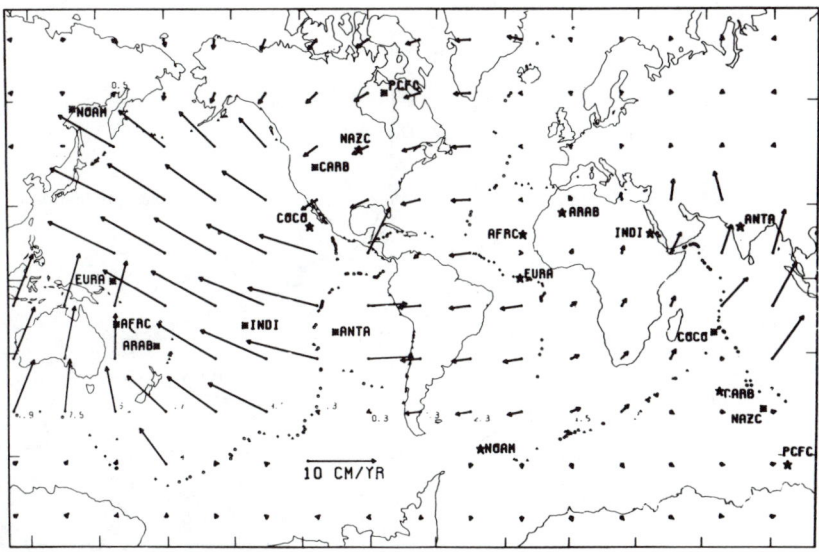

Figure 14-1. Relative *(top)* and absolute *(bottom)* plate motions. Arrows are vectors with velocity represented by the length of each arrow (from Minster and Jordan, 1980, and Uyeda, 1984).

The motion between the two is determined by vector-summing the motion of the Nazca versus the Antarctic plate plus Antarctica versus Africa plus Africa versus South America, all of which are separated by spreading centers. The resultant motion is Nazca versus South America.

But for motions fixed relative to the mantle, an *absolute plate motion* frame is needed. For the determination of absolute motions of the plates relative to the mantle, the use of hot-spot trails was proposed by Tuzo Wilson of the University of Toronto and Jason Morgan of Princeton. A hot spot is an anomalous volcanic center that is thought to be in a fixed location relative to the Earth's spin axis, with its magma coming from deep in the mantle. Thus, as a plate moves over this hot spot, an island chain is formed. A prime example is the Hawaiian-Emperor seamount chain on the Pacific plate (Figure 14-2). Currently, the island of Hawaii sits at the hot-spot center. To the northwest, one encounters a series of progressively older islands and seamounts. Thus, Oahu is older than Hawaii, Midway is older than Oahu, and so on. Near Cocos Island, which is 40 million years old, a sharp bend in the chain occurs. The Emperor Islands take off to the north at an oblique angle

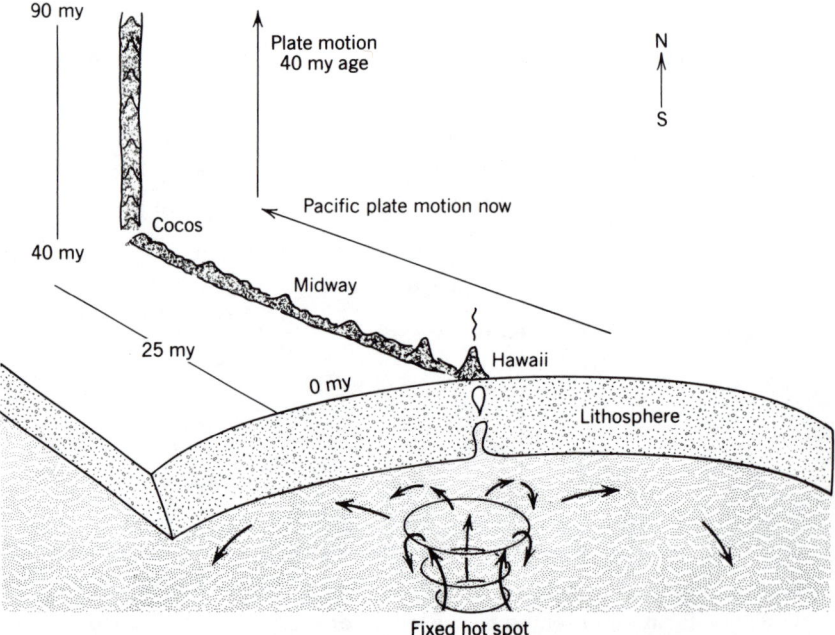

Figure 14-2. Schematic of Hawaiian-Emperor seamount chain in the Pacific. Direction of Pacific plate motion across the fixed location of the Hawaiian hot spot is recorded in the islands of the chain.

to the Hawaiian chain (Figure 14-2), until they disappear beneath the Aleutian trench. The oldest island of the Emperor chain is just now being subducted back into the mantle, and was over the hot spot, currently centered on the island of Hawaii, 90 million years ago. The direction of the Hawaiian-Emperor chain is thought to record the absolute motion of the Pacific plate relative to the mantle over the last 90 million years (Figure 14-2).

Other hot-spot trails are found propagating away from the Galapagos, Iceland, Yellowstone, the Azores, Tristan de Cuna, Easter Island, and many more volcanic centers. All locations of volcanism away from plate boundaries, and also areas of excessive volcanism on plate boundaries, are thought to be hot spots. Consequently, there are many hot spots. For example, there are nine hot spots in the Atlantic Ocean (Figure 14-3). Minster and Jordan were successful in compiling a worldwide absolute plate motion map by using the motion described by these hot spots to determine plate motions

Figure 14-3. Hot-spot locations in the Atlantic. Each is a volcanic island.

relative to the mantle (Figure 14-1), as a companion to their relative plate motion model.

Three other gross observations of plate motions are relevant to the deciphering of the forces placed upon the plates by mantle convection (Figure 14-4). First, the larger the mass of continents on a given plate, the slower it moves over the mantle. Second, there is no plate area versus speed correlation (the size of the plate has no effect on its velocity). In fact, the second fastest plate (Figure 14-4), the Pacific, is also the biggest; but the smallest, the Cocos, is even faster. Third, the more trench or subduction-zone length there is to a plate, the faster it moves. Don Forsyth of Brown University and Seiya Uyeda of the University of Tokyo concluded from these observations that the asthenosphere does not resist or drag against the plate bottom, but is instead affected itself by plate motions. They concluded that the forces on the boundaries of the plate must then determine the plate motion. They fur-

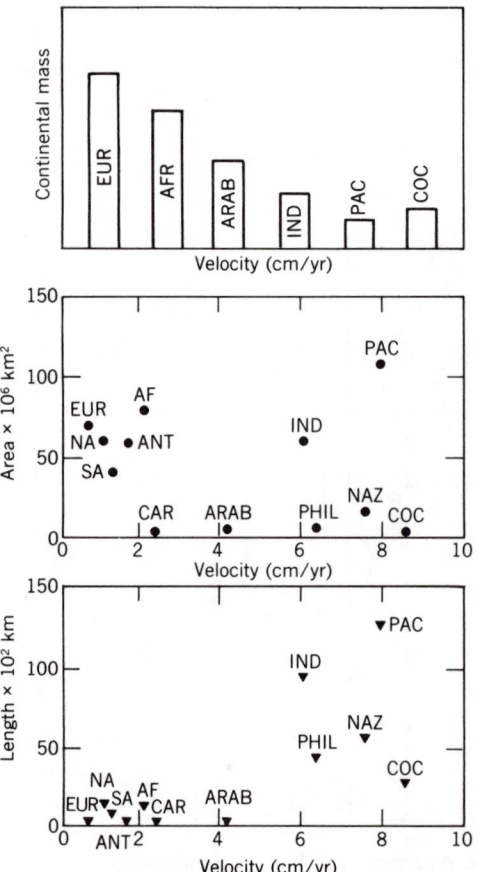

Figure 14-4. *(Top)* The volume of continental mass on each plate plotted against its velocity (absolute) relative to the mantle. *(Middle)* Area of plates versus absolute velocity. *(Bottom)* Length of trench along the boundary of each plate versus absolute velocity (from Forsyth and Uyeda, 1975).

ther proposed that the slab beneath a subduction zone exerts a dominant pull on plates because of the sheer weight of the rock hanging into the mantle beneath trenches. This would explain the trench length versus velocity correlation noted previously. The longer a plate's trench, the stronger the pull toward the mantle and the faster the velocity of the plate. An additional push comes from midocean ridges that are uphill from the rest of the plate. The rock exerts a push downhill because of gravity.

Earthquakes provide another strong constraint on the form of mantle flow. Along subduction zones, the shape of the plates plunging into the mantle is outlined by deep earthquakes. But these earthquakes never occur below a 700-km depth (see Figure 11-19). A substantial viscosity (fluidity) and density contrast must exist at 700 km (the phase change discussed in Chapter 11), which prevents deeper earthquakes from occurring. Thus the upper mantle convection layer can only extend from the base of the lithosphere (100 km) to the 700-km depth in the mantle. Convection below this depth must be decoupled to some extent from this upper mantle zone.

The Heat Source

Convection in the mantle requires some heating either from within (from radioactivity) or from below (from cooling of the core). The primary radioactive elements with half-lives long enough to still be around in appreciable quantities in the mantle (1- to 10-billion-year half-lives) are uranium (U), thorium (Th), and potassium (K). Called KUTh, as we remember from Chapter 1, their concentration in the Earth is inferred from that in surface rocks of differing compositions and from that in meteorites. Harold Urey of the University of Chicago noticed in 1956 the **chondrite coincidence,** that is, the amount of heat lost from the Earth's surface each day is equal to that which would be generated by a bulk earth full of the same amount of KUTh as in chondritic or stony meteorites. The average heat loss on the surface of the Earth was thought in 1956 to be only about two thirds of what we know that value to be today, now that we know about submarine hot springs, black smokers, and hydrothermal convection at midocean-ridge axes. Since this extra heat, unknown in Urey's time, must be from either KUTh heat generation or from cooling of the core, then either the mantle must have twice the concentration of radioactive minerals as stony meteorites or the whole Earth must have about one third more heat still to be lost.

We don't know which, and it makes a big difference in thermal convection models of mantle motion. Either the fluid mantle is heated from within (by KUTh), from below (by the core), or both. If the former, the pattern of convection is dominated by the cold, rigid upper boundary layer (the plates) and the lower boundary is relatively cold (the core). If we model such conditions in the laboratory, cold downward plumes are formed with hot material rising more diffusely around these cold spots. In the latter case, the lower boundary is hot, and upwelling hot material is concentrated in hot plumes with the downwelling of cold material diffused over a large area.

Luckily, the seismic constraint that a phase change exists at 700 km into the mantle requires that the convection be somewhat detached between the main thickness of the mantle and the base of the plate. Then the further constraint that hot spots such as Hawaii be located over hot plumes requires that the 700-km discontinuity be a hot bottom layer to the upper mantle convection pattern driving plates. That is, the lower mantle can be heated either from below or internally, and it will still provide the heat source to heat the base of this top layer of the mantle.

Mantle Convection Plan-Form

The most important parameter that determines the form of convection in the Earth's mantle is the **Rayleigh number,** which is the balance of buoyancy and heat-transfer terms in the convection equation. The Rayleigh number

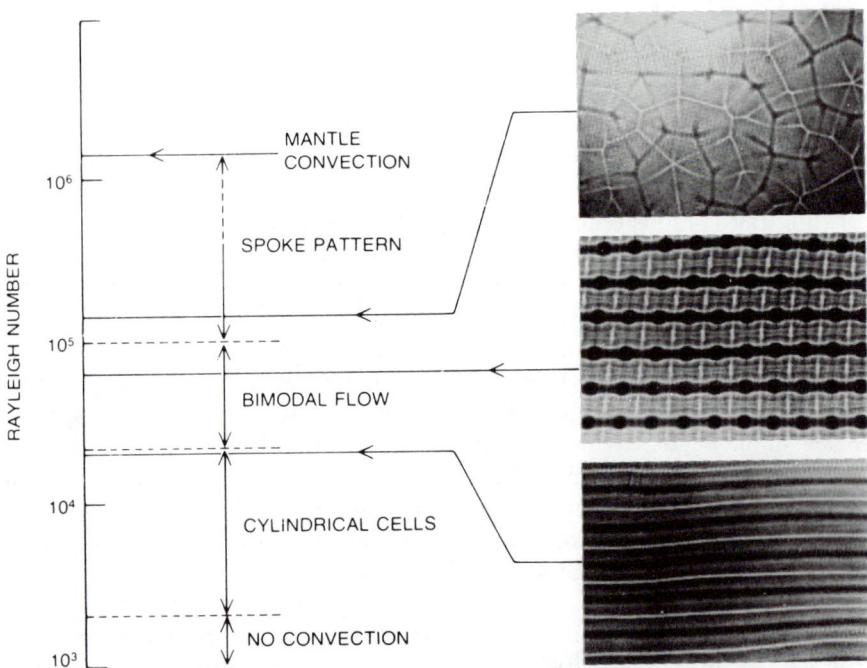

Figure 14-5. Form of convection changes from cylindrical rolls to spokelike pattern as Rayleigh number increases in the fluid (from Parsons and Richter, 1981).

gives us a quantitative measure of the buoyancy balance between thermal conductivity, viscosity, gravity, the amount of thermal expansion of the fluid, differential temperatures across the layer, and gravity. The Rayleigh number must exceed a critical value before convection will occur at all.

The interest in determining the Rayleigh number of the upper mantle is that if the basic properties of rock are the same, then layers with the same Rayleigh number will have the same form of convection. Computer and laboratory models, if scaled properly (i.e., if they can be extrapolated from small scale to Earth scale), can then be used to describe the mantle convection patterns of the earth by setting up the laboratory models which mimic the mantle.

As one increases the Rayleigh number of a system, there will be no motion until a critical value is passed. Then long convective rolls will be the first plan-form to appear; as the Rayleigh number increases further, the two-dimensional rolls will break up into three-dimensional spokelike cells (Figure 14-5).

The Parsons–Richter Two-Scale Model for Mantle Convection

Barry Parsons of MIT and Frank Richter of the University of Chicago presented, in 1981, an excellent representation of our current state of knowledge of the form of mantle convection and how it controls plate motions. The plate motions themselves (Figure 14-6) constitute the large-scale flow along the top and one side of the convection pattern—from the ridge axis to the subduction zone. The rest of the upper mantle must supply the required backflow to conserve mass. The driving force for this large-scale flow is the plate itself, since it is a cold, dense plate floating on the surface of a warm, less-dense upper mantle (remember the wet towel analogies of Chapter 11). Think of wax solidifying at the top of a hot pan during candlemaking, the liquid wax wants to move up (usually at the center of the pan) and the cold,

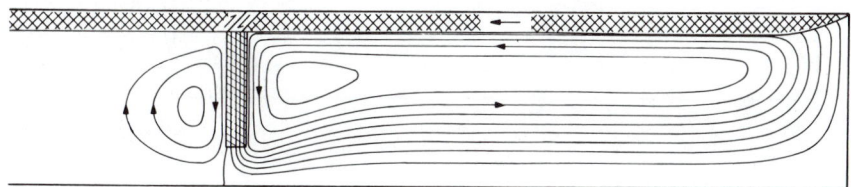

Figure 14-6. Model for large-scale flow in the mantle associated with plate motion. *(Right)* Ridge axis. *(Left)* Trench (from Parsons and Richter, 1981).

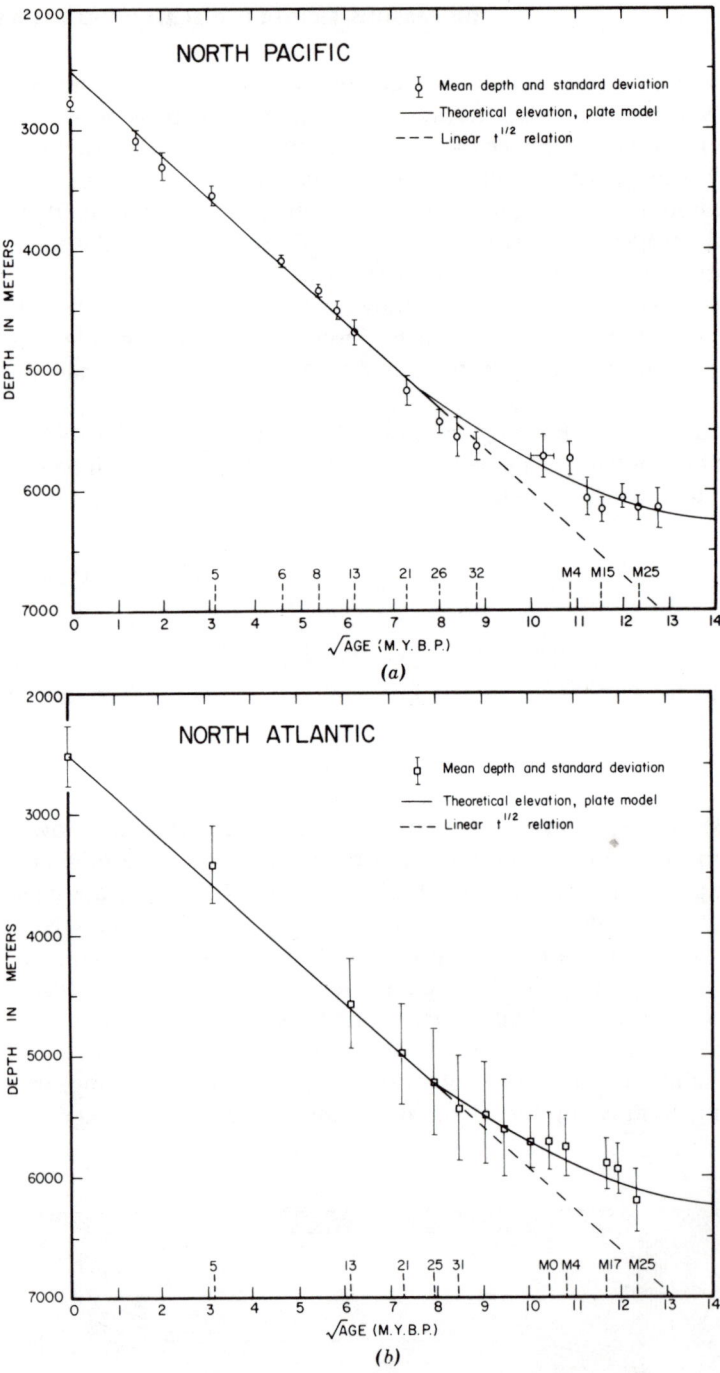

Figure 14-7. Sea-floor depths plotted versus age of the plate in the North Pacific (*top*) and North Atlantic (*bottom*). Note that both plates slow their subsidence at about 80 million years of age. From then on, the plates receive as much heat into the bottom as they lose out the top. They are in steady state (from Parsons and Sclater, 1977).

heavy and now solid wax sinks back down (usually at the edges). Like the wet towel carefully set onto a full bathtub, the downgoing slab of a subduction zone pulls the surface plate downward into the warm mantle, beginning the large-scale flow.

Small-scale convection is the second scale of flow required to conserve mass and supply material back to the accreting edges of plates. We can observe the details of this small-scale convection flow. The sea-floor depth at the top of the lithosphere was shown earlier to be a sensitive measure of the total heat content of the plate. But the plate must have a bottom (Figure 14-7) because the depth of sea floor "bottoms out" in old ocean basins. If instead, the plates were a semi-infinite solid, they would continue to cool and subside throughout their history on the surface. They would then continue to contract and deepen with age. Instead, they reach an equilibrium depth where the amount of heat entering the base of the plate from small-scale convection in the mantle equals the amount of heat lost out the top (Figure 14-7). Small-scale mantle convection is the only viable mechanism for supplying enough additional heat to the base of the lithosphere to flatten out the sea-floor depths in old oceanic lithosphere. Parsons and Richter showed that the two scales of convection can indeed exist together, at least in the laboratory (Figure 14-8). This small-scale convection, however, is caused by the plate motions.

The Rayleigh number of this small-scale flow is such that if the plate on top were not to move, three-dimensional spokes would form, but the faster a plate moves across the upper surface, the more fully developed is a two-dimensional horizontal roll pattern that is formed along the directions of the

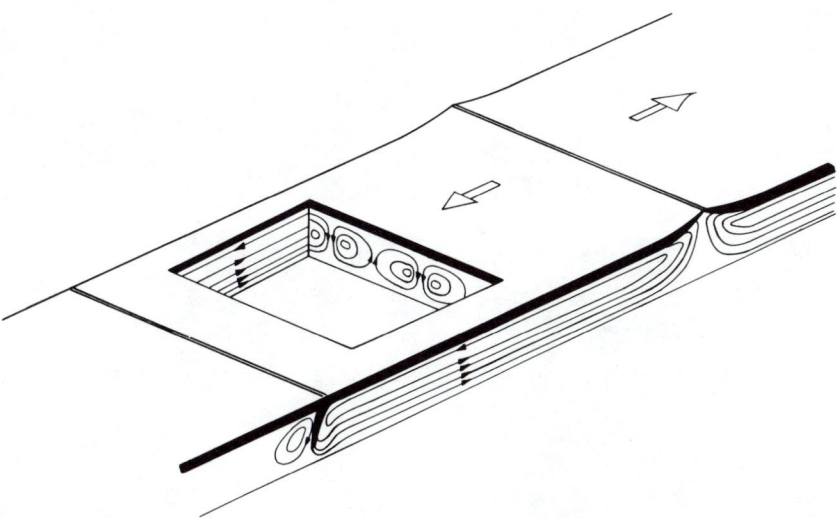

Figure 14-8. Longitudinal rolls in the mantle are caused by plate drag from the top (from Parsons and Richter, 1984).

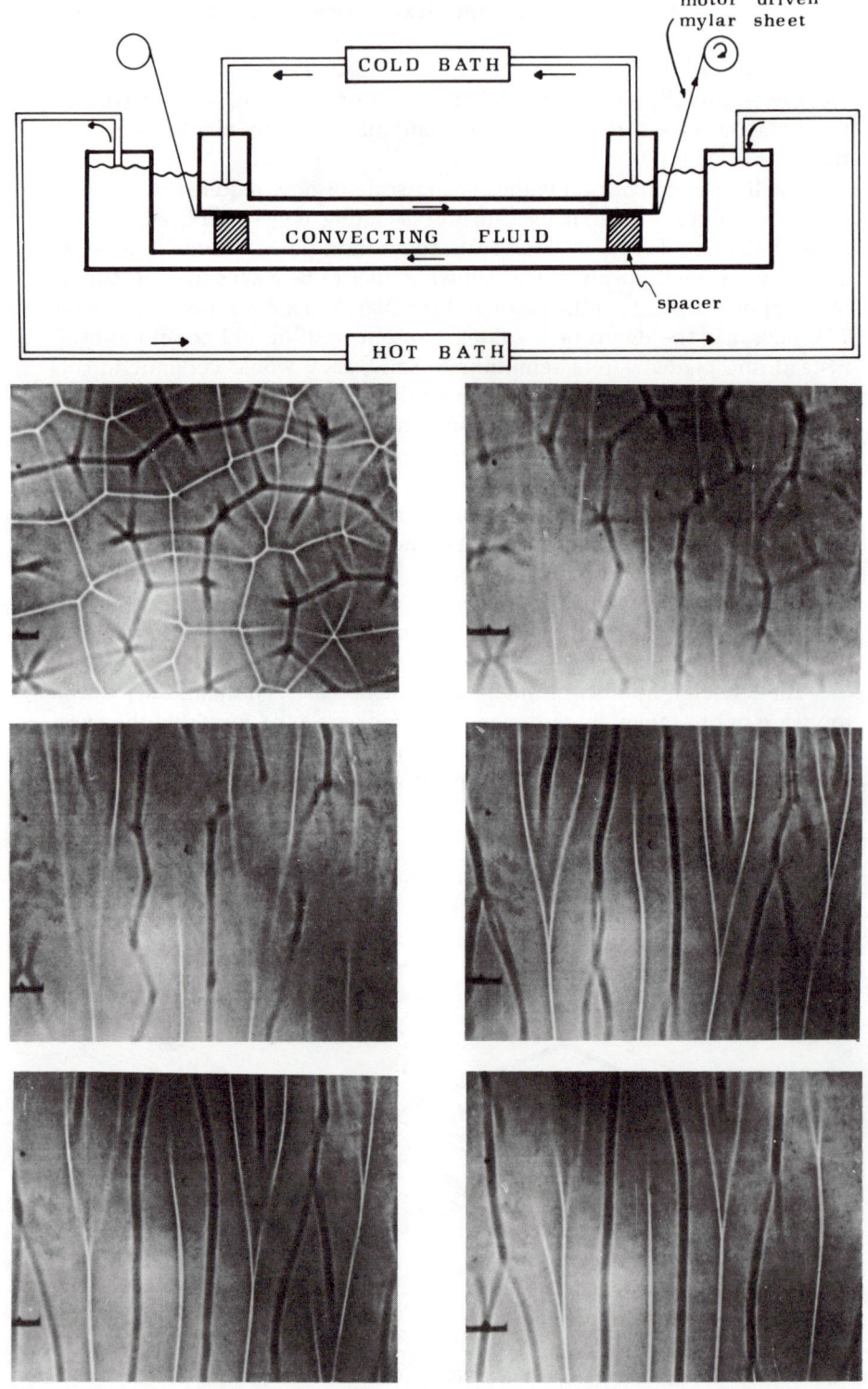

160°W HAWAII   MEXICO   110°W

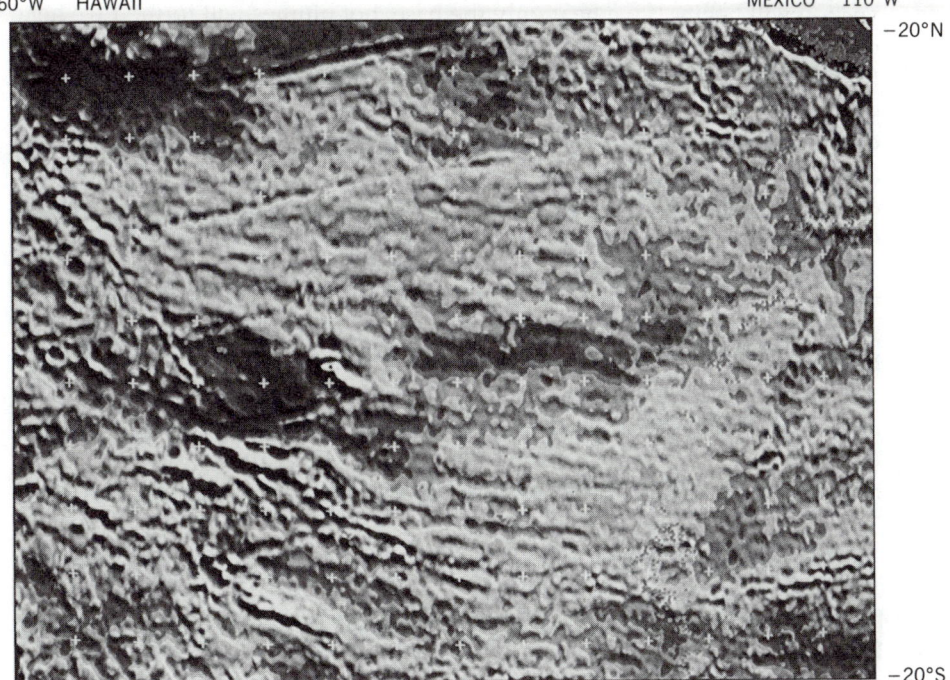

—20°N

—20°S

Figure 14-10. The northwest striking horizontal rolls under the Pacific plate can be observed from the small differences in the Earth's gravity pull between upwelling (white) and downwelling (black) limbs of the rolls. This image comes from satellite measurements of gravity (from Haxby, 1984). See also color plate, Figure 2-3. The Pacific Plate is moving to the Northwest. The fracture zones are the northeast striking scars in the plate.

plate motions (Figure 14-9). The satellite gravity field of the Pacific Ocean shows that such rolls exist in the mantle and are aligned parallel to the Hawaiian Island chain (Figure 14-10). We thus find that the absolute motion of the Pacific plate, determined from the direction of the Hawaiian chain, is parallel to the direction of mantle rolls. This observation of alignment of plate motion and convective roll direction can be duplicated in the laboratory.

Interestingly, the laboratory fluid that changes thickness (viscosity) with increasing temperature in the closest way to that of mantle rock is a particular brand of maple syrup. If we place this syrup in a fish aquarium with thin platinum heater wires both within the syrup and at the bottom, con-

Figure 14-9. Laboratory model in which a plastic sheet of mylar is pulled across the top of a convecting fluid to reproduce the horizontal rolls thought to occur beneath plates. When viewed from the top, the three-dimensional pattern at the upper left quickly converts to horizontal rolls at the lower right as the plastic is moved across the top of the tank (from Parsons and Richter, 1981).

vection will begin. If we heat only the base, hot plumes will form; if we heat only the platinum wires within the syrup, cold plumes will form. This verification of the results from computer models allows us to believe the validity of the next step more fully. We heat both from below and within, producing diffuse upwelling and downwelling. We then place a thin sheet of plastic across the top of the syrup and simulate plate motion. Gradually, rolls appear at the base of the plastic sheet, with their axes aligned in the direction of the motion of the plastic, just as is seen in the Pacific.

After motion has begun, the rolls take some time to form. This suggests that the motion of the large-scale flow precedes the formation of the small-scale horizontal convection rolls beneath the plates. They form as an **instability** rather than a stability in the large-scale flow (Figure 14-11).

The convective motions inside the mantle can actually be imaged using a technique similar to the CAT-scan mode of imaging the brain. A computerized axial tomography (CAT) scan bombards the brain with a series of X rays oriented as if to dissect the brain into slices. By successively focusing

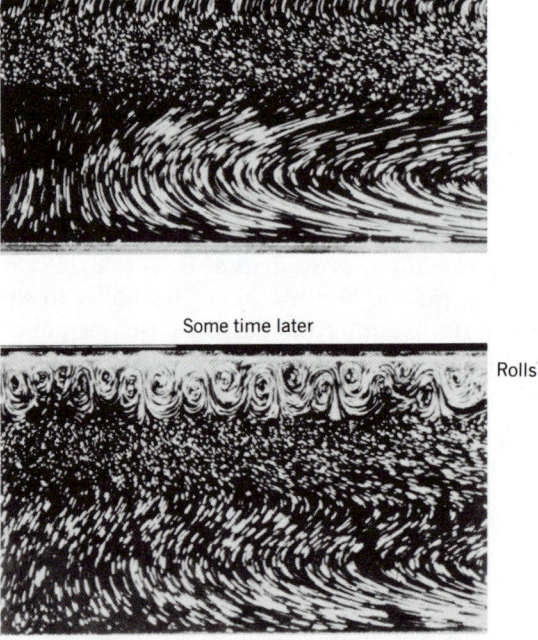

Begin plate motion

Some time later

Rolls

Figure 14-11. In this cross-sectional view small-scale rolls at the top of a large scale circulation pattern are shown here developing a short time after motion across the top is begun (from Parsons and Richter, 1981).

on predetermined planes of the brain, a CAT scan will show selected planar images in detail while suppressing the images of structures in other planes. Don Anderson of Cal Tech and Adam Dziewonski of Harvard (1984) have perfected a similar way of imaging slices through the mantle. They use variations in velocity of seismic waves from earthquakes that are recorded at over 100 seismic stations around the world. They look for lateral heterogeneities, or changes in seismic waveforms that relate to specific geographic positions within the mantle. By using sophisticated computer imaging techniques, they are able to differentiate where within the mantle areas of fast versus slow seismic energy are transmitted. Temperature and density are the physical causes of these velocity anomalies with hot, light mantle causing the slow transmission of seismic energy and cold, dense mantle transmitting energy fast.

The images of vertical slices through the mantle produced by this seismic tomography technique show that hot spots have deep roots of hot mantle that do not always remain directly below the volcanic island location (Figure 14–12a, color insert). This means that hot spots may move around on the surface to some degree. Think of a water hose spouting water at high velocity and loose on the ground. It snakes about somewhat but never strays far from the central position that the rest of the hose forces upon it. Interestingly, the ridge axes are usually above hot material in the mantle as well. But they often appear on the edges of upwelling material, particularly relative to the deep mantle (Figure 14-12b, color insert). The deep and shallow mantle, though appearing to have different convection patterns in each layer, are linked to some extent. That is, hot, deep mantle grades into hot, shallow mantle and vice versa (Figure 14-12b). The technique of seismic tomography is only in the development stages. Within the next few years, a worldwide digital seismic network is planned that will take us to a whole new level of understanding of the mantle. Since we will never be able to drill into the mantle, we must make the most of our ability to observe phenomena at the surface that tell us of processes occurring at depth.

The Hawaiian-Emperor Bend and the Driving Force for Motion of the Pacific Plate

What then can we conclude from the sharp bend in the Hawaiian-Emperor island chain? The Pacific plate appears to have abruptly changed its direction of motion relative to the mantle 40 million years ago (the age of rocks from islands closest to the bend). Prior to that time, the plate was moving due north across the Hawaiian hot spot (Figure 14-2). Then the plate abruptly turned to the northwest. Why did it change direction?

If we correctly understand the driving forces acting on the plate, then we must be able to explain such a significant change in motion of the largest plate on the planet. Trench-pulling forces must be involved somehow. If we examine the age of volcanism along all the trenches surrounding the Pacific plate, we find the answer to this remarkable puzzle. Volcanoes are going to exist above subduction zones whenever underthrusting is active. The Aleutian Islands are a volcanic arc behind the trench with rocks at least 100 million years old on many of the islands. The northward pull of the Aleutian trench was responsible for the Emperor direction prior to 40 million years ago.

What happened then to begin pulling the Pacific to the west as well as to the north 40 million years ago? There are few volcanic rocks on Japan or the Kurile Islands older than 40 million years. This fact suggests that subduction was not occurring beneath Japan prior to 40 million years ago. If subduction suddenly began then, the Pacific plate would be pulled not only to the north by the Aleutian slab, but also to the west by the Japan and Kurile slabs.

But why did subduction suddenly begin beneath Japan 40 million years ago? We do not really know because we have not yet discovered how to make a trench start from scratch. The primary cause of plate motion disruptions at that time is most assuredly the collision of India into Eurasia along the Himalayas. A chain reaction was then set off that resulted in changes in the western plate boundary configuration of the Pacific plate. The most likely candidate for this local perturbation is that convergence between Asia and the Pacific may have eliminated a small plate opening in the Japan Sea. Those two megaplates then came into contact with the Asian plate being squeezed toward the Pacific by the Indian collision. But we do not know how the first piece of the edge of the Pacific plate began to sink beneath the Asian plate. No laboratory or computer model so far produced can replicate the beginnings of subduction. It obviously happened, though, and the change in direction of the Pacific plate resulted.

Initiation of
Rifting of Continents

This intrigue involving the Pacific plate leads us to understand other unclear processes swept under the rug by plate tectonics. The concept of hot spots and absolute motions allows us to determine partial solutions to puzzles that are beyond the scope of plate tectonics. Consider the splitting of continents: What forces decide where and when a seemingly solid continent will split apart? Jason Morgan (1981) discovered a likely explanation when he backtracked the continents bordering the Atlantic Ocean along hot spot trails (Figure 14-13). Not only did the hot spots exist before the breakup, they appear to have been located along the newly forming rift valleys. Hot spots

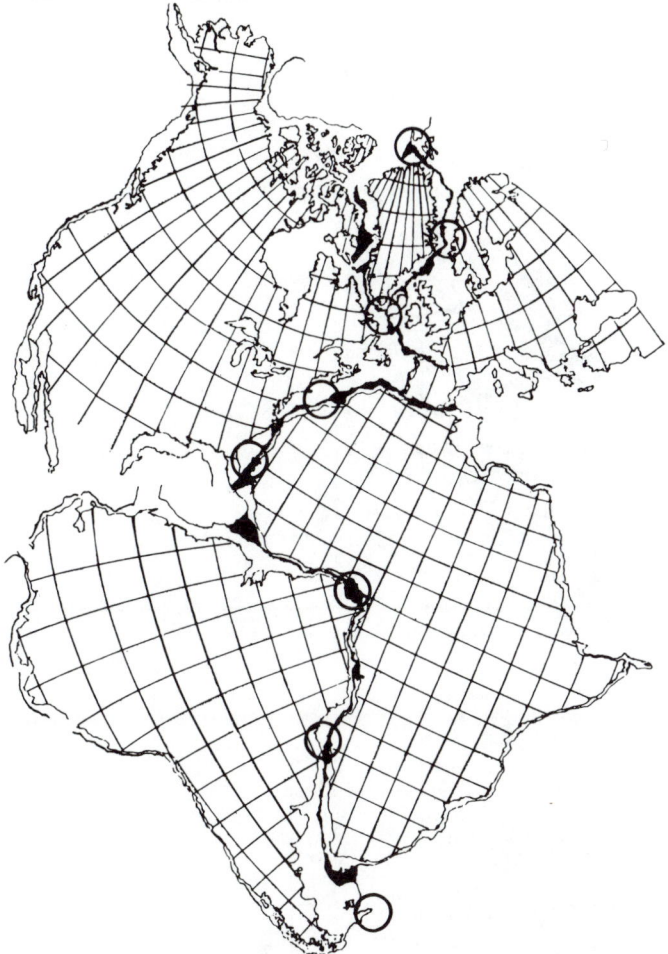

Figure 14-13. The opening of the Atlantic can be traced to the blowtorch effect of a few hot spots. Here the motion of the continents away from each other can be mapped by backtracking along hot-spot trails of islands and seamounts (from Morgan, 1981).

by their very nature would be excellent blow torches with which to cut the continents apart. Further proof that this indeed happened comes from the trace of Africa and South America across the hot spot that is now under the Island of St. Helena in the southern Atlantic Ocean. Brazil was sliced off Nigeria by this hot spot (Figure 14-13). The splitting of India, Africa, and Australia from Antarctica can be explained also by the heating and blow torch effects of hot spots now beneath Reunion, Crozet, and Kerguelen Islands in the Indian Ocean (Figure 14-14).

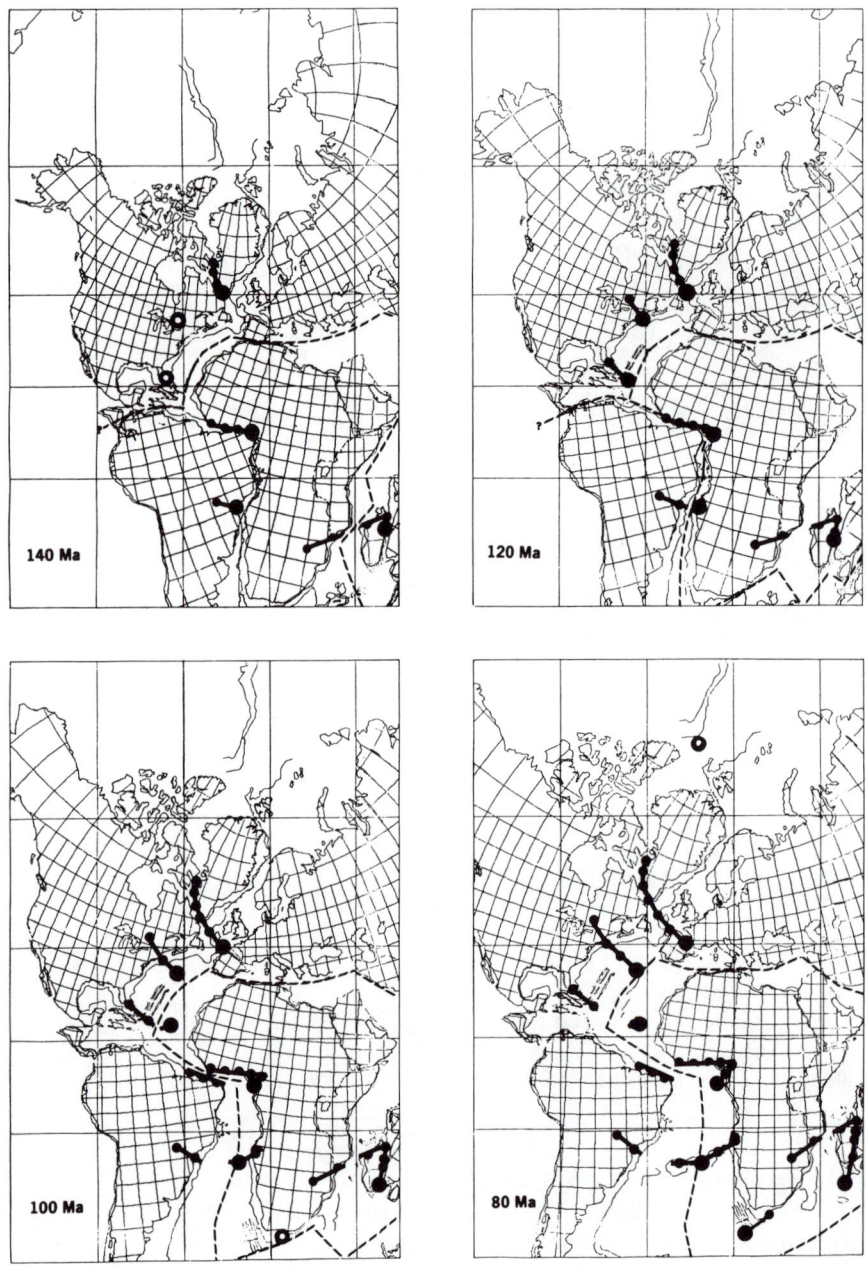

Figure 14-13. (*Continued*)

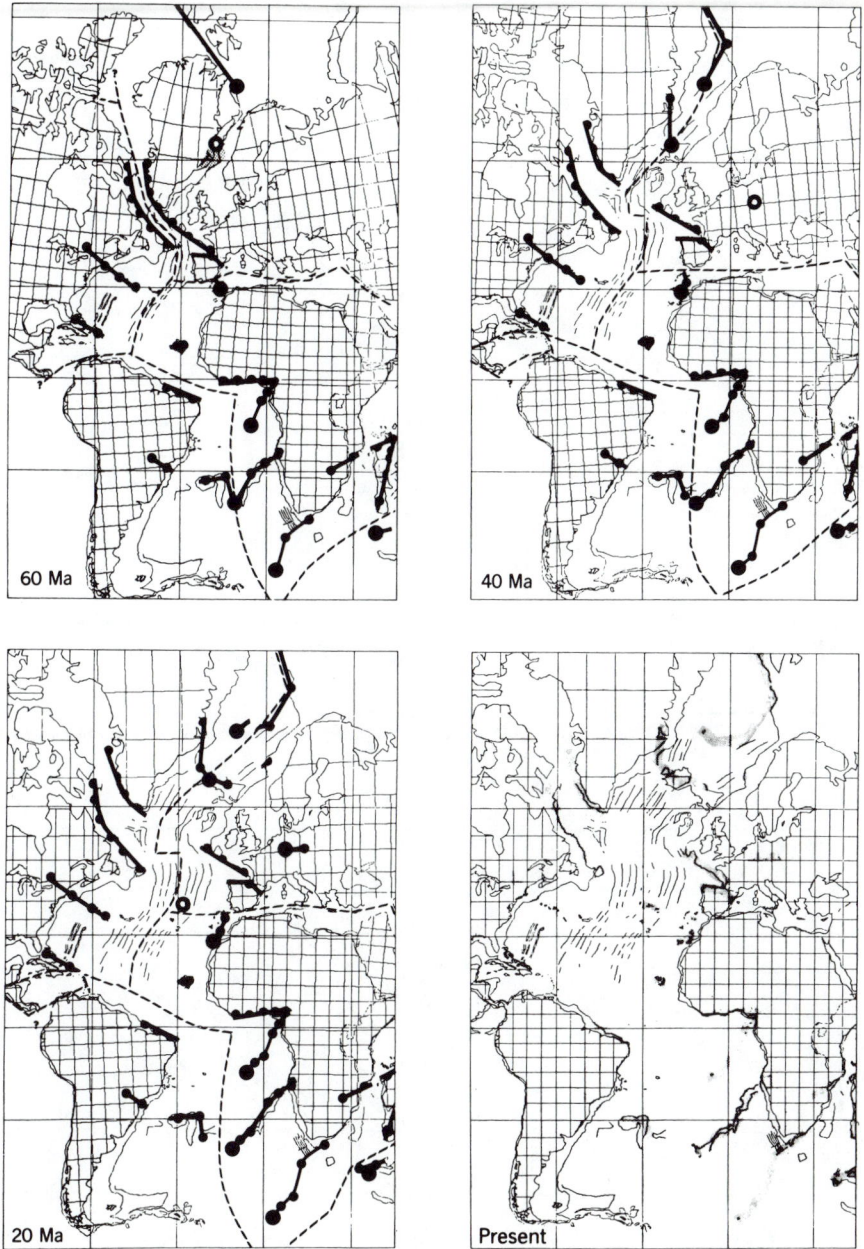

Figure 14-13. (*Continued*)

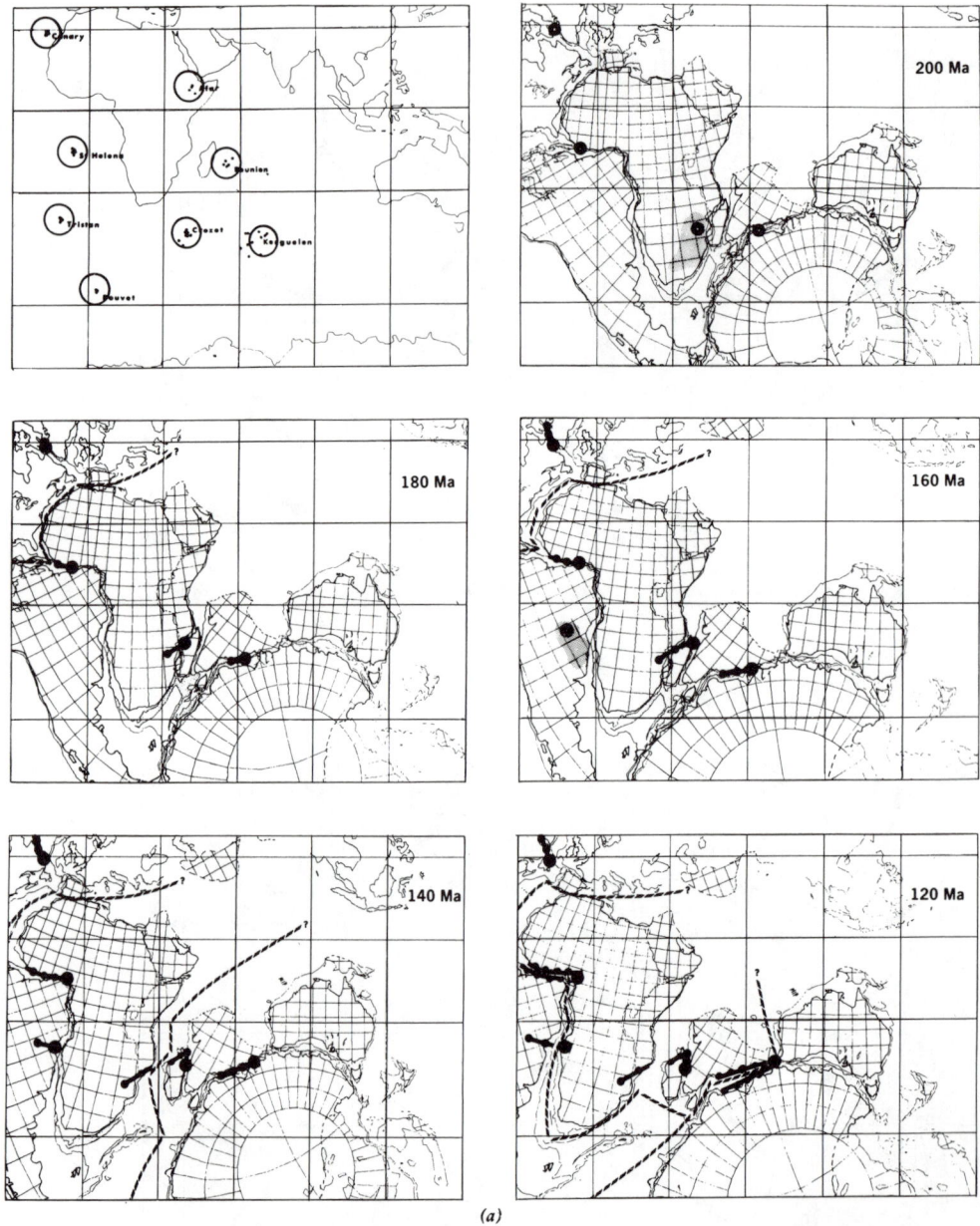

(a)

Figure 14-14. The same blowtorch effect can be seen for the opening of the Indian Ocean (from Morgan, 1981).

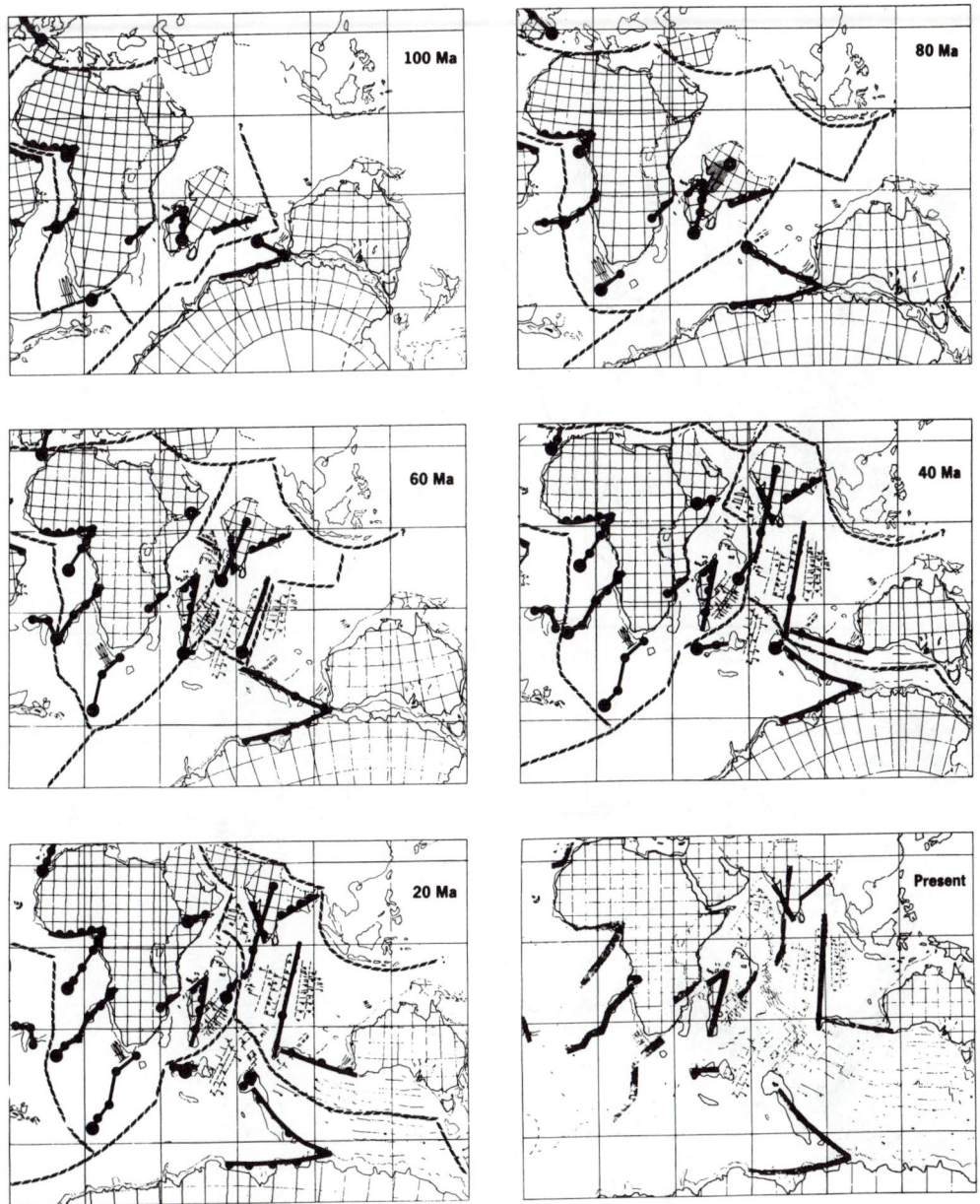

(b)

Figure 14-14. (*Continued*)

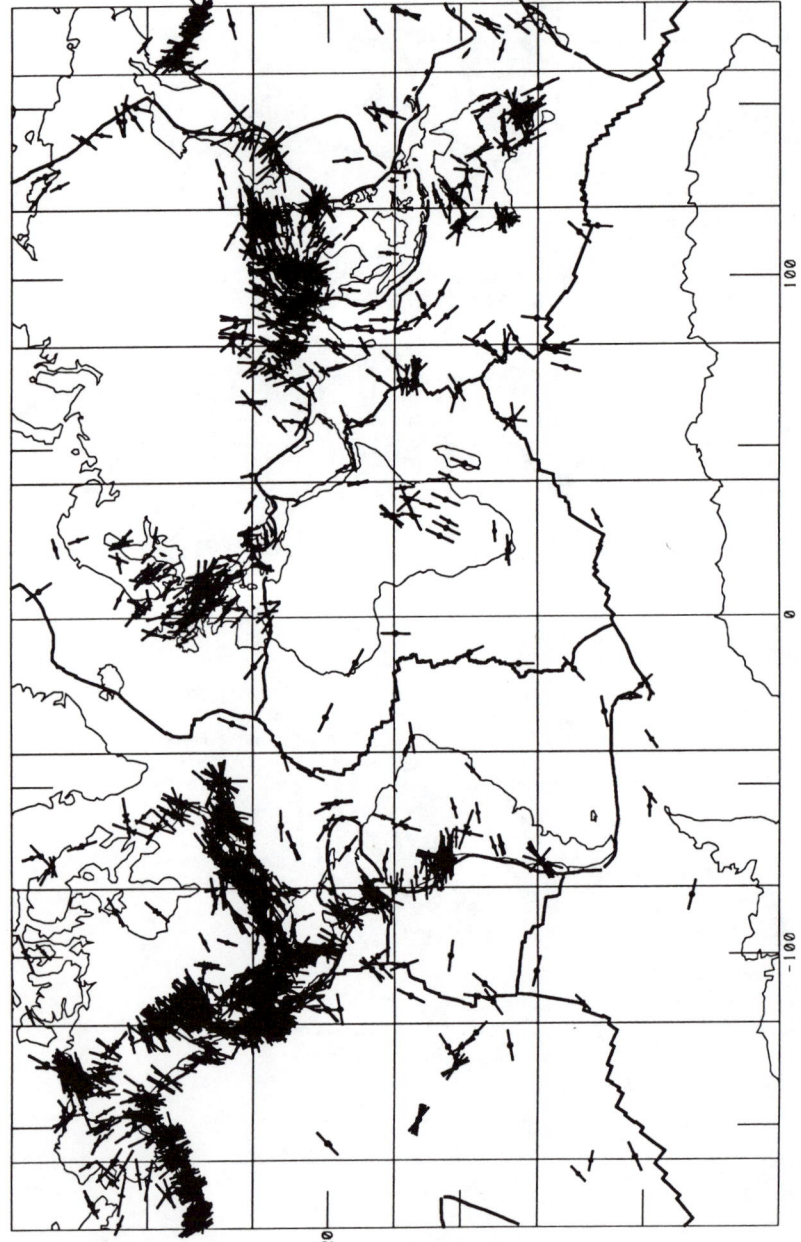

Figure 14-15. The push and pull on the plates results in the buildup of tectonic stress. The forces affecting plate motion can be mapped by measuring the state of stress along faults using earthquake focal mechanisms and in boreholes using breakouts and hydraulic fracturing (from M. L. Zoback and M. D. Zoback).

Summary

So we are left with a conceptual model, which Wegener never had, of plates moving around the surface of the earth, not randomly, but driven by density differences caused by mantle convection that produce cold, heavy plates on top of hot, light mantle. Where these plates sink back into the mantle determines in what direction and at what speed they traverse the surface. When and where they encounter hot spots determines how they will be carved up. The important concept to remember is that the plates are large, rigid slabs that respond not to any local forces but to the resultant of all forces acting on their edges and bottoms.

We can only begin to decipher these forces by determining the individual forces acting on each plate. A major step forward in this regard has recently been made by Mark and Mary Lou Zoback (1983) of Stanford University and the U.S. Geological Survey. They compiled a map of the forces pushing and pulling on North America (Figure 14-15). They used not only natural earthquake directions of maximum compression but also directions of force determined by a new technique for making artificial earthquakes in drill holes. This technique involves a method of determining direction and magnitude of maximum and minimum compression within a plate by making small earthquakes. Hydraulic fractures are induced in a well by forcing the rock to break along a newly induced fault by making a small earthquake using excessive water pressures. These measurements can be cited to determine the state of stress at a given place within the boundaries of a plate. Careful placement of hydraulic fracture measurements in gaps in natural earthquake locations allowed the Zobacks to determine the resultant of the North American plate motion. That direction is not surprisingly that of the Yellowstone hot spot (Figure 14-15). The Zoback work showed, however, that this resultant arises from the predominance of similarly aligned forces throughout the midcontinent of the United States and Canada. The bounding geological provinces each have distinctly different forces acting on them, but these other forces largely offset each other (Figure 14-15).

The future resolution of individual stress provinces within the boundaries of other plates will eventually allow us to determine the relative importance of forces other than the slab pull, and this largest remaining puzzle to how the Earth works will slowly crumble before the inquisitiveness of scientists.

Further Reading

McKenzie, D., 1983, The Earth's mantle: *Scientific American*, v. 249.

Parsons, B., and Richter, F.M., 1981, Mantle convection and the oceanic lithosphere, *in* C. Emiliani, ed., The Sea, v 7: New York, Wiley.

Glossary

Absolute plate motion The movement of a plate relative to the spin axis of the earth and the fixed (assumed) mantle.

Accretion (continental) The emplacement from elsewhere as when sediments from the sea floor are scraped off the downgoing slab and accreted onto the overthrust plate during subduction.

Accretion (planetary) Accumulation of celestial dust by gravitational attraction into a large enough mass to become a planet, planetesimal, astroid, or moon.

Accretionary wedge The scraping off of oceanic sediments onto the landward side of a subduction zone produces an inverted stratigraphic section whereby a wedge of sediments forms with the newest offscraped material underneath and wedged into the previously offscraped sediments.

Asthenosphere The partially molten mantle directly underneath the plates.

Alteration minerals The minerals formed after original solidification of a rock from magma. The thermodynamically controlled breakdown of the chemical structure of the original rock often forms alteration minerals that replace the original crystals and fill pore spaces of a rock.

Altimeter An instrument that measures the height of a body above sea level.

Alvin The name of the deep-diving submersible submarine that took scientists down to observe the black smokers and fantastic organisms at the ridge axes.

Angular momentum Mass times velocity. The heavier and faster moving a body is, the larger the force required to stop or impede its movement.

Atmosphere The air layers of the Earth above the water and rock.

Authigenic Sediments deposited or redeposited originating from the locality in which they are found.

Back-arc basin The sea floor spreading system of volcanos caused by extension behind the island arc above a subduction zone.

Back-arc spreading A sea-floor spreading center running parallel to and landward of a volcanic island arc above a subduction zone.

Backstripping Removal of the subsidence effects of loading and sea level changes to describe the thermal or tectonic subsidence.

Backtracking Tracing back through geologic history.

Baloon The focal mechanism of an earthquake can be displayed in a circle by projecting all motions onto a sphere, then onto the lower hemisphere of the sphere, and then onto the plane cutting the equator of the sphere. The center of the sphere is the earthquake location.

Basalt Black igneous rock that solidifies from magma. Chemically it contains mostly magnesium and iron silicates.

Bedrock The basement rock underneath sediments of a basin, composed usually of igneous but sometimes of metamorphic rock.

Benthic front Oceanic currents that flow along the bottom of the deep ocean.

β-Factor The degree of stretching of continental crust before rifting is completed is measured as a ratio to the total beginning thickness. Half-thickness stretching is a $\beta = 2.0$ which is stretching by 100%.

Black smoker When the superheated hydrothermal water at a mid-ocean ridge axis rises to the surface before mixing with cold water, the effluent is supersaturated with metals. Though exiting the sea floor clear, the water quickly cools and the dissolved metals precipitate, resulting in black, smokelike effluent.

Biogenic Sediments composed of the remains of plant and animal life, such as shells.

Breccia Ground up and recemented rock.

Buffer A chemical balance that is driven by the attempt to maintain equilibrium during changing conditions.

Bulk contraction Any solid will contract into a smaller volume when it cools.

b-Value The slope of the relation between earthquake magnitude and number of earthquakes. In general, there are more small than large earthquakes. The b-value measures the exact relation between the number of small versus large earthquakes.

Carbonate compensation depth (CCD)   The level in the ocean below which calcium carbonate shells dissolve back into sea water faster than they rain down from above.

Cation   Positively charged elements that combine with anions or negatively charged elements to form molecules of minerals.

Centigrade   The temperature scale that linearly increases from zero degrees at the freezing point of water to 100 degrees at the boiling point.

Chemical oceanography   The branch of oceanographic sciences that studies the chemistry of the ocean water.

Clapyron curve   The pressure-temperature relationship whereby a chemical compound reacts to become some other combination of elements.

Clay   Hydrated rock composed of platelike sheets of potassium, calcium, and sodium silicate with water chemically bound between the plates.

Compressional wave   The fastest seismic wave propagated by an earthquake or explosive charge. The P or primary wave travels by direct vibrational energy transfer away from the center of the earthquake.

Conduction   Transmission of heat by transfer of vibrational energy from one molecule to the next.

Continental drift   The concept that the continents have been drifting across the surface of the Earth throughout geological time. A subset of plate tectonics.

Continental shelf   The offshore area of a continent in shallow water.

Continental slope   The transition from the continental margin to the deep sea basin.

Convection   Transmission of heat by physical transport of the heat-bearing substance, usually by flow of a liquid from a hot area to a cold area and vice versa.

Core (sedimentary or rock)   A sample taken vertically into the earth.

Coriolis force   The spin of the earth about its axis produces a force on the ocean that is related to centrifical force and causes waters in the northern hemisphere to circulate clockwise and waters in the southern hemisphere to circulate counterclockwise.

Craton   The center, stable interior of a continent. Usually composed of the oldest rock on the continent.

Cretaceous   The geological period from 135 to 65 million years ago; the end of this period was marked by a massive extinction event that killed off the dinosaurs as well as half the other living organisms on the planet.

Crevasses   Deep canyons formed by flowing water or by faulting.

Cross section   A map representing a vertical slice through a feature.

Cylindrical rolls   Convection currents that are much longer than they are either deep or wide.

Dehydration   Under high pressures and temperatures, a hydrous mineral will lose its bound water to form a dry, dehydrated mineral plus water.

Delta   The wedge-shaped pile of sediments deposited at the mouth of a river.

Density   The weight of a rock or mineral in grams per cubic centimeter or comparable units.

Diagenesis   The chemical and other alteration of a sediment after it has been deposited.

Diapir   The buoyant rise of a rock through heavier rock toward the surface.

Diatom   The silica fossil shells of these microplants form siliceous sediments.

Differentiation   Separation of solids or liquids according to their weight with heavy mass sinking and light material rising toward the surface.

Dikes   Near vertical sheets of rock that solidified after intrusion into the rock above.

Double couple   The mechanism by which an earthquake shakes the Earth. For every force outward, there must be an equal and opposite force on the opposite side of the earth that compensates for it. Consequently the earth moves in quadrants during an earthquake.

Double plane   Earthquakes along the downgoing slab are concentrated at the top and bottom of the rigid outer layer of the plate. Two planes of seismic activity are formed.

Downgoing slab   The subducting plate that plunges back into the mantle.

Downwelling convection cells   The cold fluid of a convection cell sinks downward because it is heavy.

Earthquake   A sudden movement of a fault caused by the breaking of the rock in contact along the fault surface when the stresses of the Earth's movements become larger than the strength with which the rock is held together.

Earthquake magnitude   The amount of energy released by an earthquake is measured logarithmically by its magnitude.

East Pacific rise   The predominant location upon which the hot springs and black smokers have been discovered to date is the mid-ocean spreading center that runs north-south along the eastern side of the Pacific.

Eclogite   Garnet- and pyroxene-bearing mantle rock with large crystals.

Electrical resistivity   The property of a solid that measures its ability to transfer or carry an electrical current.

Eolian   Pertaining to wind-blown sediments.

Epicenter   The point on the surface of the earth which is directly above an earthquake within the earth.

Evaporites   The deposition of salt, anhydrite, and gypsum from the evaporation in an enclosed basin of stranded sea water.

Exponential   The relation of one property to a second whereby the first increases as the square of the second.

Extrusion   The ejection of lava onto the Earth's surface from below.

Fahrenheit   The temperature scale increasing from 32 degrees at the freezing point of water to 212 degrees at the boiling point.

Farallon plate   The giant oceanic plate that once occupied most of the Pacific Ocean and is now broken into small plates off the coast of Oregon and Mexico. The rest of the plate has been subducted beneath North America.

First motion   The movement outward from an earthquake at the moment when each point in the Earth feels the earthquake.

Focal mechanism   The center of propagation of an earthquake about which the motions all over the world can be backtracked to define the type and form of the fault motion causing the earthquake.

Foraminifera   Calcium-carbonate secreting microorganisms that live in the surface waters of the oceans; after death their shells form the primary constituents of limestone rock and sediments deposited on the sea floor.

Fore-arc basin   Between the trench and volcanic island arc, the accretionary wedge often forms a deep sedimentary basin as the offscraped sediments are compacted, dewatered, and rise to form a barrier behind which sediments derived from landward are trapped.

Fracture front   When cold sea water convecting downward encounters hot rock of the newly solidifying crust, fractures are formed. This zone of contact moves as a front as fracturing penetrates downward after each intrusion event of new lava injected at the ridge axes.

Fractures   The cracks in rock. Anything from a microcrack to the San Andreas fault qualifies as a fracture in the Earth.

Fracture zone   The frozen trace of a transform fault captured in the lithosphere away from midocean ridges.

Gabbro   Chemically identical to basalt, but cooled and solidified more slowly so that crystals are larger.

Geochemistry   The chemistry of the Earth.

Geoid   The natural surface that a liquid will seek at the earth's surface. Since a liquid such as water can hold no shape of its own, the ocean surface defines the neutral gravity force surface of the Earth.

Geostrophic flow   Ocean currents that flow perpendicular to the coriolis flow or to the right of the boundary currents in the northern hemisphere.

Geyser   A hot spring that periodically flashes to steam and blows out at the surface.

Granite   Light-colored rock that contains sodium, potassium, and calcic silicates.

Gravitational pull   The attraction of any mass to any other mass. The force itself is a function of how much mass is present in each body.

Gravity fault   Motion along a fault plane that moves as if pulled downslope by gravity.

Greenhouse effect   Light enters and penetrates through our atmosphere to impact the surface. There it splits into its spectrum of contained wavelengths from infrared to ultraviolet. The atmosphere, particularly CO_2 in the atmosphere, prevents the infrared energy from escaping back into space. The heat is thus trapped inside the atmosphere, which in turn becomes hotter.

Guyot   An undersea volcano that reached the surface of the ocean, causing its top to be flattened by erosion. Then, as the lava and magma cool, thermal subsidence, causes the volcano to sink beneath the sea surface. The well-preserved flat top is characteristic of a guyot.

Half-life   Each radioactive element decays to half its mass in a characteristic time interval. It then decays to half of the remaining half in the same time, again and again.

Harmonic tremor   The shaking caused by liquids moving inside the earth, which is periodic and sinusoidal.

Heat flow   Heat energy flows from hot toward cold at a rate or flux equal to the temperature gradient times the conductivity of the material in between.

Hot spot   A volcanic center that has no relation to plate boundary location; an anomalous magma generation site in the mantle.

Hydrate   A rock or mineral with water chemically bound within its structure.

Hydraulic head   The force from a column of fluid.

Hydrocarbon maturation   The cooking of hydrocarbons under pressure, temperature, and time determines whether oil, gas, or if too hot, soured and useless products will develop.

Hydrocarbon migration   Hydrocarbons formed in source rock must move to be trapped in a permeable rock in order to be produced by an oil company.

Hydrocarbons   Oil, gas and other hydrogen, carbon and oxygen compounds formed by a partial degradation of organic material.

Hydrocarbon trap   The superposition of an impermeable *cap* rock over a permeable *reservoir* rock traps hydrocarbons for production.

Hydrogenous   Pertaining to sedimentary deposits from the water column.

Hydrosphere   The water layer at the surface of the Earth.

Hydrothermal circulation   The convection of cold sea water downward through the oceanic crust toward the deeper depths of the oceanic crust, where it becomes hot and is bouyantly forced back toward the surface.

Hypocenter   The actual location within the earth where an earthquake occurs.

Inert gases   Argon, krypton, zenon, and neon are examples inert gases which have their atomic structure exactly filled so that no chemical combination with any other element is ever possible.

Infrared   The short wavelength component of light energy.

Internal waves   A wave propagating at a density boundary within the ocean rather than at the surface of the water.

Intrusion   The injection of one body (e.g., magma) into another (as with a dike).

Iridium   One of the rare earth elements that is not plentiful on earth, but is more plentiful in space.

Island arc   The volcanos landward of a subduction zone, parallel to the trench, and above the melting zone of a subduction zone.

Isostatic equilibrium   The floating of the lithosphere in the asthenosphere so that equilibrium levels are maintained.

Isotherm   A line of constant temperature within the Earth.

Isotope   Most elements have several closely related atomic weights (relative masses of atoms) while having the same atomic number (protons in the nucleus).

Jurassic   The geological period from 190 to 135 million years ago that preceded the Cretaceous.

Kilometer   One thousand meters; a meter is about 39 inches long.

Kula plate   The oceanic plate that once occupied the entire northern Pacific Ocean and is now all subducted beneath Alaska, except possibly for a remnant in the Bering Sea.

KUTh   The major radioactive heat-releasing elements within the Earth are K = potassium, U = uranium and Th = thorium. KUTh is a slang term for these elements.

Lava   Magma, or rock hot enough to flow, becomes lava when it reaches the surface.

Layer 1 The sedimentary layer on top of the sea floor.

Layer 2 The basaltic crust at the top of the oceanic lithosphere but below the sediment.

Layer 2A The pillow basalts at the top of Layer 2.

Layer 2B The intermixed flows, pillows, and dikes at the center of Layer 2.

Layer 2C The dikes that intrude the crust to form the base of the basaltic layer 2.

Layer 3 The gabbro that is the solidified magma chamber below the basaltic layer but still within the crust.

Leveling Periodic measurement of the height of land above sea level.

Limestone Calcium carbonate rock formed by the accumulation of shells from dead marine organisms and the later solidification into rock.

Lithosphere The solid outer plates that form the earths outer shell. Made up of both crustal and mantle rocks.

Loading The piling of a new weight onto the lithosphere causes it to sink to its isostatic equilibrium level.

Longitudinal rolls The form of convection cells that appears as cylindrical rolls.

Lysocline The ocean depth below which the rate of dissolution just exceeds the rate of deposition of the dead shells of calcareous organisms.

Lystric fault The normal or gravity fault that begins vertically and is flattened with depth until it becomes nearly horizontal. Formed by the stretching of a brittle material.

Magma Rock that is hot enough to be liquid and flow.

Magma chamber Every volcano has deep within it a core of molten rock that supplies lava to the surface.

Magnetic anomaly After the Earth's present magnetic field is stripped away, the much smaller intensity field reversals frozen into the rock during the original cooling can be detected. These form patterns or stripes often referred to as anomalies, caused by the periodic reversal of the earth's north and south poles.

Magnetic field When rock flows within the earth, the movement of electrons within the rock causes a magnetic field to be formed. The attractive and repellant forces are the same as with a bar magnet, but the forces originate from the flow of an electrical current in the earth's core.

Magnetic stripes Long, thin stripes of alternately positively and negatively magnetized rock (north pole pointing up followed by north pole pointing down) produced by the periodic reversal of the Earth's magnetic field during the continued spreading of a midoceanic ridge volcanic system.

Magnetometer An instrument that detects the magnetic field of the Earth.

Manganese nodules Accretions from the water column of manganese and other precious metals at the sea floor in the form of rounded nodules. The ultimate source for the metals is the black smoker system at the ridge axes.

Mantle (Earth's) The portion of the Earth below the solid crust and above the core, most of which is composed of rock very near the melting temperature so that it flows slowly.

Mantle (lithospheric) The ultramafic residual rock that forms the bottom 90% of the lithosphere. It is formed when the light crust separates from the mantle (Earth's) leaving an intermediate layer of ulatramafic rocks.

Mare Lunar sea of basaltic lava.

Mass Anything with density has mass. Weight is a form of measurement of mass.

Massive sulfide The ore body deposited when the hot hydrothermal waters rich in metal sulfides mix with cold sea water. Mined on land as part of ophiolites, these ore bodies are called massive sulfides.

Metallogenesis The formation of metal concentrations from the deposition and alteration of rock and fluid.

Metasomatism The diffusion of elements through the lattice structure of solid rock in a closed geochemical system. Elements are rearranged but not removed.

Meteor A rock that falls through the earth's atmosphere from space. Most meteors come from the asteroid belt between Earth and Mars.

Meteorite Most meteors burn up in our atmosphere. If, however, the rock survives to fall to the surface, it becomes a meteorite.

Microcalorie One millionth of the amount of heat carried by one calorie, which is itself defined as the quantity of heat required to raise the temperature of one cm^3 of water by one degree Centigrade.

Mid-Atlantic ridge The sea-floor spreading ridge of volcanos that marks the extensional edge of the North American and South American plates to the west and the Eurasian and African plates to the east.

Mohorovičić discontinuity, or Moho The major seismic discontinuity separating light crustal rocks from heavy mantle rocks both on land and under the sea.

Mylar A transparent and thin plastic sheet.

Nannofossils Tiny calcareous shelled microfossils.

Nemesis The supposed sister star to the earth that resides on the other side of the galaxy now, but that periodically causes meteorites to shower the earth with space debris possibly causing extentions. It has never been seen yet.

Normal fault   Another name for a gravity or extensional fault.

Nutrients   Food for plants and animals in the ocean.

Obduction   The emplacement upward onto land of a sliver of oceanic plate to form an ophiolite.

Olivine   A magnesium iron silicate mineral that is the primary constituent of the mantle.

Oort cloud   The collection of comets that orbits close to the earth about once every 26 million years, showering the planet with meteorites possibly causing extinctions.

Ophiolite   The rock of the oceanic crust periodically is thrust upward as a sliver onto land during subduction to become an ophiolite complex.

Ore body   The accumulation of precious metal-bearing ores where the hot hydrothermal water moving upward toward the surface mixes with the cold sea water penetrating downward.

Outgassing   The loss of gas from within a planet to space.

Paleoceanography   The study of the currents and chemical structure of the oceans in the geological past.

Paleoenvironment   The study and reconstruction of the climate of past geological times.

Paleomagnetic reversal   Reversals of the Earth's magnetic field preserved within the magnetization of progressively older rocks.

Paleomagnetism   The old pole locations and magnetism of past geological rock.

Peridotite   The most common ultramafic rock type in the Earth's mantle.

Permeability   The ability to transfer fluid through cracks, pores, and interconnected spaces within a rock.

Permian   The geological period from 280 to 255 million years ago, the end of which marked the end of the Paleozoic era.

Phase change   The increase in pressure and temperature causes a mineral to reconstitute its crystal structure to more compact forms at specific thermodynamic energy states.

Physical oceanography   The branch of oceanographic sciences that studies the physics of water movements in the ocean.

Physiography   The physical description of the form or shape of land or sea floor.

Pillow basalt   Lava extruded under water quenches and solidifies faster on its edges than in its center. The result is the formation of tubes and lobate tunnels within which the lava flows. These structures are called pillow basalts because they resemble fields of piled pillows.

Plagioclase   A class of light-colored and light-weight minerals made up of alcalic silicates.

Plate tectonics   The surface of the Earth is coverd by discrete plates that move relative to the spin axis. The plates interact with each other only at their edges and move relative to each other by clearly defined geometric laws defined by the motion of rigid bodies across the surface of a sphere.

Polarity reversals   The periodic reversal of the Earth's magnetic field from the attraction end of a bar magnet pointing to the north pole, to the repulsion end pointing to the north.

Porosity   The percent of a rock consisting of pore spaces between crystals and grains, usually filled with water.

Postrift sediments   The usually deeper water sediments that fill the rift as a proto-ocean becomes a full-fledged oceanic circulation system.

Pressure   The force exerted on one object by another. In the Earth, the pressure is the force on a rock or fluid by all the rocks and fluid surrounding it.

Project Mohole   The original concept that spawned the Deep Sea Drilling Project: to drill a single deep hole beneath the sea floor into the Moho discontinuity.

Propagating rift   Periodically, plates change their motion relative to each other. Readjustments along the extensional boundaries propagate a new ridge axis that spreads across the old pattern and eventually replaces it.

Pyrolite   Theoretical composition of the Earth's asthenosphere calculated so that melting will remove one part basalt and three parts ultramafic mantle to form the oceanic lithosphere.

Quenching   The flash cooling of a liquid, such as magma, into a solid, such as lava rock erupted under the ocean.

Radioactive decay   The emission of neutrons or gamma rays by a rock with an unstable nuclear configuration within its nucleus.

Radiolaria   Siliceous-shelled microorganisms whose shells make up a large component of siliceous sediments.

Radiometric Dating   rate of decay of a radioactive rock or mineral used to determine the age of a rock.

Reef   The biological community that lives at the edge of an island or continent. The shells form a limestone deposit that is readily preserved in the geological record.

Regression   A fall in sea level that exposes continental shelves to erosion.

Relative plate motion   The movement of one plate relative to another. It has no relation to spin axis location at all.

Ridge   A linear string of mountains or volcanos.

Ridge crest   An axis of midoceanic volcanos aligned along the edge of two plates extending away from each other.

Rift   An usually long, narrow rent in the surface where two stable crustal segments are being torn apart.

Rift valley   The center of an extensional spreading center where continental or oceanic plate separation is occurring.

Salinity crisis   The removal of large volumes of salt from circulating sea water by evaporation in an isolated basin requires the input of additional salts from the hydrothermal waters of the mid-ocean ridge axis to stabilize the chemical composition of ocean water.

Scarp   A wall of rock usually formed by movement along a fault during repeated earthquakes.

Sea-floor spreading   The linear ridge of volcanos where new magma and lava are upwelling to form the newest edges of extensional plate boundaries.

Seamount   An undersea volcano that never reached the surface of the ocean and so does not have a flat erosional top (a guyot).

Seasat   The radar altimetry satellite launched by the United States in 1978 to define the ocean geoid.

Seaward bulge   The elevated seaward bulge produced by the bending of the subducting plate.

Sedimentary   Rocks formed by deposition from elsewhere.

Seismic anisotropy   Differential velocity structure of rock so that speeds of propagation of seismic waves are faster in one direction than in another.

Seismic discontinuity   A boundary within the Earth with two very different rock types in contact so that the impedance contrast produces a stepwise shift in the elastic behavior of the rock.

Seismic donut   The subduction process produces uniform stresses across the downgoing plate. However, because the faulting process is not uniform over a historical time frame, gaps in the occurrence of earthquakes occur. These areas (donuts) of no activity are particularly dangerous locales where earthquakes are more likely to occur in the future.

Seismic reflection   The mapping of seismic energy that has bounced off impedance layers within the earth.

Seismic refraction   The transport of seismic energy through rock and along impedance layers.

Seismic velocity   The speed with which seismic energy propagates through rock.

Seismic velocity   The speed with which seismic energy propagates through rock.

Seismic wave tomography   Mapping the three-dimensional form of structures with like seismic wave velocities changes such as flow in the mantle.

Seismology   The study of earthquakes and the propagation of vibrations for these earthquakes through the Earth.

Seismometer   The instrument recording seismic waves as they pass beneath the sensor; through the use of an electromagnet, in which electric vibration is converted into current.

Serpentine   A fiberous ultramafic alteration produce with a very high water content within its crystal structure.

Sertsey   An island off the southern tip of Iceland that grew from submarine volcano breaking the surface and forming an island.

Shale   The rock formed from compaction of clay into rock.

Shear wave   The secondary or S wave that propagates slower than the P wave by vibration transverse to the direction of propagation away from either an earthquake or explosive charge.

Shear-wave anomaly   The variation about some standard value of the velocity with which shear waves travel through a body.

Sheet flow   The extrusion of lava across a wide area. If intrusive, it forms a *sill*.

Siliceous   Sediments composed primarily of quartz and other forms of SiO_2.

Soluble   Refers to a substance that dissolves in water.

Sonar   Sonic energy bounced off distant objects underwater to locate and range on them, just as radar does with microwaves in air.

Spectrum   The breaking down of a wave of some form into its component parts. Power spectrum, for example, divides a complex wave into energy content of each of its frequency components.

Spinel   The high pressure, high temperature form of manganese oxide, after a phase change.

Spokelike convection   Convection currents shaped like the spokes on a bicycle wheel.

State-of-stress   The force per unit area within a body, caused by external forces acting on the body.

Stockwork   The feeder network of black and white smokers eventually is penetrated by cold water, causing precipitation of metals in the feeder fracture system under a massive sulfide. These mineralized veins are called stockworks.

Stratigraphy   Study of the order of rock strata, their age and form as well as their distribution and lithology.

Stretching   The continental crust "stretches" as extension begins. In reality, the crust breaks into normal or "lystric" faults and the continental mantle extends like taffy before a clear connection to the asthenosphere is established and sea floor spreading begins.

Strike   The direction in which a feature trends; its orientation.

Strike-slip fault   Motion parallel to the surface along a fault neither with or against gravity.

Subduction   When two plates converge at the surface, one is forced downward into the mantle where it is eventually remelted and assimilated.

Subduction complex   The subducting slab, trench, fore-arc, volcanic arc, and back-arc basin taken together.

Subduction zone   Convergence zone where two plates collide, thrusting one downward into the mantle.

Submarine canyon   The deep gorge residing underwater and formed by the underwater extensions of rivers.

Subsidence   Sinking due to loading or thermal contraction during cooling.

Superheated   Under high pressure water can be heated beyond the critical point to higher temperatures than would be possible under low pressure.

Supersaturated water   Superheated water that is able to dissolve more elements and minerals than would ordinarily be possible.

Syn-rift sediments   The sediments that fill the rift valley formed during stretching of a continent. They are derived from the weathering of the continent and from repeated evaporation of small seas that first fill the newly forming ocean.

Synthetic seismogram   A physical model reflecting our understanding of how the earth is shaking during seismic movement. A synthetic replica of that motion is then constructed to see how well it, and our model, fit the real-world motion.

Temperature   The state of excited vibration of the molecules within a body.

Tension   Extensional forces stretch the earth and form tensional forces.

Terrigenous   Sediments deposited from land to the sea floor.

Thermal conductivity   The rate at which a substance transmits heat by transfer of the vibrational energy from molecule to molecule.

Thermal contraction   During cooling, a solid will contract as it loses heat energy.

Thermodynamics   The physical description of chemical reactions. That is, the pressure, temperature, and chemical bonding energy of any chemical state can be defined by the laws of thermodynamics.

Thinning   Stretching of the continental crust that produces thinned layers of rock.

Thrust fault   Motion along this fault that is reversed from that expected from gravity forces.

Tidal friction   The loss of energy through heating caused by the movements associated with the tides.

Tidal pull   The gravity pull of the moon on our ocean.

Topography   The shape of a surface above and below a datum, like the sea level.

Tortuosity   The measure of the pathway interconnecting permeable rock; in other words, of how tortuous the path is.

Tracer   A chemical with a distinctive signature that can be used to trace ocean current movements, etc.

Transform fault   A major plate boundary formed when two plates move across each other along a fault.

Transgression   A rise in sea level that causes flooding of the shallow edges of continental margins.

Trench   The sea floor plunges to the deepest depths recorded anywhere in the oceans at the line where the subducting plate bends beneath the surface headed for the mantle. This topographic feature is called a trench.

Triple junction   When three plates meet at a point, a triple junction is formed. The evolution of and motion around the triple junction are precisely defined by Eulerian geometry.

Tube worms   Brilliant red-colored Phoganofera worms live in a long, cylindrical, chitinous tube and consume sulfur-eating bacteria at the hydrothermal hot springs at the ridge axes.

Turbidite   The slurry of mud that periodically slides down often gentle slopes toward the deep-sea floor.

Turbidity current   An undersea landslide causes the sediment caught up in the flow to intermix and stratify into a characteristic gradational pattern of coarse to fine-grained particles that flow over very gentle slopes for many hundreds of miles as a sea floor current.

Ultramafic   Chemical composition of rock with even more magnesium, iron, and other heavy cations than mafic rocks.

Ultrasonic imaging   Just as they are used in medicine, super high frequency sound waves can be bounced off a geological feature, such as the inside of a drillhole, to produce a picture of it.

Unbending   Below the trench, the subducting slab must straighten out from elastic rebound forces. This changes the forces on the bottom plane of the double seismic zone from compression to extension.

Upwelling   Fluid moving upward usually propelled by buoyancy forces.

Upwelling convection cells   The hot fluid in a convection cell rises toward the surface because it is buoyant and light.

Void spaces   The porous liquid- or gas-filled cavities between grains or crystals of rock.

Volatiles   Gases dissolved in a liquid.

Volcano   The centerpoint of magma eruption where lava flows onto the surface.

Weathering   The erosion of the continent or the high ground below sea level.

White smoker   A hydrothermal hot spring that is not hot enough to be supersaturated with metals, resulting in an effluent that consists of white sulfides instead of black sulfides.

References

Almagor, G., and Garfunkel, Z., Submarine slumping in continental margins of Israel and northern Sinai; *Am. Assn. Petrog. Geol., Bull.*, **63**, 324–340, 1979.

Alvarez, L. W., Alvarez, W., Asaro, F., and Michel, H. V., Extraterrestrial cause for the Cretaceous-Tertiary Extensions, *Science*, **208**, 1095–1108, 1980.

Anderson, R. N., Surprises from the Glomar Challenger, *Nature*, **293**, 261–262, 1981.

Anderson, R. N., and Skilbeck, J. N., Oceanic Heat Flow, in *The Sea*, Vol. 7, C. Emiliani, ed., Wiley Interscience, New York, 489–525, 1981.

Anderson, R. N., and Zoback, M. D., Permeability of the upper oceanic crust, DSDP hole 504B, *J. Geophys. Res.*, **81**, 2860–2868, 1982.

Anderson, R. N., Hobart, M. A., and Langseth, M. G., Geothermal convection through oceanic crust and sediments in the Indian Ocean, *Science*, **204**, 828–832, 1977.

Anderson, R. N., Langseth, M., and Sclater, J. G., The mechanism of heat transfer through the floor of the Indian Ocean, *J. Geophys. Res.*, **82**, 3391–4409, 1977.

Anderson, R. N., DeLong, S. E., and Schwartz, W., Dehydration and a thermal model for subduction, *J. Geol.*, 1977.

Anderson, R. N., Hasegawa, A., Umino, H., Takagi, A., Phase changes and the frequency-magnitude distribution in the double-plane seismic zone beneath Tohoku, Japan, *J. Geophys. Res.*, **83**, 1379–1383, 1979.

Anderson, R. N., Honnorez, J., Becker, K., et al., DSDP Hole 504B: The first reference section over 1 km through layer 2 of the oceanic crust, *Nature*, **300**, 589–594, 1982.

Anderson, R. N., Zoback, M. D., and Newmark, R. L., Permeability versus depth in the upper oceanic crust, DSDP hole 504B, *J. Geophys. Res.*, **84**, April 1985.

Atwater, T. Implications of plate tectonics for the Cenozoic tectonic evolution for western North America, *Geol. Soc. Am., Bull.*, **81**, 3513–3566, 1970.

Atwater, T., and Menard, H. W., Magnetic lineations in the Northeast Pacific, *Earth Planet. Sci. Lett.*, **7**, 445–450, 1971.

Ballard, R. D., Oasis form the deep, *National Geographic Magazine,* April 1979.

Ballard, R. D., and Francheteau, J., Geological processes at mid-ocean ridges and their relationship to sulfide deposits, in *Hydrothermal Processes at Sea Floor Spreading Centers,* P. Rona, ed., Plenum Press, New York, 7–26, 1983.

Ballard, R. D., Hekinian R., and Francheteau, J., Geological setting of hydrothermal activity at 12 degrees North on the East Pacific Rise, *Earth Planet. Sci. Lett.,* **69,** 176–186, 1984.

Barazangi, M., and Dorman, J., World seismicity map, 1961–1967, ESSA, *Coast and Geodetic Survey,* 1969.

Barron, E. J., and Whitman, J. M., Oceanic sediments in space and time, in *The Sea,* Vol. 7, C. Emiliani, ed., Wiley Interscience, New York, 689–733, 1981.

Berger, W. H., Deep Sea sedimentation, in *Geology of the Continental Margins,* C. A. Burk and C. D. Drake, eds., Springer-Verlag, New York, 1974.

Berger, W. H., Biogenous deep-sea sediments: production, preservation and interpretation, in *Treatise on Chemical Oceanography,* Vol. 5, J. Riley and R. Chester, eds., Academic Press, New York, 265–388, 1976.

Berger, W. H., Paleoceanography: the deep-sea record, in *The Sea,* Vol. 7, C. Emiliani, ed., Wiley Interscience, New York, 1437–1521, 1981.

Berger, W. H., and Winterer, E. L., Plate stratigraphy and the fluctuating carbonate line, in *Pelagic Sediments on Land and under the Sea,* K. Hsu and H. C. Jenkyns, eds., Blackwell, Oxford, 1974.

Bonatti, E., Metal deposits in the oceanic lithosphere, in *The Sea,* Vol. 7, C. Emiliani, ed., Wiley Interscience, New York, 639–687, 1981.

Boorstin, D. J., The Discoverers, Random House, New York, 1983.

Bullard, E. C., Everett, J. E., and Smith, A. G., The fit of the continents around the Atlantic, in *A Symposium on Continental Drift,* Phil. Trans. Roy. Soc. of London, A258, 41–51, 1965.

Burns, R. G., and Burns, V. M., Authigenic oxides, in *The Sea,* Vol. 7, C. Emiliani, ed., Wiley Interscience, New York, 875–915, 1981.

Cann, J. R., Basalts from the ocean floor, in *The Sea,* Vol. 7, C.Emiliani, ed., Wiley Interscience, New York, 363–391, 1981.

Casey, J. F., Dewey, J. F. Fox, P. J., Karson, J. A., and Rosencrantz, E., Heterogeneous nature of the oceanic crust and mantle: a perspective from the Bay of Islands Ophiolite complex, in *The Sea,* Vol. 7, C. Emiliani, ed., Wiley Interscience, New York, 305–339, 1981.

Corliss, J. B., Dymond, J., Gordon, L. I., et al., Submarine thermal springs on the Galapagos Rift, *Science,* **203,** 1073–1083, 1979.

Corliss, J. B., Barrios, J., and Suess, J., Sulfur-eating organisms from the deep sea black smokers and the origin of life, French Acad. of Sci,   1982.

Craig, H., and Lupton, J. E., Helium-3 and mantle volatiles in the ocean and the oceanic crust, in *The Sea,* Vol. 7, C. Emiliani, ed., Wiley Interscience, New York, 391–428, 1983.

Davies, T. A., and Gorsline, D. S., Oceanic sediments and sedimentary processes, in *Chemical Oceanography,* Part 5, J. P. Riley and R. Chester, eds., Academic Press, New York, 1976.

DeLong, S. E., Anderson, R. N., and Schwarz, W. M., Thermal effects of ridge subduction, *Earth Planet. Sci. Lett.*, **44,** 239–246, 1979.

Dewey, J. F., Plate tectonics, *Sci. Am.*, **266,** 56–68, 1972.

Douglas, R., and Woodruff, F., Deep-sea benthic Foraminifera, in *The Sea*, Vol. 7, C. Emiliani, ed., Wiley Interscience, New York, 1233–1329, 1981.

Dziewonski, A. M., and Anderson, D. L., Seismic tomography of the Earth's Interior, *Am. Sci.*, **72,** 4483–494, 1984.

Edmond, J. M., Ridge crest hot springs: the story so far, *EOS*, **61,** 127–131, 1980.

Edmond, J. M., Corliss, J. B., Gordon, L. I., Ridge crest hydrothermal metamorphism at the Galapagos Spreading Center and reverse weathering, in *Deep Sea Drilling Project Results in the Atlantic Ocean: the Oceanic Crust*, M. Talwani, ed., Am. Geophys Un., 383–393, 1979.

Elthon, D., Metamorphism in oceanic spreading centers, in *The Sea*, Vol. 7, C. Emiliani, ed., Wiley Interscience, New York, 285–305, 1981.

Emiliani, C., ed., *The Sea*, Vol. 7, Wiley Interscience, New York, 1981.

Farr, J., and Ryan, W. B. F., Seamark images of the Sea Floor, in *Lamont-Doherty Geological Observatory Yearbook*, Columbia Univ., 1983.

Fehn, U., Green, K. E., Von Herzen, R. P., and Cathles, L. M., Numerical Models for the hydrothermal field at the Galapagos Spreading Center, *J. Geophys. Res.*, **88,** 1033–1048, 1983.

Foreman, H. P., Radiolaria, in *The Sea*, Vol. 7, C. Emiliani, ed., Wiley Interscience, New York, 1121–1145, 1981.

Fornari, D., Ryan, W. B. J., and Fox, P. J., Evolution of craters and calderas in young seamounts near the axis of the East Pacific Rise at 10 degrees North, *J. Geophys. Res.*, **89,** 1169–1183, 1985.

Forsyth, D., and Uyeda, S., On the relative driving forces of plate motion, *Geophys. J. Roy. Astron. Soc.*, **43,** 163–200, 1975.

Fox, P. J., and Stroup, J. B., The plutonic foundation of the oceanic crust, in *The Sea*, Vol. 7, C. Emiliani, ed., Wiley Interscience, New York, 119–219, 1981.

Francheteau, J., The Oceanic Crust, *Sci. Am.*, **249,** 114–129, 1983.

Gartner, S., Calcareous nannofossils in marine sediments, in *The Sea*, Vol. 7, C. Emiliani, ed., Wiley Interscience, New York, 1145–1179, 1981.

Gass, I. G., and Smewing, J. D., Ophiolites: Obducted oceanic crust, in *The Sea*, Vol. 7, C. Emiliani, ed., Wiley Interscience, New York, 339–363, 1981.

Grassle, F., Introduction to the biology of hydrothermal vents, in *Hydrothermal Processes at Sea Floor Spreading Centers*, P. Rona, ed., Plenum Press, New York, 665–676, 1983.

Grow, J. A., Crustal and upper mantle structure of the Central Aleutian Arc, *Geol. Soc. Am. Bull.*, **84,** 2169–2192, 1973.

Grow, J. A., Deep structure and evolution of the Baltimore Canyon trough in view of the COST b-3 well, in *Geological Structure of the COST B-3 well*, U.S. Geol. Survey Circular 833, 117–125, 1980.

Harrison, C. G. A., Magnetism of the oceanic crust, in *The Sea*, Vol. 7, C. Emiliani, ed., Wiley Interscience, New York, 219–241, 1981.

Harrison, C. G. A., and Bonatti, E., The oceanic lithosphere, in *The Sea*, Vol. 7, C. Emiliani, ed., Wiley Interscience, New York, 21–49, 1981.

Hart, S. R., and Straudigel, H., Oceanic crust: the age of hydrothermal alteration, *Geophys. Res. Lett.*, **5**, 1009–1012, 1978.

Hasegawa, A., Umino, N., and Takagi, A., Double-planed structure of the deep seismic zone in the northeast Japan arc, *Tectonophys.*, **47**, 42–58, 1978.

Hayes, D. E., and Ewing, M., Pacific boundary structure, in *The Sea*, Vol. 4, A. Maxwell, ed., Wiley Interscience, New York, 29–72, 1970.

Hays, J. D., Imbrie, J., and Shackleton, N. J., Variations in the Earth's orbit: Pacemaker of the ice ages, *Science*, **194**, 1121–1132, 1976.

Haxby, W., Gravity field of the world's oceans recovered from SEASAT altimetry, Lamont-Doherty Geological Observatory Map, Columbia Univ., 1983.

Haxby, W., Karner, G., Weissel, J. K., and LaBrecque, J., Digital images of combined ocean and continental data sets and their use in tectonic studies, *EOS*, **64**, 995–1004, 1983.

Heezen, B. C., and Tharp, M., The floor of the oceans, *National Geographic Society Magazine*, 1976.

Heezen, B. C., and Tharp, M., North Atlantic Ocean: a portion of the World Ocean Panorama, Heezen and Tharp Maps, 1977.

Heirtzler, J. R., Le Pichon, X., and Barron, J. C., Magnetic anomalies over the Reykjanes Ridge, *Deep Sea Research*, **13**, 427–443, 1966.

Herron, T. J., Ludwig, W. J., Stoffa, P. L., Kan, T. K., and Buhl, P., Structure of the East Pacific Rise crest from multichannel seismic data, *J. Geophys. Res.*, **83**, 798–804, 1978.

Hey, R. N., A new class of pseudofaults and their bearing on plate tectonics: a propagating rift model, *Earth Planet. Sci. Lett.*, **37**, 321–325, 1978.

Holland, H. C., River transport to the oceans, in *The Sea*, Vol. 7, C. Emiliani, ed., Wiley Interscience, New York, 763–801, 1981.

Holland, H. C., Anhydrite in the Kuroko deposits: mode of occurrence and depositional mechanism, *Econ. Geol.*, mono 5, 329–344, 1983.

Holmes, A. *Principals of Physical Geology*, John Wiley, New York, 1978.

Honnorez, J., The aging of the oceanic crust at low temperature, in *The Sea*, Vol. 7, C. Emiliani, ed., Wiley Interscience, New York, 525–589, 1981.

Honnorez, J., Basalt-sea water exchange: a perspective from an experimental viewpoint, in *Hydrothermal Processes at Sea Floor Spreading Centers*, P. Rona, ed., Plenum Press, New York, 169–176, 1983.

Isacks, B. L., and Molnar, P., Distribution of stresses in the descending lithosphere from global survey of focal mechanism solutions of mantle earthquakes, *Rev. Geophys. and Space Phys.*, **9**, 103–174, 1971.

Isacks, B. L., Oliver, J., and Sykes, L. R., Seismology and the new plate tectonics, *J. Geophys. Res.*, **73**, 5855–5900, 1968.

Jansa, L. F., Gardner, J., and Dean, W. E., Mesozoic Sequences of the Central North Atlantic, in *Initial Reports, Deep Sea Drilling Project*, U.S. Government Printing Office, Washington, D.C., Vol. 41, 991–1031, 1978.

Jenkins, W. J., Edmond, J. M., and Corliss, J. B., Excess helium-3 and helium-4 in Galapagos submarine hydrothermal waters, *Nature*, **272**, 156–158, 1978.

Jennings, C. W., Strand, R. G., and Rogers, T. H., *Geological Map of California*, Williams and Heintz, 1977.

Jordan, T. H., and Anderson, D. L., Earth structure from free oscillations and travel times, *Geophys. J. Roy. Astron. Soc.*, **36**, 411–459, 1974.

Kastner, M., Authigenic silicates in deep-sea sediments: formation and diagenesis, in *The Sea*, Vol. 7, C. Emiliani, ed., Wiley Interscience, New York, 915–981, 1981.

Kennett, J., *Marine Geology*, Prentice-Hall, Englewood Cliffs, N.J., 1982.

Larson, R. L., Pitman, W. C. III, X. Galauchenco, Cande, S. E., Dewey, J. F., Haxby, W. F., and Labrecque, J. L., *Bedrock Geology of the World*, W. H. Freeman, San Francisco, 1985.

LePichon, X., Francheteau, J., and Bonin, J., *Plate Tectonics*, Elsevier, New York, 1973.

Macdonald, K. C., Crustal processes at spreading centers, Contr. in Tectonophys., *U.S. Nat. Rep.*, 79–82, Am. Geophys. Un., 1983.

Macdonald, K. C., and Fox, P. J., Overlapping spreading centers: new accretionary geometry on the East Pacific Rise, *Nature*, **302**, 55–58, 1983.

Macdonald, K. C., and Luyendyk, B. P., The Crest of the East Pacific Rise, *Sci. Am.*, **244**, 100–118, 1981.

Macdonald, K. C., Becker, K., and Spiess, F. N., Hydrothermal heat flux of black smoker vents on the East Pacific Rise, *Earth Planet. Sci. Lett.*, **48**, 1–7, 1980.

McCoy, F. W., and Zimmerman, H. B., A history of sediment lithofacies in the South Atlantic, in *Initial Reports, Deep Sea Drilling Project*, U.S. Government Printing Office, Washington, D.C., Vol. 39, 1047–1079, 1977.

McKenzie, D. P., The Earth's Mantle, *Sci. Am.*, **249**, 66–113, 1983.

McKenzie, D. P., and Parker, R. L., A North Pacific example of tectonics on a sphere, *Nature*, **216**, 1276–1278, 1967.

McKenzie, D. P., and Sclater, J. G., The evolution of the Indian Ocean since late Cretaceous, *Geophys. J. Roy. Astron. Soc.*, **25**, 437–528, 1971.

Maxwell, A., Von Herzen, R. P., et al., *Initial Reports, Deep Sea Drilling Project*, U.S. Government Printing Office, Washington, D.C., Vol. 3, 1970.

Menard, H. W., and Atwater, T., Changes in direction of sea-floor spreading, *Nature*, **219**, 463–467, 1968.

Milankovitch, M., Kanron der Erdbestrahlung und Seine Andwendung auf das Eiszeiten Problem, Serb. Akad. Beogr. Spec. Publ. 132, 1941.

Minster, B., and Jordan, T., Present day plate motions, *J. Geophys. Res.*, **83**, 5331–5354, 1978.

Mitchum, R., Vail, P. and Thompson, T. Seismic stratigraphy and global changes of sea level, in *Am. Assoc. Petr. Geol. Mem.*, **26**, 53–81, 1977.

Molnar, P., and Sykes, L., Tectonics of the Caribbean and mid-American region from focal mechanisms and seismology, *Geol. Soc. Am. Bull.*, **80**, 1639–1684, 1969.

Moore, G. F., and E. A. Silver, Collision processes in the northern Mollocca Sea, in

Tectonic and geologic evolution of Southeast Asian seas and islands, Part 2, *Geophysical Mono.* **27,** D. E. Hayes, ed., Am. Geophys. Un., 1983.

Morgan, W. J., Rises, great faults, and crustal blocks, *J. Geophys. Res.,* **73,** 1959–1982, 1968.

Morgan, W. J., Hotspot tracks and the opening of the Atlantic and Indian Oceans, in *The Sea,* Vol. 7, C. Emiliani, ed., Wiley Interscience, New York, 443–489, 1981.

Nelson, J. D., Granse, R. A., Significant earthquakes 1900–1979, Geophys. and Solar Terrestrial Data Center, NOAA Nat. Ocean Survey, 1979.

Normark, W. R., Morton, Delaney, J. R., Geological setting of massive sulfide deposition and hydrothermal vents along the Juan de Fuca ridge, United States Geological Survey, Open file report 82-200A, 1982.

Oldenburg, D. W., A physical model for creation of new lithosphere, *Geophys. J. Roy. Astron. Soc.,* **43,** 425–451, 1975.

Opdyke, N. D., The paleomagnetism of deep sea cores, *Rev. Geophys. and Space Phys,* **10,** 213–249, 1972.

Orcutt, J., Kennett, B. G. N., Dorman, L. M., Structure of the East Pacific Rise from ocean bottom seismometer arrays, *Geophys. J. Roy. Astron. Soc.,* **45,** 305–320, 1976.

Parker, R. L., and Oldenburg, D. W., A thermal model of ocean ridges, *Nature,* **242,** 137–139, 1973.

Parsons, B., and Richter, F., Mantle convection and the oceanic lithosphere, in *The Sea,* Vol. 7, C. Emiliani, ed., Wiley Interscience, New York, 73–119, 1981.

Parsons, B., and Sclater, J. G., An analysis of the variation of Ocean floor bathymetry and heat flow with age, *J. Geophys. Res.,* **82,** 803–827, 1977.

Pendelton, W. D., Form of subduction in the Aleutian Arc, *Tectonophys.,* **102,** 377–387, 1984.

Pratt, R. M., The seaward extension of submarine canyons off the northeast coast of the United States, *Deep Sea Res.,* **14,** 409–420, 1967.

Press, F., and Siever, R., *Earth,* W. H. Freeman, San Francisco, 1981.

Prospero, J. M., Eolian transport to the world ocean, in *The Sea,* Vol. 7, C. Emiliani, ed., Wiley Interscience, New York, 801–875, 1981.

Rona, P., Bostrom, K., Laubier, J., and Smith, S., *Hydrothermal Processes at Sea Floor Spreading Centers,* Plenum Press, New York, 1983.

Ruddiman, W., The Quaternary Climate, in *Lamont-Doherty Geological Observatory Yearbook,* Columbia Univ., 1983.

Ruddiman, W., and MacIntyre, A., Late Quaternary surface ocean kinematics and climatic change in the high-latitude North Atlantic, *J. Geophys. Res.,* **82,** 3877–3887, 1980.

Ruddiman, W. F., Pleistocene sedimentation in the equatorial Atlantic: stratigraphy and faunal paleoclimatology, *Geol. Soc. Am. Bull.,* **82,** 283–302, 1971.

Sayles, F. L., and Jenkins, W. J., Advection of pore fluids through sediments of the equatorial east Pacific, *Science,* **217,** 245–248, 1982.

Schouten, H., and Denham, C. R., Modeling the oceanic magnetic source layer, in *DSDP Results in the Atlantic Ocean,* M. Talwani, ed., Am. Geophys. Un., 1979.

Schrader, H. J., and Schuette, G., Marine Diatoms, in *The Sea*, Vol. 7, C. Emiliani, ed., Wiley Interscience, New York, 1179–1233, 1981.

Shackleton, N. J., and Opdyke, N. D., Oxygen isotope and paleomagnetic stratigraphy of equatorial Pacific core V28-238: oxygen isotope temperatures and ice volumes on a 100000 and one million year scale, *Quat. Res.*, **3,** 39–55, 1973.

Sillen, L. G., The Oceans as a Chemical System, *Science*, **156,** 1189, 1967.

Sleep, N. Hydrothermal convection at ridges axes, in *Hydrothermal Processes at Sea Floor Spreading Center*, P. Rona, ed., Plenum Press, New York, 71–82, 1983.

Smith, A. G., Bullard, E. C., *Mesozoic and Cenozoic Paleocontinental Maps*, Cambridge Univ. Press, New York, 1977.

Spiess, F. N., Macdonald, K. C., Atwater, T., et al., East Pacific Rise: hot springs and geophysical experiments, *Science*, **207,** 1421–1433, 1980.

Steckler, M., Subsidence in the Gulf of Lion, *Nature*, **287,** 425–429, 1980.

Steckler, M., and Watts, A. B., Subsidence of Atlantic type margins off New York, *Earth Planet. Sci. Lett.*, **41,** 1–13, 1978.

Stoffa, P., and Talwani, M., Exploring the crust beneath the oceans, Lamont-Doherty *Geological Observatory Yearbook*, Columbia Univ., 1978.

Sullivan, W., *Continents in Motion*, Quadrangle, 1976.

Thompson, G., Basalt-sea water interaction, in *Hydrothermal Processes at Sea Floor Spreading Centers*, P. Rona, ed., Plenum Press, New York, 225–278, 1983.

Tucholke, B., Vogt, P., et al., Initial Reports, Deep-Sea Drilling Project, U.S. Government Printing Office, Vol. 35, 1976.

Turekian, K. K., Some Aspects of the Geochemistry of Marine Sediments, in Chemical Oceanography, Vol. 2, J. Riley, and G. Skirrow, eds., Academic Press, New York, 1965.

Turekian, K. K., Geochemical mass balance and the cycle of the elements, in *Hydrothermal Processes at Sea Floor Spreading Centers*, P. Rona, ed., Plenum Press, New York 361–368, 1983.

Turekian, K. K., Cochran ,J. K., and Nasaki, Y., Growth rate of clams from Galapagos rift hotspring field using natural radionucleide ratios, *Nature*, **280,** 385–387, 1979.

Uyeda, S., The New View of the Earth, Moving Continents and Moving Oceans, W. H. Freeman, San Francisco, 1978.

Uyeda, S., Subduction zones, their diversity, mechanisms and human impact, *Geojournal*, **8,** 4–14, 1984.

Van Andel, T. H., Mesozoic/Cenozoic calcite compensation depth and the global distribution of calcareous sediments, *Earth Planet. Sci. Lett.*, **26,** 187–195, 1975.

Van Andel, T. H., Theide, J., Sclater, J. G., and Hay, W. W., Depositional History of the South Atlantic Ocean during the last 125 million years, *J. Geol.*, **85,** 651–698, 1977.

Vincent, E., and Berger, W. H., Planktonic foraminifera and their use in paleoceanography, in *The Sea*, Vol. 7, C. Emiliani, ed., Wiley Interscience, New York, 1025–1121, 1981.

Vine, F. J., and Matthews, D. H., Magnetic anomalies over oceanic ridges, *Nature*, **199,** 947–949, 1963.

Vine, F., and Wilson, J. T., Magnetic anomalies over a young oceanic ridge off Vancouver Island, *Science*, **150,** 485–489, 1965.

Watts, A. B., Ten-Brink, U., Buhl, P., and Broecker, T. M., Multichannel seismic study of lithospheric flecture across the Hawaiian-Empeor seamount chain, *Nature*, **315,** 105–111, 1985.

Wegener, A. *The Origin of Continents and Oceans*, Dover, New York, 1924.

Williams, D. W., Von Herzen, R. P., Sclater, J. G., and Anderson, R. N., The Galapagos Spreading Center: lithosphere cooling and hydrothermal circulation, *Geophys. J. Roy. Astron. Soc.*, **38,** 587–608, 1974.

Yoshii, T., Detailed cross-section of the deep seismic zone off northeast Honshu, Japan, *Tectonophys.*, **53,** 349–360, 1979.

Zoback, M. D., and Zoback, M. L., State-of-stress and intraplate earthquakes in the United States, *Science*, **213,** 96–104, 1982.

Zoback, M. D., and Anderson, R. N., Borehole Televiewer imagery of the upper oceanic crust, DSDP hole 504B, *Nature*, **295,** 345–379, 1982.

Figure Credits

Chapter 1

1-1 Karl Turekian, *Chemistry of the Earth*, 1972.
1-2 Karl Turekian, *Chemistry of the Earth*, 1972.
1-3 Tom Jordan and Don Anderson, *Geophys. Journal Roy. Astron. Soc.*, 1974.
1-4 Frank Press and Raymond Siever, *The Earth*, 1982.
1-5 NASA Photo.
1-6 (color inserts). NASA Photos.
1-8 NASA Photo.

Chapter 2

2-2, 3 William F. Haxby, Lamont-Doherty Geological Observatory, 1984.
2-4 Science and Technology Division, New York Public Library.
2-6 C. Emiliani, *The Sea*, Vol. 7, Wiley-Interscience, New York, 1981.
2-8 John Farre and William B. F. Ryan, Lamont-Doherty Geological Observatory, 1984.
2-9 Walter Sullivan, *Continents in Motion*, Quadrangle, 1978.

Chapter 3

3-1 Walter Sullivan, *Continents in Motion*, Quadrangle, 1978.
3-2 Smith et al., Cambridge Univ. Press, 1977.
3-3 From Arthur Holmes, *Principals of Physical Geology*, 1978.
3-5 John Dewey, 1972.
3-6 From Nelson and Granse, NOAA Nat. Ocean Survey, 1979.
3-7,8 From John Dewey, Oxford University, 1978.
3-9 Robert E. Wallace, United States Geological Survey.
3-10 Brian Isacks, Jack Oliver, and Lynn Sykes, *J. Geophys. Res.*, 1968.

3-11 LePichon, Francheteau, and Bonin, *Plate Tectonics*, Elsevier, New York, 1973.

3-12 A portion of the "World Ocean Floor" Panorama by Bruce Heezen and Marie Tharp, 1977 © Marie Tharp.

3-13 Jason Morgan, *J. Geophys. Res.*, 1968.

3-14 Jason Morgan, *J. Geophys. Res.*, 1968.

3-15 LePichon, Francheteau, and Bonin, *Plate Tectonics*, Elsevier, New York, 1973.

3-16 Forsyth and Uyeda, *Geophys. J. Roy. Astron. Soc.*, 1975.

3-17 Dan McKenzie and Robert Parker, *Nature*, 1967.

3-21-22 A. Hasegawa et al., Tohoku University, 1978.

3-23 Neil Opdyke et al., 1968.

3-24 James Heirtzler et al., 1968.

3-25 Vine and Wilson, 1965, after Walter Sullivan, 1974.

3-26 Maxwell, Von Herzen et al. 1970, after Walter Sullivan, 1974.

3-27 John Dewey, 1980.

3-28 LePichon, Francheteau and Bonin, *Plate Tectonics*, Elsevier, 1973.

3-29 Dan McKenzie and John Sclater, *Geophys. J. Roy. Astron. Soc.*, 1971.

Chapter 4

4-1 Don Forsyth, Brown University, 1974.

4-3 Tony Watts et al., *J. Geophys. Res.*, 1985.

4-4 Hasegawa et al., *Tectonophysics*, 1978.

4-5 Tony Watts, Lamont-Doherty Geological Observatory, 1982.

4-6 Harrison and Bonatti, *The Sea*, Vol. 7, Wiley-Interscience, New York, 1981.

4-7 Mark Zoback and Anderson, *Nature*, 1982.

4-9 LePichon, Francheteau, and Bonin, Plate Tectonics, Elsevier, New York, 1973.

4-10 Michael A. Hobart, Lamont-Doherty Geological Observatory.

4-11 Bonatti, *The Sea*, Vol. 7, Wiley-Interscience, New York, 1981.

Chapter 5

5-1,2 Casey, et al. *The Sea*, Vol. 7, Wiley-Interscience, New York, 1981.

5-3,4 Manik Talwani et al., 1983.

5-5 Gass and Smewing, *The Sea*, Vol. 7, Wiley-Interscience, New York, 1981.

Chapter 6

6-1 John Orcutt, *J. Geophys. Res.*, 1982.

6-2 Tom Herron et al., *J. Geophys. Res.*, 1982.

6-3,9,10 Ken Macdonald and Bruce Luyendyk, *Sci. Am.*, 1981.

6-4 Casey, et al., 1981.

6-5 Bob Ballard, Hydrothermal Processes at Sea Floor Spreading Centers, 1984.

6-6 Dan Fornari, *J. Geophys. Res.*, 1985.

6-8 Bob Ballard, 1984.

6-11 Walter Sullivan, *Continents in Motion*, from Oldenburg, 1974.

6-12,13,14 Ken Macdonald, *Am. Geophys. Un.*, 1983.

Chapter 7

7-1 Ken Macdonald, University California, Santa Barbara.

7-2,3,4,5 National Geographic Society, 1979, Woods Hole Oceanographic Institution, Bob Ballard, Emory Kristoff, Kathy Crane.
7-6 Ken Macdonald, *Am. Geophys. Union*, 1983.
7-7 David Williams et al., *Geophys. J. Roy. Astron. Soc.*, 1972.
7-8 Bonatti, *The Sea*, Vol. 7, Wiley-Interscience, New York, 1981.
7-9 Deep Sea Drilling Project, University of California, San Diego.
7-10 Uto Fehn et al., *J. Geophys. Res.*, 1983.

Chapter 8

8-1 W. S. Fyfe, in *Cambridge Encyclopedia of the Earth Sciences*, 1981.
8-2,3,4,5,6,7 Enrico Bonatti, *The Sea*, Vol. 7, Wiley-Interscience, New York, 1981.

Chapter 9

9-3,4 Harmon Craig and John Lupton, *The Sea*, Vol. 7, Wiley-Interscience, New York, 1981.
9-7,8,10 James Kennett, *Marine Geology*, Prentice-Hall, Englewood Cliffs, N.J., 1982.
9-9 Kennett, after van Andel et al., 1977.
9-11 Fred Sayles and Bill Jenkins, *Science*, 1982.

Chapter 10

10-1,2,10,11,17,18 James Kennett, *Marine Geology*, Prentice-Hall, Englewood Cliffs, N.J., 1982.
10-3,4,5 Vincent and Berger, *The Sea*, Vol. 7, Wiley-Interscience, New York, 1981.
10-6,8 Barron and Whitman, *The Sea*, Vol. 7, Wiley-Interscience, New York, 1981.
10-7,10,11 James Kennett, 1982 after van Andel et al., 1979.
10-9 Kennett, 1982.
10-12 Suzanne O'Connell, Lamont-Doherty Geological Observatory.
10-13 Holland, *The Sea*, Vol. 7, 1981.
10-14 Lamont-Doherty Geological Observatory photograph.
10-15,16 Stephan Gartner, *The Sea*, Vol. 7, Wiley-Interscience, New York, 1981.
10-17 Schrader and Schuette, *The Sea*, Vol. 7, Wiley-Interscience, New York, 1981.
10-18 Kennett, 1982 from Ruddiman et al., 1971.
10-19 Kastner, *The Sea*, Vol. 7, 1983.
10-20 Shackelton and Opdyke, 1973.
10-21 John Farre and Bill Ryan, Lamont-Doherty Geological Observatory 1982.
10-22 Bill Ruddiman, Lamont-Doherty Geological Observatory.
10-23 Kennett, 1982 from Hays et al., 1976.
10-24 Kennett, 1982 from Ruddiman and McIntyre, 1978.
10-26 Teschurdy, *Science*, September 7, 1984.

Chapter 11

11-1,2 Nelson and Granse, NOAA Nat. Ocean Survey, 1979.
11-3,4,5,6,7,12,13,14,16,17 A. Hasegawa, A. Takagi, Tohoku University, 1978.
11-8 Dennis Hayes and Maurice Ewing, *The Sea*, Vol. 4, Wiley-Interscience, New York, 1970.
11-9 Moore, *Am. Geophys Un.*, Mons. 21, 1982.

11-10 Dan McKenzie, *Sci. Am.,* 1984.

11-11 Iida, Nagoya Univ., 1985.

11-15 Yoshii, *Tectonophysics,* 1978.

11-18 Fisher, *J. Geophys. Res.,* 1983.

11-19 Isacks and Molnar, *Rev. Geophys. and Space Phys.,* 1971.

11-23,24 Icelandic Geological Survey, Surtsey Volcano.

11-25 Birchfield, *Sci. Am.,* 1983.

11-27 Anderson, DeLong, and Schwarz, *J. Geology,* 1977.

11-28 Moore and Silver, *Am. Geophys. Un.,* 1984.

11-30 Icelandic Geological Survey.

Chapter 12

12-1 Jennings et al., Williams and Heintz, 1977.

12-2 Tanya Atwater, and H. W. Menard, *Earth and Planet. Sci Lett.,* 1970.

12-3,9,11,12,14,15 John Dewey and Walter Pitman III, 1984.

12-4 Tanya Atwater, *Geol. Soc. Am. Bull.,* 1970.

12-5,6,7,8 Joseph Curray, Scripps Institution of Oceanography, La Jolla, Calif.

12-13 John Dewey, *Sci. Am.,* 1972.

12-11 John Maxwell, *Am. Sci.,* 1985.

Chapter 13

13-1,2,4 Windley, The evolving continent, Wiley, 1984.

13-3,5,6,7,15,16 John Dewey and Walter Pitman III, 1984.

13-6 Courtillot, *Sci. Am.,* 1983.

13-9 Michael Steckler, *Earth and Planet. Sci. Lett.,* 1980.

13-10,14 Michael Steckler and Tony Watts, *J. Geophys. Res.,* 1978.

13-11 Mitchum et al., AAPG Mons., 26, 1977.

13-12 Hutchinson et al., 1972.

Chapter 14

14-1 Bernard Minster and Tom Jordan, *Geophys. J. Roy. Astron. Soc.,* 1980.

14-3,13,14 Jason Morgan, *The Sea,* Vol. 7, Wiley-Interscience, New York, 1981.

14-4 Don Forsyth and Seiya Uyeda, *Geophys. J. Roy. Astron. Soc.,* 1975 and

14-4 Brian Isacks and Peter Molnar, *Rev. Geophys and Space Phys.,* 1971.

14-5,6,8,9,10,11,12 Barry Parsons and Frank Richter, *The Sea,* Vol. 7, Wiley-Interscience, New York, 1981.

14-7 LePichon, X., Francheteau, J., and Bonin, J., *Plate Tectonics,* Elsevier, New York, 1972.

14-10 William Haxby, Lamont-Doherty Geological Observatory, 1983.

14-12 Adam Dzewonski and D. L. Anderson, *Am. Sci.,* 1984.

14-15 Mark D. Zoback and Mary Lou Zoback, Science, 1983.

Index